Life in the Spirit

IN MARRIAGE, HOME & WORK

An Exposition of Ephesians 5:18 to 6:9

D. M. LLOYD-JONES

THE BANNER OF TRUTH TRUST

THE BANNER OF TRUTH TRUST
3 Murrayfield Road, Edinburgh EH12 6EL
PO Box 621, Carlisle, Pennsylvania 17013, USA

    First published 1974
    Reprinted 1975
    Reprinted 1982
    Reprinted 1985
    Reprinted 1992
    ISBN 0 85151 194 5

Set in 11 on 12 pt 'Monotype' Garamond
Printed and bound in Great Britain by
Mackays of Chatham PLC, Chatham, Kent

Preface

This volume follows the previous volume of sermons on the second chapter of the Epistle to the Ephesians published under the title 'God's Way of Reconciliation', (Evangelical Press). The fact that it appears rather than a volume on chapter 3 is due solely to the urgency of the problems with which it deals. My hope is that it will eventually take its place, in due course, as one volume in a series on this great Epistle.

This series of sermons was preached in Westminster Chapel, London on Sunday mornings during 1959 and 1960. The relevance of the Apostle's handling of the subjects dealt with here at a time when the very institution of marriage is being queried, the so-called generation-gap is being emphasized, parental control flouted and derided, and industrial strife is rampant, needs no emphasizing. 'If the foundations be destroyed, what can the righteous do?' asks the Psalmist (Psalm 11:3). The Apostle reminds us here of those foundations in his customary manner; and his handling of them should, in my opinion, be expounded in this expository and sermonic manner.

The sermons up to the end of chapter 5 have already appeared in print in the Westminster Record for 1968/9, but the remaining eleven, dealing with the relationship between parents and children, and children and parents, and masters and servants, in chapter 6 appear for the first time. To avoid undue length I decided to omit the sermons on chapter 5, verses 19 and 20, as they have no direct bearing on the themes handled in this volume.

Many have testified to the help already received from reading the sermons already printed, and have urged me to issue them in this more permanent form with the additional sermons. I can but pray that God will bless them, and use them to help many confused Christians and others at this present time.

January 1974   D. M. LLOYD-JONES

Contents

IV WORK *Ephesians* 6:5–9

NEW LIFE
IN THE SPIRIT

Ephesians 5 : 18 – 21

18 *And be not drunk with wine, wherein is excess; but be*
filled with the Spirit;
19 *Speaking to yourselves in psalms and hymns and spiritual*
songs, singing and making melody in your heart to the
Lord;
20 *Giving thanks always for all things unto God and the*
Father in the name of our Lord Jesus Christ;
21 *Submitting yourselves one to another in the fear of God.*

I

The Stimulus of the Spirit

Ephesians 5:18

Nothing is more remarkable about the Apostle Paul than the varied character of his ministry. He was at one and the same time an evangelist and preacher, founder of churches, theologian and teacher, and at the same time a tender-hearted and sympathetic pastor. His expositions of the great doctrines of the Christian faith are incomparable; but equally remarkable is the way in which he shows and works out the implications of those doctrines. He was as concerned about application as exposition, because, as he constantly emphasizes, Christianity is a life to be lived and not a mere philosophy or point of view.

The result of this is that he never approaches any practical problem in Christian living immediately or directly: he always does so in a doctrinal manner. He places every problem into the context of the whole body of Christian truth. So we find here that when he comes to deal with the problems of the Christian in his married and family life, and in his work, he does so by reminding us that the Christian life is a 'life in the Spirit'.

He puts it in an arresting manner in the words, 'Be not drunk with wine, wherein is excess, but be filled with the Spirit'. We can dismiss immediately, of course, any notion that he is merely dealing here with the question of drunkenness or excessive drinking. For anybody to use this verse merely as a text for what is called, I believe, a Temperance Sermon is to show a complete misunderstanding of the verse. The Apostle's object is not merely to denounce drunkenness or to prohibit drunkenness. That is certainly included in the text; but that is not the main thrust, not the main message of the verse. And if we were to stop short at that we should be in grave danger of becoming legalistic. But above all we should miss the glory of this particular exhortation.

Here the Apostle begins to give us an even more positive view of the Christian life than he has been doing hitherto. So far he has been mainly concerned to point out the difference in a negative way between the old life and the new. But now he becomes much more positive and paints the picture of the new life in the Spirit in more positive terms. But why does he make the transition in what at first may seem a strange and indeed surprising manner? It comes almost as a shock to us, in the midst of all that he has been saying, and all he is going to say, to read suddenly, 'Be not drunk with wine, wherein is excess, but be filled with the Spirit'. Why did he not go on to put this positive teaching of the life of one who is filled with the Spirit, in a direct manner? Why introduce this element of drunkenness, excessive drinking?

It seems to me that there are two main answers to that question. The first is, that there was nothing which was more characteristic of the old life which these people had been living, and which their contemporaries were still living, than drunkenness and debauchery. The ancient world at the time when our Lord came into it was characterized by this very thing. There are many classical descriptions of it. You will find it, for example, in the second half of the first chapter of the Epistle to the Romans, and also in chapter four of this Epistle itself. The life lived commonly was one of drunkenness and vice, indeed all the things that generally accompany excessive drinking. That had been the prevailing way of life of these Ephesians. But now these people have been changed. They have become new people, they are Christians, they are 'in the Spirit'; and so the Apostle is once more emphasizing the fact that the new life is altogether different. Yet even that is not enough; he is anxious to show that this new life is not only different from but indeed a complete contrast to the old life.

At the same time he also has a second object in his mind – to show that there is, in some respects, a similarity between the two states and lives. It is because of that curious fact that he has chosen to use this particular language and illustration. I have no doubt that there was in the Apostle's mind at this point the memory of what he had been told about the reaction of the citizens of Jerusalem, on the Day of Pentecost, when they found that something strange had happened to the followers of the Lord Jesus Christ. The account is given in Acts chapter 2, verses twelve to sixteen. The apostles were 'speaking in tongues'. We are told that people from different countries heard them 'speaking in our tongues the wonderful works of God. And they were all amazed, and were in doubt, saying one to another, What meaneth this? Others mocking said, These men are full of new wine'. They are drunk! 'But Peter, standing up with the eleven, lifted up his voice, and said unto them, Ye men of Judaea, and all ye that dwell at Jerusalem, be this known unto you, and hearken to my words: For these are not drunken, as ye suppose, seeing it is but the third hour of the day. But this is that which was spoken by the prophet Joel: And it shall come to pass in the last days, saith God, I will pour out of my Spirit upon all flesh'. Here were men suddenly filled with the Holy Spirit; but certain people thought that they were drunk, drunk with wine. So there is obviously a certain similarity between the two states and conditions.

I suggest, therefore, that the Apostle puts it in this way in order that he may bring out both the element of contrast and the element of similarity. There are these clear essential differences between the two lives; but there are certain respects in which they are similar. And we cannot get a true conception of the Christian life unless we bear the element of similarity in mind as well as the element of contrast. So the Apostle by putting it in this way gives us a striking and marvellous picture of the Christian life in all its fulness, and especially in some of its most essential features. We shall first take a general look at what he tells us about this life of the Christian filled with the Spirit. Then we shall go on to consider how this life becomes possible, and the exact meaning of the term 'Be filled with the Spirit'. And further, we shall proceed to consider how this kind of life shows and manifests itself.

There are two terms for us to consider before we look at the general picture. The first is the word 'drunk'. 'Be not drunk'; what does that mean? Wycliffe, when he translated the Bible, translated this by the word 'filled', 'Be not filled with wine, but be filled with the Spirit'. In other words the whole notion is not just that of a man who takes a sip of wine, or a little wine, but a man who is full of wine, 'filled with wine'. Indeed it is most interesting to observe and to discover that the very word the Apostle used here was also used for the process of 'soaking'. For instance, when they wanted to make use of the hide of an animal and were anxious to stretch it,

[13]

they found that it was very difficult to do so. The method they resorted to was to soak the hide in various oils and fats, and thus it became more supple, and they were able more easily to stretch it. Now the same word was used for that process of soaking; so it can be translated, 'Do not be soaked with wine, but be filled with the Spirit'. That is the meaning of our word 'drunk'.

The accompanying word is 'excess'. This is clearly a very important word. To understand this gives us the key to the explanation of the illustration which the Apostle is using. When he says 'Be not drunk with wine, wherein is excess' he is not simply calling attention to the amount of wine that has been consumed, but stating that being drunk with wine leads to excess, and is a condition of being in excess. What does that mean? Most interestingly we observe that it is precisely the same word that was used about the Prodigal Son. We read of him in Luke 15 that 'he wasted his substance in riotous living' – the word translated 'riotous' is exactly the same word as here. The younger, the prodigal son went to the far country with his pockets full of money; but he wasted his substance in riotous living. So we can read here, 'Be not drunk with wine, which is "riotous" '. Or you could use the word 'prodigality'. It is the behaviour of a prodigal, hence we call that parable 'the parable of the Prodigal Son'. He wasted his substance in a prodigal manner, he was guilty of 'prodigality'. You could even use the word 'wasteful', you could use the word 'profligate', you could use the word 'wanton'. But it is interesting to notice the root meaning of the word: it is a word which has a negative prefix to it, but its essential meaning is, 'to save'. 'To save' is the opposite, of course, of 'to squander'. It is 'to save' – to look after what you have, and to be careful. But here there is a negative prefix to the word, so 'excess' is that which is opposite to 'saving'. When you are guilty of 'excess' you do not save, you do not keep, you do not conserve; you 'scatter abroad' in a foolish, prodigal, profligate, wanton way; and in the end you have got nothing at all. Ultimately, therefore, the word carries the notion of destructiveness. Far from saving and conserving, it is a process of destruction. Now then we have the meaning, 'Be not soaked with wine, which leads to profligacy, wantonness, wastefulness and final destruction; but be filled with the Spirit'.

In the light of that, let us look at the positive picture the Apostle gives us here of the Christian life. The first thing he tells us about it is this: It is a controlled life, it is an ordered life. Here we have a link with what has gone before; because there he has told us that we must 'walk circumspectly', 'not as fools, but as wise'. 'Be ye not unwise, but understanding what the will of the Lord is.' Here he develops that idea. The Christian life is a controlled life, an ordered life; it is the very reverse of the condition of the drunkard who has lost control, and is being controlled by something else, as it were, and who is therefore in a state of utter disorder and disarray. Excess of wine leads to a condition which is characterized above everything by the loss of understanding, the loss of refinement, the loss of judgment, the loss of balance. That is what drink does.

Drink is not a stimulus, it is a depressant. It depresses first and foremost the highest centres of all in the brain. They are the very first to be influenced and affected by drink. They control everything that gives a man self-control, wisdom, understanding, discrimination, judgment, balance, the power to assess everything; in other words everything that makes a man behave at his very best and highest. The better a man's control, the better man he is. A man who can control his feelings and moods and states and passions is obviously a better and a greater man than he who cannot do so. A man may be very able, but, sometimes, when you are talking about some such men you have to say 'Yes, he is a wonderful man, an able man, but unfortunately he cannot control his temper', or this or that aspect of his life. There is nothing higher in a sense than just this power of control, self-control, balance, discipline. The Scripture teaches that throughout and says that this is the hall-mark of the truly 'wise' man. But drink is something which immediately gets rid of control; that indeed is the first thing it does; and the Apostle is reminding us here that there is nothing which should be more obvious about, and more characteristic of the Christian, than orderliness – this ordered quality, this balance, this refinement, this discipline. It is the 'sound mind' of which he speaks in his Second Epistle to Timothy in the first chapter and the seventh verse. It means discipline. That then, is the first thing. There should be nothing about the Christian to suggest that lack of control which is the most obvious feature of drunkenness, the excess which characterizes it.

Secondly, the Christian life is not a wasteful life, but a productive life. That is obvious in our very terms. What is the Christian? I cannot think of a better way of describing him than this; he is the exact opposite of the Prodigal Son. In that parable you really get, I believe, a most perfect commentary on this verse at which we are looking. You are given the two sides, the Prodigal Son in the far country, the Prodigal Son after he has come home; and again, the Prodigal Son, and the father. Here is this wonderful contrast. Drunkenness always leads to excess, always leads to prodigality, profligacy, wantonness and destruction. I mean that it is always wasteful, it always squanders. What does it squander? For one thing it squanders time. A man in this drunken condition has no concern for his business or for anything else; he always has time to talk, other things must wait. He squanders his time. In the same way he squanders his energy. He does things that he would not do in his sober moments. He throws away his energy just to show how strong he is, how wonderful he is. Excess, drunkenness, is prodigal, and prodigal especially in the wasteful use of energy. The drunken person throws it away, as it were, with both hands. He does it in his talk, in his actions, in everything.

But that kind of life throws other and yet more important things away. It throws away chastity, it throws away purity. Far from preserving them, it throws them away. The most precious gifts that God has given to man, it throws away – the ability to think and reason and compute and understand, and all the balance I have been talking about. It is all dissipated. That is the characteristic of this excess which is produced by drunkenness; it makes a man throw away his chastity, his purity, his morality. That is what makes drunkenness such a terrible thing. You see such a man throwing overboard the most precious things that belong to him; he is wasting them. It is always destructive.

The Christian life on the other hand is the exact opposite of all this. I shall develop this theme later. But the great characteristic of the Christian life is that it conserves, it build up, it adds to what we have. One is always gaining something, always learning something new. The Old Testament says about the godly life that it is a life which 'maketh rich' – rich in every aspect, indeed it introduces us to 'the unsearchable riches of Christ'. The Christian life does that. It is a life that preserves and conserves and increases everything that is best in man. It is the precise opposite of the kind of life that was lived by the Prodigal Son; and it is so in every respect. The Prodigal threw away his money with both hands. The Christian is not a miser, but the New Testament says that he is a 'steward'. He holds

[16]

and he conserves; he does not just throw money away with both hands without thinking what he is doing. He realizes that a solemn charge has been committed to him, and that he must carry it out in the right way. So he is truly a steward of his money, and of everything else.

Another striking contrast is this. The Christian life, unlike the life of drunkenness and excess, does not exhaust a man. That is the tragedy of that other life, is it not? The poor fellow thinks he is being stimulated; actually he is being exhausted because of this prodigal use of his energy and everything else. But the Christian life does not produce exhaustion; indeed it does the exact opposite, thank God.

A great principle emerges at this point. It applies not only to drink but to many other agencies that have the same effect exactly as drink. In simple terms, it tells us that the difference between the operation of the Spirit upon us, and any other influence that may appear at first sight to be *like* the influence of the Spirit is this, that all those other agencies exhaust us, whereas the Spirit always puts power into us.

Let me illustrate what I mean. I remember hearing, a few years ago, that a mission had been held under the auspices of a certain Christian organization during one particular term. And then I remember hearing that the following term was one of the worst terms in a spiritual sense in the history of that particular organization. Fewer people went to the prayer meetings and to the various other meetings. People were not only not turning up to prayer meetings or doing their regular Christian work, they were also not reading their Scriptures as they used to do. Someone enquired as to the cause of this strange phenomenon, and the explanation, the answer, that was given was this, that it was due to what they called 'the post-campaign exhaustion'. Every participant was tired out and exhausted. Does that not cause one to think furiously?

The Holy Spirit, I say, does not exhaust; He puts power into us. Many other agencies exhaust. If a church or Christian organization is exhausted after an evangelistic campaign I would query very much the basis on which the campaign was conducted. The Spirit does not exhaust, but the energy produced and expended by man does. Alcohol, or any artificial stimulus worked up by man, always leaves us exhausted and tired. Not so the Spirit! Drunkenness exhausts; the Holy Spirit does not exhaust, but energizes.

In the same way we can indicate that this excess, this drunkenness always impoverishes. The poor drunkard finds himself with nothing. See that in the story of the Prodigal. There he was, poor fellow, the money had ended, everything had gone, and he was trying to keep himself alive by eating the husks that were given to feed the swine. 'And no man gave unto him'. He had nothing at all, was completely impoverished. He remembers his home and his father, and he says, 'Why, the servants of my father are in a better case than I am, they have bread "enough and to spare", I have got nothing'. Here he is, exhausted; everything has gone utterly, and he is left penniless, hopeless, helpless and friendless. The Christian life is the exact opposite of that. The Apostle puts it again in writing to Timothy: 'Laying up in store for yourselves a good foundation against that time' (1 Timothy 6:19). Are we building up, are we increasing, are we growing, are we developing? That is a most searching test as to whether the Spirit is in us in His fulness or not. The old, natural, sinful life impoverishes, and leaves us with nothing.

But let me hurry on to the third principle. I have been emphasizing that the Christian life is a controlled life and an ordered life, that it is a productive life by contrast with all the others. But above all I want to emphasize that the Christian life is not merely a negative life. I believe that it was in order to say that, that the Apostle used this comparison. You may have been reading this Epistle to the Ephesians, and especially from the seventeenth verse of the fourth chapter, up to this point, and you may perhaps, reading superficially, get the impression that the Christian life is just a negative life – you must not do this and you must not do that, you must not indulge in foolish talking and jesting, and become drunk, and so on. Many think of it in that way and say, 'Your Christian life is a purely negative life; it is just a life of prohibitions, and you are always emphasizing order and control and discipline and carefulness and similar things. Is this Christian life of yours entirely a negative life?' The answer is, 'No, a thousand times, No'.

How can this be brought out and emphasized? We can put it like this. There is something about the Christian life, as we have seen, that makes an unbeliever think that a man who is a Christian is drunk: 'These men are full of new wine'. 'Be not drunk with wine, wherein is excess, but be filled with the Spirit'. No, this is not a negative life! And I believe that the Apostle was particularly concerned to bring this out. There are some who seem to think that the

Christian is a man who, to use the words of Milton, 'scorns delights and lives laborious days', that he is a sad man, almost a miserable man, and merely a moral man.

How can it be put more strongly than by this verse at which we are looking, that Christianity is not a mere negative morality? Is anybody surprised that I speak in this way of morality? I do so because morality is in many ways the greatest enemy of Christianity. It is your good moral men who today are the greatest enemies of the Cross of Christ; and therefore they are to be denounced. Christianity is not mere morality, or the absence of certain things in the life of man. There is nothing, surely, that does greater harm to the Christian faith than just that view of it. I am emphasizing this point because I am increasingly convinced that so much in the state of the Christian church today is to be explained chiefly by the fact that for nearly a hundred years the church has been preaching morality and ethics, and not the Christian faith. It is this preaching of the 'good life', of being 'a good little gentleman', and of viewing religion as 'morality touched by emotion', as Matthew Arnold put it, that has been the curse. Such men have shed the doctrines; they dislike any idea of atonement, they dismiss the whole notion of the miraculous and the supernatural, and ridicule talk about re-birth. Christianity to them is that which teaches a man to live a good life.

But that is entirely false. Christianity gives a man a new life. It is not a mere negative, mechanical kind of morality that dulls the soul and robs it of all life and vitality. The Apostle, I say, by using this comparison thunders at us this tremendous fact, that the Christian life is not just a negative life, a mere absence of evil and of sin.

Let me now put that, in the fourth place, in a positive form. Christianity is stimulating, Christianity is exhilarating, Christianity is thrilling! That is what Paul is saying, 'Do not be drunk with wine, wherein is excess' – do not go and take drink if you are looking for a thrill, or for a stimulus, or for some exhilaration – 'but be filled with the Spirit', and you will have all that and more. This is the tremendous idea which is so characteristic of New Testament teaching. Wine – alcohol – as I have already reminded you, pharmacologically speaking is not a stimulant; it is a depressant. Take up any book on pharmacology and look up 'alcohol', and you will find, always, that it is classified among the depressants. It is not a stimulus. 'Well', you say, 'why do people drink alcohol in order to receive a stimulus?' In a sense I have already been answering the question. What alcohol does is this; it knocks out those higher centres, and so the more primitive elements in the brain come up and take control; and a man feels better temporarily. He has lost his sense of fear, and he has lost his discrimination, he has lost his power to assess. Alcohol merely knocks out his higher centres and releases the more instinctive, primal elements; but the man believes that he is being stimulated. What is really true of him is that he has become more of an animal; his control over himself is diminished.

That is the exact opposite of being filled with the Spirit; for what the Spirit does is truly to stimulate. If it were possible to put the Spirit into a text-book of Pharmacology I would put Him under the stimulants, for that is where He belongs. He really does stimulate. He does not merely appear to do so, as alcohol does, and, thereby fools and deludes us. The Holy Spirit is an active, positive, real stimulus.

What does He stimulate? He stimulates our every faculty. He stimulates the mind and the intellect. I can prove that very simply. History proves that a desire for education always follows a spiritual revival and awakening. It happened at the Reformation, it happened after the Puritan Awakening, it happened in a still more striking manner after the Evangelical Awakening of 200 years ago. There were those besotted, drunken miners and others in the Midlands and in the North and round about Bristol – suddenly they were converted by this power of the Holy Spirit, and they began to clamour for schools, and wanted to be able to read. The Holy Spirit stimulates the mind. He is a direct stimulus to the mind and to the intellect. He really awakens one's faculties and develops them. He does not have the effect upon them that alcohol and other drugs have. It is the exact opposite to that; it is a true stimulus.

But He not merely stimulates the intellect. He stimulates the heart also. He moves the heart; and there is nothing which can so move the heart to its very depths as the Holy Spirit. Alcohol does not move the heart. What alcohol does, I say again, is to release the instinctual element in life; and a man mistakes it for feeling. It is not, it is hollow, it is all on the surface. He is not really responsible for what he is doing, and he is sorry afterwards for the generosity he displayed when he was drunk. It has not touched his heart at all; it has simple knocked out his higher control. He appeared to be so generous; the next day he regrets it, he wishes he could reverse his act. That is not moving the heart. But here is something that moves the heart, enlarges it, and opens it out. And likewise the will. Drink of course paralyses the will, and makes a man helpless. 'Look at him', we say, 'helplessly drunk, incapacitated'. But the Holy Spirit's influence is something that moves and stimulates the will.

Christians at all times have agreed that the Christian life they have received is the greatest stimulus conceivable. It is always leading on to something new, always leading to something greater. May I give my own personal testimony in this respect? You would have thought, perhaps, that a man having preached in the same pulpit for over twenty years would begin to feel that he had exhausted the Bible, or that it had ceased to stimulate him. My feeling, on the contrary, is that I am only just beginning. It is more and more and increasingly marvellous. I find it more and more thrilling week after week. I sometimes wish there were two Sundays in the week, and even more! It is so extraordinary; the wealth and the depth and the largeness are such that I feel I have only been in the ante-chambers; and there are these great treasures inside. I have had a glimpse of them and I want to examine them. What a stimulating, thrilling, exhilarating life this is! You are always moving in it, always moving forward, going round corners, and seeing ever nobler vistas. You had never heard of this one, and then there is another beyond it, and on and on.

> *Changed from glory into glory,*
> *Till in heaven we take our place;*
> *Till we cast our crowns before Him,*
> *Lost in wonder, love and praise!*

The Christian is a man whose mind is expanding, whose heart is moved and enlarged. And he wants to do something, he wants to make a contribution, he wants to extend the confines of the Kingdom of God, he wants others to share in it. It affects the whole of the man, intellect, emotions and will. What a stimulus!

My fifth point is that the Christian life is a happy life; it is a life that is full of joy. Why does that poor fellow turn to drink ? Because he is miserable! He wants to be happy; but he is unhappy. He thinks about life and he becomes more unhappy. He looks at other people and they look as unhappy as he is; but his whole idea is to be happy. So he takes to his drink. He is seeking for joy, he is seeking for happiness. 'Are you interested in happiness and in joy?' asks the

Apostle. Well, if so, 'be filled with the Spirit'. 'Do not be filled with wine, wherein is excess, be filled with the Spirit.' Had you thought that this Christian life was a dull life and a dreary life? If you did, you are all wrong in your notion of it. 'But', you say, 'that is the impression I get from Christian people'. So much the worse for them! God have mercy upon us if we ever represent this life as a dull and a dreary life! I say, again, that it is exciting, it is happy, it is full of joy. Listen to the Old Testament: 'The joy of the Lord is your strength'. Listen to the Apostle, writing to the Philippians, 'Rejoice in the Lord alway; and again I say, Rejoice' (Philippians 4:4). These are the great terms of the Christian life and the Christian faith.

Even more; this is not only a happy and a joyful life, this is a life that enables one to be happy and joyful even in the midst of trials and of tribulations. Listen to the Apostle Peter saying that. He has been talking about the Gospel and its blessings, and he says: 'Wherein you greatly rejoice, though now for a season, if need be, you are in heaviness through manifold temptations' (1 Peter 1:6). They were having a very hard and difficult time, they were in the midst of trials and tribulations, yet he says 'I know that you greatly rejoice'. He adds to these words in verse eight of that first chapter. Talking about Christ, he says, 'Whom having not seen, you love; in whom, though now you see Him not, yet believing, you rejoice with joy unspeakable and full of glory'. This is Christianity! Or take again the Apostle Paul putting it to the Romans in chapter five. He has been saying that, being justified by faith, we have peace with God through our Lord Jesus Christ, 'by whom also we have access by faith into this grace wherein we stand, and rejoice in hope of the glory of God. And not only so, but we rejoice in tribulations also'. Christians rejoice even in the midst of tribulations. How do we do it? Well, we have a hope, he says, and it is 'because the love of God is shed abroad in our hearts by the Holy Ghost which is given unto us'. A miserable, an unhappy life? This is the only life that is truly happy!

The Psalmist has the same message for us in Psalm 4, 'There be many that say, Who will show us any good?' Here is his reply: 'Lord, lift Thou up the light of Thy countenance upon us'. That is the answer! 'Thou hast put gladness in my heart, more than in the time that their corn and their wine increased'. Men, he says, are never so happy as at the time of harvest. They have gathered in the

corn, they have garnered the fruit and made the wine. They have
their 'harvest home', harvest festival, and rejoice and hold their
celebrations. They eat and they drink and talk, and they are happy.
The summer-autumn work is finished and they are ready for the
winter. It is a time of great joy. 'O', says the Psalmist, 'Thou hast
put a joy in my heart, greater than any joy that they have ever
known or ever can know, with all their corn and their wine.'
Natural joys often lead to misery and unhappiness, and 'the morning
after the night before', and remorse and exhaustion. The joy of the
Lord not only makes me happy for the night, but for the morning,
and the next day, and ten and twenty years later – on my death-bed
and for ever and for ever in glory. 'More than their joy, which they
have with their corn and all their wine'. This is the only joy that continues even in adversity. 'My joy', says Christ under the shadow of
the cross, 'I give unto you, and My joy no man taketh from you'.
Thank God, man cannot do so because it is the joy of the Lord, it is
the joy of the Holy Spirit.

The sixth characteristic of the Christian life is that it is a convivial
life. The other man wants boon companions, conviviality, happiness; and he argues that you cannot have conviviality without
drink. I have read serious books about this. 'Conviviality', they say,
'is impossible without the stimulus of drink' – they mean, of course,
without the soporific effect of drink! But they think they are enjoying conviviality and friendship. The Apostle's reply is that it is
only here that you really find it: 'Be not drunk with wine, wherein is
excess, but be filled with the Spirit; speaking to yourselves in psalms
and hymns and spiritual songs'. Of course Christians like the company of one another. If you do not like the company of Christian
people I cannot see that you can be a Christian at all. 'We know that
we have passed from death unto life, because we love the brethren'.
Is there anything on earth comparable to meeting with Christian
people? I would sacrifice everything the world has to offer to have
five minutes with a saint! What has the world to offer at its best and
its highest, in all its palaces, and all its refinements, and all its art
and literature, its everything, when you put it in the light of this –
the fellowship of kindred and Christian minds, the children of God
meeting together, talking together about the great deliverance, and
about the new life, and the blessed hope that lies before them,
talking about home, talking about the glory that is coming, happy
together, facing the problems together, helping one another,

strengthening one another, stimulating one another? That is the joy of Christians living in community in the life of the church. There is nothing like it as long as it is truly Christian. Church membership does not of necessity give you that, morality certainly does not. But when your church members are filled with the Spirit this is what follows; they have love, an interest in one another, a compassion, a desire to help, and are all together in a great and glorious spirit of conviviality praising the Lord, mingling their voices in song, and anticipating together what is yet in store for them!

Thus, by means of his strange comparison, the Apostle has opened a vista before us, and given us a sight of some of the essential glories of the Christian life. No, it is not merely, and not only, a life of not getting drunk, or not going to a cinema, not smoking, not doing this, that or the other. You can be clear on all those matters and still not be a Christian. The Christian is a man who is stimulated by the Holy Ghost. His personality is expanded; he is happy, he is joyful, he is convivial, he is useful. He is living the most thrilling, exciting life that a man can ever know, and it has all been produced by the Holy Spirit. Nothing else, no-one else, can produce all these things, and produce them all at the same time. A man with great will power, or a highly moral man can control himself. Yes, but he cannot make himself happy. That is why I have denounced the type of man who is merely moral, the man who gives the impression that Christianity is something negative and sad.

But let me also say this, to be fair – I denounce equally the type of Christian who tries to produce a false, counterfeit, fictitious cheeriness and breeziness. That is not the Holy Ghost's work. I am referring to those people who put on a kind of glib cheeriness and say, 'I always show that I am a happy man as a Christian'. The effect they always have upon me is to make me feel extremely miserable as I see the display of their carnality, and their failure to understand the doctrine concerning the Holy Spirit! They try to create it and wear it like a cloak. Then they try to make their meetings bright and cheerful. They are even talking about 'bright and cheery buildings' now. Some even argue that that is essential to evangelistic work! That is drunkenness, that is excess, that is like the effect of alcohol; that is man trying to produce an appearance of happiness.

There is nothing more revolting than a man trying to give the impression that he is happy! The Christian does not do that, because he is happy. This is the stimulus of the Holy Ghost, this is the joy of the Lord. There is nothing exhibitionist about it. This is not play-acting, this is not something put on. Here you do not see the man so much as the Lord who makes him what he is. It is 'joy in the Holy Ghost'. 'The fruit of the Spirit is love, joy' – that is it! So let us abominate and reprobate the kind of Christian who gives the impression that Christianity is miserable; but let us equally abominate and reprobate the kind of Christian who gives the impression that Christianity is a kind of brightness, and a breeziness, and a busy-ness, and an excitability which is nothing but the flesh, and falls into the category of the effect that is produced by excess of wine. 'Be not drunk with wine, wherein is excess, but be filled with the Spirit'.

2

The Power of the Spirit

Ephesians 5:18

As we have seen, the Apostle lays down here one of those absolutely vital and essential principles in connection not only with our understanding of the Christian faith, but indeed of the whole of our life as Christians in this world. He is reminding these Ephesians, and all Christians, that there is really only one way whereby the Christian life can be lived, indeed that there is only one way whereby the great problems that agitate the life of society, and bring it into such tragic disorder, can possibly be solved.

He starts off with this general statement: 'Now', he says, 'you must be filled, not with wine, but with the Spirit if you are to solve certain problems which are confronting you'. What are these problems? One of the first is the problem of getting on with one another. So he says in verse twenty-one, 'Submitting yourselves one to another in the fear of God'. It is not easy to get on with one another. The world is characterized by divisions, by clashes, everybody wanting to be first, everybody wanting to be important. That is, of course, the main cause of all the problems and the difficulties that are confronting the world at this present time. Now the Apostle's statement asserts that there is really only one solution to that problem, and that is, that men and women be filled with the Holy Spirit of God. It is only as they are filled with the Holy Spirit of God that they can and will submit themselves one to another in the fear of God.

Then he goes on to another great problem, the problem of husbands and wives. Here is a major modern problem. Try to estimate the misery and the unhappiness in the world today because of conflict between husbands and wives. What unhappiness is caused to men and women and children by this! Think of it as over the entire world affecting all nations – the most advanced as well as the backward. How can that problem be solved? How can it be dealt with? The Apostle's answer is that there is only one way, and that is, that men and women be filled with the Holy Spirit. It is only husbands and wives who are filled with the Spirit who will have a true view of what a husband should be, and what a wife should be, and what the relationship between them should be. It is the only way to get peace and unity and concord instead of disunity and quarrelling and separation and all that results from these evils. That is his solution for this problem also.

Then the Apostle moves on to the problem of children and parents. Again he might very well have been writing for today. This is another of our major problems, as we all know – juvenile delinquency, lawlessness amongst children, parents having less and less control over children, children utterly irresponsible, demanding rights, not recognizing any authority. Sometimes there is harshness on the part of parents, who recognize that indiscipline is wrong but do not know how to deal with the problem. There is great agony and trouble in the world today as the result of this many-sided problem of children and parents.

After that Paul goes on to the final problem that he puts before them, namely, the relationship between masters and servants. How familiar we are with this problem in terms of strikes, lockouts, and all the things that disrupt the working of society, and endanger the peace of this and other lands! Masters and servants!

My contention is that the Apostle is laying down in this verse a great universal principle. The way to deal with all these problems, he says, is to be filled with the Spirit. They can only be dealt with in that particular way and manner.

This is the principle that is taught everywhere in the Bible. This is the only way in which the ultimate problem of war can ever be solved, for war is nothing but what I have been outlining, on a grand scale. It is because so many cannot see it so, that they waste so much of their time and their breath and their energy; they cannot see that war, after all, is nothing but a dispute between two people magnified – a dispute between two people in the same family, or in the same country, a dispute between husband and wife, parents and children, masters and servants. War is just what is involved in any one of these situations multiplied and magnified. War is not something special and different, it is not a unique problem; it is but the problem of human relationships on a large scale. So here, I say, we are face to face with this most vital principle which is taught in the whole of the Bible; and here is the argument – that there is no solution to these problems apart from the solution that is provided by the Holy Spirit of God.

In other words the Apostle is trying to show these Ephesians their uniqueness as Christian people; and his argument is that because they are Christians, and are no longer what they once were, it is now possible for them to live in a true and happy manner. He is virtually saying, 'Now, because you are Christians, there should be no disputes and difficulties between husbands and wives amongst you'. He can make a special appeal to them, which he could not make to anybody else. And likewise with parents and children, and masters and servants. It is because it is possible for a Christian to be filled with the Spirit that the Apostle is writing as he does. 'Thank God', he says, 'at last there is a solution as far as we are concerned. Now then', he continues, 'put it into practice, avail yourselves of it'.

Anyone who comes to the New Testament with an open mind, without prejudice, will have to agree that such is the New Testament teaching. But of course we are all familiar with the fact that that is not what is being done at the present time, and that what is being taught in the name of Christianity and of the Christian church is often something essentially different. The idea now is, that the Christian 'ethic', as it is called, the Christian teaching, must be abstracted from the Bible, and must be presented and preached and taught to all and sundry in the world, that it must be addressed to states as well as to individuals. It is being taught that this Christian ethic is something that everybody is capable of applying and putting into practice; that the state can do so, and that the whole world can do so. That is the modern notion and idea. And so we have church dignitaries saying that a leader like Nikita Khrushchev has made a most magnificent Christian statement. That is the way in which the Gospel is misunderstood and perverted today.

The simple answer to that, is that no man can speak as a Christian unless he is a Christian. But the notion has gained currency that this is Christianity. You just take the Christian ethic and you teach it, as I say, to everybody – everybody is capable of appreciating it and

[28]

understanding it, everybody is capable of applying it and putting it into practice and operation. And so we are confronted by a teaching which, as I want to show, is a complete perversion of the New Testament teaching. Indeed I would not hesitate to go further: it is such teaching that constitutes the greatest danger to the true Christian faith; it is, ultimately, the last denial of the foundation principles of this Christian Gospel. I say that, because this view ultimately teaches that Christianity is meant to reform the world, and that though men may deny the great doctrines of the faith altogether, they can nevertheless apply this Christian ethic. We can get rid of war, we can get rid of armaments, we can get rid of all these great problems through just applying the Christian ethic; and that is the main function, they tell us, of the Christian Gospel. And so on Remembrance Sunday from thousands of pulpits that is the kind of message preached. Christianity will be represented as no more than a teaching which can be applied by the political and the social authorities; and accordingly sermons will be preached on political and social matters such as how to avoid war, and how to get rid of all our armaments, and so we shall be perfectly happy together. That is the idea of many as to what constitutes the Christian message.

I want to show that that is a teaching which is wrong from every conceivable standpoint. It is completely wrong theologically from the standpoint of New Testament doctrine; it is also entirely opposite to the practice of the early church. Thirdly, it is something which completely fails in practice, and leads to the direct opposite result from that which its proponents desire.

Let us glance at points two and three before I come to the first, which is the really important one. All this, I say, is opposed to the New Testament practice. Take the book of the Acts of the Apostles. Do you find here that the Apostles were always preaching about affairs of state? Did they spend their time in preaching about the problem of slavery? or in passing resolutions and sending them up to the Roman government and to the Emperor in Rome? That is what the modern church is doing. The time is given to politics and to social matters, and we are given the impression that unless we are constantly preaching against armaments and bombs and wars and about the race question we are really not Christian. That is certainly the impression you gather from the newspapers and from the wireless and the television. This, we are told, is Christianity: and

[29]

we must be perpetually objecting and protesting and speaking against certain things, and appealing to governments and bringing pressure to bear on them. But I ask you solemnly to put all that to the test of the New Testament. Can you imagine anything more different from what you find in the book of the Acts of the Apostles? That was not the early church's practice, and it has never been the practice of the church in periods of revival and of re-awakening. It is a contradiction of the practice of the true church. Not only so; I say it is something that even fails in practice in this way. There have been times and epochs in the history of this country when the Christian message has undoubtedly had a great general influence. I mean by that, times when Christian teaching has permeated the life of the community as a whole. When has it done that? The answer is, quite plainly, that that has always happened when there has been a large number of Christian people. The world only listens to the Christian voice when it is a powerful one. The world is interested, of course, in politics and in numbers, and when there were large numbers of Christians who could exercise a vote, the statesmen and the politicians paid attention to them. They might affect the result of an election, so they had to pay attention, and they had to give certain sops to the Christian's and the church's point of view.

In other words Christian teaching has permeated most into the general life of society in the periods that have followed great religious awakenings. So if the church is anxious that her teaching should permeate the life of society, the quickest and the shortest way to accomplish that is not to preach politics, is not to preach about social matters, is not to be for ever protesting against this and that; it is to produce a larger number of Christians. And how is that done? By preaching the pure Gospel, by preaching a Gospel that can convert people. To preach against war and against bombs does not convert anybody. So this very teaching defeats its own end. Very many of our churches are empty today because so many preachers have preached nothing but sermons on politics and social matters. They have not been preaching the Gospel, and have not been converting men and women; and so there are fewer and fewer Christians, and 'the powers that be' ignore us and can afford to forget us entirely. So from that standpoint also this perversion of the New Testament teaching is altogether and entirely wrong.

But let us come to the most important thing of all, let us see what a complete denial it is of the actual teaching of the New Testament itself. Look at it like this. The first thing which is so wrong about it is that it divorces the Christian ethic from the Christian doctrine. I often refer to this matter at the present time because one is hearing it so constantly. Only last week a person was speaking to me about a problem. It was a problem which was a purely medical one in a sense; and this good friend said to me that it had been suggested that he should have a certain type of treatment. He was very anxious to know whether the doctor suggesting this treatment was a Christian doctor, so he asked him about his attitude to these things. The doctor's reply was, 'Of course, I believe in the Christian ethic; but I am sorry I do not accept what you would regard as doctrine'. This attitude is indeed common – that you can hold to the Christian ethic but not believe in the Virgin Birth, and the two natures in Christ's one Person, in the miracles, in Christ's atoning sacrificial death, in the literal physical resurrection, in the Person of the Holy Spirit. They are not interested, they say, in these 'doctrines and dogmas', but only in the ethic, Christ's teaching, The Sermon on the Mount. 'That is what we want', they say, 'that is what we must teach people; to live like that; and then we shall banish war, and all will be well.'

There is nothing, I assert, which is so un-Christian as to speak in that way, and to think that you can take the ethic and shed the doctrine. Why do I say this? The answer is found in the New Testament itself. Look at the Apostle's method in this very Epistle which we are studying. What is it? The first three chapters are devoted entirely to doctrine; and it is only after he has laid down his doctrine that he begins to deal with its practical application. In other words, the Apostle, in a sense, is saying everywhere that he has no ethics apart from his doctrine. You will never find ethical teaching in the New Testament except in the context of doctrine. It is the second half of the epistles that contain the ethical teachings and they are always introduced by the word 'Therefore'. 'Therefore' – in the light of all that I have been saying – 'therefore'. But without that 'therefore' you have no ethics.

In other words, the basic assumption of the Apostle is this: 'Now', he says, 'I am going to talk to you about some very practical matters. I am going to talk to you about how you get on with one another, husbands and wives, children and parents, masters and servants'. And, he says 'I am very happy to do this with you because you are what you are, because you are not as the other

Gentiles still are, and as you once were; because this is possible for you'. That is his basic assumption. The Apostle was not writing a tract for the state, or people in general; this was not something to be sent up to the Roman Emperor and his government in Rome. No, he is writing to a church, to a number of churches; he is addressing Christian people. That is why he writes with complete confidence.

What the Apostle does here, is what is done by every other New Testament writer; it is what was done by our blessed Lord Himself. Take all present-day talk about the Sermon on the Mount as a kind of social charter, as the way to introduce and to legislate into the world the Kingdom of God, as the way to reform society. The Sermon on the Mount, they say, is what is needed – turn the other cheek instead of building armaments, give a great moral example, and all will be well. But read the Sermon on the Mount, and what you will find is that our Lord says that that kind of living is only possible to a certain kind of person. What kind of person is that? It is the person He describes in the Beatitudes. 'Blessed are the poor in spirit'; they are the only people who are likely to turn the other cheek. There are other people who may pretend to do so in order to bring to pass their own nefarious ends; but you will never get anybody to turn the other cheek in a biblical sense unless he is 'poor in spirit', unless he 'mourns', unless he is 'meek' and 'hungers and thirsts after righteousness', unless he is a 'peacemaker', and is 'pure in heart'.

Our Lord makes that quite plain. It is idle to ask for this sort of conduct unless a man is already a possessor of the Holy Spirit. If I may so put it, you cannot live the life of the Kingdom of God until you have entered the Kingdom of God. You cannot share the life of the Kingdom of God without being a citizen of that Kingdom. So it is wrong to talk of men who are outside the Kingdom living the life of the Kingdom; it is a contradiction of the whole of the New Testament teaching. There is no greater denial of the Christian faith than just precisely that.

Let me put it in another form. This modern teaching is a complete denial of the biblical doctrine of sin and of the depravity of the natural human heart. That is really the essence of the whole trouble. The real trouble about all this teaching, which is so popular today, is that it does not know and realize the truth about man as he is, as he is as the result of the Fall, as he is as the result of sin. Or if I may put it in another way, the whole tragedy of all this glib talk is its fatal optimism. That is what appals and alarms me about it. How any man who has ever read the Bible can have the optimism that these unbiblical preachers have passes my understanding. They really believe at the present time (1959) that a statement made by Mr. Khrushchev holds out the marvellous possibility that we are on the verge at last, in the twentieth century, of abolishing war, and that all armaments are going to be banned – they really believe that this is going to happen. What an extraordinary optimism! It is strange optimism even for people who have read something of the course of human history; but how any man who has ever read the Bible can believe that kind of thing completely passes my comprehension.

And for this reason; if you accept the biblical teaching concerning 'man in sin' you will find this, that man is a creature who is controlled chiefly by lusts and by desires. 'Ah but', says somebody, 'that is a pessimistic view to take'. But this is not a question which can be settled by just throwing epithets about, it is a question of facing facts and of being realistic. Man, according to the Bible, is a creature of lust and desire; he is not governed by his mind or by his reason; he never has been since man first fell into sin. The Apostle has stated that in the second chapter of this Epistle very clearly: 'You', he says, 'were dead in trespasses and sins, wherein in time past ye walked according to the course of this world, according to the prince of the power of the air, the spirit that now worketh in the children of disobedience: among whom we all had our conversation in times past in the lusts of our flesh, fulfilling the desires of the flesh and of the mind; and by nature were all, even as others, the children of wrath'. (Ephesians 2:1–3). That is the biblical teaching from beginning to end. Man, it says, is a selfish and a self-centred creature. What is, to me, so difficult to understand is how anybody who has his eyes open at all can possibly dispute such a proposition. Why is there such trouble in the world? Why is it difficult to live with others? 'Oh but', you say, 'it is because that other person is difficult'. Yes, but that other person is saying exactly the same about you; and the truth of the matter is that you are both right! We are all difficult; and we are all difficult because we are all selfish, because we are all self-centred, because we are all listening to something elemental that is within us that wants things for ourselves. We are all unjust, we are all unrighteous, we are all capable of

[33]

terrible dishonesty and devilry and lying – every one of us! Do you dispute that?

Such is man by nature, man as the result of what is recorded in the third chapter of Genesis. The moment man listened to the enemy, the enemy of God, he put himself in his power; and it has been a life of enmity and strife ever since. You see this at once in the children of Adam and Eve – Cain and Abel. There it is! Cain is still alive, that nature is still alive in every one of us by inheritance. It varies in its manifestations, but it is there in every one of us. 'Whence come wars among you?' asks James' epistle; and he answers his own question, 'they come even of your lusts that war in your members' (James 4:1). Why should people be surprised that a nation looks with lust upon another nation? Why should people be surprised at what China is doing to India at the present time (1959)? at what aggressive nations are doing with weaker nations? It has been the case in the history of humanity from the very beginning. Why should we be surprised at this when we know what happens on the personal level? Why should we expect a body of people to be different from individuals? They act in a similar way because they are only bodies of individuals. A state is but a gathering of individual persons, and while there is lust in the individual there will be lust in the state. It is not surprising; indeed it is something that we should expect.

Yet it is painfully, tragically clear that this is being entirely forgotten today. The idea nowadays is that man is fundamentally right in and of himself, and that his troubles are due to the fact that he is a victim of circumstances. 'Ah', they say, 'we are inheritors of these old traditions. If we only make a break and shake ourselves free from them, everything will be all right'. They believe that man desires this and that man is capable of accomplishing it.

It is not for me to enter into the realm of politics – I have already been abominating the fact that the church does so much of it – but let me put the matter in this way: It is, as I see it, the essence of the biblical teaching, that you really must not trust anybody finally who is not a Christian! Does that sound extreme? It is typical biblical teaching. Why do you lock your door at night? Why do we have a Police Force? It is because you know perfectly well that in human nature there is that which is predatory, is selfish, is unjust and unrighteous, and that therefore we need to protect ourselves. The wisdom of the world itself teaches that it is a right assumption with which to face the whole of life and its problems, that every man is a liar, and that every man is out for himself. Is this a pessimistic view? It is a realistic view.

Not only does society as it is today prove it, the whole course of history proves it. Was not the second world war very largely due to the fact that people did not realize truths such as this, but believed an obvious liar like Hitler when he said that he wanted peace, and that he was going to make a gesture? He was believed! It is almost incredible. But my point is that it is a failure to understand the Gospel that makes people fall into such colossal mistakes. The Gospel teaches us that man in sin is a very evil character, that nothing will stop him if it suits his purpose. He will appear as 'an angel of light', he will say 'banish all armaments', and so on, and so on. All I say is that, unless you have examined, not only what he is, and what he says on the surface, but also all that he is, and all that he is capable of in the depths of his being, if you believe him you are a fool!

What does this mean? asks someone. Does it mean that you are advocating war and armaments? It means nothing of the kind; but it does mean this, that you do not trust the mere statements of men, because man in sin is a liar, and he will tell any lie if it seems to further his own ends and purposes. It means that law and the power to enforce it are essential.

'Husbands and wives'; what is the cause of all the modern trouble in that realm? As I read the papers I gather that this is largely the result of failure to keep solemn vows, of lying and of pretence, and of men saying that they have not done what they have done, or that they have done what they have not done. A man will lie to satisfy his own lusts and desires. And yet the popular teaching today is that we have but to go to people with this Christian ethic, and they will rise to it; they will be ready to listen to it, and ready to believe it. Not only that, it is taught that modern man is really capable of putting it into practice. That is the final error – to believe that man as he is can practise this Christian ethic; that men as they are are ready to 'submit themselves one to another in the fear of God', that husbands and wives are ready to do this naturally, and children and parents to solve all their problems according to this teaching. You have only to say to them, 'Cannot you see that you are behaving in a wrong way? Now if you only did this and that all would be well. Come, let us all decide to do so'. And the belief is that everybody will say,

[35]

'Excellent! we agree with this; now let us set out to do it'.

I reply: if they believe that they are capable of doing it, all I ask is this – Why have they taken such a long time to put their belief into practice? This kind of thing has been taught, we must remember, for many centuries. The Greek philosophers were teaching about possible Utopias before Christ ever came. Then there is the Sermon on the Mount; it has been before the world for nearly two thousand years. If a moral example is enough, why do they not follow Christ? The simple answer is that they cannot do so, and they do not want to do so. Man is paralysed by sin; evil is the most powerful force in his nature.

There is no need to spend any more time on this, at any rate for those who are familiar with the teaching of the seventh chapter of the Epistle to the Romans. For what Paul teaches there is that the holy Law of God which He gave through angels to Moses, instead of saving men, made them worse! Listen to his words: 'The Law of God stirred up, stimulated sin within me, it produced in me all manner of concupiscence' (vv. 5, 8). 'God's Law, which is holy, and just and good', says Paul, 'led me into deeper and deeper sin, it killed me, it slew me'. Why? It is not because there is anything wrong with the Law, he says, it is because of this 'sin that is in me'; 'sin, that it might appear sin, working death in me by that which is good, that thereby sin might be shown to be exceeding sinful'. And yet in spite of all that, what is preached so regularly is simply the Christian ethic, and appeals are made to states and governments to put it into practice. We are told, 'if only' we all do this, war will be banished and all will be well.

It is because men believe the dangerous fallacy that man in sin is ready to respond to a moral example. You are familiar with the argument. They say, Let this nation, let just one nation destroy all its armaments, and the other nations will look on in amazement and say 'What a wonderful thing. We must all rise up and do the same'! They believe that, they believe that that will happen. You may remember how, before the second world war, a war began between Japan and China, when a well-known clergyman proposed to go out there to stand between the two armies, because he believed that when both sides saw him they would say, 'This is so wonderful, we cannot go on fighting'! He believed that man in sin can be so moved by a moral example that he will say, 'Oh, how wrong I have been; I must give up all this. I am now going to live this new, this wonder-

ful life'! If that were true, the Son of God would never have come
into this world; His coming would not have been necessary. Divine
teaching, and the examples of men would have been sufficient.

So I come to my last point. What is finally wrong with such
teaching is that it is a complete denial of the biblical doctrine of the
Holy Spirit. The Apostle Paul does not tell people to 'submit themselves one to another' – 'husbands and wives' to submit themselves
one to another in the right way, and in the right spirit, and likewise
'children and parents' and 'masters and servants' – he does not ask
them to do that, without saying to them first of all, 'Be filled with
the Spirit'. He says that such conduct is quite impossible without
that essential preliminary condition. But people today do not believe in the Holy Spirit; they do not believe in the Person of the
Holy Spirit. They talk about the 'Christian spirit' and the 'spirit of
brotherhood and goodwill' and so on. That is not Christianity; that
is morality, that is pagan teaching.

Here we have a doctrine about the third Person in the blessed
Holy Trinity, the Holy Spirit of God. The biblical teaching is that
there is no hope for man apart from Him. What has He to do? The
first thing He does is to 'convict the world of sin, and of righteousness, and of judgment.' The world does not believe in sin, it needs
to be convinced of it. The Holy Spirit is sent to do that. In spite of
the fact that Christianity has been preached for nearly two thousand
years the world still does not believe in sin, it does not believe in
righteousness, it does not believe in judgment. It believes in itself,
in man, in the power of man and the goodness of man. It is the
exact opposite of the teaching of Christ. What else does the Holy
Spirit do? Why has He been sent? Let me remind you of this blessed
teaching. After convicting us of our sin, and after revealing to us
the salvation that is in Christ 'through His blood', what does He do?
He gives us life anew – regeneration. There it is in our Lord's
teaching to Nicodemus! Listen to Him. He says in effect to Nicodemus, 'Stop talking, stop asking questions, Verily, verily, I say
unto you, except a man be born of the Spirit he cannot see the
Kingdom of God; you must be born again, you must be born of the
Spirit.' (John 3:3–8.) I cannot discuss My kingdom with you, said
our Lord to that excellent, moral, religious man Nicodemus; I cannot discuss it with you because you cannot possibly understand it as
you are. 'Marvel not that I said unto thee, Ye must be born again.
That which is born of the flesh, is flesh; that which is born of the

[37]

Spirit is spirit'. You are trying to understand, but you cannot. You have to be born again before you can enter this kingdom; then you will begin to understand. And yet men still advocate the teaching of the Christian ethic to godless, atheistic states, and to men and women who are not born again, who are not Christians.

Such conduct is a denial of the whole basis of Christianity. The Holy Spirit is sent to regenerate men, to give them a new nature, a new mind, a new outlook, a new everything. There is no hope apart from that. He is, likewise, sent in order to promote our sanctification – 'Be filled with the Spirit'. It is only those who are controlled by the Holy Spirit of God who can live in peace with one another. This is the solution to the marriage problem, to the home problem, to the industrial problem. Once men are governed and filled by the Spirit, they understand, they see the evil that is in them, they curb and control themselves, they 'grow in grace, and in the knowledge of the Lord', amity and concord become a possibility. But only as we are 'filled with the Spirit'. Without the Spirit it is impossible. So the Holy Spirit is meant and sent to promote our sanctification, and to control us, to enable us to live the life that God would have us live.

Finally, the Holy Spirit is sent in order to produce revival and religious re-awakening. I said at the beginning that the periods when the Christian ethic has had its greatest influence on the life of society in this country have always been the periods that have followed revival, the reason being that at such times thousands of people had become Christian. The Victorian era, and the benefits it brought to so many, is to be explained in terms of the Evangelical Awakening of 200 years ago. It was because so many people were Christian, and because in so many chapels and churches this message was being preached and so many believed it, that the Christian church counted. The very numbers produced 'the Nonconformist conscience' and statesmen had to listen. The Holy Spirit is sent in such power in times of revival that large numbers of people are converted at the same time. When He is 'shed abroad' thousands can be converted in a day. The whole state of society can be changed, public houses shut, and so on. People begin to think in a new way, and they really do begin to try to apply these principles to the whole of life. You will never influence politicians and parliaments without the numbers; and so, you see, while increasing numbers of preachers have been preaching about politics and social matters, the main result has been to empty the churches. The life of society has gone

[38]

from bad to worse, and the position becomes increasingly hopeless.

There is only one way to live the truly Christian life; it is to be 'filled with the Spirit'. It is a waste of breath to appeal to people to be better, it is a waste of breath to appeal to people in terms of Remembrance Sunday, the horrors of war, and so forth. They may become a little emotional, and be better for the rest of the day, perhaps it will cover even the next day. But it will soon be gone like the morning dew, just as our New Year's resolutions are forgotten every year with such constant regularity. Man cannot do it. Man needs a new nature. He needs to be changed; and the Spirit of God alone can do that. Man needs to be 'filled with the Spirit'. Then he will be able to do these things, and not until then.

Christian people, it is our chief business at a time like this to make clear to all with whom we come in contact what Christianity really is. The prevailing, the popular view is a denial of the Christian faith. Let us enlighten men and women. But above all let us continue instant in prayer for revival, for re-awakening, for a mighty outpouring of the Spirit of God, that His truth may be authenticated, that large masses of people may be brought to life and to the faith, and may proceed to demonstrate it in practice, and thereby influence the general life of society. 'Be filled with the Spirit,' the Spirit of the living God.

3
The Control of the Spirit

Ephesians 5:18

We return to the consideration of this verse because of its crucial importance in the Christian life. We have already seen that it reminds us of the essential characteristic of the Christian life, namely, that it is a life of power, and of vigour, and of joy and happiness – conviviality. And we have also seen that it is a life which can only be lived in and by and through the power of the Holy Spirit.

We proceed now to look at it more directly. We must discover what it means to be 'filled with the Spirit', and we must try also to discover how we can be filled with the Spirit.

Those who are familiar with this text, and familiar in general with evangelical teaching will know that this verse, unfortunately, has become a matter of controversy. This is so, very largely, because it has become almost the slogan of a school of teaching with respect to sanctification and holiness. It is always dangerous to turn a text into a slogan. It generally means that it has been taken out of its context, and has therefore been treated with a certain element of violence from the standpoint of exposition. So let us bear that in mind, and let us try to rid ourselves of slogans and prejudices, and points of view which we are concerned to defend at all costs, so as to prove that we are right. Let us try to get rid of all that and come to the statement in its own setting and context.

Let us look at it, first of all, in the light of similar usages in the Bible. That is always a wise procedure. Whenever we come across a statement or a phrase which is in any way difficult, the first thing to do is to look for it elsewhere in the Scriptures, to look for parallels. As we do so we at once make certain discoveries.

The first point, it seems to me, that we have to get clear in our minds is that to be 'filled with the Spirit' is not the same as being 'baptized with the Spirit'. Now it is just there that most of the confusion tends to arise. To be filled with the Spirit is not the same as being 'sealed' with the Spirit, which I would regard as synonymous with being 'baptized with the Spirit'. And I say that for this reason, that the Apostle is exhorting people to become, and to go on being 'filled with the Spirit' of whom he has already said in the first chapter (verse thirteen) that they have been 'sealed' with the Spirit. In that verse we read: 'In whom ye also trusted, after that ye heard the word of truth, the gospel of your salvation: in whom also, after that ye believed – or, having believed – you were sealed with that Holy Spirit of promise'. This, therefore, cannot be the same thing as the 'sealing of the Spirit'. And he has reminded them of the same thing in the fourth chapter (verse thirty), where he says: 'And grieve not the Holy Spirit of God, whereby you are sealed unto the day of redemption'.

It is important to keep these things clear. The 'baptism' with the Spirit, the 'sealing' of the Spirit, is a definite concrete experience. It is mainly concerned with the question of assurance and of certainty – it is a very definite experience. It is not something that you 'receive by faith'; a man knows whether he is sealed with the Spirit or not. One cannot be baptized with the Spirit without knowing it. That is seen very clearly in the second chapter of Acts, and in various other chapters also in that same book. Now the purpose of that baptism, primarily, is to enable us to witness with power and with boldness. That was the immediate effect of the baptism of the Spirit as is seen clearly in that second chapter of Acts. Given this great assurance, given this clarity of vision, this immediate, direct knowledge of God and of Christ, a man is enabled to witness. That, of course, was the promise given to the apostles by our Lord – 'Ye shall be witnesses unto Me', after this had been done to them. (Acts 1:8) The confusion tends to arise for this reason, that in the second chapter of the Acts of the Apostles – which is an account of how the Apostles and others were baptized with the Holy Ghost – the term that is actually used is that they were all 'filled' with the Spirit. People therefore jump to a conclusion – 'Ah', they say, 'we are told there that they were "filled with the Spirit", and here they are exhorted to be "filled with the Spirit", so it is the same thing.' That is where and how the confusion comes in.

[41]

What is described in the second chapter of Acts is 'baptism with the Spirit'. Now the 'baptism with the Spirit' clearly includes being 'filled with the Spirit'; but it is more than that. There, it seems to me, is the essential difference. You cannot be 'baptized with the Spirit' without being 'filled with the Spirit'; but you can be 'filled with the Spirit', and full of the Spirit, without experiencing 'the baptism with the Spirit'. Baptism is a distinct, concrete, special experience; whereas this, as I am going to show, is meant to be a continuous state, a condition in which one should always be.

That, then, is the point at which we draw our most important distinction – sealing and baptism is a very definite experience, while 'being filled with the Spirit' is rather a condition which is continuous. The two things are not identical, and they differ in that way. However, that will become clear, perhaps, as we proceed.

As we come to the actual term 'filled', which we thus differentiate from the baptism or the sealing, we find again that this term itself is used in two different ways. Once more it is vital that we should have these two ways distinct and clear in our minds. One way in which it is used is the following: You read that certain people were filled with the Spirit in order to perform some special or peculiar task which had been allotted to them. You find it, for instance, in the Old Testament, in the case of a man called Bezaleel who was expert in working with various metals, and who was therefore used in the building of the Tabernacle. You read of that in Exodus 31:3. God says to Moses, 'And I have filled him with the Spirit of God, in wisdom, in understanding, and in knowledge, and in all manner of workmanship.' This man Bezaleel was filled with the Spirit of God in order that he might do that particular work. It was a special enduement, a special filling with the Spirit, in order that he might perform that task. But there is further interesting evidence of how people were thus filled with the Spirit before the day of Pentecost. The prophecy given concerning John the Baptist, in Luke 1:15, is this: 'he shall be filled with the Holy Ghost, even from his mother's womb'. Then we are told about Elisabeth, the mother of John: 'And Elisabeth was filled with the Holy Ghost, and she lifted up her voice, and she spoke' (Luke 1:4). We are told the same about Zacharias, the father of John the Baptist, in verse sixty-seven: 'And his father Zacharias was filled with the Holy Ghost, and prophesied'.

In each of these cases, you observe, these people were filled with the Holy Ghost in order that they might speak or do something. It is an enduement of power for a special purpose.

The next use of the term in the New Testament is, as I have said, in Acts 2:4: 'And they were all filled with the Holy Spirit, and began to speak with other tongues, as the Spirit gave them utterance'. That is a unique statement because the two things happened together. There is the baptism plus, or including, the filling; and it is this that enables them to speak with other tongues as the Spirit gave them utterance. But here is an interesting point. The Apostle Peter, with all the other Apostles, and with their followers on that day of Pentecost, were baptized and filled with the Spirit. But in Acts 4:8 we read this: 'Then Peter, filled with the Holy Ghost, said unto them. . . .' Here is another filling. The man who has already been baptized and filled on that day of Pentecost is filled again, filled for a special object. The special object in Acts 4 was that he and John who had been arraigned before the authorities, and were on trial because of their healing of the impotent man who had been sitting at the Beautiful Gate of the Temple, had to speak. The Holy Ghost came upon Peter, and he was filled with the Spirit, in order that he might speak with authority and power to these authorities who were trying him. The same Peter is filled again. I am establishing the point that there is this essential difference between the baptism and the filling. But still we are dealing with the filling of the Spirit in terms of capacity and power given to perform a given task.

Then take another example. After their trial, Peter and John went back to their company, to the church, and reported what had been done with them, and they all began to pray together. Then, we are told, in the thirty-first verse of the fourth chapter of Acts: '. . . the place was shaken where they were assembled together; and they were all filled with the Holy Ghost, and they spake the Word of God with boldness'. It is the same thing again. These people had already been baptized, they had been filled as they were baptized, but they are filled again. This is something that can be repeated many times. Indeed there is another striking example in connection with the Apostle Paul. The account of his conversion and the account of his being baptized with the Spirit is given in the ninth chapter of the Book of Acts. But in the thirteenth chapter we find that Paul is speaking, and this is what we are told in verse nine: 'Paul, filled with the Holy Ghost, fixed his eyes on him'. Luke the historian is dealing with the man who was a sorcerer, and who attended a certain Roman official. The Apostle determined to rebuke this man for what he said. So we are told that Paul, filled with the Holy Ghost, fixed his eyes on him.' He was 'filled' in order that he might speak to this man, and sternly rebuke him.

In the light of all that, it is obvious that we are dealing with some clear-cut experience. All these persons were conscious of the fact that the Spirit had come upon them, that they had been endued with new power and with authority. They knew exactly what had happened. So this is an experience describing something that happens to us, our consciousness of an access of power for a specific purpose. This is something, therefore, which is quite distinct and clear.

But this is not confined to the New Testament, thank God. Read the biographies of the great preachers in the church throughout the centuries, and especially in times of revival and re-awakening, and you find this kind of thing repeated endlessly. A man who is preaching suddenly becomes aware that the Spirit of God has come upon him, and has taken hold of him. He is taken out of himself, he is given a luminosity and an understanding and a power and an ability to speak with conviction; and tremendous things happen. The man himself is very conscious of it, so are those who are listening to him. There are very many instances of this during the long story of the Christian church.

Thank God, this is not confined to past history. By the grace of God this is something that still continues to happen. There are men still alive who know of this, and who rejoice in it, men who serve God with honesty and sincerity and who are aware of this experience from time to time. That, then, is one way in which this term is used; these various people were filled with the Spirit, and they were given an unusual power and ability.

Now the question arises – Is that the meaning of this statement here in Ephesians 5:18? I suggest that it is not, and that we must not be misled by the mere similarity of the expression. What, then, is this? I suggest that this is a description of a state or a condition. Perhaps the best way to understand it is to recall what we are told of our Lord Himself, in the first verse of the fourth chapter of the Gospel according to St. Luke. We read that, 'Jesus, being full of the Holy Ghost, . . . was led by the Spirit into the wilderness' to be tempted of the devil. Now that is a statement about our Lord, that He was 'full of the Holy Spirit'. Likewise we are told about Him in

[44]

the third chapter of John's Gospel that 'God giveth not the Spirit by measure unto Him'. He was always full of the Spirit in all His fulness.

But notice certain other statements. Take, for instance, what we read about Stephen in the Acts of the Apostles. He was one of the men chosen, as we are told in the sixth chapter, to deal with various matters in order that the Apostles might give themselves to prayer and to the preaching of the Word. And this is what we read about him: 'Stephen, a man full of faith and of the Holy Ghost'. He was full of the Holy Ghost. This is not a statement that at a given point he was filled with the Spirit to do a certain thing. No, he was chosen to do this work because he was a man who was already 'full of the Holy Ghost'. But take another statement about him in chapter seven of Acts in verse fifty-five. Here Stephen is on trial for his life, and we read: 'But he, being full of the Holy Ghost, looked up steadfastly into heaven and saw the glory of God, and Jesus standing on the right hand of God, and said . . .'.

Now that is to me a doubtful statement, doubtful in this sense, that I am not sure whether to put it into the category we are now considering or into the previous category. Indeed it fits equally well into both categories. Stephen was full of the Holy Ghost habitually, but because of the peculiar circumstances, because of the crisis in which he found himself, though he was full of the Spirit, he was 'filled with the Spirit' again. It means that though he was full of the Spirit there was a further manifestation, a further 'access' of power, a further 'filling' to overflowing, and a particular ability was given to him to meet his traducers and accusers, and to speak the Word of God with boldness and with conviction. That therefore is an interesting statement. But look also at the statement about Barnabas, the companion of Paul. We read about Barnabas in Acts 11:24, 'He was a good man, and full of the Holy Ghost and of faith'; a man like Stephen. He was full of faith, and he was also full of the Holy Ghost. I end with a statement about the disciples as a company. In Acts 13:52 I read: 'The disciples were filled with joy, and with the Holy Ghost'.

You see the distinction. In these cases – and regarding Acts 7:55 as rather a special one – we are not now looking at people being filled with a 'power' to do a particular task. We are being given a description of the normal state of these people, their condition. Here we have a description of a moral and a spiritual 'state'. It is

[45]

not so much a question of power now, as a question of how a man lives. Stephen was chosen – why? Because he was a man who was 'full of faith and full of the Holy Ghost'. That is how people spoke of him, and so when they came to choose the deacons they said, Well now, here is a man who is full of faith, and full of the Holy Ghost. Barnabas was chosen for the same reason. And we read about the general company that they were 'full of joy and of the Holy Ghost'.

There is then an obvious difference between these two statements which seem so similar at first sight; and what makes it so important to differentiate between them is, that we are not to expect always that the expression indicates special filling for a task. That comes, that goes. But we are meant to be 'filled with the Spirit' always. Hence the importance of differentiating between the two. Thus there is another point which we have established. A man who is full of the Holy Ghost can suddenly be filled with the Holy Ghost for a special purpose. I have illustrated that in the case of Stephen on trial. I have illustrated it also in the case of the disciples themselves on the day of Pentecost.

In the light of all these Scriptures, is it not clear and obvious that what we are dealing with in this verse – Ephesians 5:18 – is the second usage? Here, we are given an account of a state or condition. Indeed I think this can be proved beyond any doubt in this way: 'Be not drunk with wine, wherein is excess, but be filled with the Spirit'. The tense of the verb is most important, and here it is the present, the present continuous. The true translation of this verse is this: 'Be not drunk with wine, wherein is excess, but go on being filled with the Spirit – be perpetually filled with the Spirit. Let it go on, let it continue, let it be your constant condition'. It is the present continuous. I argue that because it is the present continuous it cannot carry the first meaning, which, clearly, is something that comes, and comes again and again, as it did to Peter, as it did to Stephen, and as it did to the Apostle Paul in various trying or critical circumstances. The being filled for a task is something that comes and goes; this being filled with the Spirit is meant to be a constant permanent condition which does not vary and which does not change. In other words, what we are told here is that we are meant to be always like Stephen, like Barnabas, like Paul and others 'full of the Spirit'.

It is vital that that should be established, otherwise there will be

[46]

nothing but confusion. There is great confusion about all this, and people are waiting for an experience of being filled because they have a wrong conception of this particular teaching. We have established, then, what it means in terms of the typical usage of the New Testament. But what does it mean in actual practice? Here is the practical matter for us.

The way to approach this, it seems to me, is to remind ourselves that the Holy Spirit is a Person. The Holy Spirit is not just an influence. So many seem to talk about being filled with the Spirit as if the Holy Spirit were some kind of liquid. They talk about having an 'empty vessel', an empty jug, and having the Spirit poured in. That is entirely wrong because it forgets that the Holy Spirit is a Person. He is not a substance, not a liquid, and not a power like electricity. We all tend to fall into this error. We even tend to refer to the Holy Spirit as 'it', forgetting that the Holy Spirit is the third Person in the blessed Holy Trinity. Our ideas about being 'filled with the Spirit' go entirely wrong just because we have forgotten that He is a Person. But if that is so, why does the Bible use these terms 'poured out', 'shed forth' and so on? These are but figures, of course. The Scriptures are anxious to convey the idea that the influence of the Spirit upon us is a power. We talk about the 'influence' of a man's personality; but that is not a substance, it is the man who is producing the influence. These are but terms and expressions used in order to put the truth to us in a vivid way, in order that we may realize the variations in the strength of the personal influence and power. When this influence is powerful it is, as it were, 'poured out', 'poured forth'; but we must not literalize an analogy or an illustration and begin to think of it in some kind of materialistic way. The influence is the influence of the person, the Person of the Holy Spirit Himself.

What does it mean then to be 'full' in this sense? I am going to quote a definition which is found in Thayer's Greek Lexicon, which is standard and authoritative. It puts it like this: 'What wholly takes possession of the mind is said to fill it'. That is a current expression. Anything that takes possession of my mind is said to fill my mind, so we, in ordinary parlance, talk about being 'full' of something. Someone has suddenly taken up a new interest – 'Ah', you say, 'he is full of it, he never talks about anything else.' Now that is it – he is full of this thing. Or we talk about this in terms of persons. If you find a person always talking about another person, what you say is

'Ah, he is absolutely full of So-and-so'. You are talking about the influence of person 'A' upon person 'B', and you say about person 'B' that he or she is full of 'A', always talking about that person, cannot stop talking about that person. That is how we state, in other words, the controlling influence of one person upon another.

There it is entirely in terms of persons. But let me put it this way: Take the Apostle's own analogy here – 'Be not drunk with wine, wherein is excess, but be filled with the Spirit'. What do you say about a man who is 'drunk'? You say, 'he is under the influence of drink'. So what the Apostle is saying in a sense is this: 'Do not be under the influence of wine; be under the influence of the Holy Spirit' – that is exactly what it means. 'To be filled' means 'to be under the influence of'. A man who is full of wine, wherein is excess, a man who is 'soaked' with wine, is under the influence of wine. Very well, says Paul, do not be under the influence of wine, but be under the influence of the Holy Spirit. It is exactly the same expression.

To be 'under the influence' means that the whole of our personality – our mind and heart and will – is being controlled by this other influence or power. A man who is under the influence of drink is totally under its influence – his mind is affected and influenced, so are his heart and his will. Do not be worried about the exact pharmacology of this – this is a pictorial expression. As we have seen, actually what happens in the case of the man with the wine is that it is not so much that he is under the influence of the wine as that the wine removes the highest and best influence which he has within him. It comes to the same thing in actual practice. But here is the analogy – as that man's mind and heart and will are affected by that wine, so we are to be influenced and affected in mind and heart and will by the Holy Spirit. The man who is under the influence of wine can no longer control himself. Very well, says Paul, let the Holy Spirit control you. That is what it means to be filled with the Spirit. It is not something poured into me so that I have to try to empty the vessel first and thus receive. ... That manner of thinking is quite wrong, it does violence to the Person of the Spirit. No, the exhortation is, 'Go on being controlled by the Holy Spirit'. As you become full of a subject or full of a person in whom you are interested, so be filled full of the Holy Spirit.

If that, then, is what it means, the next question that arises is, How does this become possible? How can one be filled with the

Spirit? Here is a most important matter. The first thing we notice is that it is a command, an injunction, 'Be filled', 'go on being filled', with the Spirit, 'go on being controlled by the Holy Spirit'. It therefore follows of necessity that it is not an experience. Because it is a command, it is not an experience; because it is in the continuous present it is not some crisis, it is not some critical experience; and therefore it is not to be sought as 'a blessing'. There are many people who go round from meeting to meeting seeking, hoping to get 'the blessing' of being 'filled with the Spirit'. They are sometimes invited to come forward at the end of a meeting to 'receive' the fulness of the Spirit. But surely that is to do utter violence to the language used here and to the whole analogy of the teaching of the Scripture. This is not a critical experience, this is a state or a condition in which we are to live always, permanently. This is how you always ought to be, says the Apostle; and he commands us to be like this. So I deduce that this is not something that happens to us; this is something which we control, and which we determine. As a man decides and controls whether he is going to be filled with wine or not, so it is he himself who controls and decides whether he is going to be controlled by the Spirit or not. He is therefore given a commandment, an injunction, an exhortation. We must therefore cease to think of it in terms of 'having an experience'.

Again, let me put it like this in order to make it clear. What happened to the disciples on the day of Pentecost was an experience, and not only did they know it, but everybody else knew it. What happened to Cornelius and his household when the Holy Spirit fell upon them was an experience, and everybody else knew it. What happened to those people in Samaria, when Peter and John went down from Jerusalem and laid their hands upon them and prayed for them was an experience, and they and everybody else knew it. Likewise with the people in Acts 19:1–6. To be 'sealed', to be 'baptized' with the Spirit is a definite experience. We do not control that; that is entirely the action of our Lord. It is something He does to us. But this filling is something which patently we control; and therefore it is put to us in the form of a command or an exhortation, 'Go on being filled and controlled by the Spirit.' In other words, we must get rid of all notions of passivity here; you do not just wait for this to happen. It is in your power and mine to determine whether we are filled with the Spirit or not. Is that clear? It is not in our power to determine whether we are going to be regenerated or not, it is not in our power to determine whether we are going to be baptized with the Spirit or not, but it is in our power to decide whether we are going to go on being filled with the Spirit or not. To confuse this last with the baptism with the Spirit is nothing but a grievous perversion of the Scripture. This is no experience that you wait for, or pray for, or long for. Rather, you and I have certain things to do if we are anxious to go on being filled with the Spirit. What are they?

Let me put them negatively first. If I am to go on being filled with the Spirit I must not 'grieve' the Spirit. We meet that expression in chapter four, verse thirty: 'Grieve not the holy Spirit of God, whereby ye are sealed unto the day of redemption.' What does it mean? It means that if you and I yield to anything that is opposed to the Spirit, we shall not be under the control of the Spirit. If I allow my lusts and passions to control me, then the Holy Spirit is not controlling me. 'The flesh lusteth against the Spirit, and the Spirit against the flesh, and these are contrary the one to the other' (Galatians 5:17). If I want to be filled and controlled by the Spirit I must see to it that my lusts and passions and evil desires are not controlling me. Neither must the devil control me. I must resist the devil, and I must also resist 'the world'. That is obvious; I must not grieve the Spirit. If I am living a life of sin He is grieved; and He does not control me when He is grieved. He withholds Himself. We are dealing, remember, with a Person. Therefore I must be very careful, negatively, not to grieve Him in any shape or form. He is compared to a dove – gentle and sensitive.

In the same way I must not 'quench' the Spirit. The Spirit is within, stimulating, giving ideas, producing thoughts, making suggestions. Every time I refuse them or reject them, every time I say 'No, wait a minute, I want to do this first, and then . . .', I am quenching the Spirit; and to that extent I am not being controlled by the Spirit. This is voluntary, this is within my control. If I deliberately reject Him, if I deliberately do things that He tells me not to do, well, I am not being controlled by the Spirit; and I shall not enjoy the results of the blessing of being controlled by the Spirit.

But turn to the positive – this is what is most important. The negative, surely, is self-evident. You cannot be filled with wine and the Holy Spirit at the same time; you cannot be filled with sin and the Holy Spirit; they are incompatible. 'There is no communion

[50]

between light and darkness, God and Belial' (2 Corinthians 6: 14–16). That is elementary, surely. We must stop grieving the Spirit, we must resist the devil, we must keep under the body, we must fight against the relics and remnants of sin that are within us. That is the first part, but it is negative.

What is the positive? It is this – and nothing can be more important than this – we must realize that He is within us. The Holy Spirit is in every Christian. 'Know ye not', says the Apostle to the Corinthians, 'that your bodies are the temple of the Holy Ghost that dwelleth in you, which ye have of God, and ye are not your own?' (1 Corinthians 6:19) That is the first thing; and it is because we so constantly forget this that we are not filled with the Spirit, and not controlled by Him. To use the words of a hymn, He is within us – 'a gracious, willing guest'.

Have you noticed how our Lord put it? He was going to leave His disciples, and they were crestfallen. He said, 'Let not your heart be troubled' – don't be grieved. 'I shall not leave you comfortless'; which means, 'I am not going to leave you as orphans, I will send another Comforter.' (John 14) 'I am going to send Someone to you who will do for you what I have been doing whilst I have been with you. You have turned to Me when you were in difficulties, you have asked Me your questions. I was always here to answer. Because I say I am going away, you say, "What are we going to do now?" But do not be troubled, I am going to send you "another Comforter", I am going to send you another Advocate, Someone who will be with you always, in you, with you at all times ever to guide you and to direct you, and to do all that you need.' The way to go on being controlled by the Holy Spirit is to remember that He is there, 'a gracious, willing guest' within us, dwelling within us. We have to do this quite deliberately. We have to repeat these Scriptures to ourselves. We should start our day by saying something like this to ourselves, 'The Holy Spirit is dwelling within me, He is in my body; my body is the temple of the Holy Spirit who is living and dwelling within me. I must remember that.'

Let me use a simple illustration. What do parents who have young children do when they have a guest or a friend staying with them? The children tend to wake up early in the morning. What do you parents say to them? You say, 'Keep quiet, you must not disturb our guest'. You remind them that this guest is in the house, and you say to the children, 'Now be careful, don't shout, keep quiet, realize who is staying here'. That is precisely what you and I have to do if we are to go on being controlled by the Holy Spirit – remember that He is there, He is in you, He dwells within you. Without that realization we shall never be controlled by Him. We have to recollect this, to remind ourselves of it, and to keep on doing so.

More than that; we have to desire Him, and thirst for Him and His fellowship and His communion. Have you noticed how often the New Testament speaks about 'the communion of the Holy Ghost'? Look at the benediction: 'The grace of the Lord Jesus Christ, the love of God, and the fellowship, the communion, of the Holy Ghost be with you' (2 Corinthians 13:14). We have to be reminded of this fellowship, we have to remind ourselves of it, and to seek it. If He is within me, I must not only realize the fact, I must commune with Him, I must have fellowship with Him. I must consult Him, I must consider His presence and ask Him to manifest Himself more and more to me. That is how one is filled with the Spirit.

Then, too, I must pay very careful heed to all His promptings: 'Work out your own salvation with fear and trembling; for it is God that worketh in you, both to will and to do'. How does He do that? Through the Holy Spirit! He 'worketh in you, both to will and to do'. If ever you feel a sudden desire to read the Word of God, that is the Holy Spirit working in you. He is in you, He is prompting you. Obey Him; go and do it. If you feel called to prayer, go and do it. Stop what you are doing; do not postpone obedience. HE has asked you, so let everything be dropped; do what He asks of you. Let us be sensitive to His promptings. That is the way to be more and more controlled by the Spirit. The more we obey Him the more He will indicate His desires, the more He will prompt us. So we must be careful and punctilious in obeying His every behest or request, every prompting and every urge that comes to us from Him.

All this is happening within us constantly. He would lead us on, He would guide us. He is always doing it, He is always anxious to show us more and more of the Lord Jesus Christ. Let Him do so. Are we not all guilty of quenching promptings about attending God's house, about reading the Scriptures, about prayer, and a thousand and one other things? These are the promptings of the Holy Ghost who would lead us and guide us and control us and direct us. Listen to Him. Let Him do it. That is the meaning of this exhortation.

You do not receive this as an experience. I almost said, Would to God that we could! How much easier it would be! But this is God's way. It is a question of a personal relationship; and as Christians we are responsible creatures. He is not going to do it all for us while we just remain in passivity. It is not all done marvellously for us, and there is no more struggle. There is a struggle! The world and the flesh and the devil are still there, and we have to resist them. And we also have to listen to Him positively and give time and attention to doing so.

There are no short cuts in these matters. You do not receive this in a packet tied up, 'ready-made', everything complete. No, that is the way of the Cults; that is not the New Testament teaching. That is psychology; it is not the teaching of the Scripture.

Listen to the Spirit's promptings, and then listen to the Word, the Scriptures. What is this Word? It is the Word of the Holy Spirit. He is the Author. 'Holy men of God spake as they were moved by the Holy Ghost' (2 Peter 1 :21). None of this is of private interpretation; this is not of man; this is God's Word. Read it, I say, study it, devour it, understand it, give your time and attention to it. Are you taking advantage of every opportunity of understanding this Word? Is one service in a week enough? How often do we pay attention to public exposition, and to private study in order to understand it? That is the way to be led of the Spirit. To know His Word and all its injunctions, to listen to them; to be sensitive to them, and then to obey them! To obey the Word of God! The Holy Spirit is pleased when any one of us takes a word in the Scriptures and puts it into practice, when we allow it to govern our decisions, our actions, and all our behaviour.

There, then, are some of the principles. I have merely mentioned the main headings of the ways in which we are to be filled with the Spirit. It is a submission, voluntarily, to be controlled in the whole of our lives, mind and heart and will, by the Holy Spirit of God.

To what does it lead? That is what the Apostle goes on to say. It means that the fruit of the Spirit will be manifest in us. Where He is in control the fruit is evident and obvious – 'love, joy, peace, longsuffering, gentleness, meekness, goodness, faith and temperance'. There they are! they become evident. And also all the things the Apostle goes on to say from the next verse, the nineteenth verse

of this fifth chapter of Ephesians – all about how we conduct ourselves in the house of God, how we get on together, husbands and
wives, fathers and children, masters and servants. When men and
women are controlled by the Holy Spirit in mind and heart and will,
that is the sort of life they lead. Go on, keep on being controlled by
the Holy Spirit that dwelleth in you as 'a gracious, willing guest'.

4
Submission in the Spirit

Ephesians 5:21

There is one technical point about this statement to which I must refer before we proceed with our consideration of it; and that is, that all are agreed that it should be, 'Submitting yourselves one to another in the fear of Christ'. It is not a matter of translation, but rather of manuscripts; and beyond all doubt the best manuscripts have here, 'in the fear of Christ', not 'in the fear of God'. Of course ultimately it comes to very much the same; but it does give an additional emphasis to what the Apostle says, as we shall proceed to see.

Here is a statement which we must be very careful to take in its setting and its context. It is important that we should do so in order that we may truly understand what the Apostle is actually saying. In other words, the connection must engage our attention for a moment. There are those who would so translate this as to make it a new and separate injunction. They say that in this section the Apostle is giving a series of separate exhortations. But that is quite unjustifiable. He did not say 'Submit yourselves one to another'; he said 'Submitting yourselves one to another'. So we must not regard it as an independent statement or exhortation. Others say that it is merely and only an introduction to what follows, as if he were saying, 'Submitting yourselves one to another in the fear of God. Wives, submit yourselves unto your own husbands as unto the Lord' – and so on, with 'children', and 'servants'. Thus they make it a kind of introduction to what is to follow. But surely both of those suggestions are wrong. The second is less wrong than the first. Nevertheless, quite patently, what the Apostle is doing here is to

[55]

continue what he has already been saying, and at the same time to introduce what he is going to say. That seems to me to be the only right way of interpreting this statement. It is a kind of link between what has gone before and what is to follow. In other words it is a further illustration of what he has laid down as a fundamental principle in verse 18, 'Be not drunk with wine, wherein is excess; but be filled with the Spirit'. I argue that he still has that in his mind, and is addressing men and women who are filled with the Spirit. He has already told them certain things about themselves which are inevitably true if they are filled with the Spirit. Here, then, is another. So we interpret this statement in the light of verse 18 with its exhortation to us to go on being filled with the Spirit.

I am emphasizing this because no man can possibly do what the Apostle tells us to do in this verse unless he is filled with the Spirit. It is useless to go to the world and say, 'Submitting yourselves one to another in the fear of Christ'. The world not only does not do that, the world will not do it, the world cannot do it. This is a meaningless exhortation to anybody who is not filled with the Spirit. I therefore argue that here the Apostle is carrying forward the two ideas he has in his mind in verse 18, 'Be not drunk with wine, wherein is excess'. A man who is drunk is not going to submit himself to anybody. He is asserting himself. That is the characteristic of such a man. He is lacking in control and especially in this respect. He is boasting, and praising himself, and thinks he is wonderful. If we are to submit ourselves one to another we must be entirely different from those who are filled with wine, and who go to that excess. And, on the other hand, we must be filled with the Spirit.

There, I suggest, is the essential connection. There is the basic idea. We have to be unlike what we were, we have to be unlike the world, we have to be altogether different in our essential characteristics from men and women who still belong to that realm. We are to be filled with the Spirit. How do we show that? So far the Apostle has been illustrating it in our relationship to God. He has been dealing with our worship, 'Speaking to yourselves (to one another) in psalms and hymns and spiritual songs, singing and making melody in your heart to the Lord; Giving thanks always for all things unto God and the Father in the name of our Lord Jesus Christ'. You are filled with the Spirit, he says, and you meet together to have your meetings, your convivial meetings of happiness

[56]

and of joy. You are to express all that together in worship of God and praise and adoration. But, he says, not only that, you are to manifest this same spirit in your dealings with one another, in the fellowship that you have with one another on the purely human and earthly level. So he is emphasizing his basic theme by showing that men and women who are filled with the Spirit are to show that characteristic in their dealings with one another.

That is the way to approach this particular verse. It is essential that we should understand exactly what it means, because the Apostle is going to illustrate this truth in three particular respects. He lays down the principle, then having done so, he says, applying that in particular, 'Wives, submit yourselves unto your own husbands as unto the Lord . . . Children, obey your parents in the Lord: for this is right . . . Servants, be obedient unto them that are your masters according to the flesh'. These three are, as we shall see, separate and particular illustrations of this fundamental principle that should always govern the relationship of Christian people one with another.

'Submitting yourselves one to another'. Notice that the very way in which the Apostle puts it confirms what I have just been saying about the connection of this verse with the immediately surrounding verses. 'You who are filled with the Spirit, must therefore sing together, and submit yourselves one to another, and behave as follows in the crucial relationships in life'.

But what does 'submitting yourselves one to another' mean? A better translation, perhaps, would be, 'Being subject one to another'. The idea that he obviously has in mind, in view of the word he uses, is something like this: It is the picture of soldiers in a regiment, soldiers in a line under an officer. The characteristic of a man in that position is this, that he is in a sense no longer an individual; he is now a member of a regiment; and all of them together are listening to the commands and the instructions which the officer is issuing to them. When a man joins the army he is as it were signing away his right to determine his own life and activity. That is an essential part of his contract. When he joins the army or air force or the navy, or whatever it is, he no longer governs and controls himself; he has to do what he is told. He cannot go on a holiday when he likes, he cannot get up at the hour in the morning when he likes. He is a man under authority, and the rules dictate to him; and if he begins to act on his own, and independently of the others, he is guilty of insubordination and will be punished accordingly. Such is the word the Apostle uses; so what he is saying amounts to this – that we who are filled with the Spirit are to behave voluntarily in that way with respect to one another. We are members of the same regiment, we are units in this same great army. We are to do that voluntarily which the soldier is 'forced' to do.

How does this work out in practice? It is not enough merely to use the words; these things have to be applied. As our Lord put it to the disciples: 'If ye know these things, happy are ye if ye do them.' What does it involve? What does it mean to say that we have to submit and to subject ourselves one to another? Negatively, it clearly means certain things. We must not be thoughtless. Most of the troubles in life, and most of the clashes, are due to the fact that people do not think. Impetuous action is the greatest cause of clashes and of disputes and of unhappiness in every realm of life. If only people thought before they spoke, or before they looked, or before they acted, what a difference it would make! But the trouble with the natural man is that he does not think; he gets an idea and he expresses it; he has a feeling and he wants to put it into operation at once; an impulse comes and he acts. Putting it negatively, therefore, the Apostle is saying that the Christian must never be a thoughtless man, must not live that sort of instinctive, intuitional kind of life. As he has already been telling us at great length, the Christian is a man who is governed by truth, governed by principles; he is wise. He has put it earlier, 'But as wise'. And again, 'Therefore be ye not unwise, but understanding what the will of the Lord is'. A wise man is a man who thinks; he looks before he leaps, he thinks before he speaks. He is a man who is governed by thought and by understanding, by meditation and a spirit of consideration.

And the moment he begins to think, he will discover another very important negative, namely, that he must not be selfish and self-centred. The real trouble with selfish and self-centred people is that they never think at all – except, of course, about themselves. But this really means that they are not thinking; they are acting as animals. An animal is always out for itself, it does not think, it acts according to its instincts. To speak generally, that is the trouble with the non-Christian; he is selfish and self-centred, because he does not think.

Or, remembering the Apostle's word and the illustration it suggests, let me put it another way. The Christian, while he is still an individual, must never be individualistic. The moment you are individualistic you are wrong. This principle, this characteristic of being individualistic is impossible, as I say, in an army. That is the first thing that has to be repressed in a man who goes into the army. It can be a very painful process; but he has to realize that he can no longer act as formerly. Perhaps he was a spoilt child at home – the moment he wanted a thing he always had it, he was the ruler. But all that has to stop. In the army he has to submit to others. It would be impossible to run an army if it consisted of a series of people who were individualistic. All that has to be submerged.

To express the matter in another way – we must cease to be self-assertive. Self-assertion is the very antithesis of what the Apostle is saying: 'Submitting yourselves one to another in the fear of Christ'. A man who pursues that course is never self-assertive. Self is the root cause of all our troubles. The devil understood that at the very beginning when he first tempted man: 'Hath God said that you must not eat of this? Of course He did so because he knew you would be as gods. That is insulting to you; it is keeping you down. Do not submit to that, assert yourself'. Self-assertion! Oh, the havoc that is being wrought in the world because of self-assertion! It has been the cause of the two world-wars we have had in this century. It can be national as well as in the individual – 'My country right or wrong' – hence wars and clashes! But it is the same on the level of individual relationships; all trouble springs out of this horrid self which is always anxious to have its own way.

Yet another way of putting it is to say that the Christian must never be opinionated. A Christian has, and must have, opinions; but he must never be opinionated. What a difference there is between a man who has opinions, good opinions, strong opinions, and the man who is opinionated – self-conscious and proud of his opinions! We must never be opinionated because that again is another manifestation of self. The opinionated man is much more interested in the fact that he believes than in what he believes; he is always looking at himself; he parades his beliefs. The way in which he does so, of course, always betrays the man. He shows that he is proud of his knowledge. That is because he really does not understand the subject about which he knows a little. If he did it would humble him. But he is not really interested in truth, he is interested in his relationship to it, his knowledge of it. Opinionated people always cause clashes.

[59]

This, in turn, leads to another trouble. Such a person always tends to be dictatorial – one more manifestation of self – and (to use the expression of the Apostle Peter), to 'lord' it over others. Peter writes in his first Epistle, chapter 5: 'The elders which are among you I exhort'. He is addressing elders because this is the particular temptation that confronts a man who becomes an elder. He is a man with ability, and he has elements of leadership in him, therefore he gets into this position; and by reason of his eldership he is particularly exposed to this danger. 'The elders which are among you I exhort . . . Feed the flock of God which is among you, taking the oversight thereof, not by constraint, but willingly; not for filthy lucre, but of a ready mind; neither as being lords over God's heritage, but being ensamples to the flock'. There are to be none that 'lord' it in the church; elders are to be ensamples to the flock. It is always the temptation, the danger, to such men; and the clearer a man's ideas are, the more exposed he is to this particular temptation. But you must not fall into it, says the Apostle; you must 'submit yourselves one to another'.

This theme can be illustrated almost endlessly. We can perhaps sum up what we have been saying by putting it like this; the Christian must never be self-seeking. I have been explaining the manifestations of self-seeking; self-centredness always leads to self-seeking. Then, to work it out still further, because this man of the world with whom the Apostle is contrasting the Christian, is essentially self-seeking and self-centred, he is thoughtless and unconcerned with respect to others. He is so anxious about himself that he never has a moment for other people. He wants something, but it does not occur to him that somebody else might want it also. He wants to get on, but the other man wants to get on also. Now he doesn't realize that; so, because he is so self-centred and thoughtless, he is particularly thoughtless and unconcerned with respect to the position and the needs and the desires and the welfare of others. Indeed probably he will go further and will even tend to despise others, and to treat them with a certain amount of contempt. There is a fine illustration of this in Paul's First Epistle to the Corinthians. The evil I have been describing was the real trouble there; that is why he had to write the twelfth chapter about the church as the Body of Christ. Those who were the 'more comely parts' were despising those who were 'the less comely parts', and the latter were jealous of the former because of their ostentation and their importance, and the honour that was

being paid them. Thus there was a fundamental failure to understand this principle.

A final way in which we can put this negative consideration is to
say that the man who is thus self-centred, and selfish, and individualistic, and thoughtless, and self-seeking, is almost invariably, at the
same time, a man who resents criticism, and is impatient of other
points of view. If I am very proud of my opinion then the fact that
anyone should dare to question it or to query it is a gross insult to
me – not to the truth, but to me. It is what *I* believe that matters. So
this man resents criticism, and is impatient of other points of view.
He does not want to hear them, and indeed resents them. He is
hyper-sensitive. What an extraordinary thing this 'self' is! What a
foul disease is self-centredness! Notice the multiplicity of the symp-
toms. It affects the whole of a man's outlook, every part of him – his
thinking, his emotional, affective life, his action, his will, the voli-
tional part – everything is involved. Look at this picture of this
person – selfish, self-centred, opinionated, tending to be dictatorial,
hyper-sensitive. What happens next? The next thing is that he is
always threatening resignation. He feels that he is being queried,
that people do not trust him, that they are not doing what he says,
or appreciating what he thinks. It is unfair – so he is going out, he is
going to resign! The Apostle is writing about church life, and he
says: You must not be like that, you will make havoc of the church
if you are like that, and if you are always 'walking out'. That, then,
is the negative way of interpreting the words, 'Submitting yourselves one to another in the fear of Christ'.

But what do the words mean positively? They are, of course, the
exact antithesis of all I have been saying; but yet more. 'Be filled
with the Spirit'. This means that 'the eyes of your understanding
are enlightened' with respect to the truth. What does that lead to?
This is how it works. Here is a solution to all our problems – personal, individual problems, inter-relationships in marriage, work,
business, professions, in the State with the various classes and
groups, and races, and all else. How easy it would be for us to illustrate this, for instance, in terms of anti-Semitism. That is but one
illustration of this great principle. It happens to be a political matter
and often in the public eye; but men cannot see that it is the
principle behind it that matters. If you are right concerning the
principle you will solve not only that problem but many others as
well.

The Christian way works like this. If the eyes of our understanding are truly enlightened the first thing we learn is the truth about ourselves. That means that we realize that we are all hopeless, we are all lost, we are all damned, we are all sinners – every one of us. 'There is none righteous, no, not one'. The man who sees that that is true stops boasting about himself immediately. He does not boast about his morality, his goodness, his good works, his good deeds, his knowledge, his learning or anything else. If we but knew the truth about ourselves these problems of relationships would be soon solved. It is the Gospel alone that does that; nothing else can. The Gospel reduces us to the same level, every one of us. There is no difference, 'all have sinned and have come short of the glory of God'. 'Jew and Gentile' are all one; no master race, no superior people, none at all – all are the same. Whatever may be true of us individually we are all reduced to the same level.

Paul puts that superbly in writing to the Corinthians (1 Corinthians 4:7): 'For who maketh thee to differ from another? and what hast thou that thou didst not receive? Now if thou didst receive it, why dost thou glory, as if thou hadst not received it?' Is not that wonderful? And yet how slow people are to understand it! Here is a man boasting of his great brain, his great mind, his great ability, and despising others. Wait a moment, says Paul, what are you so proud of? Have you produced that brain of yours, have you generated it, have you brought it into being? 'What hast thou that thou didst not receive? what makes thee differ from another?' Have you made the difference? Of course you have not; everything you have got you have received; it is a gift from God. If you have a great brain, well, do not boast of it, but thank God for it. And that will keep you humble. Some are proud of their good looks; but have they themselves produced them? Others are proud of their ability in some respect – in music, art, or in speech – but where did they get it? The moment you realize that all are gifts you stop boasting, you stop being proud in this foolish manner.

But it is the Spirit alone that can bring a man to this point. The world does the exact opposite; it grades men. It has its honours, its glittering prizes, and it looks at these things; these are everything, and they are proud of them and are flushed with pride and with their success. 'You are not to be like that', says Paul – 'that is being drunk with wine, wherein is excess. Be filled with the Spirit, and if you are filled with the Spirit you will realize that all you have got is given to

[62]

you by God, and you have nothing to boast of. In any case the Spirit will lead you to see this, that with all you have got you are still very poor, you are still very ignorant, you are still very fallible, and you still fail a great deal. You', he says to the people in Corinth, 'you who are puffed up with your knowledge, what do you really know? You are but babes in Christ still. I could not feed you with meat, I could only give you milk, because you are babes – and yet you are puffed up with your knowledge'. The way to solve these difficulties in relationships is to know the truth about ourselves. The moment we begin to know this truth we see that we are but babes, we are but at the beginning. The man who thinks that his head is packed full of knowledge, when he comes to face the truth as it is found here in the light of the Spirit, feels that he knows nothing, that he is but a beginner, a babe, and that he is full of failures and of faults.

So the Apostle can go on to say 'Who art thou that judgest another?' Indeed our Lord had already said it all in these words: 'Judge not, that ye be not judged. For with what measure ye mete, it shall be measured to you again'. Realize, says our Lord, that you are under someone else. You who have set yourself up and are looking down upon others, look at the God who is looking down upon you, and you will realize that you are nothing. The trouble is, of course, that we tend to think in inches instead of in miles, and our little hillock which happens to reach a thousand feet seems a marvellous mountain to us because so many people are at sea level. Put it in the light of Mount Everest, put it in the light of heaven, and you will stop boasting about your little mole-hill. That is the way the Spirit works. He opens our understanding.

But not only that. He helps us to realize that we are members together of one body. This has been an earlier theme in this Epistle. 'Submitting yourselves one to another' – Why? Because you are all like the different parts and members of a body. The Apostle introduced that notion at the end of chapter 1, he has worked it out in chapter 4 verses 11 to 16. And, as I have already said, it is the great theme of 1 Corinthians 12: 'Ye are the body of Christ, and members in particular'. (v. 27) If you realize that, you will realize also that what really is important is not that you are a part, but that you are a part of a whole. It is the whole that matters most and not the part. And that, again, is a way of solving all our problems. In other words, it will lead you always to consider the body and its good, rather than just your own particular and personal good. Surely half the troubles today are due to the fact that we are too individualistic in our whole notion of salvation. Thank God it is individual, as we must always emphasize; but we must not think of it individualistically. People are always thinking of themselves and looking at themselves. They come to the church of God to get something for themselves. Let us try to get a true conception of the church, this great thing into which we have been put. We are but little parts and members and portions; so let us think of the whole, not the part. The man in the army is not fighting for himself, he is fighting for his country – that is the argument.

The moment a man begins to realize all these things he will be ready to forego his rights, his personal individualistic rights. He needs to understand this conception of the church as the Body of Christ, and the great privilege of being just a little part or portion in it. He will not then think of his rights primarily: he will now be interested in the development and the advancement of the whole, of every other part also – his neighbour, and the one who is next to him, and so on. Together they see this great unity, this organic vital unity of the whole. The man who sees this does not worry any longer about his rights as such, and talk about them, and always be watching them and guarding them – that goes out. Furthermore, he is ready to listen, and he is ready to learn. Realizing that he does not possess a monopoly of all the truth, and that other people have their opinions and ideas also, he is always ready to listen, he is always ready to learn. He does not automatically reject things; he is patient, he is understanding, and if a man says 'But now, wait a minute, I think . . .' he will listen to him, he will give him a proper hearing. He will not cut him off at once; he will give the man a full opportunity of expounding his position. Then he will deal with it as best he can. In other words he is the antithesis of the man I have been describing in negative terms.

But we can go further. I say that this is a man who is ready to suffer, and ready even to suffer injustice, if necessary, for the sake of the truth, for the sake of the cause, for the sake of the Body. Paul puts that once and for ever in his great statement in 1 Corinthians 13: 'Love suffereth long, and is kind; love envieth not; love vaunteth not itself, is not puffed up, doth not behave itself unseemly, seeketh not its own, is not easily provoked, thinketh no evil; rejoiceth not in iniquity, but rejoiceth in the truth; beareth all

[64]

things, believeth all things, hopeth all things, endureth all things. Love (charity) never faileth'. That is what the Apostle tells us to put into practice here: 'Submitting yourselves one to another in the fear of Christ.' Do not be puffed up, do not boast, do not be suspicious. Get rid of self, be filled with love, believe, hope all things, never fail, be patient and longsuffering. Indeed I can summarize it all by putting it like this: The only man who can submit himself to another in the fear of Christ is the man who really is filled with the Spirit, because the man who is filled with the Spirit is a man who shows and displays the fruit of the Spirit. And the fruit of the Spirit is 'love, joy, peace, longsuffering, gentleness, goodness, faith, meekness, temperance'. If a man is full of those characteristics there will be no difficulty with him, there will be no trouble. He will be the sort of man who will submit himself readily, willingly, voluntarily, always for the sake of others and for the good of the whole cause. The only man who can do this is the man who is showing the fruit of the Spirit because he is filled with the Spirit.

This shows itself in an endless number of ways. Let me give just one illustration, a very practical one. In 1 Corinthians 14 the Apostle writes at verse 29: 'Let the prophets speak two or three, and let the other judge. If anything be revealed to another that sitteth by, let the first hold his peace. For ye may all prophesy one by one, that all may learn, and all may be comforted. And the spirits of the prophets are subject to the prophets'. What a perfect illustration! The trouble in Corinth was this: A man rose to his feet and began to speak. He was so full of matter, and felt that he alone had it, that he went on and on. But another man had a truth, and he wanted to speak; yet the first man would not give way to him. Now, says the Apostle, that is wrong. 'But,' says the first man, 'I am filled with the Spirit, I cannot help myself, I am full of matter, and I cannot refrain'. But you can, says Paul, 'the spirits of the prophets are subject to the prophets'. Control yourself, and when you see that the other man has something to say, and you have had your opportunity, sit down, let him speak. And then let that man in turn do the same with the next: 'Let two or three speak, and let the other judge; consider it together'. That is the way, says the Apostle, to avoid these problems, 'Submitting yourselves one to another in the fear of Christ'.

That, then, is the exposition of what the Apostle is saying. But if I were to leave it at that I should be doing something that could be extremely dangerous, indeed I should be doing what is, perhaps,

[65]

one of the most dangerous things a man can do at the present time. I have been expounding what the Apostle Paul is saying; but remember what I said at the beginning, that this must be taken in its context, and that it is only true in its context. I mean this – that this is the sort of text that is being so much abused today. 'Submitting yourselves' they say, 'one to another in the fear of Christ'. 'Quite so; you angular evangelicals that will not join in with the Anglo-Catholics, you people who say "No, we cannot do that, we will not join with the Church of Rome", you, and your refusal to submit to one another are the whole cause of the trouble'. 'Look at Communism', they add, 'look at the opponents of Christianity: what is needed today is a great united world church including Roman Catholics, Eastern Orthodox, liberal modernists, conservatives, everybody'. Indeed some would even go further, and add 'everybody who believes in God – the Mohammedans, the Hindus, the Jews. Bring them in; this is no time for asserting particular beliefs'. 'Submitting yourselves one to another in the fear of Christ' means, they say, that you must not stand out in that way, and if you do you are denying your own doctrine.

This text is being abused in that way today. Again they say, did not Christ pray the great High Priestly prayer 'that they all may be one'? So they ask, 'why do you not submit to this?' They believe that a text like this is the final argument for the ecumenical movement, and for the submerging of all divisions and differences and distinctions, and having a great world church. You see therefore the importance of taking a statement like this in its context. Do you imagine that the Apostle Paul in this verse is preaching peace at any price, and saying that a man should ride lightly and loosely to the truth, and that he should be pliable and accommodating and compromising as regards doctrine? Is he teaching a false humility here? Is he saying that loyalty to institutional Christianity comes before everything, and that a man must put his opinions on one side and conform to the general line and say what everybody else is saying? Does the Apostle's teaching run on those lines? The answer is this: the Apostle who wrote this verse had already written chapters 1, 2 and 3 of this Epistle, in which he has laid down basic, essential, fundamental Christian doctrines. This statement is only addressed to people who are agreed about doctrine. He is not discussing here the relationship between people who disagree about doctrine. He assumes that they are on 'the foundation of the apostles and prophets' and that they are 'in the unity of the faith'. A heretic was not allowed to remain in the church; he was to be put out, they were not to have fellowship with him.

To apply a statement like this to the 'church' as she is today, is to misunderstand completely the whole of the New Testament. Paul is writing here to people who are agreed about doctrine. He is dealing with the spirit in which they apply the common doctrine about which they are agreed. If you interpret it in the other way you will find that scripture contradicts scripture. Scripture tells us 'earnestly to contend for the faith'. The Apostle thanks the Philippians that they had stood with him for 'the defence and confirmation of the Gospel'. If that other interpretation is right they would have been wrong so to do. Then you will remember what we read in the second chapter of Galatians about what Paul did to Peter. Peter was not quite as clear in his mind, and in his understanding, as Paul over the question of eating with those who had not been circumcised. The Peter who had been so prominent was wrong in his teaching at this point. What did the Apostle Paul do? Did he submit himself to Peter, in the fear of Christ, and say, 'Well, who am I to argue with Peter? After all, he was one of the innermost three in the circle that were with Christ. I was never with Christ in the flesh; I was then a blasphemer and a Pharisee. Who am I to stand up against a great man like Peter? I must just say nothing, I must listen in silence and pray; and then we must work together in a spirit of amity and co-operation?' How monstrous! On the contrary Paul says, 'I withstood him to the face'. He corrected Peter in public because Peter was wrong, and the whole future of the Church was in jeopardy. You see how important it is to take a statement in its context, and how extremely dangerous it is to extract any statement like this out of its context. It can lead to a denial of the New Testament teaching. Let me give one final example of this, taken from the Second Epistle of John, where the matter is put so clearly: 'If there come any unto you and bring not this doctrine, receive him not into your house, neither bid him God speed: for he that biddeth him God speed is a partaker of his evil deeds'. That means guilt by association, and we must not submit to him.

'Submitting yourselves one to another in the fear of Christ' does not mean that you accommodate yourself to wrong teaching and doctrine, that you say nothing when falsehood is being propagated. No! for that is a denial of all the New Testament. Not only that, it is

[67]

a denial of some of the most glorious epochs and eras in the Christian church. What are the mountain peaks in church history? Here is one: *Athanasius contra mundum*. Athanasius had to stand alone against the whole world on the doctrine of the Person of Christ. Martin Luther – what was he doing? Well, here was a man standing absolutely alone against the great Papist church and fifteen centuries of tradition. Of course what people said to him was this: 'Who are you? Why do you not submit yourself in the fear of Christ?' ' "Submitting yourselves one to another in the fear of Christ" – Who are you?' And yet he stood and said, 'I can do no other, so help me God'! Why? Because the Spirit had enlightened him. Luther was right, the church was wrong.

God forbid that we should misinterpret a text like this. This statement must be taken in its context. Paul is writing to people who are agreed about the truth, and what he is saying is this: You who agree about the truth, do so in the right way; do not be opinionated; listen patiently to the other side; do not lose your temper; know how to be indulgent in argument; let the others speak, let them put forward their ideas; do not be censorious; do not condemn a man for a word; be prepared to listen; be charitable; go as far as you can; but when it comes to vital truth, stand, but always do so in the right way, in the Spirit. Do it with humility, do it with charity, do it with understanding, do it with hopefulness. Do not be offensive and bad-mannered; do not be opinionated; 'submit yourselves one to another in the fear of Christ'.

There, it seems to me, is the meaning of what the Apostle says in this important and vital statement. There is still the last phrase, 'in the fear of Christ'. We shall have to go on to that. But above everything let us be sure that we understand the context in which the Apostle makes this statement. There are certain fundamental, essential things about which there must be no question or query. There is an irreducible minimum to Christianity; and on that we must stand. We do not submit there; we fight, if necessary, even unto death. And we must do so in the right way and in the right spirit. But when you come to matters about which there cannot be certainty and finality, it is then, especially, that you have to remember this exhortation. The members of the church at Corinth in general were agreed about the fundamentals and the vital matters, the foundational principles of Christianity. The Apostle does not have to instruct them about these principles, but only to remind them.

[68]

(Chapter 15:1–4) In what respect does he have to instruct them? About the way they were talking about one another, about the fact that some were eating meat offered to idols and others not doing so, and so on. They were agreed about the way of salvation, about the deity of Christ, and about the atonement. They were all agreed there, otherwise they would not have been in the church. But you can be agreed about those truths and still divide the church and be guilty of schism, about other matters. And it is just here that we have to learn to submit ourselves one to the other in the fear of Christ. If you have no opinions you are not a Christian; but if you are opinionated you are a bad Christian. God grant us the ability to draw that distinction! We are not told not to have opinions or to sell them lightly. We are told to have, and to hold them, but never to be opinionated. We are to hold them as 'filled with the Spirit', manifesting love, joy, peace, longsuffering, gentleness, goodness, meekness, faith, temperance – glorious fruits of the blessed Holy Spirit. 'Be not drunk with wine, wherein is excess' – do not boast, do not be bombastic, do not be violent. 'Be filled with the Spirit'; hold and preach and teach the truth in love, and then personal relationships will be sweet and loving and lovely, and the Name of God will be glorified throughout the world.

5
The Spirit of Christ

Ephesians 5:21

The Apostle in this great injunction which is to control the whole of our Christian living does not stop at saying 'submitting yourselves one to another'. There is this further addition to which I now call attention – 'in the fear of Christ'.

Here we are told exactly how and why we are to submit ourselves one to the other. In other words, this last phrase of the Apostle's provides us with the motives for submitting ourselves one to the other. We can divide it in the following way. Let us first observe why we are to submit ourselves one to another – the reason for doing so. It is, 'in the fear of Christ'. Now this is not just a casual addition, not just a phrase to round off the injunction; it is not something that Paul wrote without thinking about it, almost accidentally, as we are sometimes guilty of doing. Those who would have us know their spirituality often intersperse their conversation with certain clichés and phrases. They keep on saying 'praise the Lord' after almost every sentence. That is not the way in which the Apostle added this phrase, 'in the fear of Christ'; it is not done thoughtlessly and glibly and superficially.

It is obviously done because it is an essential part of his teaching. I can prove that quite easily. He is laying down here his general principle – we are to live a life which is characterized by this, that we submit ourselves one to another. Then he takes this up in three particular instances, wives and husbands, children and parents, servants and masters. But what is so interesting to observe is that in each of the three instances, as here in the general statement of the principle, he is very careful to make this addition.

[70]

First we see it in the general principle, 'Submitting yourselves one to another in the fear of Christ'. Then in the first application in verse 22: 'Wives, submit yourselves unto your own husbands, as unto the Lord'. He does not stop at saying, 'Wives, submit yourselves unto your own husbands', he adds 'as unto the Lord'. Then in the second application, in the case of children, 'Children, obey your parents in the Lord'. (Chapter 6, verse 1) Still the same addition! He does not merely say, 'Children, obey your parents, for this is right', he says, 'obey your parents in the Lord: for this is right.' And then in the third application with regard to the servants and the masters we have the same thing in chapter 6 verses 5 and following: 'Servants, be obedient to them that are your masters according to the flesh, with fear and trembling, in singleness of your heart, as unto Christ; not with eyeservice, as men-pleasers; but as the servants of Christ, doing the will of God from the heart; with good will, doing service, as to the Lord, and not to men: knowing that whatsoever good thing any man doeth, the same shall he receive of the Lord, whether he be bond or free. And, ye masters, do the same things unto them, forbearing threatening; knowing that your Master also is in heaven; neither is there respect of persons with Him'.

The whole passage shows that this is clearly a controlling principle; and it is idle for us to go on to consider the duties of wives towards their husbands, or of children to parents, or of servants to masters, unless we are clear about this over-riding principle concerning the way in which we do these things, the reason why we must do them.

What, then, exactly does this mean? We can put it first in a general form. This is the motive which is to govern the whole of Christian living. Everything the Christian does is to be done 'in the fear of Christ'. He emphasizes that, by repeating it each time in the individual instances. Here is something which we ignore at our peril; all is to be 'in the fear of Christ'.

Let me first put the matter negatively. We are to submit ourselves one to another, and do all the things that come out of that, not because this is good in and of itself, and because not to do so is bad. There are men of the world who do this kind of thing because they believe it is a right thing to do. But that is not the reason why the Christian behaves in this way. The thing that marks off the Christian from the man who is not a Christian is not merely that he believes in the Lord Jesus Christ unto salvation, and trusts Him and His atoning work, but that, in addition, the life of the Christian is governed altogether by this Person. Jesus Christ is Lord; and the Christian believes in the Lord Jesus Christ. You cannot believe in Him as Saviour without believing in Him as Lord. If you have any belief in Him at all you believe in the whole Christ; and therefore He becomes the Lord of your life. The Christian does not merely do things because they are good and right, and because it is wrong to do certain other things; the differentiating mark of the Christian is that he does everything 'as unto the Lord', 'in the fear of Christ', because Christ is his Lord.

This revolutionizes all our thinking. Let me put it therefore in the form of another negative. 'Submitting yourselves one to another'. 'Here', says somebody, 'is a principle with which I am in entire agreement. I have no use for your talk about the blood of Christ, atonement, and so on; but when you say that we should all submit ourselves one to another, I agree. That is the basis of an egalitarian state; it is the doing away with all classes and divisions and distinctions so that we all may become one, and all men be equal – "submitting yourselves one to another".'

But that is not what the Apostle says. We are not to submit ourselves one to another because of some political or social teaching which we may hold. There are people who hold that teaching, that egalitarian philosophy – that all are to be reduced to the same common level. Irrespective of what they are, or who they are, all are to be brought to that level. That is not what the Apostle says at all. 'Submitting yourselves one to another'. Why? Not because it is your political or social theory, but 'in the fear of Christ' – something altogether different.

In so speaking I am not expressing my opinion of political and social and philosophical theories. All I am concerned to emphasize is that the Christian motive for doing these things is altogether different from that which applies in the case of the non-Christian. Furthermore, to confuse Christian teaching with, or to reduce Christian teaching to the level of political theory, to socialism or whatever else it may be, is a travesty of the Gospel. I am not concerned, I say, about the politics, but I am concerned to show that the Christian position is always this – 'in the fear of Christ'. Though by Acts of Parliament you may reduce all men to a common denominator, you do not make them Christians thereby. If it is not

[72]

for the reason given by the Apostle it is of no value at all spiritually.

Or take another negative. We are not to submit ourselves one to another simply because it is the thing to do in certain circles and under certain conditions. There are social conventions that call on us to do this; you stand back politely and make way for others – submitting yourselves one to another. That is not what the Apostle is talking about. He does not say that you are to put on a kind of social uniform, or affect the manners of a certain class or group, that you are to give the impression that you are submitting yourselves whereas, in fact, the whole time in your heart you are doing the exact opposite. The trouble with that apparent submission is that it is actually a sign of your superiority, and you are proud of your position and your social manners. But this is not 'etiquette'! The world appears very wonderful. You look on and you see a man standing back and bowing and making way for another. But the question is, What about his heart ? why is he doing that ? Is he doing it 'in the fear of Christ ?' Social conventions are not in the mind of the Apostle at all, because they are always superficial, and generally unreal. The Christian is moved by a profound and a deep motive; it is 'the fear of Christ'. This is what governs him, this is what always rules him.

But let me proceed to one other negative. I wonder whether this will come as a shock. We are to submit ourselves one to the other – in the matter of wives and husbands and children and parents and servants and masters – not even for the sake of keeping the law, even the Law of God. That is not the Christian's primary motive. The motive of the Christian is always, 'in the fear of Christ'. Some of the things he is told to do, of course, have already been stated in the Law. Take children, for instance: 'Children, obey your parents in the Lord: for this is right. Honour thy father and mother; which is the first commandment with promise'. The commandment said it, and the Christian is to do that which is indicated in the commandment. Yes, but he has another reason, and a new reason for doing so. The Jew is meant to keep the commandment, but the Christian does it 'in the Lord', 'in the fear of Christ'. He is not merely concerned about keeping the Law, he has this higher motive, it is 'in the fear of Christ'.

This then is always the differentiating mark of the Christian. The Christian does not think of himself in terms of the Law any longer, he always thinks of himself in this relationship – 'not as being

[73]

without law, but as being under law to Christ', 'in the fear of Christ', in terms of this personal relationship to his Lord and Saviour. The Apostle therefore keeps on repeating this in order to impress it upon us; and, of course, it is essential for this reason, that it is only as we are governed by this motive that we shall be able to do all this. A man who is filled with the Spirit is a man who is always remembering the Lord Jesus Christ. The Spirit points to Him, the Spirit glorifies Him, the Spirit always leads to Him; and so the man filled with the Spirit will ever be looking at Him. This is his one grand motive – 'in the fear of Christ'. Having this at the centre of all his thinking he is enabled to do these various things.

I sum it up by putting it in this form. The difference between the Christian and the non-Christian is this: the Christian always knows why he does a thing, he always knows what he is doing. As we have already been reminded, the Christian is 'not unwise, but understanding what the will of the Lord is'. That is in verse 17 and that is the difference. The other man does not know why he does things, he conforms to a pattern, he imitates others, he watches what they do and he does the same. He does not know why, he has no real philosophy of the thing, he just does it – he is always conforming. But the Christian, on the contrary, thinks, and reasons; he has wisdom, and knows exactly what he is doing; and the reason always is 'in the fear of Christ'.

How does all this work out? What are the Christian's particular reasons and motives? The first is obviously this: The Christian submits himself to others, and does these other things, because this is something that has been plainly and clearly taught by the Lord Jesus Christ Himself. It would be a simple matter to quote many passages out of the Gospels which make this plain and clear. There is one in the 20th chapter of Matthew's Gospel which illustrates and illuminates this whole subject. Look at that statement beginning at verse 20: 'Then came to Him the mother of Zebedee's children with her sons, worshipping Him, and desiring a certain thing of Him. And He said unto her, What wilt thou? and she said, Grant that these my two sons may sit, the one on Thy right hand, and the other on the left, in Thy kingdom. But Jesus answered and said, Ye know not what ye ask. Are ye able to drink of the cup that I drink of?', and so on. Matthews account then goes on to say, 'And when the ten heard this they were moved with indignation against the two brethren'. But why? Because they desired to be in that supreme position themselves. They were annoyed with the two brothers because they had got in first, as it were. We are all so clear about these deficiencies in others; so the ten were filled with indignation. 'But Jesus called them unto Him, and said, Ye know that the princes of the Gentiles exercise dominion over them, and they that are great exercise authority upon them. But it shall not be so among you: but whosoever will be great among you, let him be your minister; and whosoever will be chief among you, let him be your servant: Even as the Son of man came not to be ministered unto, but to minister, and to give His life a ransom for many'. There, our Lord has given explicit teaching on this very subject. The Christian need be in no doubt or hesitation; this is one of the clearest commandments and pieces of teaching ever given by our blessed Lord.

Then there is that other extraordinary illustration of it in John 13 verse 12. Here is our Lord on the very eve of His death. We are told that 'having loved His own which were in the world, He loved them unto the end'. And then this remarkable thing happened: 'So after He had washed their feet, and had taken His garments, and was set down, He said unto them' – you remember what had preceded. 'Jesus knowing that the Father had given all things into His hands, and that He was come from God, and went to God; knowing that, He riseth from supper and laid aside His garments; and took a towel, and girded Himself. After that He poureth water into a basin, and began to wash the disciples' feet, and to wipe them with the towel wherewith He was girded'. The disciples could not understand this, and Peter so objected to this that our Lord had to rebuke him and teach him. 'So after He had washed their feet, and had taken His garments, and was set down again, He said unto them, Know ye what I have done to you?' Do you understand what I have been doing? Do you see its meaning? Do you see its significance? 'Ye call me Master and Lord; and ye say well, for so I am. If I then, your Lord and Master, have washed your feet, ye also ought to wash one another's feet. For I have given you an example, that ye should do as I have done to you. Verily, verily, I say unto you, The servant is not greater than his lord; neither is he that is sent greater than he that sent him. If ye know these things, happy are ye if ye do them'. There was never plainer teaching than this. There is no need to argue about this, there is no need to be in any difficulty or in any doubt or darkness with respect to it. Our Lord, once and for ever,

[75]

in that act of washing the disciples' feet, has placed it before us. He has done something, and so the picture should ever be before us.

That is why we submit ourselves one to another – because He has taught us to do so. Hear Him saying again, 'By this shall all men know that ye are my disciples if ye have love one to another'. That is how they are going to know it. Indeed, He says it again in the great High Priestly prayer, where He prays that they all may be one as He and the Father are one, that all men may know that they are His disciples, and that the Father has sent Him. So our first great reason for paying great heed to this is, that our Lord has gone out of His way to teach us. Here He is, the Lord of glory; but He humbled Himself. Lord and Master – yes! but He is not like the princes of the world. He is in a different category. We must get rid of all human thinking here. He is the Son of God who has come down to be our minister. 'The Son of man came not to be ministered unto, but to minister, and to give His life a ransom for many'.

The second reason for doing these things, or the second explanation of why we are to do these things, is in order to show our gratitude to Him. If we really believe what we claim to believe, as Christians, our supreme desire in life should be to show our gratitude to Him. Do we really believe that He is the Son of God, and that He came down from heaven to earth in order to save us; that He saves us not only by living His perfect life, but especially by going deliberately to the Cross and taking our sins upon Him, and bearing our sins and their punishment; that He gave His life, that He died that we might be forgiven, that we might be reconciled unto God? The argument is that, if we really believe that, our supreme desire should be to please Him, to show our gratitude to Him. He has done that for us; what does He desire of us? He asks us to keep His commandments in order that His name might be magnified and glorified amongst other people.

Once more we find in the great High Priestly prayer that He put it like this. Praying to the Father He says: 'I have glorified Thy name in the earth'; and then – 'I am glorified in them'. This is the thing that should always govern all our practice, that the Lord Jesus Christ be glorified in us and through us. This is not a matter of argument, it is not a matter of whether we like it or not; He has said it and it is obviously true. Men and women outside judge the Lord Jesus Christ, and form their assessments of Him, by what they see in us. If they look at us and see conduct and behaviour which is identical with that in the world – every man striving for superiority, every man trying to show himself and to call attention to himself – they will say, 'This is the world, that is what the world does'. The world does not work in harmony; there are always clashes; the world is full of individualists who are always asserting themselves that they may call attention to themselves. That is how the world lives, and does everything; so if they see the same things in us, how can they possibly believe in, and worship, the Lord Jesus Christ? His claim is not only that He has died for us, but that He gives us new life, that He creates us anew, that He regenerates us, that we are essentially different, that we are filled with the Spirit that was within Him – 'I am glorified in them'. So the Christian is a man who always remembers this. He does not ask, 'What do I want to do, what would I like to do, what pleases me?' He has lost himself in his love for Christ, in gratitude to Him. His desire is to show his gratitude; he has a zeal for the Name of the Lord; he wants others to believe in Him. And he knows that the way to do that is primarily to live in the way which the Apostle outlines here. It is useless to talk to people if you deny it in your practice; my preaching is in vain if I deny the message in my life. People look at us and what we are and what we do. Therefore, Paul says, 'Submitting yourselves one to another in the fear of Christ'. This is to be our governing over-ruling motive.

But let me take the case a step higher. Our desire is to please Him and to show our love to Him. But Paul uses the word 'fear' – 'in the fear of Christ'. That means, among other things, the fear of disappointing Him, the fear of grieving Him. The Epistle to the Hebrews tells us that Christ says: 'Behold, I and the children which God hath given Me' (2:13). We are His possession, we are His people. His name is upon us, we are His representatives, we are the people whom He has 'purchased', and the relationship between us is one of love. So the Christian is a man who is governed by such thoughts. He is looking down upon us; His reputation, as it were, is in our hands – 'I am glorified in them'. He says, 'I am the light of the world', but also, 'ye are the light of the world'. The world does not see Him, it sees us, and we are the light, the only light that it has. The Christian is a man who lives and walks and does all he does in the light of that realization. 'Are we disappointing Him?' That is how love thinks, is it not? That is the kind of fear that comes

[77]

into the realm of love. It is altogether higher than law. This is the fear of hurting or of grieving or of disappointing someone who loves you, and who has faith in you, and who trusts you, and is fond of you, who has done so much for you. This is the marvellous thing about love.

This is why love is the greatest power and the greatest motive force in the whole world. A man is enabled to do things for love which he cannot do by his own will power or anything else. Love is the grandest and the greatest motive; and it operates partly in that way. Is there anything more terrible than to realize that we are disappointing the One who so loved us that He gave Himself for us; that we should grieve, that we should be unworthy of Him? Parents have this feeling about their children, and children should have the same feeling about their parents. This is the way the Christian lives. It is not, I say, the putting on of a uniform, neither is it based on some political or social theory. It is His love to us, and our relationship to Him, and our fear, our dread, lest in any way we should grieve Him or disappoint Him.

But I have to take it even a step beyond that. There is a fear that should govern all we are and all we do, that should govern us in the matter of living and sanctification, and in all our service. It is something which is stated frequently in the New Testament. I wonder how much we are influenced by this particular fear to which I am now going to call attention. The Apostle puts this to the Corinthians in the First Epistle chapter 3, beginning at verse 9: 'For we are labourers together with God: ye are God's husbandry, ye are God's building. According to the grace of God which is given unto me, as a wise masterbuilder, I have laid the foundation, and another buildeth thereon. But let every man take heed how he buildeth thereupon. For other foundation can no man lay than that is laid, which is Jesus Christ. Now if any man build upon this foundation gold, silver, precious stones, wood, hay, stubble; every man's work shall be made manifest: for the day shall declare it, because it shall be revealed by fire; and the fire shall try every man's work of what sort it is. If any man's work abide which he hath built thereupon, he shall receive a reward. If any man's work shall be burned, he shall suffer loss: but he himself shall be saved; yet so as by fire. Know ye not that ye are the temple of God, and that the Spirit of God dwelleth in you? If any man defile the temple of God, him shall God destroy; for the temple of God is holy, which temple ye are'. Now there we are dealing with a different type of fear – 'the day shall declare it'.

Let us look at some other examples of this before we draw the doctrine out of it. Take what Paul says at the end of chapter 9 in that First Epistle to the Corinthians from verse 24 to the end. 'Know ye not that they which run in a race run all, but one receiveth the prize? So run, that ye may obtain. And every man that striveth for the mastery is temperate in all things. Now they do it to obtain a corruptible crown; but we an incorruptible. I therefore so run, not as uncertainly; so fight I, not as one that beateth the air: But I keep under my body, and bring it into subjection, lest that by any means, when I have preached to others, I myself should be a castaway'. Then in the Second Epistle to the Corinthians, chapter 5, at verse 9: 'Wherefore we labour, that, whether present or absent, we may be accepted of Him. For we must all appear before the judgment seat of Christ; that everyone may receive the things done in the body, according to that he hath done, whether it be good or bad. Knowing therefore the terror of the Lord, we persuade men; but we are made manifest unto God, and I trust also are made manifest in your consciences.' 'Knowing the terror of the Lord, we persuade men'. 'Submitting yourselves one to another in the fear of Christ' – 'The terror of the Lord'! Go on to chapter 7 of that same Second Epistle to the Corinthians, the first verse: 'Having therefore these promises, dearly beloved, let us cleanse ourselves from all filthiness of the flesh and spirit, perfecting holiness in the fear of God'. Again, in Galatians chapter 6, from the 1st verse: 'Brethren, if a man be overtaken in a fault, ye which are spiritual restore such an one in the spirit of meekness; considering thyself, lest thou also be tempted. Bear ye one another's burdens, and so fulfil the law of Christ'. And again: 'If a man think himself to be something, when he is nothing, he deceiveth himself. But let every man prove his own work, and then shall he have rejoicing in himself alone, and not in another. For every man shall bear his own burden'. Then we have that great statement in Philippians 2:12 and 13: 'Wherefore, my beloved, as ye have always obeyed, not as in my presence only, but now much more in my absence, work out your own salvation with fear and trembling'. That is how you are to work it out, that is why you are to submit yourselves one to another in the fear of Christ. 'Work out your own salvation with fear and trembling'. Then in writing to Timothy, Paul says exactly the same in the Second Epistle, chapter

2, verse 19: There are people, he says, who are saying and doing things that are wrong – 'Nevertheless the foundation of God standeth sure, having this seal, The Lord knoweth them that are His. And, Let every one that nameth the Name of Christ depart from iniquity'. But in many ways the supreme example of all is at the end of chapter 12 of the Epistle to the Hebrews in verses 28 and 29: 'Wherefore we receiving a kingdom which cannot be moved, let us have grace, whereby we may serve God acceptably with reverence and godly fear: for our God is a consuming fire'.

All this, of course, has nothing to do with our justification; this has nothing to do with our receiving salvation. This is different; this is a fear concerning the matter of reward. Take the Apostle's statement in that first quotation from 1 Corinthians 3. He says: 'Every man's work is going to be tried, and if a man has built upon the foundation wood and hay and stubble it will all be burned'. There will be nothing left, 'he shall suffer loss, but he himself shall be saved; yet so as by fire', This is a great mystery. I do not pretend to understand it; nobody understands it. But the teaching seems to be clear, and it applies to all the other passages. Not one of those passages has reference to a man's salvation, but they do have reference to the reward that he is going to receive. It is possible for a man to be saved 'yet so as by fire', He may arrive in eternity with nothing at all, nothing that he has done which is of value – nothing! It has all gone, it has been destroyed by the fire of judgment. He himself is saved, 'yet so as by fire'. And it is exactly the same in all these other passages. It does not mean that a man can fall from grace; but it does mean this – that a man who is saved can know 'the terror of the Lord'. 'We must all appear before the judgment throne of Christ, and give an account of the deeds done in the body, whether good or bad'. (2 Corinthians 5:10)

Therefore, says the Apostle, 'Submit yourselves one to another in the fear of Christ'. Christian people, we are going to stand before Him and look into His eyes, and into His face. Can you imagine what it will be like to feel at that moment: 'Ah, yes, I believed that You died for me, I believed in Your shed blood; and I traded on it, I did what I wanted, I did not obey Your commandments, I did not do what You had told me, I did not perfect holiness in the fear of God. I did not submit myself to others, I asserted myself, I was so much the natural man still'!

Can you imagine what it will be like just to look into His eyes?

I can give you some conception of it. We are told in the Gospels that our Lord had warned the Apostle Peter that He would deny Him three times before the cock crowed, and of how Peter protested. Then the time came at our Lord's trial when the servant maid challenged Peter, and he, anxious to save his skin in his cowardice, denied his Lord. But remember what we are told afterwards? 'The Lord looked upon Peter; and he went out and wept bitterly'. The Lord did not say a word to him, but just looked at him. He looked at him with a look of disappointment, with a look of sorrow, because Peter had failed Him; not with a look of reprimand. Peter could not stand that; He would have preferred words, he would have preferred a thrashing, he would have preferred to be thrown into gaol. It was that look that broke him, and almost killed him. 'The Lord looked upon Peter'. Add the element of judgment to that, and you have – 'knowing the terror of the Lord'. 'Submitting yourselves one to another in the fear of Christ'. 'Wives and husbands', there is no need to argue; 'children and parents', there is no argument or discussion; 'servants and masters'; He has told us what His will is; and He has given us an example. We are without excuse. Therefore, let us 'submit ourselves one to another in the fear of Christ'. It is the only motive; and it is a sufficient motive.

But thank God, He gives us encouragement, He gives us an incentive. We have this glorious encouragement. What is it? It is His own example. Paul has already used it at the beginning of this fifth chapter. 'Be ye therefore followers of God, as dear children; and walk in love, as Christ also hath loved us, and hath given Himself for us an offering and a sacrifice to God for a sweet-smelling savour'. Then take that most glorious statement of it in Philippians chapter 2: 'Let nothing be done through strife or vainglory; but in lowliness of mind let each esteem other better than themselves. Look not every man on his own things, but every man also on the things of others. Let this mind be in you, which was also in Christ Jesus'. Is it difficult to submit to others in the way we have indicated? Is it difficult to control ourselves and submerge ourselves, and get rid of that antagonism, and so on – is it difficult? Well, if you find it difficult, as a Christian here is your answer: 'Let this mind be in you, which was also in Christ Jesus, who, being in the form of God, thought it not robbery to be equal with God: but made himself of no reputation, and took upon Him the form of a servant, and was made in the likeness of men: and being found in

[81]

fashion as a man, He humbled Himself, and became obedient unto death, even the death of the Cross'.

If that does not enable you to submit yourselves, nothing can do it. 'Submitting yourselves one to another in the fear of Christ', 'that ye should follow His steps: Who did no sin, neither was guile found in His mouth . . . when He suffered He threatened not, but committed Himself to Him that judgeth righteously: Who His own self bare our sins in His own body on the tree, that we, being dead to sins, should live unto righteousness: by whose stripes ye were healed'. (1 Peter 2:21–24) 'Submitting yourselves one to another in the fear of Christ.' We are to live this life, not because it is the thing to do, not because it is a 'uniform' we put on now that we are saved and converted, not because others are doing it; indeed, not for any reason other than this one and only reason – 'in the fear of Christ'. And, thank God, that is not only enough, it is more than enough. 'Let this mind be in you, which was also in Christ Jesus'.

MARRIAGE

Ephesians 5:22-33

22 *Wives, submit yourselves unto your own husbands, as unto the Lord.*

23 *For the husband is the head of the wife, even as Christ is the head of the church; and he is the saviour of the body.*

24 *Therefore as the church is subject unto Christ, so let the wives be to their own husbands in every thing.*

25 *Husbands, love your wives, even as Christ also loved the church, and gave himself for it;*

26 *That he might sanctify and cleanse it with the washing of water by the word,*

27 *That he might present it to himself a glorious church, not having spot, or wrinkle, or any such thing; but that it should be holy and without blemish.*

28 *So ought men to love their wives as their own bodies. He that loveth his wife loveth himself.*

29 *For no man ever yet hated his own flesh; but nourisheth and cherisheth it, even as the Lord the church:*

30 *For we are members of his body, of his flesh, and of his bones.*

31 *For this cause shall a man leave his father and mother, and shall be joined unto his wife, and they two shall be one flesh.*

32 *This is a great mystery: but I speak concerning Christ and the church.*

33 *Nevertheless let every one of you in particular so love his wife even as himself; and the wife see that she reverence her husband.*

6
Basic Principles

Ephesians 5:22–33

We come now to what I have been describing as the practical application of the principle which the Apostle laid down in the twenty-first verse, 'Submitting yourselves one to another in the fear of Christ'. There was the general principle, and now, as is his invariable custom, he comes to its particular application.

There can be no question at all that that is what the Apostle is doing. We can prove it in three different ways. The first is, the word 'submit' which is found in the Authorized or King James' Version, and also in other versions. 'Wives, submit yourselves unto your own husbands'. Actually in the original the word 'submit' is not there at all, it is just 'Wives, unto your own husbands, as unto the Lord'. How do we explain the omission of the word? It means that the Apostle is carrying over the injunction about 'submitting' from verse 21 into verse 22. The very fact that the word is not actually repeated is therefore a proof that verse 22 is a continuation of verse 21, and that he is still dealing with the same theme, the general principle of submission. He knows that that will be in the minds of his readers, and therefore he says: 'Wives (in this matter of submission) unto your own husbands'. So the mere absence of the word 'submit' in the original is a proof in and of itself that that is what the Apostle is doing here.

But there is a second proof. It is found in the fact that he mentions the wives before the husbands. That is not accidental; neither is it done merely out of politeness or on the principle of 'Ladies first'. The Bible never does that. The Bible, as we shall see, and as the Apostle expounds, invariably uses the other order. Indeed the law of the land does so, and we all do so in general parlance. We do not say Mrs. and Mr. So-and-so; we say Mr. and Mrs. – and so on. So when the Apostle puts the wives first in his consideration of the relationship of husbands and wives he has a very good reason for doing so. The reason is that he is particularly concerned about this question of submission – 'submitting'. That is the principle which he has outlined in verse 21. Now in the married relationship the aspect of submission, as he shows, applies particularly to the wives. There is another aspect that applies to the husbands – and he deals with that, because his statement is a full one and a balanced one – but as he is primarily concerned about the question of submission, he inevitably and quite naturally puts the wives first. So there we have a second proof of the claim that what we are dealing with here is an outworking of the general principle laid down in verse 21.

Another, and a third, argument for this is, that he uses the expression 'unto your own husbands.' Note the emphasis, 'Wives, submit yourselves unto your own husbands.' In verse 21 he has laid down the general principle of submission on the part of all Christians to others – 'Submitting yourselves one to another'. The argument, then, is this: If you do that in general, if you do that to everybody as it were, how much more so should wives do it to their own husbands in this peculiar relationship which has been defined so adequately in the Old Testament.

I am taking the trouble to emphasize this, because if we are not clear that verse 21 really is the controlling principle, we cannot possibly understand his detailed teaching correctly. Having cleared that point, let us now proceed.

Before we come to this vital and most important subject – especially so in these present days – it is most important that we should first of all look at the Apostle's statement in general. Let us observe his method. I have many reasons for doing this. What the Apostle does here we shall find him doing also in the case of 'children and parents' and 'servants and masters'. You notice the order in each case. The children come before the parents. Why? Because he is concerned about submission. Children do not come before parents; but in this matter they do, because it is a question of submission. The servants come before the masters, again for the same reason. I am arguing that when we study a portion of Scripture such as this – and as I have said, I am concerned at the moment to treat the matter in general – we shall find that the Apostle employs his customary

[86]

method; and if we succeed in grasping his method in one particular instance we shall find a key to the understanding of his other writings. Not only that; if we study exactly how the Apostle deals with any one problem, if we really have discovered his method, then when we are confronted by a problem we shall find that all we need to do is to apply the method, and as we apply the method we shall be able to discover the answer. What we are doing then, primarily at the moment, is to study the Apostle's method. Having done that we shall come to the particular subject with which he is dealing.

There are certain things which stand out very clearly in this particular paragraph which illustrate the Apostle's method. Here is the first: The fact that we have become Christians does not mean that we shall be automatically right in all we think and in all we do. There are some people who seem to think that that is the case. The moment a man becomes a Christian, according to them, everything is perfectly plain and clear. Evangelists are often responsible for that, because in their anxiety to get results, they make extravagant statements, and they thereby leave many, many problems for pastors and teachers. The impression is given that you enter into some magical atmosphere; nothing is the same, everything is different, no problems, no difficulties! All you have to do is to take your decision, and the story will be, 'they all lived happily ever afterwards' – there will never be any problem or difficulty. Of course that is quite wrong. If that were true there would never have been a single epistle in the New Testament. The fact that we have become Christians, that the basic matter of our relationship to God has been put right, does not mean that we are now automatically right everywhere in all we think, and in all we say and do. The very paragraph we are looking at is proof, in and of itself, that we need instruction about particular matters.

The second principle of this: Not only is it true, as I have been saying, that the Christian is not automatically right about everything, because he is a Christian; we can even say that the fact that a man has become a Christian will probably raise for him new problems which he has never had to confront before. Or if it does not do that, it will certainly present to him problems that he has never faced before in this way. He now sees situations as he has never seen them before. Whereas he did not really think before, he is now compelled to think. And the moment he thinks, and because he thinks, he is confronted by new problems.

[87]

This was very much the case in the early church. It worked like this. Take the case of a wife. A husband and wife had been living together as pagans. Neither being Christians, they lived their married life as pagans did at that time. We shall have to refer to that later. But now the wife becomes converted and becomes a Christian. The temptation that immediately confronted such a wife was to say, 'Well now of course I am free. I understand things as I never understood them before. The Gospel has told me that "there is neither barbarian, Scythian, male nor female, bond nor free". Therefore I do not continue to live now as I used to do. I have an understanding which my husband has not got'. The danger was for the wife to misinterpret her new life in such a way as to upset the marriage relationship. It was the same with children and parents, and it still tends to be the same. Very often when children are converted, and their parents are not, and have an understanding which their parents have not got, they misinterpret the new situation, and are led by the devil to misuse and abuse it. So in the end they are to be found breaking the commandment of God which tells the children to honour their parents. Thus, almost inevitably, with the enlightenment that comes with Christianity, new problems arise which had never to be faced before. So we gather from this passage that the great change which takes place in regeneration has a tendency to raise new problems. The result is that we have to think very carefully, to discover exactly what is right in this new life, and how we are to apply this new teaching to the new situation in which we find ourselves.

The third principle is this: Christianity has something to say about the whole of our life. There is no aspect of life which it does not consider, and which it does not govern. There must be no compartments in our Christian life. Very often, as you know, there are. The danger to these early Christians was, that these persons – husband and wife, or children or parents – on being converted, and becoming Christians, should say to themselves, as it were: 'Well of course, this is something that appertains to my religious life only, to the element of worship in my life; it has nothing to do with my marriage, it has nothing to do with my work, it has nothing to do with my relationship with my parents' – and so on. Now that is quite wrong according to this teaching. There is nothing so wrong and nothing so fatal, as to be living a life in compartments. Sunday, morning comes and I say, 'Ah, I am a religious man'. So I take up my religious bag. Then Monday morning comes and I say to myself, 'I am now a businessman', or something else, and I take up another bag. So I am living my life in compartments; and it is difficult to tell on Monday that I am a Christian at all. Of course I showed it on Sunday when I went to a place of worship. This conception is entirely wrong. The Christian life is a whole; the Christian faith has something to say about every realm and department of life.

Every one of these points is most important and could be greatly elaborated. There are those who say – and up to a certain point I am prepared to agree with them – that the present state of our churches, and of Christianity, is very largely due to the fact that many of our Victorian grandfathers were excessively guilty of the particular failure to realize that Christianity governs the whole of a man's life, and not only a part of it. Many of them were very religious people; some of them had prayers in their works or in their office in the morning, and then, having had the prayers, they became hard and grasping and unkind and unfair and legalistic. Undoubtedly they antagonized many against the Christian faith, because, so often, there was this kind of dichotomy, this failure to realize the wholeness of the Christian life, and that the Christian must never live a life in compartments. My Christianity must enter into my married life, into my relationship to parents, into my work, into everything I am, and into everything I do.

I come now to a fourth principle, which is again a most important one from the standpoint of doctrine and theology, and because of that, in ordinary life also. Christian teaching never contradicts or undoes fundamental biblical teaching with respect to life and living. I mean that there is no contradiction between the New Testament and the Old Testament. This needs to be emphasized at the present time because of the common attitude towards the Old Testament. People say glibly and superficially, 'Ah well, of course, we are not interested any longer in anything said in the Old Testament; we are New Testament people'. Some are foolish enough to say that they do not believe in the God of the Old Testament. They say 'I believe in the God and Father of our Lord Jesus Christ'. Christian preachers, so-called, say from their pulpits, and it is applauded, that they do not believe in the God of Sinai, the God of the Ten Commandments and the Moral Law. They dismiss the Old Testament teaching and say that we must be guided by the New Testament teaching only. Some of them even go further than that, and say that we are not even to be governed by the New Testament, because we know so much more by now.

There is this tendency to dismiss the whole of the biblical teaching. My answer is this: that the New Testament, the specifically Christian teaching, never contradicts, never sets aside the fundamental biblical teaching with regard to human relationships and the orders of life. I am referring, of course, to subjects like marriage, as we shall see here. The Apostle's argument is based partly upon what is taught in the Old Testament, even in the Book of Genesis. It is the same with regard to the family, it is the same with all these fundamental orders in life. The fact that you become a Christian does not touch those at all. What it actually does is to supplement the Old Testament, to open it out, to give us a larger view of it, to help us to see the spirit behind the original injunction. But it never contradicts it.

This is a most important and vital principle. I am emphasizing it because as a pastor I have so often had to deal with it. People somehow get hold of the notion that, because they are new beings in Christ, the old fundamental principles no longer hold. The answer of the New Testament is that they do. Notice how the Apostle quotes the Old Testament in all these instances, in order to show that the original teaching came from God, and that it must always be observed, however much it may be supplemented by this newer teaching.

Let us go on to the fifth principle. The New Testament always gives us reasons for its teaching. It always gives us arguments – and there is nothing about it that I rejoice in so much as just that. The New Testament does not merely throw a number of rules and regulations at us and say, Now then, keep those. No! It always explains, it always gives us an argument, it always gives us a reason. The kind of Christianity that simply imposes rules and regulations on people is a departure from the New Testament teaching; it is to treat us as children. Alas, there are such types of Christianity! It becomes a putting on of a uniform; and all Christians are 'like peas in a pod'. There they are, just going through their 'drill'. That is not Christianity! We should always know why we are behaving in this way; we should always understand the reason for it. We should be clear and happy about it; and therefore there should be no contradiction, there should be no 'kicking against the pricks', or working against the grain, or feeling that I have to do it but wish I had not to do it, but rather wishing to get as far away as I can from it. That is not Christianity. The Christian is a man who rejoices in the way he is living. He sees it clearly, he does not want anything else; it is inevitable, his mind is satisfied.

That is why I say that a man who is not a Christian does not know truly what it is to be a man. There is no teaching in the world that pays us such a compliment as this Word of God. It does not treat us as children and govern us by rules and regulations. It puts it to your reason, puts it to your understanding. That is true holiness teaching – not something you receive in a packet, not something that comes when you are more or less passive and unconscious. It is reasoning out the teaching, taking a principle and working it out, as the Apostle does here. That is the New Testament method of holiness and sanctification. Thank God for it!

The sixth principle which I observe here is a most glorious one. How wonderful is this Scripture! To me it is amazing that as you look at this teaching you think at first, O well, that is of course merely teaching about marriage, husbands and wives. But then you begin to discover the treasures that are here; you go from room to room and it becomes more wonderful as you go on. Have you noticed, as you have read this passage, the intimate relationship between doctrine and practice? Doctrine and practice must never be separated, because each helps the other and each illustrates the other. There are certain respects in which this passage we are looking at is, to me, one of the most astounding in the whole of the Bible. I am not saying it is the greatest, but I say it is one of the most astounding. Here we are in this Epistle to the Ephesians in chapter 5, and towards the end of the chapter. What is happening in this part of the Epistle? Well, says everybody, you are now in the practical section of the Epistle. The great doctrinal section, of course, was chapters 1, 2 and 3. A little came into chapter 4, but now we have come down into the realm of practicalities and ordinary relationships, and most ordinary matters. Never was the Apostle more practical than he is in your section – wives and husbands, children and parents, servants and masters – a purely practical section of his Epistle. Yet you notice – and have not you always been amazed at this when you have read it for yourself, or when you have happened to be in a marriage service and this section of Scripture has been read – have not you been astounded and thrilled to the very marrow of your being as you find that the Apostle in dealing with this most practical matter suddenly introduces us to the most exalted doctrine? In telling wives and husbands how to behave towards one another he introduces the doctrine of the nature of the church and the relationship of the church to Christ. Indeed I must go further. In this very section the Apostle gives us his most exalted teaching of all about the nature of the church and the relationship of the church to Christ. This is something that we should never lose sight of. When you are reading this Epistle be prepared for surprises. Do not say to yourself, 'Oh well, I need not pay much attention to this, this is of course practical and simple and direct'. Suddenly, when you are least expecting it, he will open a door, and there you will be confronted by the most magnificent and glorious doctrine you have ever met with in your life.

That leads me to make this practical comment. Beware of superficial analyses of Scripture. You know the type of person who says 'Chapter 1 – this; chapter 2 – that. All so perfect and neat and tidy!' If you try to do that with this chapter of the Epistle to the Ephesians you will find yourself bewildered, and your little scheme upset. Here, in this most practical of sections, Paul suddenly introduces this tremendous doctrine of the nature of the church, and the relationship of the church to the Lord Jesus Christ. But what we must bear in mind – because it comes out of all that – is that doctrine and practice are so intimately related that they cannot be separated. Anyone, therefore, who says, 'I am only interested in the practical', is really denying the essence of the Christian message. This great passage demonstrates that in a perfect manner.

Having said those six things, I say in the seventh place: Obviously in the light of all this, when you are confronted by any problem, never approach it directly, never start by considering the thing *per se*, in and of itself. That is what we all tend to do. How often have I found this in discussion groups and meetings! A question is put forward – a practical problem in somebody's daily life and living – and I put it to the meeting. The tendency is for people to get up at once and to speak directly on the question, and to give their opinions on it. And for that reason, of course, they are generally wrong; because that is not the way to approach a problem.

The Apostle does not approach this problem of husbands and wives, and wives and husbands directly, immediately *per se*, as if it were an isolated question. His method is this – you must always approach it indirectly. It is, once more, 'the strategy of the indirect approach'. When I am confronted by a particular question I must not immediately apply my mind directly to it. I must first ask the question, Is there any principle, is there any doctrine in the Scripture that governs this kind of problem? In other words, before you begin to deal with the individual problem, as it were, that is in front of you, you say: Well, what family does he belong to? You might go even wider and say: What nation does he belong to? Get hold of a big classification, and having discovered the truth about the group or the class or the great company, you then proceed from that to apply the principle to that particular instance or example. That is what the Apostle does here. He starts with the general and then comes to the particular.

I have often used the following illustration. Anyone who has ever done any chemistry and who has been asked to identify a substance will at once recognize the method. How does he proceed? He does the very thing I have just been saying. He starts with the most general tests, the big group tests. Thus he can exclude certain groups; and he narrows it down to one group. Then he has to divide it up into divisions, the sub-divisions of the group; and then he narrows it down and down and at last he comes to the particular individual substance. That is the Apostle's method here, as it is indeed his method everywhere. It is 'the strategy of the indirect approach', the movement from the general to the particular. Never jump at a problem, never tackle it in and of itself; get hold of the great principle or governing doctrine.

The last point I make is this, and again it is a very practical one. I deduce it from all that has gone before. Notice the spirit in which the Apostle conducts the discussion. Here he is taking up the problem of the relationship of wives and husbands, and husbands and wives; but notice his method, notice the spirit in which he does it. This subject is one of the standing jokes of the world, is it not? This is something that can always raise a laugh. The poorest comedian tries to make something of this when he has nothing else – marriage relationships, husbands and wives. I need not point out that the Apostle does not handle it in this way. You cannot handle any Christian problem like that.

But there are other negatives also. Not only does he not handle it jocularly, flippantly and lightly, there is a complete absence of a partisan spirit here. There is nothing heated, nothing assertive, no standing for rights, no anxiety to prove that one is right and the other wrong. That is how matters are normally dealt with, is it not? And that is why there is so much trouble. The Apostle evades all that, as I have been saying, by lifting it up and putting it into another context; and by doing that he avoids all these difficult-ies.

His method, positively, is this; it is the principle 'in the fear of Christ' that he has already laid down in verse 21: 'Submitting your-selves one to another in the fear of Christ'. Then he repeats it: 'Wives, submit yourselves unto your own husbands, as unto the Lord'. Before you begin to take your stand on the one side or on the other – and if you do, you are already doomed to failure because you are in a partisan spirit – he prevents all partisan spirit, he raises both immediately 'to the Lord'. Every subject that is discussed by Christians should be discussed in that way. A Christian who loses his or her temper in an argument should not speak. Whether you prove your point or not you have lost everything by losing your temper. It is 'in the Lord', 'in the fear of Christ'. Paul is talking about submission, and his point is that before we consider the merits of these two people, both of them must submit themselves unto the Lord, 'Submitting yourselves one to another in the fear of Christ'. And as both do that, you will have your argument 'on your knees'. What a difference that makes! If I may use a vulgarism, you must not get up on your hind legs; you must get down on your knees. If only we conducted these difficult matters upon our knees what a difference it would make!

This is not only true concerning the question of husbands and wives. Take the heat that is generated over the argument about pacificism, and the various other matters that are engaging people today – the heat, the partisan spirit, the animosity! The method, says the Apostle, the spirit, is that we must do it always in sub-mission to the Lord, with a desire to please Him, with a readiness always to be taught and to be led by Him and by His Word.

There, we have seen eight general principles which not only govern this particular matter but govern every problem that can ever arise in your Christian life. Having done that, let us go on to the particular matter. All I have been saying is illustrated to per-fection in the Apostle's treatment of the Christian view of marriage, the Christian teaching concerning marriage. But, once more, we must follow the method. Before we come to the details let us look at what he tells us in general about this.

The first big thing he tells us is, that the Christian view of marriage is a unique view; it is a view that is entirely different from every other view; it is a view that you only find in the Bible. How does the Christian view marriage? What is the teaching? Let me start again with a negative. The Christian's way of viewing marriage is not the way in which marriage is generally viewed by the vast majority of people. Have you ever thought of this? What if I asked you at this point to write an account of the Christian view of marriage. Have you ever done that? Shame on us who are Christians if we do not have a clear and well-defined view. Have we discovered the uniqueness of the Christian view, have we realized how it differs so essentially from the general view? What is that general view?

Unsavoury though it is, I must remind you of it. The common view of marriage is a purely physical one. It is something which is based almost exclusively on physical attraction, and the desire for physical gratification. It is a legalizing of physical attraction and physical gratification. So often it is nothing but that – hence the scandal of mounting divorce. The parties have not even thought about it, they have no view of marriage at all; they are governed entirely by instincts and impulses; it is all purely on the animal level, and never rises above it. There is no thought whatsoever about marriage in and of itself; it is but a legalizing of something that they are anxious to do.

Then there is a second common view which rises a little higher than the first. It is a little more intelligent than that because it regards marriage as a human arrangement and a human contrivance. Anthropology teaches us this, they say. There was no doubt a time, they say, when human beings were more or less like animals; they were promiscuous and behaved as animals behave. But as man began to develop, and to evolve, he began to realize that certain arrangements were necessary, that promiscuity led to confusion and to excess, and to a lot of trouble; so after a long process of agonizing and of development, and of experiment, and of trial and error, human nature in its wisdom, that is, civilization, came to the conclusion that it would be right and well and good that you should have monogamy – one man marrying one woman. It is a matter of social development – that is the teaching of anthropology. But the whole time it is something that man has discovered. As he passes

[95]

Acts of Parliament to control traffic and parking and so on, so he has discovered a way of solving this problem of man and woman and their relationships to one another, and to children. It is something entirely on the human plane. That is probably the common assumption which is made by the vast majority of people. Alas, I find it at times even among Christian people!

Another characteristic of this view – and it arises because it has not a fundamentally correct view of marriage – is that the whole approach to marriage is one which almost expects trouble. That was very true of the pagan world. Husbands tended to tyrannize over their wives and to make slaves of them, and the wives acted deceitfully. The atmosphere was one of jealousy and antagonism, leading to strife and quarrelling of necessity. Instead of this common submission to the Lord, each one stood for his or her rights. Not a true partnership, but a kind of agreement that for certain purposes they were going to do certain things together; but actually there was an under-lying bitterness and antagonism of spirit and sense of opposition.

Examine the commonly held view of marriage, and of the marriage state and relationship. You see it in the cartoons, you see it in the reports of the cases in the courts, you see it, I say again, in the popular jokes. Why should it be thus? How has this come to be so current? It is because of this completely wrong view of what marriage really means. Today the whole question has become aggravated because of the modern notions of equality between men and women resulting from the so-called feminist movement. This has aggravated the whole problem; and it makes the subject we are dealing with particularly urgent at the present time. There has been this modern movement of feminism which claims that men and women are equal in every respect, and that there should be no division or distinction at all, but complete equality. Now while, on the one hand, there are aspects of that teaching with which any Christian man, leave alone any sane intelligent man, must agree with the whole of his being, on the other hand, taking it in general, and as a principle, it goes against the plain teaching of the Scripture at this point. It is without any question the cause of much confusion, much trouble, and much damage, not only to the marriage state, but also to the family as a fundamental unit in life. The result is that discipline has gone, order has gone, and children are not given a chance. Why? Because their parents are not in the right relationship to one another; and the child is bewildered at seeing this competition, this conflict, where there should be unity. This modern feminist movement has tended to becloud the whole issue; and, alas! it seems even to be seeping into the thinking of many who call themselves evangelical, and who claim to believe in the Scripture as the infallible Word of God and our only authority.

We see at once here that that is not the Christian approach to marriage. The Christian view of marriage is governed entirely and solely by the teaching of the Scripture – the Old Testament and the New Testament, both. The Apostle derives his argument from the Old Testament as well as from Christ. So a man who claims to be a Christian does not say, 'Now, well, what I think about marriage is this'. He says rather, 'What does the Bible say about marriage?' Thus, there is a complete difference at the very beginning – he 'submits' himself to the teaching of this Book. He does not say 'Of course by now we have developed and advanced so much. Women were virtually thought of as slaves even by the Apostle Paul, you know. He was so right on the atonement, but not on the subject of women!' The moment you say that, you no longer believe the Scriptures, and you have no right to say that you believe they are the infallible Word of God. No, the Christian says 'I know nothing apart from what the Scripture tells me'. So he submits to the Old Testament and to the New Testament. His whole life is to be governed on that principle – in the matter of thought as well as conduct.

Secondly, we discover that marriage is not a human contrivance or arrangement, but God's ordinance, something instituted by God, something that God in His infinite grace and kindness has appointed and ordained and prepared and established for men and women. It is of God and not of man. The teaching of the anthropologists is based on speculation and imagination; it is not true. The teaching of the Bible is the truth about this matter; it is God's contrivance and God's ordinance.

Thirdly, the terms of the relationship, as we shall find, are clearly and plainly stated.

Fourthly, marriage can only be fully understood as we understand the doctrine of the Lord Jesus Christ and the church. You notice that that is central; the Apostle carries on the argument about Christ and the church right through the paragraph. In other words it comes to this; if we are not clear about the Lord Jesus Christ and the church, and the relationship of the church to Him, we cannot understand marriage. It is impossible because it is only in the light of that doctrine that we really understand the doctrine concerning marriage.

I therefore draw these two deductions. It is only the Christian who truly understands and appreciates marriage. That is one of the wonderful results of being a Christian. Christianity not only deals with your soul, and your final salvation, your avoidance of hell and your going to heaven; Christianity touches the whole of your life while you are still in this world. I think I can say honestly that in my pastoral experience, there has been nothing more wonderful than to see the difference Christianity makes in the husband/wife relationship. Where there was a tendency to part and to drift from one another, and an antagonism and almost a bitterness and a hatred, the two people on becoming Christians have discovered one another for the first time. They have also discovered for the first time what marriage really is, though they may have been married for years. They now see what a beautiful and what a glorious thing it is. You cannot understand marriage unless you are a Christian.

May I venture to put it like this? In the light of all this, the wonder is, not that there are so many divorces, but that there are not many more. Is it not amazing and astounding that in the general absence of thought, and even with wrong thinking when they do begin to think, marriages hold even as they do? No man, no woman has a true conception of marriage who is not a Christian; but if we are Christians there should be no difficulty about knowing what marriage is, and what it means. There should be no argument, there should be no disputation. If you believe the doctrinal teaching the view of marriage is inevitable. Not only is it inevitable, you are very glad that it is inevitable. It is so wonderful, it is so glorious, it is so exalted. There is no difficulty, there is no haggling, there is no argument. You have submitted yourself to Christ; so has the other. And you have both submitted yourselves not only to one another, but to all the other members of the church, the community to which you belong. You are governed by a higher loyalty, by loyalty to Him who did not consider His own rights and prerogatives, but who considered you only, and your desperate and appalling need. He humbled Himself, laid aside His rights and prerogatives, and took upon Him even the form of a servant, and even went to death, yea the death of the Cross. Looking at Him, and seeing how He came not only to save you from hell, but to give you life, and to give •

you life more abundantly, and to fill out your understanding of everything to His own glory – seeing that, you see marriage anew, you see everything anew. You do not object to the biblical teaching, you not only submit yourself to it, you rejoice in it, and you praise God for it.

There, then, is our introduction to the detailed teaching of the Apostle Paul in Ephesians Chapter 5 with regard to Christian marriage. We can now go on to consider the teaching in detail.

7
The Order of Creation

Ephesians 5:22–24

We now come to a more detailed consideration of the teaching of this passage, indeed the teaching of the New Testament and of the entire Bible, with regard to marriage. We have looked at it in general, and have done so because of the way in which the Apostle presents it to us; and it is essential that we should bear all that in mind.

The spirit in which we approach this matter is most important. Everything that is done in the realm of the church is different from what is done outside. The world in its debating societies debates the subject of marriage, and does so in a particular way and manner – two sides, for and against, the supporters and partisans. But that is not the way in which the church faces the problem; it does not face any problem like that. Here, we are confronted by the authority which we have in the Word. We are not concerned to express our own opinions; our one purpose is to understand the teaching of the Word. And we do so together – not one group and another, opposition and government as it were, defence and attack. We all come together in order to discover the teaching of the Holy Scripture; and we have seen that certain great principles are laid down so clearly that all this is at once lifted up to the level of Christian doctrine at its highest. We are confronted by some of the most profound teaching found anywhere in the Scriptures concerning the nature of the Christian church.

Having looked at those general principles we can now proceed to the particular application. You notice that the first thing is an injunction which is given to wives. You remember we saw that the wives are put before the husbands for one reason only, that the Apostle is dealing with the question of submission. The principle is in verse 21: 'Submitting yourselves one to another in the fear of Christ'. In this matter of submission, he says, first of all, 'Wives, submit yourselves, or be subject to your own husbands, as unto the Lord'. The matter we have to consider is this 'submission' of wives to husbands. The Apostle not only reminds them of that, but he tells them very plainly and clearly that it is their duty to do this – as it is the duty of all of us to submit ourselves one to another. This is a very special thing, he says, 'Wives, submit yourselves unto your own husbands'. This is still more obvious because they are their husbands, their own husbands, and because of the teaching with respect to the whole question of marriage. The big point, Paul says, that emerges here is this question of submission – that is what he is emphasizing. We must therefore look into this; and fortunately the Apostle helps us to do so. It is not just an injunction thrown out at random.

Paul gives us first of all a great motive for this submission: 'Wives, submit yourselves unto your own husbands, *as unto the Lord*'. We must be clear about this phrase because it can be, and has been, misunderstood. It does not mean, 'Wives, submit yourselves unto your own husbands in exactly the same way as you submit yourselves unto the Lord'. It does not mean that, because that is going too far. The submission of every wife, and indeed of every Christian believer, male or female, to the Lord Jesus Christ is an absolute one. The Apostle does not say that about the relationship of the wives to the husbands. We are all the bond-slaves of Jesus Christ, the 'slaves' of Christ; but a wife is never told to be the slave of her husband. Our relationship to the Lord is one of complete, entire, absolute submission. Wives are not exhorted to do that.

What, then, does it mean? It means: 'Wives, submit yourselves unto your own husbands because it is a part of your duty to the Lord, because it is an expression of your submission to the Lord'. Or 'Wives, submit yourselves to your own husbands; do it in this way, do it as a part of your submission to the Lord'. In other words, you are not doing it only for the husband, you are doing it primarily for the Lord Himself. It is a repetition of the general point made in verse 21, 'Submitting yourselves one to another in the fear of Christ'. You do not do it, in the last analysis, for the husband's sake; the ultimate reason and motive does not rest there; the submission is 'unto the Lord'. You are doing it for Christ's sake, you are doing it because you know that He exhorts you to do it, because it is well-pleasing in His sight that you should be doing it. It is a part of your Christian behaviour, it is a part of your discipleship. 'Whether ye eat, or drink' says the Apostle using the same sort of argument in writing to the Corinthians in the First Epistle in chapter 10, 'Whether ye eat, or drink, or whatsoever ye do, do it as unto the Lord'. Everything we do is done for His sake, to please Him, because we know that He would have us do this.

Thus at the beginning the Apostle lifts this matter up from the realm of controversy and enables us to approach it in the right spirit. If, he says, you are anxious to please the Lord Jesus Christ, and to carry out His behests and His will, submit yourselves unto your own husbands. There can be no more compelling motive for any action than this; and every Christian wife who is concerned above everything else to please the Lord Jesus Christ, will find no difficulty in this paragraph; indeed it will be her greatest delight to do what the Apostle tells us here. I would go further. Never, perhaps, have we as Christian people had a greater opportunity of showing what Christianity really means than precisely at this present time when the life of the world is showing itself increasingly in its true colours. Its life is becoming more and more chaotic in this matter of the marriage relationship and in every other respect. Here is a glorious opportunity for us to show the difference it makes to be a Christian. So, Christian wives, says the Apostle, you have a wonderful opportunity; you can show that you are no longer pagans, that you are no longer irreligious, that you no longer belong to the world. And these other people – living as they do, asserting their own rights, and displaying the arrogance which leads to all the chaos that characterizes life – when they look at you will see something so different that they will say, 'What is this? Why do you behave like this? What is the reason for it?' And your answer will not be 'Well, I just happen to be born like this', but 'I am behaving like this because it is the will of my Lord'. So you immediately get an opportunity for preaching and stating the Gospel.

That is why the Apostle exhorts them to this. The point of his entire exhortation, as we see in the whole of this chapter and most of the previous chapter – is that these Christian people are to show in every detail of their lives that once you become a Christian you are different in every respect. So this great characteristic of the Christian life can be displayed by the wives submitting themselves to their own husbands. That is the grand motive; and unless we are moved by it, and animated by it, no other argument will appeal to us. If we are not already submitted to the Lord Jesus Christ, and concerned about His Name and His honour above everything else, all other arguments will leave us untouched. The Apostle puts that first; and we have to put it first.

But having said that, Paul then goes on to give us particular reasons, additional reasons. Here again we note the wealth and the glory of the Scripture. There are two great subsidiary reasons, he says, why every Christian wife should submit herself to her own husband. The first is what we may call 'the order of creation'; the second, that this is something which belongs to the realm of the relationship of the church to the Lord Jesus Christ. Both reasons are in the twenty-first verse: 'For (because)' – here is the first reason – 'the husband is the head of the wife'. The second reason is, 'even as Christ is the head of the church: and he is the saviour of the body'.

Look at the first reason. It is that this is a part of the order of creation, a part of God's ordinances, of God's decree, of God's will, of what God has stated with regard to this relationship between men and women. This is teaching which is to be found in various portions of Scripture. You find it first in the second chapter of Genesis right back at the creation; and you notice how the references in the New Testament all lead us back there. That is what I mean by saying that it belongs to the order of creation. Before you come to consider marriage from the specifically Christian standpoint you must go further back, because the New Testament sends you back. It sends you back to the Book of Genesis and to the whole question of creation. It also refers us to the question of the Fall. The account of that is found in the third chapter of Genesis. The crucial verse is the 16th verse, which tells us what God said to the woman as the result of her listening to Satan and his temptation, and her eating of the forbidden fruit. 'Unto the woman He said, I will greatly multiply thy sorrow and thy conception; in sorrow thou shalt bring forth children; and thy desire shall be to thy husband, and he shall rule over thee.' That is an addition to Genesis chapter 2, and we must pay careful attention to it.

In order to summarize the Scripture teaching concerning this most important matter of marriage and of the family, we may extract the principles that are put before us in these various portions of

Scripture. Remember that we are dealing essentially with 'marriage' and not with the status of woman (or of all women) as such. Certainly we have to deduce from the Scriptures the teaching with regard to women in general, and such matters as the question of women entering the professions and so on. But I am not dealing with that, I am dealing only with the question of marriage. That is what the Apostle does here; he is addressing wives. He is not addressing unmarried women at this point. There is teaching about that, but it does not come within our province here except indirectly.

The teaching is the following: First, you notice that the emphasis is put constantly upon the fact that the man was created first, not the woman. So there is a natural priority for man. The Scriptures also emphasize the fact that woman was made out of the man, taken out of the man, and meant to be a 'help' for man, a help for man that was 'meet' for him. None of the animals could supply that need. 'Adam gave names to all cattle, to the fowl of the air, and to every beast of the field; but for Adam there was not found an help meet for him.' And it was because there was no help meet for man amongst the animals, that woman was created.

That is the basic teaching, and notice that the Apostles lay great stress upon it. Man was created first. But not only that; man was also made the lord of creation. It was to man that this authority was given over the brute and animal creation; it was man who was called upon to give them names. Here are indications that man was put into a position of leadership, lordship, and authority and power. He takes the decisions, he gives the rulings. That is the fundamental teaching with regard to this whole matter.

The Apostle Peter underlines all this in that significant phrase of his, where he tells the husbands to give honour to the wife 'as unto the weaker vessel'. (1 Peter 3:7) What does he mean by 'weaker vessel'? Clearly he means what is taught so plainly in the early chapters of Genesis, and, indeed, everywhere in the Bible. It means primarily this whole question of man's headship and leadership. Man, physically speaking, is naturally stronger than woman; he was made to be such, and he is such. I could enter into this in great detail. I could establish all this with extreme ease, not merely from the standpoint of anatomy, but still more from the standpoint of physiology. Woman was not meant to be as strong as man physically, nervously, and in many other aspects. She is constituted in a different manner; and when the Apostle says that she is the 'weaker vessel' he is not speaking in any derogatory sense at all. He is simply saying that she is essentially different from man, and that man must ever bear that in mind. He must not treat the woman as if she were his equal in these respects. He must remember that she has been made differently, and that he is to respect her and to honour her, to guard and to protect her accordingly.

Here, then, is this basic fundamental teaching – the man is to be the head of the wife, and he is to be the head of the family. God made him in that way, endowed him with faculties and powers and propensities that enable him to fulfil this; and so made woman that she should be the 'complement' of man. Now the word 'complement' carries in itself the notion of submission; her main function is to make up a deficiency in the man. That is why these two become 'one flesh'; the woman is the complement of the man. But the emphasis, therefore, is this, that man is responsible not only for himself, but for his wife, and for his family in all ultimate matters. The wife is to help him, to support him, to aid him, and to do everything she can in order to enable him to function as the lord of creation, into which position God has placed him. She is brought into being in order to help man to perform that great and wonderful and glorious task. That is the basic teaching with regard to the relationship of husbands and wives as laid down in the very order of creation, the fundamental rules with regard to the life of man in this world.

But we must go further. That is how it was before the Fall. While man and woman were still perfect, while they were still in Paradise without any sin, without any defect in them, that was how God ordained it. But unfortunately something happened – the Fall. Its importance is made very clear, especially by the Apostle Paul in the First Epistle to Timothy, in the second chapter, verse 11 to 15, at the end of the section. Notice that the Apostle makes a great deal of the fact that it was the woman who was deceived and fell first, and not the man. So the Fall has made a further difference – Genesis 3:16 establishes that. Here it is again: 'Unto the woman He said, Because of what thou hast done I will greatly multiply thy sorrow and thy conception'. From that one can but deduce that childbirth would probably have been painless had it not been for sin and the Fall. 'In sorrow thou shalt bring forth children.' But, for our purpose now – 'thy desire shall be to thy husband, and he shall rule over thee'. Here is something additional. It not only reiterates the lordship, the leadership and the headship already established before the Fall; it underlines it – 'he shall rule over thee'. There is a new element here; woman's subordination to man has been increased as the result of the Fall. Now it is arguable that God's edict was promulgated for this reason – that the very essence of the Fall, of what happened to Eve, was that Eve, being confronted by the insinuation and the suggestion of the Devil, instead of doing what she should have done, what she had done hitherto, and been taught to do, namely, to go to Adam and to consult him about the question, took the decision upon herself, and put herself into the position of leadership. She dealt with the situation, and as the result of her dealing with the situation, instead of taking it to Adam, as she should have done, she fell. She involved him in the fall likewise, and so the whole human race fell. So that, in a sense, the original sin was that woman failed to realize her place and her position in the married relationship, usurped authority and power and position, and thereby brought calamity and chaos to pass. That is not only stated in Genesis 3:16, it forms the whole basis of the Apostle's argument with regard to women taking authority, and teaching and preaching, in the First Epistle to Timothy, in the second chapter.

That is the teaching in its essence. But, at once, there is an objection, an objection that one reads and hears so frequently – and, alas, often from evangelical people who claim to believe the Scriptures as the infallible inspired Word of God. What one hears so often is this: 'Ah, but that is only the view of the Apostle Paul. He was obviously an anti-feminist, a man who held the view that was so commonly taken of women at that time.' It is emphasized that at that time woman was in a very debased position. Everybody throughout the world then held that view; woman was but 'goods' as it were, a slave. And as this was true even of the Jews, the Apostle was just a typical Rabbinical Jew. So runs the argument.

It is not surprising that people who do not believe the Scriptures as the Word of God say such things. They do not hesitate to say, not only that Paul was wrong, but that the Lord Jesus Christ was wrong. They are the authority; they know, they understand. I do not argue with such people; I simply say that I cannot have any discussion with them at all, because it is not merely a question of putting up my opinion against theirs. There is nothing else to say about it – it is not Christian at all. The Christian is a man who submits himself entirely to the biblical revelation; he knows nothing apart from this. So when we hear this argument, we not only bemoan it and regret it, we have to answer it, and we answer it in this way. To speak generally, it is perfectly true to say that the view of woman at the time of our Lord and of the Apostle Paul was debased. But it was not the Jews' view, for they had these Scriptures and believed them. And it most certainly was not the Apostle Paul's view. Have you noticed what he says in 1 Corinthians 11:11? His words run: 'Neither is the woman without the man, nor the man without the woman, in the Lord'. This great Apostle gloried in the fact that in Christ Jesus there was neither barbarian nor Scythian, bond nor free, male nor female. It was a vital part of his preaching of the Gospel to say: 'In this matter of salvation men and women are equal, and woman has an equal chance in salvation with man'. He gloried in that, and there is no man who speaks more delicately or more gloriously about womanhood, and of the true glory of womanhood, than the Apostle Paul. Further, notice that he does not limit himself to giving us an account of the duty of the wives towards the husband only, he always tells us about the duty of the husband to the wife also; and he shows that the Christian husband's view of womanhood, and of woman, and of his wife, is more exalted than anything the world has ever known. He puts everything into its right position. He always gives us the two sides.

But apart from all that, the Apostle never puts these things forward as his own opinion; he always goes back to Genesis, and to the order of creation. He says, in effect, It is not my opinion, this is what God has laid down. The Apostle's only concern is that the truth of God should be known, and that what God ordained should be put constantly into practice. So this tendency to say that it is 'only Paul's opinion' is a denial of the Scripture. We must be quite clear about this. If you say you believe that the Bible is the infallible and inspired Word of God, then you must not speak in the world's way about the Apostle Paul; because when he writes he not only quotes the Scripture, he also writes as an inspired Apostle. When he gives his own opinion he is always careful to say so, and if he does not say it is his own opinion, it is inspired. Remember how the Apostle Peter tells his readers to listen to the Apostle Paul. He says that some people wrest Paul's arguments and his writings to their own destruction 'even as they do also the other Scriptures' (2 Peter 3:16). What Paul writes is Scripture; so the critics are not arguing with Paul, they are arguing with God, they are arguing with the Holy Ghost. At the same time they are putting themselves into the contradictory position of saying that they believe the Bible only as long as it does not contradict what they happen to believe as creatures of the twentieth century. That is a denial of a belief in the authority of the Scripture.

Having dealt with that foolish objection – and there is nothing that is more foolish than such talk – let me sum up the position again. Woman, according to this teaching, the wife, is given a certain status. To be subject to her husband does not mean that she is the slave of her husband, it does not mean that she is inferior to her husband as such – no, not for a moment! We shall see this still more clearly when we come to consider what the Apostle says about the duty of the husband to the wife. What he is saying is that the woman is different, that she is the complement of the man. What he does prohibit is that woman should seek to be manly, that is, that a woman should seek to behave as a man, or that a woman should seek to usurp the place, the position, and the power which have been given to man by God Himself. That is all he is saying. It is not slavery; he is exhorting his readers to realize what God has ordained. Therefore the wife should rejoice in her position. She has been made by God to help man to function as God's representative in this world. She is to be the home-maker, the mother, the helper of man, his comforter, the one to whom he can speak and look for comfort and encouragement – she is a help meet for man. Man realizes the truth about himself, she also realizes the truth about herself, and thus she complements him and aids him; and together they live to the glory of God and the Lord Jesus Christ.

An illustration may help at this point. The idea of leadership or headship stumbles certain people, because they seem to think that that of necessity carries the idea of an inherent and essential inferiority. But it is not so. This whole notion of the headship of the man, the husband, in the married relationship is comparable in many ways to that of troops to their leader. An army would be completely chaotic if each one had the right to decide what is going to be done next. As I have said previously, the moment a man joins the armed forces he is subjecting himself, he is saying that he is going to obey the command that comes down to him, no matter what he may think of it; it is his business to do so. He is granting this right of command to the one who is set above him; and though he may have his own ideas and opinions, he now foregoes them; he submits and he is in subjection.

Or, if you like, think of a number of men in a team playing football or cricket. The first thing they have to do is to appoint a captain. They are not all captains; if they were they would never win a match. The first thing they do is to appoint one amongst themselves as a captain. He may not even be the best player in the team, but they decide that on the whole he has the greatest gift of leadership. So they put him into the position of captain, and having done that they have to submit themselves to him. If they fail to do so, chaos has returned again.

Or imagine a committee being appointed to consider a subject. A number of men are appointed. The first thing they do is to appoint a chairman. Of course! Why? Because you must have some authority. You cannot transact business unless there is a Chair to address, and you have to abide by the ruling of the Chairman. Here again the question of inferiority does not come in. It simply means that in order to do this thing efficiently you must have a leader. Take a new House of Commons. The first thing they do is to appoint a Speaker; and the business of the Speaker is just to sit in the Chair and exercise control, and to give his ruling. Again, it does not mean that he is the greatest man in the House of Commons, and that they are all inferior to him. No! In their wisdom, and because business cannot be transacted apart from this, they set someone in this position of authority. Now the Bible teaches that God has set man, the husband, in that position. So the Apostle says to the wives, 'Wives, submit yourselves to your own husbands' for the reason that the husband has been appointed the head.

But a still greater argument is found in 1 Corinthians 11, where we are told that the man, the husband, is the head of the wife, that Christ is the Head of the man, and that God is the Head of Christ. This is an argument that cannot be disputed. In what sense is God the Head of Christ? The answer is what we sometimes call the Economic Trinity. The Father, Son and Holy Spirit are co-equal and co-eternal. How then can the Father (God) be the Head of Christ? For the purpose of salvation the Son has subordinated Himself to the Father, and the Spirit has subordinated Himself to the Son and to the Father. It is a voluntary subordination in order that salvation may be carried out. It is essential in the carrying out of the work. The Son said, 'Here am I, send Me'. He volunteered. He lays aside this aspect of equality, He becomes a servant of His Father, and the Father sends Him – 'the Head of Christ is God'. That is the way in which the Apostle puts it: 'As the Head of Christ is God, so Christ is the Head of the man, and so the man is the head of the woman;' therefore 'Wives, submit yourselves unto your own husbands, as unto the Lord'.

That is the positive exposition of this tremendous teaching which alone gives us a true view of marriage. Incidentally, I have been dealing with an argument, a foolish argument again, that is so often brought forward. Somebody says, 'You know, this is quite wrong, I know many instances where the wife is a much abler person than the husband, much more gifted in every respect. Are you saying that such a brilliantly gifted woman has to subject herself to her husband, to a man who is altogether her inferior?' There is only one answer to that argument; the person who frames it is arguing against God. God knows all about such cases. What God says is that if that gifted, brilliant woman is not subjecting herself to her own husband she is sinning. Whatever her gifts she is to submit to her partner in marriage.

At this point I would make two comments. No woman, whatever her gifts, has a right even to contemplate marrying a given individual unless she is prepared to submit in that way. It is a voluntary submission, it is the way in which Christ submitted and subordinated Himself. She is to behave in the same way, and unless she is prepared to do so, unless she is convinced that she can submit herself to this man, she should not marry him. If she enters into marriage with any other idea, it is against the will of God, and she is committing sin.

My second comment is this. I sometimes think that one of the most wonderful things I have ever been privileged to witness was a case of this very thing to which I am referring actually being put into practice. It was my custom for a number of years to go and preach in a certain church in the provinces, and after preaching to spend the night in the manse with the minister and his wife. It was always most interesting for this reason, that it was so obvious to me on the first visit, that from the standpoint of sheer ability there was no comparison between the husband and the wife. The wife was an exceptionally able and brilliant woman. The husband was not without his gifts, but his main gifts were in the matter of personality – he was an exceptionally nice and friendly and kind and gracious man. But as regards sheer intellectual ability there was no comparison. Indeed their academic record – they were both graduates – had proved this. The wife had a degree in a subject that very few women took up at that particular time, and she had taken First Class Honours. The husband, taking a much easier subject, only had a Second Class. There was no question, I say, as to the ability – her grasp of intellectual matters, her understanding, struck me immediately, and became more and more evident as I got to know them. But what I wish to say is that I do not know that I have ever seen anything more wonderful than the way in which that woman always put her husband into his true Scriptural position. She did it in a very clever and subtle way. She would put arguments into his mouth; but she always did so in such a way as to suggest that they were his, and not hers! There is an amusing aspect to the matter, but I am reporting it as one of the most moving and tremendous things I have ever experienced. She was not only an able woman, she was a Christian woman, and she was putting into operation this principle that the husband is the head. He always had to state the decision though she had supplied him with the reasons. She was acting as a help meet for him. She had the qualities that he lacked; she was complementing, she was supplementing him. But the husband was the head, and the children were always referred to him. She was guarding his position.

Let me show the importance of realizing and grasping and understanding this teaching. Why is all this so important, and especially today? Why is it more important that I should have been doing what I have been doing rather than giving my opinions on politics or some international problem? It is because the failure to understand and to implement this very teaching is the cause of most of the problems in the world today. The basic problem in the world today is the problem of authority. The chaos in the world is due to the fact that people in every realm of life have lost all respect for authority, whether it be between nations or between parts of nations, whether it be in industry, whether it be in the home, whether it be in the schools, or anywhere else. The loss of authority! And in my view it all really starts in the home and in the married relationship. That is why I venture to query whether a statesman whose own marriage has broken down really has a right to speak about the world's problems. If he fails in the sphere where he is most competent, what right has he to speak in others? He ought to retire out of public life. The real breakdown starts in the home, and in the married relationship. I am asserting that the appalling increase in divorce which has taken place since the second world war (I am told it is coming down a little at the moment, but I suggest that that is only temporary and can be explained) is due to one thing only, namely, that men and women do not understand this Scriptural teaching about marriage and about husbands and wives.

The same lack of understanding is also the explanation of the breakdown in family and in home life, which is again so obvious at the present time. The family is ceasing to be the centre that it used to be. The members of the family are always out somewhere, and often out at all hours of the night. Family life with its wonderful cohesion – this fundamental unit in life – is disappearing. We find here, too, the explanation of the unruliness and the indiscipline amongst children, and therefore the main explanation of juvenile delinquency. This can be proved even from statistics! Children who have become delinquents are almost invariably the children of broken homes, broken marriages. They have never been given a chance, as we say. They have been brought up in an atmosphere of uncertainty, indecision, and conflict, where wife is against husband and husband against wife, and they become cynics in their tender years. They have no respect for either father or mother, or for anybody or anything. The place where a child should have confidence, and should be able to look for authority and leadership and guidance has gone; there is nothing there, and so the poor child becomes a delinquent. He has been brought up in this atmosphere of conflict between father and mother, husband and wife.

Indeed, there are other aspects of this trend that seem to me to be even more sinister. Is it not a fact that, increasingly, men have been abrogating their position and retiring out of it, and not doing their duty as husbands and as fathers as the result of sheer laziness and selfishness? Husbands are increasingly leaving the discipline of home-life to the wives, to the mothers. They cannot be bothered; they come home tired from work and ask their wives to keep the children from them, and to answer their questions. Is not this happening increasingly? The husband is deliberately vacating the position in which God has put him. It is happening among Christian people, but it is happening still more among non-Christians. The husband is evacuating his position, and leaving it in his laziness to the wife.

This is happening today in many other directions also. So many Christian people today will not touch politics because they say it is a 'dirty game'. But what an appalling argument! It is their duty as citizens of the country to be interested and concerned. But, here, we are particularly concerned with this realm of marriage.

Then, on the other side, feminism has led to aggressiveness on the part of the wife, the mother. She is setting herself up as an equal, and undermining the influence of the father in the minds of the children. The unhappy result is the totally false and wrong approach to the whole question. I do not say this in a spirit of criticism. We are seeing this increasingly in this country, but to nothing like the extent to which they are seeing it in the United States of America. There, you have what may more or less be called a matriarchal society, and the man is becoming increasingly regarded merely as the one to provide the dollars, the wage-earner, the man who brings in the necessary money. The woman, the mother, is the cultured person, and the head of the home; and the children look to her. This false unscriptural view of man and woman, and father and mother leads to a matriarchal society, which, it seems to me, is most dangerous. The result is, of course, the growth of crime and all the terrible social problems with which they are grappling in that country. Then, because they influence every other country through their films and in various other ways, this attitude is being spread throughout the entire world. A matriarchal society with the woman as the head and centre of the home is a denial of the biblical teaching, and is, indeed, a repetition of the old sin of Eve.

The problem is being recognized increasingly. That is why Marriage Guidance Councils and suchlike bodies have been formed. But, alas, they generally approach the problems in terms of psychology. Yet if you examine the married life of many of these psychologists you get a shock. These people who give advice as to how marriages are to be entered into, how they are to be preserved and kept, cannot apply the teaching in their own marriages. Of course, they cannot! It is not a matter of psychology. What is needed is not just a little common sense and wisdom and the spirit of comradeship, and give and take. Men and women know all about that, and have known all about it always; but they cannot practise it. No, there is only one hope. Until God is the Authority, and man and wife submit themselves to Him, until they do all things 'as unto the Lord', and realize that it is the same sort of headship as that of God over Christ, and Christ over man, there is no hope. It is as men and women in the last hundred years have increasingly departed from the authority of the Bible that this terrible social blight and problem has become more and more evident. I know that I shall be told, 'You obviously want to go back to that stern, repressive, autocratic Victorian husband and father'. That is quite wrong! I know that much of the modern problem is due to a reaction against Victorianism, and I condemn Victorianism as much as the present position. We must come back to the Bible. I am not advocating a return to the Victorian idea. I say, Come back to God, come back to Christ, come back to the revelation in the authoritative Word of God. Look again at His perfect plan – man, and the woman by his side complementing him, his help meet; loving one another, revering, respecting, honouring one another, but never confusing the two spheres.

May God in His grace enable us not only to see the teaching, but to submit ourselves to it, and thereby bring honour and glory to the Name of the blessed Lord. 'As unto the Lord.'

8
The Analogy of the Body

Ephesians 5:22–24

We come back to this statement, because so far we have been able to look at one aspect only of it in detail. The Apostle gives us two great particular reasons why wives should submit themselves to their own husbands. We have considered the first, which is that it is a matter of the order of nature. He says: 'For the husband is the head of the wife', God ordained it so when He made man and woman at the beginning; and we have seen how the New Testament not only confirms that but constantly goes back to that original ordinance of God. So here we are dealing with something that is basic and fundamental to the whole of man's life on earth, and to his wellbeing.

Now in all this, we have not yet been saying anything that is peculiarly and specifically Christian. That was the teaching of the Old Testament, that is something that everybody should recognize, whether they are Christians or not. This is God's ordinance with regard to the whole of life. As we have recognized the family we are to recognize this. The God who ordained the family ordained marriage, the God who ordained the State ordained marriage; and as we should submit ourselves to the State, so we should pay heed to this fundamental ordinance of God with regard to the relative positions of husbands and wives, and the relationship that should subsist between them. Now all that, so far, is general. The fact that we are Christians does not mean that we have no interest in what is general; the fact that we are Christians does not mean that we do not need the Old Testament. It is still there as a foundation; we build upon it; that is why the Apostle puts it first.

But now he goes on to his second reason, which is a peculiarly Christian one, 'The husband is the head of the wife'. Then comes the Christian addition – 'even as Christ is the Head of the church'. This takes us further; it does not do away with the first, but it adds to it, and indeed it helps us to understand the first. That is what the Christian faith does with regard to the whole of life. It is only a Christian who can really appreciate life in general in this world. I mean that it is only a Christian, in the last analysis, who can really enjoy nature. The Christian sees nature in a different way from the man of the world. There is a newness about it. He does not merely see the thing in and of itself, he sees the great Creator and the wonder of His ways, the variety, the colour and the beauty. In other words, being a Christian means that your whole outlook upon life is enriched. It does not matter what it is, every gift that man has, and which he manifests, can only be truly appreciated by the Christian. He sees with a greater depth, he has a fuller understanding. That is to say, the Christian message not only adds to what we had before but it greatly enriches what we had before, and gives us a deeper insight into it. Here we shall find that this specifically Christian addition not only helps us to understand the order of nature already laid down, but that further, on top of that, it adds a new quality, another aspect as it were, another emphasis to it all.

Here is the statement: 'The husband is the head of the wife, even as Christ is the Head of the church: and he is the saviour of the body'. What we are looking at here is something that only a Christian can understand; no-one else can. A man who does not believe in the Lord Jesus Christ, and who does not know the way of salvation, obviously cannot understand what Scripture means in saying that 'Christ is the Head of the body, which is the church'. It is meaningless to him; he does not understand it at all. Such a person therefore cannot understand this specifically Christian view of marriage. This is a deduction from the Christian doctrine of the church; and therefore if a man does not understand the Christian doctrine of the church, according to the Apostle he cannot finally understand the Christian view of marriage.

This leads us at once to draw certain conclusions. The first is, that obviously a Christian should never marry a non-Christian. We are told that specifically in the Second Epistle to the Corinthians: 'Be ye not unequally yoked together with unbelievers' (2 Corinthians 6:14). That is undoubtedly a reference to this question of marriage. And if we needed a reason for accepting that exhortation we have it here. If believer marries unbeliever the position would be that one of the people getting married would have this exalted Christian view of marriage, while the other would know nothing at all about it. Already there would be a defect in the marriage. They are not one in it; they are not entering into it in the same way; there is already a division; the one has something the other has not got. There is already the seed of discord, as the Apostle proves in that same statement in 2 Corinthians chapter 6.

The second deduction I would draw is that a Christian service in connection with marriage is only appropriate for Christians. This is a very large subject, it is a part of the subject of the discipline of the Christian church. The position has become quite chaotic, and people who know nothing at all about Christianity are given a Christian service in which this statement is read out about the husband being the head of the wife 'even as Christ is the Head of the church'. It is quite meaningless to them. I deduce therefore that that should not be done. You do not teach high Christian doctrine to those who are not Christians; to them you preach nothing but repentance and the need of belief. They cannot possibly understand the doctrine concerning marriage. You have to be in the Christian life before you can understand it. I am arguing therefore that a Christian service at a wedding should be reserved only and exclusively for Christians. It is to make a farce of it to have such a service for any others.

Thirdly, I deduce that such a service is appropriate and right, and should be taken and conducted, when Christian people are being married. I mean this. Some of the Puritans, 300 years ago, in their violent reaction against Roman Catholicism, decided that there should be no service at all in connection with marriage. Marriage, they said, is nothing but a legal contract. Now we can well understand their reaction and we are in great sympathy with it. The Roman church had taught the false and unbiblical view that marriage is a sacrament so the Puritans felt that they must get as far away as they could from that idea. Hence they ceased to have a service at all. But surely, in the light of the Apostle's teaching here, that was quite wrong! It was too violent a reaction, so violent that it became unscriptural. There are aspects of marriage which demand a service – the teaching and the understanding of this particular scripture, and others. And as the teaching is that marriage is something comparable to the mystical union between Christ and His church, I say that it is an occasion for worship and for a truly Christian service. Marriage is not only a legal contract, and we must be very careful, as I have been pointing out, that we do not allow people whose thinking is wrong to govern our thinking and our behaviour. The Christian must never be merely a reaction against anything; he must be positive, he must be scriptural. But there are those who in their hatred of Roman Catholicism go so far to the other side that they end by denying the very Scripture that they claim to uphold.

However, let me go on to assert that, though the Christian view of marriage immediately suggests those three things, it does not here, nor anywhere else, teach, as the Roman Catholics teach, that marriage is a sacrament. There is no teaching whatsoever anywhere in the Bible to support that idea. I defy anyone to produce such a Scripture. Marriage is not a sacrament. What then is the teaching? It is that which is given here, namely, this whole idea of the mystical union. The relationship between husband and wife, and wife and husband, is comparable to that between Christ and the church and the church and Christ. The Apostle for our comfort says later on, 'This is a great mystery'! The relationship between Christ and the church is a mystery. It is a fact, but it is a great mystery – this mystical union between the church and Christ and the individual believer and Christ. But being fact, we must increasingly try to understand it. Paul says that the relationship between husband and wife, and wife and husband, is comparable to that fact. It belongs to that order, and that is the way in which we must begin to think of it. We are introduced here to the realm of this high doctrine concerning the Christian church.

The Apostle, with his logical mind, knows that there should be no difficulty about this in the minds of these Ephesians, because he has already taught them about that very doctrine. He did so in chapter 1 where he prays at the end that they might know 'what is the exceeding greatness of God's power toward them'. He says it is the power 'manifested in Christ when He raised Him from the dead . . . And hath put all things under His feet, and gave Him to be the Head over all things to the church, which is His body, the fulness of Him that filleth all in all'. There, Paul has introduced them to the doctrine of the church; here he is applying it. People who rush to the end of an Epistle without reading the beginning are always in error. What we have here are deductions. He did the same thing again and added a little more to the definition, in chapter 4 in verses 15 and 16 where he says: 'Speaking the truth in love, may grow up into Him in all things, which is the Head, even Christ: from whom the whole body fitly joined together and compacted by that which every joint supplieth, according to the effectual working in the measure of every part, maketh increase of the body unto the edifying of itself in love'. He now draws upon that teaching in order that they may understand the true nature of Christian marriage.

What is the point? It is essentially this. He is emphasizing the organic, the vital union, the intimate relationship. He has referred to 'bands of supply' in chapter 4:16, those 'sheaths', as it were, the nerves and the arteries, which bring sustenance from the head, from the centre, to every part of the body. That is a way of stressing this vital organic union that exists between a husband and a wife. It is one life, and it is one life in the same way as the life of the church in her relationship to the Head, which is Christ. Here, of course, the Apostle is particularly interested in one aspect of all that, the aspect of dependence: 'Wives, submit yourselves unto your own husbands, as unto the Lord. For the husband is the head of the wife, even as Christ is the Head of the church'. He is dealing with this aspect of dependence and of submission, and he introduces this further element in order that we may have a clear understanding of how it comes in, and why it comes in inevitably. Later on he will deal with the other side of it, the husband with respect to the wife.

As we consider this great statement we are confronted at once by a problem. Look at it again: 'For the husband is the head of the wife, even as Christ is the Head of the church – and he is the Saviour of the body'. The problem that engages so much of the attention of the commentators, and rightly so, is this. Why did the Apostle add this further statement? Why did he not say, 'The husband is the head of the wife, even as Christ is the Head of the church . . . Therefore as the church is subject unto Christ, so let the wives be to their own husbands in everything'? Why did he add, 'and he is the Saviour of the body'? There are those – and they are in the majority, and they include great names, for example, Charles Hodge – who do not hesitate to say at this point that this is a purely independent addition, and that what the Apostle is referring to when he says 'he is the Saviour of the body' is clearly that the Lord Jesus Christ is the Saviour of the church. They go on to say that this has nothing to do with the husband. Why then did Paul say it? Well, they say, he said it for this reason. He had committed himself to this, that the husband is the head of the wife, even as Christ is the Head of the church, and the very mention of the name of Christ makes him cry out 'and he is the saviour of the body'. It has nothing to do with what he is arguing at the moment, but the very mention of the name of Christ makes him say this wonderful thing. So, they argue that this is an independent phrase, and that it does not apply to the husband's relationship to the wife.

Their arguments are these: They ask, Can you say that the husband is the saviour of his wife as Christ is the Saviour of the church? That, they say, is nonsense. Christ, we know, died for the church. He saves us by His atoning death and by His resurrection; but you cannot say that about any other relationship. It is quite unique. The Apostle was just carried away by the depth of his feeling, and put in this independent phrase which obviously has nothing to do with the husband/wife relationship.

What do we say with respect to that? We have to grant, of course, that if you read a statement like this superficially and without examining it carefully, you would have to agree with it. There is no need to argue about this. Christ as Saviour of the church, in that sense, is unique, and that obviously does not apply to the husband.

But that is not the whole of their argument. They have a further argument to which they attach very great importance. It is based upon the word translated 'Therefore' at the beginning of verse 24. The verse runs thus: '*Therefore* as the church is subject unto Christ, so let the wives be to their own husbands in everything'. The point they make here is this. They say that the translation 'Therefore' is quite wrong; and, indeed, they are right in saying that. But then they go on to say that the word which is translated 'Therefore' should in reality be translated 'Nevertheless'. It is a word of contrast, and it always presents a contrast. So they say that we should read it like this: 'For the husband is the head of the wife, even as Christ is the Head of the church and He is the Saviour of the body. 'Nevertheless' – though that is not true of the husband with respect to the wife, in spite of that – 'Nevertheless let the wives be subject to their own husbands in everything'. So they feel that the case is quite unanswerable; that the Apostle himself says in effect, 'Now when I said that He is the Saviour of the body I had forgotten for the moment my analogy between the relationship of Christ and the church, and the husband and the wife – "Nevertheless" – in spite of that, though that is not true in the realm of husband and wife, the wives should still submit themselves to their own husbands, even as the church is subject unto Christ.'

It seems to me that there is an adequate answer to all this argumentation. First of all, it confines the meaning of the word 'Saviour'. The word 'Saviour' does not always carry that one meaning, of Christ giving His life for the church, and His blood being shed. It is the common meaning, but it is not the only meaning; there is a wider meaning to this term 'Saviour'. There is an example of this in the First Epistle to Timothy, chapter 4 and verse 10: 'For therefore', says the Apostle, 'we both labour and suffer reproach, because we trust in the living God, who is the Saviour of all men, specially of those that believe'. Now that is exactly the same word as is used here about 'the Saviour of the body'. There we are told that God, the living God, is the Saviour of all men, especially of those that believe. You cannot say that that means that all men enjoy salvation in a spiritual sense, because that would make you universalists. Of course not! Well then, it means that the word 'saviour' there has a different connotation. What it means there is 'preserver' – that He looks after, that He cares for. He is the Preserver of all men, especially of those that believe. We are reminded by our Lord, 'He causes His sun to rise upon the evil and the good, and He sends rain upon the just and upon the unjust'; yes, and gives food to all. It is in that sense He is the Saviour of all men. So why not give that meaning to the word 'Saviour' here? He is the One who looks after and safeguards the body. That is one reply which we can put up against the argument quoted.

But I have further reasons for rejecting that exposition which would confine this little phrase solely to the Lord Jesus Christ and His saving work. My second reason is this: I would argue that verses 28 and 29, which are to follow, insist upon our interpreting this phrase as applying to the husband and wife as well as to Christ and the church: Paul says, 'So ought men to love their wives as their own bodies. He that loveth his wife loveth himself. For no man ever yet hated his own flesh.' Well, what does he do? 'He nourisheth and cherisheth it' – yes, he is acting as a saviour to it, he is looking after it, he is preserving it. 'No man ever yet hated his own flesh; but nourisheth and cherisheth it, even as the Lord the church, which is His body' – and so on. He says the husband ought to deal with his wife as his own flesh, his own body. He does not neglect his own body, he nourishes it and cherishes it. In other words he is 'the saviour of the body'. How important it is always to take a verse in its context! Even the mighty can fall at this point. I argue that those two verses insist upon this other interpretation here, and that this is not an isolated independent phrase, true only of the Lord Jesus Christ. Paul is still talking about husbands and wives, 'The husband is the head of the wife, even as Christ is the Head of the church: and he is the Saviour of the body'. It is true of both.

But what of the word which is translated 'Therefore' at the beginning of verse 24? Now this is really interesting. I have gone to the trouble of consulting some of the best Lexicons on the point. It is a Greek word, 'Alla', and I find that it need not be translated always as a kind of antithesis to something which is an opposite and a contrast. Take, for instance, the Greek/English Lexicon of the New Testament (edition 1952), by Arndt and Gingrich, one of the best and most authoritative. They actually say this: that what it really means is 'Now' or 'Then'. I quote them. They say, 'It is used to strengthen the command', not to imply a contrast or a difference, to strengthen the very command that he is giving. And they actually pick out Ephesians 5:24 as an illustration of this particular use of the word. Grimm-Thayer has a similar statement.

It seems to me therefore that on all these grounds we must reject the interpretation which says that this is an independent phrase referring only to the Lord. Indeed, if it were that, it would be quite purposeless at this point; it would be sheer confusion. This Apostle is not given to doing that kind of thing. So what we read, therefore, is that 'the husband is the head of the wife, even as Christ is the Head of the church; and he is the Saviour of the body'. Then – 'As the church is subject unto Christ, so let the wives be to their husbands in everything'.

What, then, is the doctrine? It is clearly this. The wife is the one who is kept, preserved, guarded, shielded, provided for by the husband. That is the relationship – as Christ nourishes and cherishes the church, so the husband nourishes and cherishes the wife – and the wife should realize that that is her position in this relationship. The husband is the preserver, he is the saviour of the body. The wife then should start with this idea, and she should always act in the light of it.

But we can go further. What is the relationship of the body to the head? What is true of the church in relation to Christ is true of the wife in relation to the husband. Let us take the illustration that Paul uses here and in the previous instances I have given of the church as the body of Christ such as in 1 Corinthians chapter 12 and Romans chapter 12. What is the teaching? The wife is to the husband what the body is to the head, what the church is to Christ. It is the idea of the 'complement' again. The essential thing in the Christian concept of marriage is this idea of wholeness, completeness. We met with it in Genesis chapter 2 – 'help meet', someone taken out of Adam, a part of him; yes, but complementing him, making up a wholeness. That is the very idea that you think of inevitably as you think of your body, the body as a whole. The body is not a collection of parts, not a number of fingers and hands and feet and toes stuck on, and limbs loosely attached together. That is a completely false notion of the body. It is an organic, vital unity; it is one, it is whole. Now that is the very idea we have here. The husband and wife are not separate; they are not like two kingdoms which have diplomatic relationships, but are always in a state of tension, and always in danger of a quarrel. That is quite the opposite of the Christian concept of what a marriage really is. Christ and the church are one as the body and the head are one. But this ideal allows for differing functions; and that is what we are to grasp – differing functions, different purposes, special duties that only each part can perform. But it is vital that we should remember that each part is a part of a whole and that all the separate actions are part of a unified action which leads to a corporate result.

But let us work this out a little more in detail in order to illumine this question of the marriage state and relationship. How important all this is! I have given some reasons for that already. I believe that much of the irreligion of today is partly a reaction against that Victorian type of life in which many husbands and wives appeared to be great Christians, but of whom people said, 'If only you knew them in their private life!' Nothing does more harm to Christianity than that a man should not be the same at home as he is in the church or out on the street or in his office. It is in the home you really know a man. What are the relationships there? These things are important for that reason, not only in and of themselves, but as a part of our general testimony as Christians.

What, then, does this teach us about the relationship of the wife to the husband in this matter of subjecting herself? It seems clear that it does not teach a mere and a sheer passivity; the wife is not to be entirely passive. It is a mis-interpretation of this picture to say that the wife should never speak, never give an opinion, but be mute or dumb and utterly passive. That is a pressing of an analogy and an illustration to a point at which it becomes meaningless. But what it means is this: the wife should never be guilty of independent action. The analogy of the body and the head insists upon that. The business of my body is not to act independently of me. It is I who decide to act with my mind and brains and will. My body is the means through which I express it. If my body begins to act apart from me, I am suffering from some sort of 'convulsions'. This is exactly what 'convulsions' means; that parts of a man's body are moving in an irrational manner. It is not purposive action; he does not want them to act, but he cannot stop them; they are acting independently of his mind and will. That is chaos, that is convulsions. Here is the analogy, 'Wives, submit yourselves unto your own husbands; be subject and obedient to them in everything'. Why? Because as wife, and in this relationship, you do not act independently of your husband. If you do, it is chaos, it is convulsions.

Or let me divide it up still more. The wife must not act before the husband. All the teaching indicates that he is the head, that he ultimately controls. So she not only does not act independently of him, she does not act before him. But let me emphasize this also; as it is true to say that she must not act before him, it is equally true to say that she must not delay action, she must not stall action, she must not refuse to act. Go back to the analogy of the body. Think of somebody who has had a 'stroke'. This person wants to act, but the limb is paralysed, so he cannot. Though the person is willing movement there is no movement – the arm is not healthy, it resists movement. This is a part of the teaching; the subjection involves the idea that she does not act before her husband, nor does she delay, she does not hinder action, she does not paralyse action. These points are all vital in this whole relationship of marriage; and it is because people do not realize and know these things that marriage is breaking down round and about us. Independence, acting before, not acting, stalling, refusing, is all wrong; and it is all because men and women do not understand this Christian view of marriage.

We can sum it up thus: The teaching is that the initiative and the leadership are ultimately the husband's, but the action must always be co-ordinated. That is the meaning of this picture – co-ordinated action but leadership in the head. There is no sense of inferiority suggested by this. The wife is not inferior to her husband; she is different. She has her own peculiar position, full of honour and respect. That is why the man is later to be told to cherish and to nourish and to love and to care for, and to respect and honour his wife. There is no inferiority involved. What Paul is teaching is that any Christian woman who realizes all this will love to please her husband, to be useful to him, to help him, to aid him, to enable him to function. She will not cavil at saying 'and obey' in the marriage service. What a sad thing this is! I was told by a friend recently that a clergyman who was going to take a marriage service had said that he would not have the word 'obey'. He thought he was being modern, that he was appealing to 'the man in the street' – showing that, after all, Christianity is not narrow! He did not realize that he was denying the biblical doctrine. And how utterly inconsistent such people are! Such a man, I suppose, if he was in a football match, would boast of the fact of the team spirit. Though they are all playing individually and all have ability, they start off by saying that there is only one man who is captain. Each says 'I am not captain, I am submitting myself to the captain'. That is marvellous, that is the team spirit; each player is going to obey the captain. But you must not say that with regard to marriage! That is derogatory to woman, that is old-fashioned, that is Paul, that is the hard pharisee, that is legalistic, that is the Old Testament! But that denies the whole doctrine, and is even inconsistent in its supposed modernity. The Christian wife, understanding these things, wants to say 'and obey', 'to love, cherish and obey'. Of course! Why is she getting married? Is it not in order to produce 'one flesh', wholeness? Is it not in order to enjoy this co-ordinated action, this completeness, which is to be demonstrated to the world? That is not slavery; that is living as the church does with respect to her Lord; that is manifesting the essential spirit of Christianity.

But let me say a final word. Did you notice that the end of the exhortation was, 'Therefore (then, now then) as the church is subject unto Christ, so let the wives be to their own husbands in everything'. 'Everything!' Does it really mean that? Here we answer again in terms of the analogy of Scripture in its entirety. When the Scripture makes a sweeping general statement like that it always expects us to interpret it in the light of its own teaching. So when we read here that the wife is to be subject to her own husband in everything, it is exactly the same as saying that the Christian is to be subject to the State, to the powers that be, as in Romans chapter 13 and in other places. Does it mean, then, that the wife has to do literally everything her husband tells her to do in all circumstances and conditions? Of course not! That would be to make the Scripture ridiculous. There are qualifications here. What are they? Here is one: It is a fundamental rule of the Scripture that nobody should ever act against his or her conscience. This exhortation does not tell a wife that she has to act against her own conscience. Within the conjugal relation, within the terms of marriage, the husband has no right to dictate to a wife's conscience.

Here we might cite a number of very interesting cases. There is a great deal of confusion sometimes between obeying conscience and holding on to an opinion. They are not the same thing. The Scripture exhorts us to obey conscience in all circumstances; but that is not necessarily the same thing as holding on to your own opinion. Let me give you one illustration of this. I remember reading in the book on Scottish Theology by Dr. John Macleod, of a very interesting case that teaches this very point. There was a dispute in Scotland in the eighteenth century over the relationship of the Christian to the local government, and part of the Church divided into two sections known as the Burgher and the anti-Burgher sections. This was a matter of great controversy. There was a minister of the name of James Scott who had a very remarkable wife whose name was Alison. She was the daughter of that very remarkable man Ebenezer Erskine, one of the founders of the original Secession in Scotland. She was a very strong character and also the wife of a very able man. Mr. Scott and his wife disagreed at this point – Mr. Scott belonging to the anti-Burgher party, Mrs. Scott belonging to the Burgher party. Many difficult cases arose, and Mr. Scott was in a synod which actually reprimanded and deposed his wife's father and uncle and brother-in-law – a very courageous act on his part. Then, having done that in the synod he had to go home and tell his wife what he had done. In response, Alison Scott made this famous statement: 'James Scott, you are still my husband but you are no longer my minister'. She also put that into practice, so that as every Sunday came she did not go and worship in the church where her own husband was leading the service and preaching, she went to one of the Burgher churches. What do you make of a case like that? I would not hesitate to say that Alison Scott was entirely wrong, because she was putting opinion in the place of conscience. There, surely, is an instance where, for every reason, she should have submitted to the leading and the guidance of her husband. She would not have been violating her conscience; it was a pure matter of opinion. We must never, I say, make the mistake of confusing conscience and opinion. The wife can give her opinion, but when she sees that the husband is determined, she should abide by his ruling.

Let me give you another illustration to counter-balance this one. One of the most remarkable and moving experiences I have ever had since I have been the minister of Westminster Chapel happened some eighteen months ago, if I remember rightly. I was preaching in the chapel on the first Sunday night after I had come back from my summer vacation, and on the text 'We are ambassadors for Christ'. I was emphasizing the aspect of the call of the ambassador, and so on. I went out of the pulpit into my room, and a lady was ushered in immediately, obviously in a state of agitation. What she had to tell me was this, that she was quite certain that that sermon had been preached for her. She and her husband had been married for some ten years. He had the feeling that he was being called to the ministry, and he was giving up his work as a school teacher. She did not agree at all. She had done everything she could to hinder her husband, but still the husband was certain and was going forward, and there was a real crisis in their married life. But during the service that woman had been deeply convicted about this matter, and just came in to confess it to me and to tell me that she was rushing immediately to the nearest telephone to phone her husband who was down in the West Country, and who had to sit an examination for entrance into the ministry the very next morning. She saw how wrong she had been to stand on her opinion and thus to thwart God's purpose in her husband's life. That was not conscience, that was standing on an opinion. I say that we should never violate conscience, but I also say that we must be ready to submit in the matter of opinion. The wife's position in the married relationship is not to be pressed to the extent of going against her conscience; neither must she allow her husband to make her commit sin. If the husband is trying to get the wife to commit sin she must say 'No!' Not to say this is to make the Scripture ridiculous. Should the husband lose his mental balance and become insane, obviously she is not to obey him in everything. The Scripture is never ridiculous; the Scripture carries its own meaning with it; and there are these inevitable limits.

[127]

The fourth point I would make is that the wife is not to submit to the husband to the extent of allowing him to interfere with her relationship to God and the Lord Jesus Christ. She must do everything short of that, but not that!

Fifthly, adultery breaks the marriage relationship; and if the husband has been guilty of adultery the wife is no longer bound to give him obedience in everything. She can divorce him, she is allowed to do so by the Scripture. She is entitled to do so because adultery breaks the unity, breaks the relationship. They are now separate and no longer one. He has broken the unity, he has gone out of it. So we must not interpret this Scripture as teaching that the wife is thus irrevocably, inevitably bound to an adulterous husband for the rest of her life. She may choose to be – that is for her to decide. All I am saying is, that this Scripture does not command it, it does not make it inevitable. In other words, there are these limits to these matters.

There, then, as I see it, are the main deductions from this wonderful illustration. The big point that is emphasized is that the wife must go to the extremest limit of submitting herself to her husband for Christ's sake, for the reasons given, short of violating the principles which we have just been laying down. To any wife who is in trouble in this matter let me suggest certain practical helps. If you are in trouble, ask yourself the following questions: Why did I originally marry this man? What was it then? Cannot that be restored? Try to re-capture that in the spirit of Christ and the Gospel. 'Ah but,' you say, 'it is impossible, I cannot'. Well then, I say, as a Christian, feel sorry for the man, pray for him. Put into practice the teaching of the Apostle Peter, in his First Epistle, chapter 3, where he tells the wives so plainly to subject themselves, and not only to those who are Christians: 'Be in subjection to your own husbands; that if any obey not the Word, they also may without the Word be won by the conversation of the wives; while they behold your chaste conversation coupled with fear'. Try to put that into practice; try in humility and meekness to win your husband. 'Whose adorning let it not be that outward adorning of plaiting the hair, and of wearing of gold, or of putting on of apparel; but let it be the hidden man of the heart, in that which is not corruptible, even the ornament of a meek and quiet spirit, which is in the sight of God of great price'. Do all you can, go to the limit, go beyond the limit short of these principles. And, finally, ask yourself this question – Can I honestly go in my present attitude and condition into the presence of the Lord, who, in spite of me and my vileness and my sinfulness, came from heaven and went to the Cross of Calvary and gave Himself and His life for me? If you can face Him all is well; I have nothing to say. But if you feel condemned, in His presence, about your attitude, about your relationship in any aspect, go and put it right. So that when you go back to Him again, it will be with a quiet conscience, an open spirit, and you will be able to rejoice in His holy presence. This is a Christian matter; it is like the relationship of the church to Christ, the body to the head. As long as we look at it in those terms there are no problems; it is a great privilege, it is something which God looks down upon with pleasure and with delight. 'Wives, submit yourselves' – 'a meek and a quiet spirit is in the sight of God of great price', and however much you may have to suffer here, your reward in heaven will be very great.

9
True Love

Ephesians 5:25–33

So far we have been looking at what the Apostle has to say to wives; now we come to what he has to say to husbands. It is found in the remarkable statement he makes from verse 25 to the end of the chapter. It is remarkable in two main respects; in what it tells us about the duties of husbands, and, still more remarkable, in what it tells us about the relationship of the Lord Jesus Christ to the Christian church. That is one of the astounding things about this man's letters always; you never know when you are going to find a pearl, a pearl of greatest price. Here, in this essentially practical part of this Epistle, he suddenly throws out the most exalted and wonderful statement he has ever made anywhere about the nature of the Christian church and her relationship to the Lord Jesus Christ. You observe that in treating this matter of husbands, and how they are to behave towards their wives, he also treats that other subject, and he gives both this wonderful treatment.

The two things, you will notice, are intertwined; so our first business is to arrive at some kind of a division of the matter. He moves from one to the other and then back to the first. That is often his method; he does not always make a complete statement on the one side and then apply it; he gives a part of his statement, applies it, and then another part, and applies that. I suggest this classification. In verses 25, 26 and 27 he tells us what Christ has done for the church, and why He has done it. Then in verses 28 and 29 he gives us a preliminary deduction from that as to the duty of a husband towards his wife, especially in terms of the union that subsists between Christ and the church, and the husband and the wife. Then

[130]

in part of verse 29 and in verses 30 and 32 he develops sublime doctrine of the mystical union between Christ and the church. Then in verses 31 and 33 he draws his final practical deductions.

That seems to me to be the analysis of the verses we are studying. But in order that we may grasp his teaching more clearly, I suggest that we approach it in this way. First, we start with his general injunction: 'Husbands, love your wives'. That is what he desires to emphasize above everything. In other words the controlling idea with regard to the husband is to be love. You remember that the controlling idea with respect to the wives was submission – 'Wives, submit yourselves.' Submission on the part of the wife, love on the part of the husband! We must be clear about this. This does not mean, of course, that it is the husband alone that is to love. 'He does not say a word here about the wives loving their husbands', someone may remark. To say that is to misunderstand the Apostle's object altogether. He is not giving us an exhaustive treatise here on marriage. In his idea of the wife submitting herself love is implicit. We must realize what the Apostle is concerned to do. He is really concerned about one basic point only, namely, harmony and peace and unity as they are displayed in the married relationship and in the home. That being his leading theme he picks out on the two sides the element that needs to be emphasized above every other. What the wife is required to keep her eye on, in maintaining the harmony, is the element of submission; while the husband has to keep his eye on the element of love. So Paul is picking out the chief characteristic, the chief contribution that is to be made by each of the partners in this wonderful relationship which can demonstrate the glory of the Christian life so clearly. The word addressed therefore to husbands is, 'Love your wives'.

This is most important, particularly in connection with the previous teaching. It safeguards the previous teaching, and it is important that we should look at it in that way. He has been emphasizing that the husband is 'the head of the wife, even as Christ is the head of the church'. We have seen that he is in the position of leadership, that he is the lord of the wife. That is the teaching of the Old Testament and the New, and the Apostle has been emphasizing it. But immediately he adds this: 'Husbands, love your wives', as if to say, 'You are the head, you are the leader, you are as it were the lord in this relationship; but because you love your wives the leadership will never become a tyranny, and though you are "lord" you will never become a tyrant'. That is the connection between the two precepts.

This is something which is found very generally in the teaching of the New Testament. Let me give an example. In many ways the best commentary on this matter is to be found in Paul's Second Epistle to Timothy, chapter 1 and verse 7, where he says, 'God hath not given us the spirit of fear; but of power, and of love, and of a sound mind' (discipline). There you have the same thing again. 'God has not given us the spirit of fear'. Well, what has He given? It is a 'spirit of power'; but lest a man should think that this is something tyrannical he adds, 'and love'. It is the power of love. It is not naked power, it is not the power of a dictator or a little tyrant, it is not the idea of a man who arrogates to himself certain rights, and tramples upon his wife's feelings and so on, and sits in the home as a dictator. I was referring in a previous study to what was perhaps the greatest defect in the Victorian outlook upon life, and even its Christianity; and it was just this very thing. They tended to emphasize one side at the expense of the other. And so many of our problems today are due to a reaction, a violent over-reaction against the false emphasis of that particular period.

We must always maintain this balance therefore. We must remember that power is to be tempered by love; it is to be controlled by love, it is the power of love. No husband is entitled to say that he is the head of the wife unless he loves his wife. He is not carrying out the Scriptural injunction unless he does so. These things go together. In other words, it is a manifestation of the Spirit, and the Holy Spirit not only gives power but He gives love and also discipline. So as the husband exercises his privilege as the head of the wife, and the head of the family, he does so in this way. He is to be controlled always by love, and he is to be controlled by discipline. He must discipline himself. There may be the tendency to dictate, but he must not do so – 'power, love, sound mind' (discipline). All that is implicit here in this great word 'love'.

So the reign of the husband is to be a reign and a rule of love; it is a leadership of love. It is not the idea of a pope or a dictator; it is not a case of 'ipse dixit'; he does not speak 'ex-cathedra'. No, it is the power of love, it is the discipline of the Spirit, guarding this power and authority and dignity which are given to the husband. That is clearly the fundamental and the controlling idea in the whole of this matter – 'Husbands, love your wives'.

But now we must proceed to consider in general the character or the nature of that love. This again is very much needed at the present time. There are two things which stand out in a glaring manner in the world today – the abuse of the idea of power, and the still greater abuse of the idea of love. The world has never talked so much about love as it does today. But I wonder whether there has ever been a time when there has been less love. These great terms have become so utterly debased that many people have no idea as to the meaning of the word 'love'.

'Husbands, love your wives'. What is this love? Fortunately for us the Apostle tells us; and he does so in two ways. 'Husbands, love your wives, even as Christ also loved the church'. There are two definitions there. The first is in the word 'love' itself. The very word the Apostle has used here for 'love' is most eloquent in its teaching and its meaning. In the Greek language as used in the days of the Apostle Paul there were three words which can be translated by the English word 'love'. It is most important that we should be clear about this and differentiate between them; because much of the loose thinking today in this realm is due to the failure to appreciate this. One of the three – it does not occur in the New Testament – is the word 'eros' which describes a love that belongs entirely to the flesh. The adjective 'erotic', as commonly used today, reminds us of the content of the word. Of course it is a kind of love. But it is a love of the flesh, it is desire, it is something carnal; and the characteristic of that kind of love is that it is selfish. Now it is not of necessity wrong because it is selfish, but that kind of love is essentially selfish; it is born, as I say, of desire. It wants something, and it is mainly concerned about that. That is its level. It is, so to speak, the animal part in man. And that is what generally passes as 'love' in the world today. The world glories in its 'marvellous' romances, and tells us how wonderful they are. Nothing is said, mark you, about the fact that the man has been unfaithful to his wife and vice versa, and that little children are going to suffer. 'A wonderful romance' has come into the life of the man and the woman he is going to marry. That they are both guilty of breaking their vows and desecrating sanctities is not mentioned; what is publicized is this wonderful 'love match', this wonderful romance! You find that kind of thing in the papers every day. It is nothing but this erotic, selfish, fleshly, lustful desire. But I am reminding you that 'eros' is certainly regarded as love by the world today.

As for the two words translated 'love' in the New Testament

[133]

(Authorized Version) one of them, 'phileo', really means 'to be fond of'. It comes in as a root in such words as 'philanthropic' and 'Philadelphia'. The classic illustration of its use is found in the last chapter of the Gospel according to St. John in the incident which tells how Peter and the others had gone fishing at night and, coming back, had suddenly seen our Lord on the seashore. There He cooked a breakfast for them, and began to speak to them. This is what we read: 'So when they had dined, Jesus saith to Simon Peter, Simon, son of Jonas, lovest thou Me more than these? He saith unto Him, Yea, Lord; thou knowest that I love Thee. He saith unto him, Feed My lambs'. Now the interesting point there is that when Peter says, 'Thou knowest that I love Thee', the word he used was 'Thou knowest that I am fond of Thee'. Our Lord, using the third word to which we have not yet come, asks him if he really loves Him, but Peter replies, 'Thou knowest that I am fond of Thee'. 'He saith unto him again the second time, Simon, son of Jonas, lovest thou Me? He saith unto Him, Yea, Lord, Thou knowest that I love Thee' – which means, 'Thou knowest that I am fond of Thee' – 'He saith unto him, Feed My sheep'. Then we come to verse 17: 'He saith unto him the third time, Simon, son of Jonas, lovest thou Me?' Now here our Lord does a very interesting thing, He does not use the word He had been using before; He now uses the word that Peter had been using. 'He saith unto him the third time, Simon, son of Jonas, are you really fond of Me?' He has lowered the conception, 'Art thou really fond of Me?' 'Peter was grieved because He said unto him the third time, Lovest thou Me? And he said unto Him, Lord, Thou knowest all things, Thou knowest that I love Thee'. Peter was grieved that the Lord seemed to doubt whether he was even fond of Him, so in the light of his failure he could but trust himself to the Lord's knowledge and say, 'Thou knowest that I am fond of Thee'. But let us keep these things in mind – the word translated as 'love' may mean 'being fond of'.

The other New Testament word rises to a much greater height. This is the word that is always used in the Bible to express God's love to us. 'God so loved the world' – 'Agapao'. Now this is the word which is used in the text we are considering. 'Husbands, love your wives' in that sense, love as God loves. There is nothing higher than this. Or, to put it in another way. Take the list describing the fruit of the Spirit in Galatians 5:22. The Apostle is contrasting the works of the flesh and the fruit of the Spirit, and he says,

'The fruit of the Spirit is love' – not erotic feeling, not merely being fond of, it is the love that resembles God's love – love, joy, peace, and so on. That is the love, says the Apostle, which husbands should have and show towards their wives. You see how it all links up so perfectly with the 18th verse: 'Be not drunk with wine, wherein is excess, but be filled with the Spirit'. If you are filled with the Spirit you will be filled with the fruit of the Spirit, and the fruit of the Spirit is 'love'.

The Apostle is addressing people who are filled with the Spirit, for they alone can show this love. It is idle to say this to a man who is not a Christian. He is incapable of it; he cannot love with this kind of love. But the Apostle says that Christians should manifest this kind of love because they are filled with the Spirit. So one of the ways in which I show that I am filled with the Spirit is not so much that I go into ecstasies and manifest certain phenomena; it is the way I behave towards my wife when I am at home, it is this love which is 'the fruit of the Spirit'.

The very word the Apostle selects leads us immediately to the precise idea he is anxious to convey. Let me put it in these terms therefore. Let us get this whole question of marriage and the marriage relationship into focus. I am not saying that the Apostle teaches that that first element which belongs to the flesh should not come in at all. That is quite wrong. There have been people who have so taught. The Roman Catholic teaching concerning celibacy is ultimately based on that misconception. And there are many Christians, I find, who are in trouble over the matter. They seem to think that the Christian is no longer human, no longer natural; and they regard sex as evil. Now that is not only not Christian teaching, it is error, it is wrong. That element of 'eros' is to come in, it is included. Man is man. God made him thus. God has given us these gifts, sex included. There is nothing wrong in the erotic element in and of itself; indeed I go further, I say that it should be present. I refer to this because I am so often asked to deal with these things. I have known Christian people who very honestly, because of this wrong view of sex, and of that which is natural, have more or less come to the conclusion that any Christian man can marry any Christian woman. They say that the only thing that matters and counts now is that we are Christians. They do away altogether with the natural element. But the Bible does not do so. Though we are Christians it is right that we should feel more attracted to one than to another.

The natural comes in and you must not exclude it. We must never take up the position that any one of us could quite rightly marry any other. You could live together, but that would be to exclude this natural element.

I have been at pains to show that the Christian teaching never does away with the natural, with the way in which God has created us. And God has so created us that one feels an attraction to one person more than to another person; and it is mutual. That is right; do not set it aside. It is being assumed here. The Apostle is assuming that this man and this woman, because they were attracted to each other, because, if you like, to use the common phrase, they 'fell in love', are married. Christians should behave in that way like everybody else. This is not something mechanical. A Christian does not say, 'Now that I am a Christian I am going to look round and decide whom to marry' in cold blood, as it were. That is not biblical teaching. This may sound eccentric and amusing to some, but there are many Christians who have acted on that very principle. I am speaking out of pastoral experience. They are very honest people, but regarding sex as evil, they get into this false position. But we are not to exclude the natural. The Apostle is assuming that this man and this woman have felt this mutual attraction, and that they have been drawn together on that basis.

More than that, the Apostle is assuming that they are fond of each other. What I mean by that is that they like the companionship of each other. Let me emphasize that that also is to come into Christian marriage. There are certain natural affinities, and we ignore them at our peril. Again, I have often seen this. Two people have imagined that because they are Christians nothing else matters, and they get married on that basis. But it is very important in the married state that the two persons should be fond of each other. If they are not fond of each other, and have married on the basis of the physical only, it will soon go. That has no permanence in it; but on the other hand, one of the things that has permanence is that the two are fond of each other. There are certain imponderables in this married state. It is good that people who are married should have the same affinities, the same interests, should be attracted by the same things. No matter how much they love each other, if there are fundamental differences in this respect, it will lead to trouble. The problem of married life and living in harmony will be very much greater. It is important, I say, that this second element, the word that

Peter kept on using, 'I am fond of Thee', should play its part.

The Apostle is assuming both considerations. It is probable that some of the Christians had married while they were pagans, and that the marriage included both 'eros' and 'phileo'. Very well, says Paul, this is where Christianity comes in. Now, because you are Christians, the further element comes in; and it lifts up the other two, it sanctifies them, it gives a glory to them, it gives a splendour to them. That is the difference that Christ makes to marriage. It is only the Christian who is able to rise to this level. There can be happy and successful marriages without this; they do happen still, thank God. There are happy marriages on the natural human level, and they are based on the first two words which I have been using. If you get the first element, plus this fondness for each other, and a certain temperament, they can produce very happy and successful marriages. But it will never rise to this higher level. Yet this is the point to which the Apostle wants us to rise. Over and above what is possible to the natural man, there comes in this true love, this love that is of God, the love that he defines in 1 Corinthians 13.

It is clear that the Apostle in choosing his word has told us a great deal. It is therefore the duty of every husband who hears or reads this exhortation to examine himself in the light of this word. Are the three elements present in you? Is everything crowned and glorified by this 'love' that can be attributed even to God Himself?

But lest we be in any trouble about this, the Apostle proceeds to give us a further illustration in the second point he makes. He says, 'Husbands, love your wives, even as' – 'even as Christ also loved the church'. Here again, he shows how anxious he is to help us. The very mention of the name of Christ leads him at once to elaborate the statement. He cannot barely say 'even as Christ loved the church', he must go further and say 'and gave Himself for it; that He might sanctify and cleanse it with the washing of water by the Word, that He might present it to Himself a glorious church, not having spot, or wrinkle, or any such thing; but that it should be holy and without blemish'. He says all that to help the husband to love his wife as he ought to love his wife.

Why, then, does he elaborate the matter in this way? I believe that there are three main reasons. First, he wants every one of us to know Christ's great love to us. He wants us to realize the truth about Christ and ourselves and our relationship to Him. Why is he so concerned about this? His argument is clearly this – it is only as we realize the truth about the relationship of Christ to the church that we can really function as Christian husbands ought to function. That this might be clear he ends by saying, 'This is a great mystery: but I speak concerning Christ and the church'. But why is he speaking concerning Christ and the church? Why has he led us into that mystery? In order that husbands might know how to love their wives. And that is where the glib and superficial people who jeer at doctrine show their folly and their ignorance. 'Ah', they say, 'those people are only interested in doctrine; we are practical people'. But you cannot be practical without doctrine, you cannot love your wife truly unless you understand something about this doctrine, about this great mystery. 'Ah', say others, 'it is too difficult, I cannot follow it at all'. But if you want to live as a Christian you have got to follow it, you have got to apply your mind, you have got to think, you have got to study, you have got to try to understand, you have got to grapple with it. It is here for you, and if you turn your back on this you are rejecting something God gives you, and you are a terrible sinner. To reject doctrine is a terrible sin. You must never put practice against doctrine because you cannot practise without it. So the Apostle takes the trouble to elaborate this wonderful doctrine about the relationship of Christ and the church, not simply for the sake of stating it, important as it is, but in order that you and I at home may love our wives as we ought to love them – 'even as Christ loved the church'.

So we can now look at the problem in the following way. The principle which is to control our practice is that the relationship between husband and wife is the same in essence, and in nature, as the relationship between Christ and the church. How do we approach it therefore? We must start by studying the relationship between Christ and the church, and then, and then only, can we look at the relationship between the husband and the wife. That is what the Apostle is doing. 'Husbands, love your wives, even as Christ loved the church'. This said, he tells us exactly how Christ has loved the church. Then, he says, Go and do the same; that is your rule. That is the first great doctrine.

We start then by considering the relationship of Christ and the church. Here is something that concerns all, not husbands only, but all people. What we are told about the relationship of Christ to the church is true of every single one of us. Christ is the husband of the church, Christ is the husband of every single believer. You ask,

Where do you find this teaching? I find it, for instance, in the Epistle to the Romans, chapter 7 verse 4: 'Wherefore, my brethren, you also are become dead to the law by the body of Christ; that you should be married to another, even to Him who is raised from the dead, that we should bring forth fruit unto God'. Christ is the Husband of the church, the church is the Bride of Christ. Every one of us can in that sense look upon the Lord Jesus Christ as our husband, and collectively we do so as members of the Christian church.

What does the Apostle tell us about this? The first thing he tells us is about the attitude of the Lord Jesus Christ to the church, of how He looks upon her. Here is instruction for husbands. What is your attitude? How do you look upon your wife? Just here the Apostle tells us some marvellous things. Christian people, have you realized that these things are true about you as members of the Christian church? Look at the characteristics of our Lord's attitude towards his bride, the church. He loves her: 'even as Christ loved the church'. What an eloquent expression! He loved her in spite of her unworthiness, He loved her in spite of her deficiencies. Notice what He has to do for her. She needs to be washed, she needs to be cleansed. He saw her in her rags, in her vileness; but He loved her. That is the height of the doctrine of salvation. He loved us, not because of anything in us; He loved us in spite of what was in us, 'while we were yet sinners'. He loved the ungodly, 'while we were yet enemies'. In all our unworthiness and vileness He loved us. He loved the church, not because she was glorious and beautiful – no, but that He might make her such. Take note of the doctrine, and see what it has to say to husbands. A husband comes up against deficiencies, difficulties, things he feels he can criticize in his wife, but he is to love her 'as Christ loved the church'. That is the kind of love he must show. So much for the first principle.

The second principle is this: 'He gave Himself for her'. He was not only ready to sacrifice Himself for her. He actually did sacrifice Himself for her. Such is Christ's love for the church! He could only save her by giving His life for her; and He gave His life. That is the characteristic of His love.

Then take notice of His great concern for her, and for her wellbeing. He is looking at her. He is concerned about her. He sees the possibilities in her, as it were. He desires her to be perfect. That is why Paul goes on to say, 'That He might sanctify her and cleanse her with the washing of water by the Word, that He might present her

[139]

to Himself a glorious church, not having spot, or wrinkle, or any such thing.' You see His interest in her, His love for her, His pride in her. Those are the characteristics of Christ's love to the church – this great desire that she should be perfect. And He is not going to be satisfied until she is perfect. He wants to be able to present her to Himself a glorious church, 'not having spot, or wrinkle, or any such thing'. He wants her to be perfect, beyond criticism. He wants the whole world, as it were, to admire her. So we were told in the third chapter of this Epistle, in verse 10, that He has done all this 'to the intent that now unto the principalities and powers in heavenly places might be known, by the church, the manifold wisdom of God'. It is this pride of the bridegroom in his wife; he is proud of her beauty, proud of her appearance, proud of all that pertains to her; and he wants to show her to the family, to all His creatures. That is the sort of relationship that exists between the Lord Jesus Christ and His church. I am extracting the principle out of the details first, because they give us an understanding of this wonderful mystical relationship. And so the picture is of our Lord rejoicing in the relationship, happy in it, triumphant in it, glorying in it. There is nothing that He will not do for His bride, the church.

Such is the first great matter that emerges in the Apostle's treatment of this vast and exalted subject. We have to start with this picture of Christ and the church. You see how He looks upon her, and what He does for her because He looks upon her in that way, what He has in view for her – His ultimate objective. And because of all this there is the extraordinary concept of the mystical relationship, the unity, the idea that they are one flesh, and that she is His body. 'Husbands, love your wives, even as Christ loved the church'.

There, then, is our first great principle – Christ loving the church. The relationship between Christ and the church is that which should exist between husband and wife. So start with that. Look at the great doctrine of the church. Come all of you, married and unmarried. This is true of all of us because we are in the church. How wonderful to realize that we are in this relationship to Christ! That is how He looks at you, that is His attitude towards you. The principle is this; this love, this God-like love, is altogether above the erotic and philanthropic which is the highest the world can know. The great characteristic of this love – and this is where it is essentially different from the others – is that this is not so much governed by the desire to have, as by the desire to give. 'God so loved the world'. How? 'That He gave'. There is nothing wrong with the other types of love – I have said this previously – but even when you have them at their best they are always self-centred, they are always thinking of themselves. But the characteristic of this other love is, that it does not think of itself. He gave Himself; He died for her – 'even unto death'. Sacrifice is the characteristic of this love. This love is a love that gives; it is not always considering what it is going to have, but what it may give for the benefit of the other. 'Husbands, love your wives like that, even as Christ loved the church.'

Having looked thus in general at Christ's attitude towards the church, we can proceed to show how that attitude manifests itself in practice; and then beyond that to its ultimate objective, and finally to the mystical relationship and union. Let us thank God that when we come to consider marriage, which is so common, and apparently so ordinary, we discover, if we are Christians, that we have to consider it in such a way that it brings us into the very centre of Christian truth, into the heart of theology and doctrine, into the mysteries of God in Christ as seen in and through the church. May God bless that consideration to us!

10

The Bride of Christ

Ephesians 5:25–33

The Apostle's fundamental proposition, so we have seen, is that we cannot understand the duties of husbands and wives unless we understand the truth about Christ and the church; we have therefore started with that truth, as the Apostle does. The husband is to love his wife, 'even as Christ loved the church'. We have reminded ourselves of the content of the word 'love'. It is the highest word that the Bible knows. It is the same sort of love wherewith Christ loved the church; indeed, wherewith God has loved the world. Therefore we are concentrating upon this love of the Lord Jesus Christ for the church. We have only looked at it in general so far. We have looked at His whole attitude towards the church. His concern about her, His pride in her, the way in which He shields her and guards her and protects her. That is brought out here.

But we must proceed beyond that aspect, because the Apostle is at pains to remind us that this attitude of Christ toward the church is something which manifests itself in practice. That is the matter we now take up. 'Husbands, love your wives, even as Christ also loved the church, and gave Himself for it.' It is not enough to consider His attitude towards the church, the way He looks at the church and regards the church. That is something, says Paul, which has manifested itself in practice. And we must emphasize this, because it is the Apostle's emphasis here.

The principle, therefore, is that love is not something theoretical. Love is not something merely to be talked about; love is not just something to be written about, not something merely about which you write poetry. Love is not merely the theme of some great aria in an opera, or some great song, or this miserable 'crooning', or whatever it is called. Love is not something which you look at theoretically or externally. Love is the most practical thing in the world. That is the great principle we are taught here. There is no word, perhaps, that is being more debased at this present time than the word 'love'. Many people obviously have no idea as to what it means. The world, perhaps, has never used terms of endearment so freely; but there has never been so little love. Everybody addresses everybody else in terms of endearment; the superlatives are all being used. People who scarcely know one another bandy these tender terms about; but there is no content to them. That is why people whom, if you listen to their talk, you would imagine to be the greatest lovers the world has ever known, really know nothing about love and may well be divorced almost the next day. For some reason the idea is widespread that love is something to be talked about, to be sung about. This is where the poets can be so dangerous. Have you ever noticed the extraordinary contrast between the things the poets sing about in their poems, and their actual lives. Is it not tragic that that can be true about men who can write so beautifully and marvellously about love? When you read the biographies of these men you are shocked, you are amazed, and feel the facts are scarcely possible. It is all because they have never understood the meaning of love. They think of it in a theoretical manner, as something very beautiful, but the truth about love is that it is the most practical thing in the world.

Such is the teaching of our Lord Himself. 'He that hath my commandments and keepeth them, he it is that loveth Me' (John 14:21). How prosaic it sounds to us with all our so-called romantic view of love! It is, of course, not romantic at all, it is ridiculous, it is sentimental, it is carnal. 'This is love,' Christ says, 'that a man keep My commandments.' For it is not what you and I say that finally proves whether we are truly manifesting love; it is what we do. This is certainly the essential matter in the relationship between husband and wife. The question is not whether the man can write marvellous letters and use great expressions and protestations of his love; the test of the man's love is his conduct in the home day by day. Not what he was like before they were married, not what he is like on the honeymoon, not what he is like during the first few months of married life. The vital question is, What is he like when there are problems and difficulties, and trials, and illness, and when middle age and old age come along?

Many marriages break down because people do not realize what love means, at the beginning. Remember the Apostle's description of it in 1 Corinthians chapter 13, in which he emphasizes its essentially practical character. He tells us that it does not do this, that it does do that; and sums it all up by saying, 'Love never faileth'. That is the test of love! If you want to test whether a man's love to his wife is what it should be, do not listen to what he says, observe what he does, and what he is. That is the test!

The Apostle brings all that out here, and he does so in this most amazing manner. 'Husbands, love your wives, even as Christ also loved the church'. How do we know that He loved the church? Here is the answer: 'and gave Himself for it'. That is love – 'He gave Himself for it'. But he does not stop at that. 'Husbands, love your wives, even as Christ also loved the church, and gave Himself for it; that (in order that) He might sanctify and cleanse it with the washing of water by the Word, that (in order that) He might present it to Himself a glorious church, not having spot, or wrinkle, or any such thing; but that it should be holy and without blemish'.

Let us look at it carefully and analyse it. There are three strands, surely, in what the Apostle says here. This love of Christ, this attitude of Christ towards the church displays itself in practice in three main respects. First, there is what He has already done for the church. Christ loved the church and gave – He has done it – 'gave Himself for it'. Here, of course, we are at the very heart and centre of Christian truth. There would be no church apart from this. This was the first thing that was absolutely essential; this is the foundation. And so the Apostle says, in writing to the Corinthians, 'Other foundation can no man lay'. It is just Jesus Christ and what He has done. That is why he determined not to know anything among them 'save Jesus Christ and Him crucified'. There would have been no church at Corinth but for that, nor anywhere else. And, of course, this is a truth which is emphasized everywhere. Call to mind the story of the Apostle saying farewell to the elders of this church at Ephesus. You find the account of it in the twentieth chapter of the Book of the Acts of the Apostles. He says, 'Feed the church of God, which He hath purchased with His own blood'. That is part of the great romance of Christ and the church, the Bridegroom and the Bride. He had to buy her before He could have her as His Bride. The Apostle puts it here in terms of the church as a whole, but let us remind ourselves, and be quite sure of this in our minds, that this is true of every single one of us, every Christian, every member of the Church. The Apostle does not hesitate to say so in his own case. He says in Galatians chapter 2, verse 20, 'the Son of God, who loved me, and gave Himself for me'. Christ loved the Church and gave Himself for her – yes but also 'for me', for every one of us as individuals.

The Apostle has already introduced this great theme in this very Epistle. He did so in the first chapter in verse 7 where he says: 'In whom we have redemption through His blood, the forgiveness of sins, according to the riches of His grace'. It is also the great theme in the second chapter: 'But now in Christ Jesus ye who sometimes were far off are made nigh' – How? – 'by the blood of Christ.' 'He is our peace, who hath broken down the middle wall of partition'. He has abolished it. How? 'In His flesh'. 'And that He might reconcile both unto God in one body by the Cross, having slain the enmity thereby' – and so on. And, indeed, in this very chapter we are considering, the fifth chapter, he has introduced the same thought in the second verse: 'Be ye therefore followers of God, as dear children, and walk in love, as Christ also hath loved us, and hath given Himself for us an offering and a sacrifice to God for a sweetsmelling savour'. He keeps on repeating it; and we must keep on repeating it. Some foolish people say, 'Ah, the Cross only applies to my conversion, my original salvation, I then go on. . . .' No! Believers never go from this! This is something we should never desire to forget; it is something that continues. It is not only foundation and basis, it is the source of the life and the power that continues – 'loved the church, and gave Himself for it'.

What Paul is saying then is this – and it is supreme doctrine; there is no higher doctrine – all that the Lord Jesus Christ did, He did for the church. 'Christ loved the church, and gave Himself for it'. Our Lord reminds His Father of this in His great High Priestly prayer recorded in the seventeenth chapter of John. He puts it in this way: 'Father, the hour is come; glorify Thy Son, that Thy Son also may glorify Thee. As Thou hast given Him power over all flesh, that He should give eternal life to as many as Thou hast given Him.' They are His people, they are the church. He says, 'I pray not for the world, but for them whom Thou hast given Me'. And here we are reminded that He died for the church. We must never lose sight of this. He died for the church; He died for nobody else. His death, as Calvin and other expositors remind us, because it was eternal and

[145]

because He is the Son of God, is sufficient for the whole world; but it is efficient only for the church. His purpose in dying was to redeem the church. He gave Himself for the church, for all who belong to her when she will be complete and perfect and entire. All was known to God from eternity, and the Son came, and gave Himself for the church.

What we have to remember, therefore, is that we could never be His at all, and we could never be enjoying any of the benefits of this Christian life, unless He had done this. You and I have to be rescued and to be redeemed before we can belong to the church. Nothing else makes us Christian. Let us remind ourselves of this in passing. You may be the best moral man in the world, but that will never make you a Christian; it will never make you a member of Christ, never make you a member of the church. There is only one thing that puts a man into the church, and that is that Christ has purchased him with His own blood, that He has died for him, redeemed him. This is the only way of entry into the true church – not the visible church, but the true church, the invisible, the spiritual Body of Christ. We are saved 'by His precious blood'.

But notice that the Apostle's great concern here, particularly, is to emphasize the truth from the standpoint of showing the greatness of Christ's love to the church. Why did He do these things, and how did He do these things for us? We have the answer in many places in the Scripture. How should a husband love his wife? As Christ loved the church and gave Himself for it. What did that involve? Perhaps the best statement concerning that matter is in the Epistle to the Philippians, chapter 2, verse 5. 'Let this mind be in you, which was also in Christ Jesus: who, being in the form of God, thought it not robbery to be equal with God: but made Himself of no reputation, and took upon Him the form of a servant, and was made in the likeness of men: and being found in fashion as a man, He humbled Himself, and became obedient unto death, even the death of the Cross.' What does that mean? It means that that is how Christ loved the church, and gave Himself for it. He did not consider Himself. That is the first point. 'He thought it not robbery to be equal with God'; which means that He did not regard His equality with God as a prize to be held on to. He was the eternal Son of God, He had been sharing that glory with His Father and the Holy Spirit from all eternity, but He did not hold on to that and say, 'Why should I go to earth, why should I lay aside the signs of My glory,

[146]

why should I go down and be buffeted and spat upon?' No! 'He thought it not robbery to be equal with God', He did not regard it as something which He must hold on to at all costs because it was His by right. Instead, 'He made Himself of no reputation.' There was no need for Him to do so; there was no compulsion at all apart from the compulsion of love. If the Lord Jesus Christ had considered Himself, if He had considered His own eternal glory and dignity, there would never have been a church at all. He was the One through whom all things had been created; all the angels worshipped Him, and all the great powers and principalities did their obeisance to Him. They worshipped Him as the Son and glorified Him. What if He had said, 'O, I cannot, I cannot put any of that aside; I must have this respect that is due to me, I must have my position.' He did the exact opposite, 'He made Himself of no reputation', He was born as a babe in the likeness, the form, of a man. Not only that, He even became a servant. He did not think of Himself at all. If He had done so, none of us would have been saved, and there would be no church. He did not talk about His rights; He did not talk about His dues; He did not say 'Why should I suffer, why must I humble myself?' He did not consider the cost, He did not consider the shame. He knew what was to be involved, He knew that He would be buffeted by those Pharisees and Scribes and Sadducees and Doctors of the Law, that people would jeer at Him, and throw stones at Him, and spit upon Him – He knew that all that was to come though He had not done anything to deserve it. Why then did He do it? For the church; because of His love for the Church. 'He humbled Himself and made Himself of no reputation'. He had but one thought, that was the good of the church, the body that was to become His Bride. He was buying her, purchasing her, thinking of nobody but her. Not Himself, but her! 'Let this mind be in you also', you husbands! 'Husbands, love your wives, even as Christ also loved the church, and gave Himself for it.'

But there is another aspect of this which we must emphasize in order to bring out the depth of the teaching. Our Lord did that for us, for the church, while we were yet sinners, while we were ungodly, while we were enemies. Paul's argument in Romans chapter 5 uses these very terms, 'In due time Christ died for the ungodly', 'while we were yet sinners'. 'If, while we were enemies we were reconciled to God by the death of His Son, much more, being reconciled, we shall be saved in His life.' Notice the terms. We were 'ungodly', we were 'enemies', we were 'sinners', we were vile, there was nothing to recommend us at all. You who feel you must read romances, and delight in the story of Cinderella, look at this. Look at the church in her vileness, in her rags, in her sin, in her enmity, in all her ugliness. The Son of God, the Prince of Glory, loved her while she was like that, and in spite of it; loved her even to the extent of giving Himself for her, dying for her. 'Husbands, love your wives, even as Christ loved the church.' We are not called to do what He did to that extent. But He, in spite of everything, loved to that point of giving Himself; His blood was shed literally, for us.

'Now', says the Apostle, 'you who are in this married relationship find things in each other that you do not like and do not approve of – deficiencies, faults, failures, sins – and you are critical, and stand on your dignity, and condemn, and quarrel, and separate. Why? Simply because you fail to remember the way in which you yourselves have been saved, and have become Christians and members of the Christian church'. He reminds them that if the Lord Jesus Christ had reacted to them as they react to one another there would never have been a church. 'Love never faileth', love goes on loving in spite of everything. That is the love wherewith Christ has loved the church.

Is there anything so wrong, I ask again, as to separate doctrine from practice? How guilty we all are of that! How many of us have realized that we are always to think of the married state in terms of the doctrine of the atonement? Is that our customary way of thinking of marriage – husbands, wives, all of us? Is that how we instinctively think of marriage – in terms of the doctrine of the atonement? Where do we find what the books have to say about marriage? Under which section? Under Ethics. But it does not belong there. We must consider marriage in terms of the doctrine of the atonement.

The most foolish of all Christians are those who dislike doctrine, and decry the importance of theology and teaching. And does not that explain why they fail in practice? You cannot separate these things. You must not relegate the doctrine of the atonement simply to your conversion or to the study. Why is it that so many Christian people do not attend an evening service? 'Oh', they say, 'the sermon is going to be about the Cross, it is going to be about forgiveness, that is the beginning of the Christian life. I have been a Christian for years now, and of course that has nothing to say to me'.

Foolish Christian! have you got tired of hearing about the Cross? Do you know so much about it, do you understand it so exhaustively, that it cannot any longer move you? 'Ah', you say, 'I want the higher teaching now, I want the detailed teaching now as to how I am to live the sanctified life'. You will never live the sanctified life unless you are always there by that Cross, and unless it is governing the whole of your life, and influencing the whole of your outlook and your every activity. We are here in what is called the practical section of the Epistle to the Ephesians, the second half, where Paul takes up these ordinary questions; yes, but it is in this very context that he suddenly brings us face to face with the doctrine of the church, and the doctrine of the atonement. You cannot leave the Cross behind, you are never such an advanced Christian that that is a mere beginning as far as you are concerned. That is the way to make shipwreck of marriage, and everything else. No! 'Love so amazing, so divine, demands my soul, my life, my all' – always! I start there, but I continue there; and woe unto me if I ever cease to be there!

That is the first point the Apostle makes – the love of Christ. But then he goes on to a second point – that which Christ, because of this great love of His, is doing, or continues to do for the church, He puts that in the 'gave Himself for it; that He might sanctify and cleanse it with the washing of water by the Word' (verse 26). Here is another of these great and most vital statements. Notice that this verse has two main functions. The first is the one I have already mentioned, that it reminds us of what the Lord Jesus Christ is continuing to do for the church. But it has a second object also. It tells us why He did the first thing. 'He gave Himself for it; that (in order that)' – this is His object. Why did Christ die? He died 'in order that He might sanctify and cleanse it with the washing of water by the Word'. That is the teaching we have here concerning the doctrine of sanctification. It is all here – atonement, justification; and now sanctification.

The first point which we establish and emphasize in this: Forgiveness and deliverance from condemnation, and from hell, are never an end in and of themselves, and must never be considered to be such. They are but a means to a further end. You cannot stop at forgiveness and justification.

Let us take a closer look at what the Apostle teaches here about this great doctrine of sanctification. The first principle is that there is nothing which is so utterly unscriptural as to separate justification and sanctification. There are many who do so. They say, 'You can believe on the Lord Jesus Christ as your Saviour, and your sins will be forgiven, and you will be justified. And you can stop at that'. They add, 'Of course you should not do so, you should go on to the second step. But there are many Christians', they say, 'who stop at that. They have believed on Christ unto salvation and they are justified and forgiven; they are certainly Christians, but they have not taken up sanctification'. So then they exhort them to 'take' sanctification as they had previously 'taken' justification. Such teaching is a complete denial of what the Apostle says here, and is utterly unscriptural. The death of Christ is not merely to bring us forgiveness, and to justify us, and to make us legally righteous in the sight of God. 'He gave Himself for it; that (in order that) . . .' It is only the first move in a series; it is not a last move in any sense, and you can never stop there.

The Apostle not only teaches this truth to the Ephesians; he teaches it to all the churches. You find the same in the Epistle to the Romans, chapter eight, verses 3 and 4. It also appears in Titus 2:14: 'He gave Himself for us, that He might redeem us from all iniquity, and purify unto Himself a peculiar people, zealous of good works'. That is why He gave Himself for us; not merely that we might be forgiven, not merely to save us from hell, but to purify and to separate unto Himself this peculiar people who are zealous of good works. Our Lord said it all in His High Priestly prayer (John 17:19): 'For their sakes I sanctify Myself, that they also might be sanctified through the truth'.

To stop at justification is not only wrong in thought; it is impossible for this reason, that it is something which Christ does; it is He who does this in us. He gave Himself for the church. Why? That He might sanctify and cleanse the church. He is going to do it. The whole trouble arises from the fact that some persist in regarding sanctification as something that we decide to go in for. That is never taught anywhere in the Scriptures. The teaching of the Scripture is this – Christ has set His heart and His affection upon the church. There she is, under condemnation, in her sin, and in her rags and in her vileness! He came, the Incarnation had to happen, He took on Him 'the likeness of sinful flesh'. He took her sins upon Him, and He bore them in His own body on the tree. He has taken the punishment, He has died, He has made atonement, He has reconciled us to God. So the church is delivered from condemnation. But that does not satisfy Him. He wants her to be a glorious church, He wants to 'present her to Himself a glorious church, without spot, or wrinkle, or any such thing'. So He immediately proceeds to prepare her for that destiny. He cannot stop at the first step; He goes on to sanctify her. In other words, His death upon the Cross for us, and our sins, was simply the first step in this great process. And He does not stop at the first step. He has a complete purpose for the church, and He will go through it all step by step.

I would put this very strongly. In the last analysis you and I have no choice in this matter of sanctification. It is something that Christ does. He died for you, and then, having died for you, He is going to wash you, sanctify you, cleanse you – and He will do it. Let there be no mistake about this. If he has died for you He will go on with the process of sanctification in you, He will finally make you perfect. There is something alarming about this; but it is essential biblical teaching. If you and I do not submit voluntarily to this teaching He has another way of cleansing us; and He will use it – 'Whom the Lord loveth He chasteneth, and scourgeth every son whom He receiveth' (Hebrews 12:6). He will not allow you to remain where you were in your filth and vileness, saying 'I am all right, Christ has died for me, I am forgiven, I am a Christian'. He will not have that! He has loved you, you belong to Him; and He will make you clean. If you will not come voluntarily, and in the right way, He will put you into that gymnasium of which we read in Hebrews. He will get rid of the corners, He will get rid of the filth and the vileness, He will wash you. It may come about through an illness which He will send upon you. These 'faith-healers' who say that God never sends an illness are simply denying the Scriptures. As one of His methods, He chastises. Your circumstances may go wrong, you may lose your job, or someone dear to you may die. Christian! because you belong to Him, because Christ has died for you, He will make you perfect. Fight against Him as you will in your folly, He will knock you down, He will cleanse you, He will perfect you. That is the teaching; it is something He does. Sanctification is not something that you and I determine – 'He gave Himself for it, that (in order that) He might sanctify it and cleanse it with the washing of water by the Word'. The first principle therefore which we must grasp is that sanctification is primarily and essentially something that the Lord Jesus Christ does to us. He has His ways of doing it. It includes, of course, obedience on our part. But you must not put your primary emphasis there. The decision for sanctification is not ours; it is His. It was taken in eternity before the foundation of the world. It is His activity, it is His operation; and having died for you, He will do it. Resist Him at your peril. He will bring every son who has been called, into that final and everlasting glory. As Hebrew 12 puts it, if He does not deal with you in this way, you are 'a bastard' and not a true son (Hebrews 12:5–11).

That then is the great principle which forms the basis of this apostolic teaching. How does Christ carry it into effect? The answer is to be found in the word 'sanctify', 'Even as Christ also loved the church, and gave Himself for it; that He might sanctify'. This word 'sanctify' is used in many different ways in the Bible, but its primary meaning is, 'to set apart for God, for His peculiar possession and for His use.' You will find, for instance, in Exodus 19 that the mount on which God met with Moses and gave him the Ten Commandments was 'sanctified' in that way. It is called the 'holy mount' because it was set apart. There was no change in the mountain, but it was set apart for God's purpose, for God's use, for God's peculiar possession. The vessels that were used in the Temple ceremonial were likewise sanctified, or set apart. There was no material change in the cups and the platters, but as they were to be used in the Temple and for God's service only, they could not be turned to common use. To be sanctified means to be set apart for God and for His special use and purposes, as His peculiar possession. So we are 'people for His own possession'.

Then a secondary meaning emerges. Because they are thus set apart they are also 'made holy'. Now here in our passage there can be no question as to the meaning of this word 'sanctification'. It carries that first connotation. 'That He might sanctify it'. It has the meaning of 'set apart for Himself', 'separate from everything else, for His own possession, for His own use, for His own delight'. It does not mean more than that here, for we note that the Apostle adds the word 'cleanse', supplying the second meaning of sanctify. He divides it up into two steps. Here is the church in her rags, in her filth and vileness! Christ has died for her, He has saved her from condemnation. He takes hold of her where she was and sets her apart for Himself. She is 'translated from the kingdom of darkness, into the Kingdom of God's dear Son' (Col 1:13) – that is to say, she is moved out of the world into the special position which, as the church, she is to occupy.

This is a wonderful thing. This is what the Lord Jesus Christ has done with the church. The same occurs when a man finds his affections and his love set upon one girl out of thousands. He chooses her for himself, and he selects her from all the others. 'She is to be mine', he says. So he separates her, isolates her, 'sanctifies' her, puts her there quite on her own. He wants her for himself. That is the simple truth about every one of us who is a Christian, and a member of the Christian church in a real sense. Had you realized it – that the Lord of glory, the eternal Son of God, has set us apart, has isolated us for Himself, that we might be 'a people for His peculiar possession'?

Let me remind you again of the ninth verse in the Second chapter of the First Epistle of Peter which states this truth so gloriously. Do you know what is actually true of you at this very moment? 'Ye are a chosen generation, a royal priesthood (kingdom of priests), an holy nation (set apart)'. We are not perfect and sinless, but we are 'an holy nation' in the sense that we are a group, a nation of people set apart. And Peter goes yet further, 'a peculiar people' – 'a people for His own personal and peculiar possession' – 'that ye should shew forth the praises of Him who hath called you out of darkness into His marvellous light'. That is what Christ has done for the church. He has called us out. That is one meaning of the word 'ecclesia' – the 'called out ones'. We are called out of the world, put together here to form this body, this bride for Christ. And then Christ proceeds to deal with us.

In other words, to use the language of Peter in that same chapter again, you and I as Christians are now only 'strangers and pilgrims' in this world. Notice how he puts it. 'Dearly beloved, I beseech you as strangers and pilgrims' (v. 11). We do not belong to this world any longer. We have been taken out of it, we have been separated, sanctified. We are only strangers and pilgrims here; we do not belong to that realm as once we did. The Apostle Paul has already said all this at the end of the second chapter of this Epistle to the Ephesians. He says: 'Ye are no more strangers and foreigners, but fellow-citizens with the saints, and of the household of God'. You were strangers to this before, but now you are in this and strangers to that – sanctified, set apart for Himself. That, being interpreted, means that the bride is now no longer free to do some of the things she did before, but lives for her husband and he lives for her. The husband does not look at other women, because his bride is the one he has selected, separated, sanctified for himself. That is how Christ looks at the church. That is how a husband should regard his wife. And we, as the bride of Christ, should think of ourselves as no longer free, no longer belonging to ourselves, no longer deciding what we do, no longer belonging to the world.

Let me leave all this in the form of a question. I am addressing Christian members of the church. We shall come to the application to the husbands later. Here is the practical question which I address to every one who claims to be a believer in the Lord Jesus Christ, to everyone who says 'I believe Christ has died for me and for my sins, to rescue me'. Are you aware of the fact that Christ has separated you, that He is sanctifying you? Because, believe me, if you are not, you are deluding and fooling yourself in thinking that He has died for you. When Christ dies for an individual He always takes that individual, and moves him (or her), and puts him into this peculiar position. 'He gave Himself for it, that (in order that)' – It was the first step in the move; but He never stops at that. That is the preliminary that leads to sanctification. So it is idle to claim that Christ has died for us unless we know that He has separated us. Do you know of a surety that you no longer belong to the world, that there has been a change in you, that you have been moved, that you have been 'translated from the kingdom of darkness into the Kingdom of God's dear Son'? Do you feel that you are a stranger here? Do you say with Paul, 'Our citizenship is in heaven'? (Philippians 3:20) 'He gave Himself for her, that (in order that) He might put her on one side for Himself, His own peculiar possession.' O the privilege of being a Christian, of belonging to this company for whom Christ died, and whom He is preparing for Himself – set apart from the world for the glory which we are to enjoy with Him! Husbands, love your wives in that way.

I I
The Purification of the Bride

Ephesians 5:25–33

In our consideration of the statement which the Apostle makes concerning the duty of husbands towards their wives we are giving attention to the teaching concerning our Lord in His relationship to the church. We have seen His concern for her, His attitude with respect to her; and we are emphasizing how this attitude and concern have expressed themselves in action, in practice. We have seen what the Lord has done for the church – 'He gave Himself for it'. We have also considered what He is still doing for the church. He has done that first thing once and for ever – He gave Himself for it. But He does not leave it at that; He goes on doing something to the church and for the church.

We have been looking also at the word 'sanctify' and its meaning. The Lord has set the church apart for Himself; we are His 'peculiar people', a people for His own peculiar, special possession, His bride. He has set her aside and apart in order that He may do certain things for her.

From that point we now proceed. The next word we come to is the word 'cleanse'. 'That He might sanctify and cleanse it with the washing of water by the Word.' It is by way of this word 'cleanse' that the idea of purifying – what we normally call 'sanctification' – really comes in.

Here we must be careful to note the full content of this word 'cleanse'. There are some who would confine it solely to our being washed from the guilt of our sins. But that, clearly, is not enough. We have already found that aspect in the statement that

[155]

He gave Himself for the church and separated her. There is implicit in that the idea of our being delivered from the guilt of sin, but I am not disposed however to quarrel with those who want to include it in this word 'cleanse'. Christ certainly cleanses us from the guilt of our sin; but this word takes us still further. I think I can prove that it is not merely a matter of opinion. The very fact that Paul adds that the cleansing is effected 'with the washing of water by the Word' is proof that it is a continuous and continuing process. The washing from the guilt of sin is once and for ever. That is a single action; but here is a continuing action, 'That He might cleanse her with the washing of water by the Word'. That statement shows that it is not merely a matter of getting rid of the guilt. But then the 27th verse establishes the matter still more positively – 'That He might sanctify and cleanse it with the washing of water by the Word, that He might present it to Himself a glorious church, not having spot, or wrinkle, or any such thing; but that it should be holy and without blemish'. These words define Christ's ultimate objective – that the church should not only be delivered from the guilt of sin, but that she should be delivered entirely and completely from sin in every shape and form. Surely Toplady states this idea to perfection when he puts it thus:

> Be of sin the double cure,
> Cleanse me from its guilt and power.

The New Testament never stops at the guilt; it always goes on to this further idea of our being cleansed from the power of sin also. Indeed I want to add even to that. This cleansing is not only from the guilt of sin, and from the power of sin, it is also from the pollution of sin. That third aspect is very frequently forgotten. You will find that many Societies in their 'Basis of faith' mention the power of sin, but leave out the pollution of sin. Yet in many ways the most terrible thing about the Fall is that it has polluted our nature. Sin is powerful within us very largely because of our polluted nature. This is what the Apostle describes so graphically in the 7th chapter of the Epistle to the Romans. 'I know', he says, 'that in me (that is to say, in my flesh) dwelleth no good thing'. Now that is pollution; that is not power. It leads to power; but it is because our natures are polluted, and are tarnished, and are soiled, and made unclean by the Fall, that sin is so powerful within us. Therefore we need to be cleansed not only from the guilt, and not only from the power, but in particular from this terrible pollution of sin – the stain of it all and the perversion.

Sin has entered into the warp and woof of human nature; our very natures are vile and twisted and perverted. How vitally important it is that we should realize that that is true of all of us by nature! It is not that we are neutral by nature, and that we are tempted from the outside. No! we are 'born in sin', we are 'shapen in iniquity'. 'In sin did my mother conceive me' – that is the teaching of the Scripture (Psalm 51:5). The Apostle has already stated this clearly at the beginning of his second chapter, where he says, 'we were dead in trespasses and sins' – and so on, and he talks about 'the lusts of the flesh and of the mind'. That is another way of describing this 'law within my members'. It is not only a power, it is an infection, it is indeed, as I say, a pollution. It is like a stream polluted at its very source, rather than one which becomes polluted during its course. That is the thing from which we have to be cleansed before we can be presented by the Lord to Himself 'as a glorious church, not having spot, or wrinkle, or any such thing; but that it should be holy and without blemish'.

The question for us therefore is – How is this accomplished? The Apostle says that it is done 'with the washing of water by the Word'. Here we have an important and a very difficult phrase – a phrase which has often been misunderstood and misinterpreted. There are many who see here the teaching of what they call 'baptismal regeneration' – that we are delivered and cleansed entirely from sin by baptism. It was an error which crept into the church in the first centuries; it is an error which is perpetuated by the teaching of the Roman Catholic church, and other forms of Catholicism, even until this present time. I am not going to enter into all that, because it seems to me that it is such an utterly artificial interpretation of the words, imposing a meaning upon them which, taken naturally, and at its face value, they never would have suggested. It was introduced, of course, in the interests of the power of the church; and all who still teach it, whatever form of Catholicism they may claim to have, are still guilty of the same error. The point here is not some magical action which takes place in baptism, neither is it the particular formula which is used. Some have emphasized the latter by saying that it is the word spoken by the man who is baptizing the infant that matters, and that the formula supplies the efficacious power. Again, that is but sacerdotalism; it is nothing but a way of bolstering up the authority of a priesthood.

What then does this word teach? Obviously there is a reference here to baptism, to the fact and the act of baptism. That of course is not surprising, because here we are dealing with people who were once pagans. They heard the Gospel, they believed it, and then before they were admitted into the church they had to be baptized; and having been baptized they were received into the membership of the Christian church. Therefore baptism did stand out in their minds as something which was meant to represent this cleansing, this deliverance from one realm and 'translation' into another realm. And so you find the Apostle Paul putting it thus in writing to the Church at Corinth (1 Corinthians, 6:9–11): 'Know ye not', he says, 'that the unrighteous shall not inherit the kingdom of God? Be not deceived: neither fornicators, nor idolaters, nor adulterers, nor effeminate, nor abusers of themselves with mankind, nor thieves, nor covetous, nor drunkards, nor revilers, nor extortioners, shall inherit the kingdom of God. And such were some of you: but ye are washed, but ye are sanctified, but ye are justified in the name of the Lord Jesus, and by the Spirit of our God.' There again the same idea of 'washing' is used. He says, 'You were like that; you are no longer in that condition; you are now saints in the church – you have been washed'. One of the purposes of baptism is to represent that change.

The Apostle Peter has very much the same thought in his First Epistle, the 3rd chapter, verse 20 and following. He is talking about 'the spirits in prison, which sometime were disobedient, when once the longsuffering of God waited in the days of Noah, while the ark was a-preparing, wherein few, that is, eight souls were saved by water. The like figure whereunto even baptism doth also now save us (not the putting away of the filth of the flesh, but the answer of a good conscience toward God), by the resurrection of Jesus Christ: who is gone into heaven, and is on the right hand of God.' There, clearly enough, is the idea with which we are dealing in this statement that is before us. Baptism is a figure, and is a representation in symbolic manner, of what the Lord Jesus Christ does for us in this process of sanctification. The object of baptism, therefore, is to represent that, and to seal that to us, to our minds and to our hearts. It does no more. Baptism in and of itself does nothing. Merely to be baptised does not change us as such. That is the false idea of sacraments. The technical term used by the Roman Catholics, and all Catholic teaching, is that sacraments act and are effective 'ex opere operato'. In other words, that they act in and of themselves apart from any activity on the part of the recipient. The very act of baptism makes a child regenerate, or an adult regenerate.

There is no such teaching in the Scripture. Baptism is, as Peter says, 'a figure', a 'like figure whereunto'; it is a dramatic representation. It is the same, of course, with the Lord's Supper. We do not believe that the bread is turned into the very body of Christ. It is a representation. Our Lord says in effect, Look at this bread; when you come to eat it, let that remind you of, let that represent and figure to you My broken body. And likewise with the wine; 'this cup is the new testament'. That is our answer to the Roman Catholics who say that the wine is turned into the blood. They say that we must take these words literally. Well, if you take them literally, what our Lord said was 'This cup'; He did not say 'This wine', He said 'This cup is the new testament in My blood', proving that it is simply representative and symbolical.

So it is with baptism. What does baptism represent? Clearly it represents our being washed from the guilt of sin. There we were, sinners, and in sin, under the wrath of God. We have been delivered from that by our faith in the Lord Jesus Christ, by what He has done for us. Baptism reminds us of that deliverance. Secondly, it reminds us of the fact that we are being cleansed from the power and pollution of sin. It is a sort of 'washing', a symbolical representation of a process of cleansing. It includes that idea also. And thirdly, it stands for the whole concept of our being baptized into Christ by the Holy Spirit. You remember how Paul, in writing to the Corinthians (1 Corinthians 10) says that the Israelites were baptised unto Moses by the 'cloud' which was there over them. They were not immersed into the cloud, the cloud was over them. And in the same way baptism represents the fact that we are thus baptised into Christ by the Holy Spirit. That is the whole idea that Paul has in his mind here – our union with Christ. 'We are members' he says, 'of His body, of His flesh and of His bones.' How does that happen? It happens because 'we are baptized by one Spirit into Christ'; baptism stands for that also. So here it is! It is an external symbolical representation of the three things which the Apostle is emphasizing so prominently in this particular section.

Obviously then Paul's main object here is to show us how Christ is cleansing the church and preparing her for Himself; and that He does so through the Holy Spirit. Clearly it is not accidental that when our Lord was standing there in the Jordan at His own baptism, the Holy Spirit came down upon Him in the form and the shape of a dove. So always in baptism we should be thinking of that aspect, of the coming of the Holy Spirit into us and upon us in order that He may baptize us into Christ and proceed with this work and process of sanctification.

So much then for our consideration of the phrase and its actual terms. It is a very difficult phrase, and it has always caused a good deal of discussion – 'the washing of water'. But the really important term here is, of course, 'the Word'. 'That He might cleanse it with the washing of water by the Word or (if you find a change in the order of the phrases helpful), 'That He might cleanse it by the Word through the washing of the water'. The vital thing is this expression 'by the Word', which should be joined to the word 'cleanse'. There is a representation of it in baptism, but it is no more than a representation. The real work of sanctification is done by or through the Word, and the Holy Spirit does this work in us by means of the Word. This is a most important truth for Christian people to grasp and to understand. The instrument which is used by the Holy Spirit in our cleansing is 'the Word'.

This is the essential New Testament teaching on holiness and sanctification; it is something which is done in us by the Holy Spirit using the Word. And let us emphasize that this is a process. It is a progressive cleansing until we shall be free from every spot, or wrinkle, or any such thing; free from every blemish we shall be entirely holy. There are people who teach that what happens to the Christian is that he is a saved man, but that he remains in his sin. As long as he 'abides in Christ' he will be kept from sinning, but there is no change as regards the pollution of sin. That is only dealt with when he comes to die. But that, clearly, according to this teaching, is quite wrong. We read here of a process of cleansing; it goes on. As a man goes on in the Christian life there should be less and less of the pollution of sin in him; he should be becoming progressively sanctified as this process goes on. He is not merely enabled to resist the power of sin, he is being cleansed from the pollution of sin; he is progressively being brought into a state in which he will be finally perfect. And this is done by means of the Word. 'By the Word.'

The great principle which we must lay hold of is that the operations of the Holy Spirit in us are generally in and through 'the Word'. That is why it is always dangerous to separate the Holy Spirit from the Word. Many have done this, and there have often been grievous excesses. Indeed the virtual departure of the people called Quakers from the Christian faith is due to this very thing; they put such emphasis upon the 'inner light' that they ignore the Word. They tend to say that the Word does not matter; it is this inner light that matters. And they have reached the point at which they are more or less detached from New Testament doctrines, and the Lord Jesus Christ is scarcely necessary to their system. And there are others who have emphasized the Holy Spirit to such an extent that they have separated Him from the Word. They do not want to be taught, they do not want instruction; they live in the realm of feelings and moods and experiences, and go off into ecstasies that often lead not only to the 'shipwreck of their faith' but to gross immorality and excesses and failures. The Word and the Holy Spirit generally go together. The Word has been given by the Spirit, and He uses His own Word. This is the instrument that He uses. I am not denying that the Spirit can speak to us directly; but I am saying that that is exceptional. And I go further; I say, that anything that we may think is the work of the Spirit within us must always be tested by the Word. The Holy Spirit will never do anything contradictory to His own Word. So we are exhorted to 'prove the spirits', to 'try the spirits', to 'test the spirits'. Not all spirits are of God; you therefore need a proof and a test of any particular spirit. What provides such a proof? It is the Word. So this work is done by the Spirit, but it is done through and by means of the Word.

Let me further establish this point because it is such a vital one. To show how nearly all the work that the Spirit does in a believer is done by means of the Word, let us start with our regeneration. James puts it in this way: 'Wherefore lay apart all filthiness and superfluity of naughtiness, and receive with meekness the engrafted Word, which is able to save your souls'. The Word! Again, James puts it like this: 'Of His own will begat He us with the Word of truth, that we should be a kind of first-fruits of His creatures' (James 1:21, 18). Peter teaches the same thing – 'Being born again', he says, 'not of corruptible seed, but of incorruptible, by the Word of God, which liveth and abideth for ever' (1 Peter 1:23). Regeneration is the work of the Holy Spirit, but He does it by the Word – 'being born again, not of corruptible seed, but of incorruptible, by the Word of God'. It is the Word as used by the Spirit that gives us this new life. Again, take Paul in the First Epistle to the Thessalonians chapter 2 and verse 13: 'For this cause also thank we God without ceasing, because when ye received the Word of God which ye heard of us, ye received it not as the word of men, but as it is in truth, the Word of God which effectually worketh also in you that believe'. This Word is effectually working in us that believe. It brought us into eternal life, it is continuing to work effectually in us. 'Work out your own salvation, with fear and trembling; for it is God that worketh in you both to will and to do'. (Philippians 2:12–13). How does God do so? Through the Word.

Let me give further examples of this self-same thing. Our Lord Himself taught this very plainly and clearly. In the eighth chapter of John's Gospel you will find an account of how our Lord was preaching one day, and we are told that when they heard His words many believed on Him. Then we read this (verse 31): 'Then said Jesus unto the Jews which believed on Him, If ye continue in My Word, then are ye My disciples indeed; and ye shall know the truth, and the truth shall make you free'. You notice that they have to 'continue in His Word', and if they do so 'the truth shall make them free'. Or listen to Him again in John 15, verse 3: 'Now', He says, 'are ye clean through the Word which I have spoken unto you'. It is the Word that cleanses. And then there are two examples of it in the seventeenth chapter of John's Gospel. The first is in verse 17: 'Sanctify them through Thy truth: Thy Word is truth'. He is leaving His disciples in the world, and the enemy is attacking. He says, 'I pray not that Thou shouldest take them out of the world, but that Thou shouldest keep them, (cleanse them, deliver them) from the evil'. 'Sanctify them through Thy truth: Thy Word is truth'. And then you notice that tremendous statement where He says: 'And for their sakes I sanctify Myself.' He is talking now about setting Himself aside for the death on the Cross. Why is He going to do it? 'That they also might be sanctified through the truth.' This, then, is the great principle that we find taught everywhere in the New Testament. Christ is cleansing the church through the work of the Holy Spirit whom He has sent, and who uses this Word in doing the work.

But that leaves us with this vital question: What is this Word which the Holy Spirit uses? We are to be sanctified by means of this 'Word'. What is the Word of sanctification? What is the teaching which leads to our progressive sanctification and deliverance from the power and the pollution of sin? Here, again, is a vital point in this whole question of the doctrine of sanctification; because there is very real danger of our narrowing down this message concerning sanctification, and confining it to some special teaching or formula about sanctification. We are all familiar with such teaching. There are those who say that sanctification (and this is their own term) is 'quite simple'. They have, they claim a special message about sanctification and holiness which they say is 'quite simple'. It really just comes to this: 'Trust and obey'; 'Let go and let God'. They say that that is the teaching of the Scripture concerning sanctification. So you will find that they present their teaching quite frequently, not to say generally, in terms of some Old Testament stories about which they can let their imagination run riot. They are only concerned to present this formula, this simple formula, they say, about sanctification. 'It is quite simple, you just cease to struggle and to fight, and just "trust and obey"; you "receive it by faith", believe that you have got it, and you go on.' They say there is no more to be said or done.

But is that true to the Word? Is that 'the Word' that leads to our sanctification? Is sanctification represented anywhere in the Scripture as merely some 'formula' which you devise, and then more or less ignore all the New Testament Epistles and their teaching, and find illustrations of this simple process in various narratives in the Old Testament? Surely that is to mutilate the scriptural teaching. What is this Word that teaches us sanctification, and which sanctifies us? The answer is, of course, that it is the whole Bible, the whole of the truth that you find in the Bible or in any one of these New Testament Epistles. Why did the Apostle Paul ever write this letter to the Ephesians? He wrote it in order that their sanctification might be promoted. They had believed the truth, as he reminds them in chapter one. But he wants them to grow in grace, he wants them to develop, he wants them to be rid of sin – in its guilt, its power and its pollution. He wants them to see that the objective is that

[163]

they might be perfect and holy, entirely blameless and without spot; and he writes in order that they might be brought to that point. They must go through this process. The whole of this Epistle is about sanctification. This is 'the Word'. It is not some little formula which is 'quite simple' which you just apply, and then you have got 'it'. Not at all! You have to enter into all that you have in this Epistle. In other words, the Word by which we are sanctified is the whole of the biblical teaching. It is, in particular, all the great doctrines which are taught throughout the Bible; and it is only as we realize this that we see how that other idea which would narrow down and confine sanctification and holiness teaching to just one little formula is, in the last analysis, an ignoring of most of the Bible.

What is this Word by which the Holy Spirit sanctifies us? First and foremost it is the Word about God. When you are teaching sanctification you do not start with man. But that is how it is commonly done, is it not? They say, Is there any failure in your life? Are you unhappy? Are you being tripped by something? Are you ill at ease? Are you living a defeated life? They start with that. 'Listen', they say, 'you can be delivered from these troubles. All you need to do is to surrender that problem; just give it to the Lord and He will deliver you from it. He will take it out of you, and then all you do is to abide in Him, and He will keep you right'. Is not that typical of much sanctification and holiness teaching? It starts with man and his problem – 'How can I be made happier?', 'The Christian's Secret of a Happy Life', and so on. But that is not how the Bible teaches sanctification.

How does the Bible teach sanctification? You start by looking up into the face of God! You do not start with man; you start with God. There is no profounder way of teaching sanctification and holiness than simply to teach the doctrines concerning the being, the nature and the character of God! You do not start with yourself and your problems and needs; you start with God. You do not start with your desires, you start with the Almighty – 'Holy, Holy, Holy, Lord God Almighty'! Is there anything that promotes sanctification and holiness as much as that? The Bible is full of this teaching. Call to mind that great statement about the call of the prophet Isaiah, as it is recorded in chapter 6. 'In the year that king Uzziah died I saw also the Lord sitting upon a throne, high and lifted up, and His train filled the temple. Above it stood the seraphim: each one had six wings; with twain he covered his face, and with twain he covered his feet, and with twain he did fly. And one cried unto another, saying, Holy, holy, holy, is the Lord of hosts: the whole earth is full of His glory. And the posts of the door moved at the voice of him that cried, and the house was filled with smoke. Then said I, Woe is me! for I am undone; for I am a man of unclean lips, and I dwell in the midst of a people of unclean lips: for mine eyes have seen the King, the Lord of hosts.' That is the way in which the Bible teaches holiness and sanctification!

Why are we as we are? Why is there so much failure in our lives and so much sin? The answer is found there; we just do not know God! 'Holy Father', said our Lord, 'the world does not know Thee: but I have known Thee.' 'Oh', He said, 'if they had but known Thee they would not live as they do, but they do not know Thee!' They talk about God and they argue, but they do not know Thee! 'Holy Father, the world doth not know Thee!' The trouble even with us who are Christians is that we do not know God. Forget about your formulae, forget about yourselves and the thing that is worrying you, the thing that gets you down. That is not your trouble. Your very nature is polluted, and if you get rid of that particular problem you will have something else to fight. The real trouble is that we do not know God. It is the men who have sought God, and the face of God, who have been most holy. What we need primarily is not some experience, it is this knowledge of God, of the attributes of God – His glory, His ineffability, His holiness, His almightiness, His eternity, His omniscience, His omnipresence. If you and I but had the realization that wherever we are, and whatever we do, God is looking at us, it would transform our lives! So the Bible, this Word about which our Lord is speaking, is the Word about God, the 'Holy Father'.

This in New Testament teaching concerning holiness. You start with this first, central, all-controlling doctrine. You see it not only in Isaiah; Ezekiel shows us this same thing. He had this vision of God, and felt the same uncleanness, and fell down. Job, we find, had been talking much about God, and criticizing; but now he sees, and he says 'Mine eye seeth Thee'. He now says 'I will lay mine hand upon my mouth', and 'I abhor myself and repent in dust and ashes' (40:4 and 42:5–6). Have you heard much teaching about the being and the character of God in your holiness and sanctification meetings? How often have you heard sermons about the nature and the being and the attributes of God? All that is taken for granted. We start with ourselves and our problems, and we want to know how we can get rid of the problems or have some special blessing. The approach is wrong. The Word – 'Thy Word' – is the essential thing. And it is a Word about God to start with, a revelation of the being and the character of God. 'With the washing of water by the Word'.

The same Word also reveals to us our state in sin. It tells us what man was like originally. There is no better way of preaching sanctification than preaching about Adam as he was before the Fall. That is what man was meant to be. How often have you heard sermons about Adam in meetings concerning sanctification and holiness? Or sermons about the Fall, the fall of man and its terrible and terrifying consequences? Sanctification? Read the Epistle to the Romans chapter 5, verses 12 to 21 – our being in Adam and our being involved in his sin. There is the root of the problem; and we must understand it well. The Word teaches us about it all. That is New Testament teaching about sanctification – this high doctrine in these Epistles, rather than stories about some Old Testament characters which we can use as illustrations for our theory! Sanctification is based on the exposition of the truth – concerning God's hatred of sin, and the punishment that God threatens upon all sin. What next? The Ten Commandments! They establish the fact of sin, they pinpoint it, they focus it, they bring sin home to us – so they are part of this teaching. We do not stop at the 'ten words', but they come in, in order to convince us of our need. The Law was a 'schoolmaster to bring us to Christ', a revelation of God's holiness. That is why the Fathers used to paint the Ten Commandments on the walls of their churches. The Law is not a way of salvation, but it is a way of showing us our need of it, and the continuing need of being cleansed. Next, God's gracious purpose of redemption, the covenant of redemption before the foundation of the world, the Father and the Son and the Holy Spirit together planning man's deliverance. Paul has already told us about it at the beginning of this Epistle: 'Blessed be the God and Father of our Lord Jesus Christ' – that is how you start preaching sanctification! – 'who hath blessed us with all spiritual blessings in heavenly places in Christ, according as He hath chosen us in Him before the foundation of the world; that we should be

[166]

holy and without blame before Him in love'. That is it! And next, all about the person and work of the Lord Jesus Christ Himself, all that He has done, and all that He has endured. Indeed there is no better way of preaching sanctification than preaching on the Cross, for if I look at the Cross, and 'survey' it, I come to this conclusion:

> *Love so amazing, so divine,*
> *Demands my soul, my life, my all.*

'Ah but', they say, 'we are concerned now about holiness; we have finished with the beginning of salvation, we have finished with the forgiveness of sins. You do not preach the Cross in a holiness convention. Of course not! We are interested now in formulae for sanctification. You do not preach the Cross here!' But is there anything so calculated to promote holiness and sanctification as the Cross?

> *When I survey the wondrous Cross,*
> *On which the Prince of glory died,*
> *My richest gain I count but loss,*
> *And pour contempt on all my pride.*

It is because we have never truly seen the full meaning of the Cross that we are what we are. That is the cause of our failure and our weakness. We have never realized His love to us. If only we really saw the meaning of the Cross! If we but had the experience of Count Zinzendorf who, looking at that picture of the Cross, cried out – 'Thou hast done this for me,
> What can I do for Thee'?
Looking at that he also said, 'I have one passion, it is Christ and Christ alone'.

This is the Word – all the great doctrines, including also the Holy Spirit, His person, His work, His power. What then? His baptising us into Christ, our union with Christ! Then this doctrine of the church. This is the Word that promotes sanctification. And we must go with all these doctrines up to the doctrine of The Second Coming. It is here in verse 27: 'That He might present it to Himself a glorious church, not having spot, or wrinkle, or any such thing; but that it should be holy and without blemish'. When did you last hear a sermon on the Second Coming of Christ in a holiness convention? 'But', they say, 'that is wrong. You go to a Second Advent

[167]

meeting for that; you do not go to a holiness meeting for the doctrine of the Second Coming!' Thus you see how we have departed from the Scripture. We have introduced a number of special departments into the life of the church. Holiness? 'You do not need the Cross here, you do not need the Second Advent here; you just need this one thing, "quite simple"!' It is only as I realize His purpose for me in that glorious day which is coming, when He will present the church to Himself as a glorious church, not having spot, or wrinkle, or any such thing, that my sanctification is promoted. It is that teaching that urges me to be sanctified.

This is how the apostle John says the same thing: 'Beloved, now are we the sons of God, and it doth not yet appear what we shall be: but we know that when He shall appear, we shall be like Him; for we shall see Him as he is'. And then 'And every man that hath this hope in Him purifieth himself even as He is pure'. (1 John 3:1-3). The doctrine of the Second Coming leads to sanctification, to purification. The Word about which the Apostle is speaking here, is the entire Word of the Scripture – every doctrine, the whole of redemption from beginning to end, the entire Bible. 'With the washing of water by the Word.'

Having presented this glorious doctrine, I end with a word of exhortation. Because all this is true, what sort of people should we be? Because all this is true, as Paul has been explaining it, you cannot be as you once were; you must separate yourselves. Go on with your sanctification, 'cleanse yourselves from all pollution of the flesh and of the spirit, perfecting holiness in the fear of God'. 'Cleanse and wash your hands, ye double-minded' – these are the exhortations of the Scriptures. But they all arise from the great doctrines.

So we find here that the process of sanctification which is carried on by the Lord Jesus Christ through the instrumentality of the Holy Spirit whom He has sent, is done by, and in, and through the Word. 'Sanctify them through Thy truth; Thy word is truth.' And no matter at what point you look at it, it will humble you, and it will lead to your sanctification. But above all, start with God: 'Blessed are the pure in heart, for they shall see God'. Have we any time to waste or to spare? What we need is not to get rid of that little problem in our lives; it is to be ready for the glory. It is as we look into the face of God that we see the need of sanctification, and are shown the way whereby our sanctification can be achieved; and it is the function of the Spirit to do this. He leads us to the Word, He opens the Word to us, He implants it in our minds and hearts and wills. He reveals the Lord to us, and so our sanctification, our cleansing, proceeds from day to day, and week to week, and year to year. And as we shall yet see He will go on with it until the work is completed, and we shall be holy and without any blemish in His holy presence. This is the work which the Lord is continuing to do in His people, in the church.

12
The Marriage-Supper of the Lamb

Ephesians 5:25–33

We are still looking at this most remarkable statement in which the Apostle's primary object is to teach husbands their duties towards their wives; and he does this in terms of the relationship of the Lord Jesus Christ to the church. The Apostle passes from one to the other, but we have decided that the better procedure, in order to understand his teaching, is to take them separately. We have considered first of all what he says about the relationship of Christ to the church, in order that, having seen that doctrine in its entirety and fulness, we may then be in a position to apply it to the husbands in their relationship to the wives.

We have considered how our Lord died for the church, gave Himself for her, and how, having done that, He proceeds to separate her unto Himself, (sanctify, put on one side, set His peculiar affection upon the church), that He might cleanse her and continue with this process of spiritual purification.

There are still two expressions to consider in connection with this continuing treatment which our Lord gives to the church. They are the two words found in the 29th verse, where we read that 'no man ever yet hated his own flesh, but nourisheth and cherisheth it, even as the Lord the church'. Paul does not say that 'in the past He has nourished and cherished the church'; the whole purpose is to show that He goes on doing that work. This is entirely in line with what we have been told about the cleansing, which is clearly a continuing process of sanctification. This nourishing and cherishing is also something that continues, and is not merely an action once and for ever accomplished in the past. That is why those who would confine

[170]

what we have been dealing with hitherto in verse 26 to a past action only seem to me to be missing the entire run and teaching of this whole section. The death of our Lord is once and for all, but all the rest is continuing, with this ultimate objective in view.

Let us then look at these two words; they are most interesting. 'He nourisheth.' This explains itself. Its essential meaning is that of feeding, providing food, providing nourishment. Christ is concerned about the health and the growth and the development and the well-being of his church, so He nourishes her. The Apostle has, in a way, been dealing with this theme in the 4th chapter where he expresses it in these terms: 'He gave some, apostles; and some, prophets; and some, evangelists; and some, pastors and teachers'. What for? 'For the perfecting of the saints'; for this process that continues. It is something that keeps going on 'for the work of the ministry, for the edifying' – the building up – 'of the body of Christ. Till we all come . . .' – there is the ultimate objective again! So here, we have another way of saying the same thing, and it is wonderful for us to realize as members of the Christian church that the Lord is thus nourishing the life of the church.

It is an expression of His love for us, and of His care for us, that He provides us with the spiritual food we need. The Bible is given by God, by the Lord Jesus Christ, through the Spirit, as food for the soul. It is a part of His nourishing of us. And all the ministry of the church, as chapter 4 reminds us, is designed for the same end. In other words, there is no excuse for the church when she is ignorant or under-developed or weak, or marasmic. There is likewise no excuse for any individual Christian. The Lord Himself is nourishing us.

Peter, in his Second Epistle, tells us that 'All things that are needful or necessary for life and godliness have been provided'. That is what makes the position of the complaining Christian such a serious one. We shall never be able to plead the excuse that there was not sufficient food because we were in a wilderness. The food is available, the 'heavenly manna' is provided; everything one can ever need is here in the Bible. Here is nourishment, concentrated, unadulterated, as Peter again puts it in his First Epistle in the 2nd chapter: 'The sincere (unadulterated) milk of the Word, that ye may grow thereby'. The Lord has provided it. This is a wonderful thing for us to contemplate – that the Lord is nourishing the church. The husband in his care for his wife works to provide food and all that she needs. Parents take care that their children have the right food, and plenty of it, and at the right time. What concern they show in that respect! The Lord is doing that for us in an infinitely greater way.

How are we responding to it? Do we realize that He is nourishing us? A part of His care is to provide acts of public worship. Public worship is not a human institution, a contrivance of man. It is not something that is run like an institution; and people do not come to the house of God – at least they should not – as a matter of duty. They should come because they realize that they cannot grow if they do not come. They come to be fed, to find food for the soul – 'nourishment'. The Lord has provided it. God knows, I do not enter the pulpit because I just choose to do so. If it were not for the call of the Lord I would not be doing it. All I did was to resist that call. It is His way. He calls men, He separates them, He gives them the message, and the Spirit is present to give illumination. All this is a part of our Lord's way of nourishing the church.

Then take the word 'cherisheth'. Here is a word which is only used twice in the New Testament. It is a word that conveys a very definite idea, generally that of clothing. What the child needs above everything is food and clothing. What the bride, the wife, needs is the same. Those are the first two things you think of, the food and the clothing – 'cherishing'. But it conveys a further idea, namely that of caring for, looking after, guarding. It is an expression of solicitude. When you nourish and cherish a person you show, by a constant watchfulness a care and an anxiety that he or she should thrive and develop and grow. Such are the ideas that are conveyed here by this term 'cherisheth' which is added to the term 'nourisheth'.

Our chief trouble is that we have no true conception of our Lord's interest in us and His concern about us. That is our fundamental lack, we do not know His love. People are often concerned, and rightly of course, about their love to Him; but you and I will never love Him until we begin to know something of His love to us. You cannot 'work up' love. You can work up excitement or something carnal, but you cannot work up love. In the case of the church love is always a response, a reaction: 'We love Him because He first loved us'. We are helpless until He suddenly shines down upon us the beams of His love; and as we realize that, we begin to love. And we come to realize it in this very practical way of understanding something of what He has done for us, and what He provides for us

[172]

in 'the nourishing' and 'the cherishing'. The more we see that, and realize it, the more shall we be amazed at it, and the more we shall love Him in return.

We must not stop at His work for us at the Cross. We begin there, but we see that, having finished that work, He goes on to make all this vast and ample provision for us, and to care for us in providence, in things that happen to us, in leading and guidance. In a thousand and one ways He is nourishing and cherishing the life of the church for whom He died. This does not mean that we forget the Cross, or turn our backs on it, but that in addition we realize this further work of His for us.

Why does the Lord do all this? Why did He die for the church? Why this process of sanctification and of cleansing? Why the nourishing and the cherishing? What is it all designed for? The answer is found in the tremendous statement of verse 27: 'That He might present it to Himself a glorious church, not having spot, or wrinkle, or any such thing: but that it should be holy and without blemish'. Everything is designed to that end. All we have been looking at is the immediate object, but having in sight that ultimate object. That is the purpose, that is the grand end for which the Lord has done, and is continuing to do, the things we have been considering.

But to get the full force of this expression we must vary the translation a little. The truer translation, surely, is this: 'That He Himself might present it to Himself'. You have got to introduce an additional 'Himself' there. And it is added for this reason, that we are reminded at once that every analogy, even the analogies of Scripture, are inadequate. They are only attempts to give us some glimmer of an understanding of what the truth really is. But no illustration is sufficient. The Apostle, here, is illustrating this relationship between Christ and the church in terms of a husband and wife; and yet, at once, we meet something which shows that the analogy is inadequate, and does not go far enough. We all know that the normal procedure is that someone else presents the bride to the bridegroom, the father or a relative or friend. He brings the bride to the bridegroom in the service. Having been helped in all her preparations by others – her upbringing and education and even her clothing and so on – the bride is presented to the bridegroom by someone else. But not so here. Here, He will present His bride to Himself. 'He Himself might present it to Himself'.

This is just another way of emphasizing what is the great theme of the Bible throughout – that the whole of our salvation is of the Lord. It is His doing. He even presents His Bride to Himself because nobody else can do so, nobody else is adequate to do it. He alone can do it. He has done everything for us from beginning to end, and it will end in His presenting us to Himself in all this glory which is here described.

The picture before us, therefore, is that of our Lord and Saviour looking forward to the moment, to the day when He will present the church to Himself. And what will she be like? She will be 'a glorious church' – which means a church characterized by glory. Here is a term with which we are familiar, in the individual sense, in the Scriptures. The ultimate destiny of each of us, the ultimate issue of all our individual salvation is glorification – justification, sanctification, glorification. Sometimes it is described as 'redemption', as in the great statement, for instance, in 1 Corinthians 1 verse 30: 'Who of God is made unto us wisdom, and righteousness, and sanctification and redemption'. That really means 'glorification'. Or as Paul puts it in Romans 8: 'Whom He justified, them He also glorified'. (Romans 8:30). That is the end. Or as you have it in the Epistle to the Philippians at the close of the third chapter: 'Our conversation is in heaven; from whence also we look for the Saviour, the Lord Jesus Christ: who shall change our vile body (or the body of our humiliation) that it may be fashioned like unto His glorious body (the body of His glorification) according to the working whereby He is able even to subdue all things unto Himself'. This is to happen to us individually; but the church also, as a whole, is to be glorified.

That is what is meant by the phrase 'glorious church'. She will be in a state of glory. The Apostle helps us to understand it first by describing what she is like externally. He describes this in terms of two negatives. The church, in her glory, will have neither spot nor wrinkle upon her. There will be no stain, there will be no blemish. It is very difficult for us to realize this. While the church is walking in this world of sin and shame she gets bespattered by mud and mire. There are therefore stains and spots upon her. And it is very difficult to get rid of them. All the medicaments that we are familiar with, all the means of cleansing are inadequate to remove these spots and these stains. The church is not clean here; though she is being cleansed, there are many spots upon her still.

But when she arrives in that state of glory and of glorification she will be without a single spot; there will not be a stain upon her. When He presents her to Himself, with all the principalities and powers and the serried ranks of all the potentates of heaven looking on at this marvellous thing, and scrutinizing and examining her, there will not be a single blemish, there will not be a spot upon her. The most careful examination will not be able to detect the slightest speck of unworthiness or of sin. The Apostle has already introduced us to this idea in chapter 3 and verse 10, where he says: 'To the intent that now unto the principalities and powers in heavenly places might be known by the church the manifold wisdom of God'. These principalities and powers will be looking on; and He, in His pride, will not only present her to Himself, but before them. The Bride and Bridegroom will stand before the hosts of eternity, and He will invite their inspection. He will ask them to look at her, and they will not be able to find a stain or a single spot or blemish upon her – 'without spot'.

Yes, and thank God, 'without wrinkle' – 'not having spot or wrinkle'. Wrinkles, as we all know, are a sign of age, or a sign of disease, or a sign of some sort of constitutional trouble. Wrinkles are a sign of imperfection. As we all get older we develop wrinkles. The fat disappears from the skin. Disease too can deprive us of this layer of fat, and so it can make us look prematurely old. It does not matter what the cause is – any kind of trouble or anxiety leads to wrinkles. It is all a sign of strain and of decay, of advancing age and failure. The church in this world has many wrinkles upon her; she gets to look old and aged. But, thank God, Paul says, when the great day comes on which Christ will present the church to Himself in all her glory, not only will there not be a single spot, there will not be a wrinkle left. Everything will be smoothed out, her skin will be perfect, whole and rounded. It is impossible to describe this perfection. The whole idea is, in a sense, suggested in Psalm 110, where the Psalmist looking forward prophetically is given some glimpse of this state of perfection: 'Thy people' he says in the third verse, 'shall be willing in the day of Thy power, in the beauties of holiness from the womb of the morning; thou hast the dew of thy youth.' The church will have renewed her youth. Dare I put it like this? The Beauty-Specialist will have put his final touch to the church, the massaging will have been so perfect that there will not be a single wrinkle left. She will look young, and in the bloom of youth, with colour in her cheeks, with her skin perfect, without any spots or wrinkles. And she will remain like that for ever and for ever. The body of her humiliation will have gone, it will have been transformed and transfigured into the body of her glorification.

This is what we are told in general here about the church. But let me remind you again that in Philippians 3, verses 20–21, Paul tells us that the same thing is going to happen to us individually. This is a wonderful thing to contemplate. These bodies of ours individually, yours and mine, are going to be glorified. No infirmities will remain, no vestige of disease or failure or sign of age; there will be a grand renewal of our youth. And we shall go on living in that eternity of perpetual youth, with neither decay nor disease, nor any diminishing of the glory which belongs to us. That is what the church is going to look like externally. Do not forget that the idea the Apostle is anxious to convey is this, the pride of the Bridegroom in His Bride. He is preparing her for 'the Day'. There is going to be His great celebration; He intends to show her to the whole universe.

But not only will that be true of her externally, she will be the same internally. Psalm 45 in a most remarkable manner is a perfect prophetic description of all this: 'The King's daughter is all glorious within'. The Psalmist is not content with saying that 'her clothing is of wrought gōld' and that 'she shall be brought unto the king in raiment of needle-work', he emphasizes that she shall be 'all glorious within' also.

The Apostle brings that out here – 'but that it should be holy, and without blemish'. She will be positively holy. The Apostle's declaration is essentially positive. The holiness, the righteousness of the church is not the mere 'absence' of sin and sins; it is the sharing of the Lord's own righteousness.

This is where the merely moral men are left without any understanding at all. They have no conception of anything but a negative morality; morality to them means that you do not do certain things. That is not what the Bible means by righteousness; the biblical term means 'to be like God'! God is holy, and the church becomes holy with this positive shining righteousness, this perfection. It is much more than a mere absence of evil. It is essentially positive uprightness, truth, beauty, and everything that is glorious in all its essence as it is in God. The church partakes of that. She is clothed with the righteousness of Christ now. Thank God, He sees that, and not us! But, then, there will be more than that. She will indeed be like Him, positively, entirely holy and righteous.

[176]

And then, to make sure that we understand it, the Apostle says, 'without blemish' – which means 'without blame'. He has already said all this in verse 4 of the first chapter: 'Blessed be the God and Father of our Lord Jesus Christ, who hath blessed us with all spiritual blessings in heavenly places in Christ: according as He hath chosen us in Him before the foundation of the world'. What for? 'That we should be holy and without blame before Him in love.' There was the Overture, as it were. You always get the leading themes in the Overture. Paul has now taken up that theme which he just mentioned there; here in the fifth chapter he works it out more fully. The church, then, is going to be in this glorious state.

Let me sum it up in the following way. The terms used by the Apostle are designed to convey perfection of physical beauty, health and symmetry, the absolute perfection of spiritual character. Think of the most beautiful bride you have ever seen. Multiply that by infinity, and still you do not begin to understand it. But that is what the church is going to be like. There is never any perfect beauty in this world. A beautiful face, perhaps, but ugly hands. There is always something, some sort of blemish, is there not? But there will be none there. And that is, I suppose, the supreme quality of this beauty that is being described – its symmetry, its absolute perfection in every respect.

This is the thing, surely, we should long for most of all. We are all so lop-sided. Some people are full of head knowledge, the theoretical knowledge of doctrine, and they never move any further. Others have no doctrine, but they talk about their activities and about their lives – they are equally defective. A man who has only a theoretical understanding of these things, and who does not show their power in his life is a very unworthy representative of his Lord. And so is the other! The practical man, so-called, has no time for doctrine, the other has nothing but doctrine: they are both equally at fault. Thank God for a day which is coming when we shall be complete and entire with nothing lacking, and proportionate, balanced. Oh, the glory of this beauty which is here described, and for which our blessed Lord and Saviour is preparing us day by day, week by week, month by month, and year by year! I speak to Christians. Had you realized this about yourselves? Had you realized what a privilege it is to be members of the Christian church? This is what it means to be a Christian! You who are so ready to run to your beauty parlours, do you run to Christ's beauty parlour? That

[177]

is what the church does. Have we a real understanding of the church as the Bride of Christ for whom He has died, and for whom He is continuing to do all these things? Do you know that He cherishes you? Do you know that your name is written in His heart, as well as written upon His very hands? He has loved us with an everlasting love, He has died for us, He has set us apart for Himself, He has made all this provision for us, in preparation for that great day when He will present us to Himself a glorious church not having spot, or wrinkle, or any such thing, but that we should be holy and without blemish.

This is the process that is going on. And let me remind you again that it will go on until it is finished. Nothing can stop it, nothing will be allowed to stop it, because she is His Bride. And if I may venture on such an anthropomorphism, His pride in Himself and in her is such that He cannot allow anything to stop the work or to hinder it! It is going on, I say; and it will go on. Here is the biblical guarantee. The Apostle has given it already in chapter 3, in verses 20 and 21: 'Now', he says, 'unto Him that is able to do exceeding abundantly above all that we ask or think, according to the power that worketh in us, unto Him be glory in the church by Christ Jesus throughout all ages, world without end'. That is the power that works in us, and will continue to work. He did not stop at His death; He does not stop at justification; He is continuing to work within us. He does all the Apostle has been describing in order that 'Unto Him be glory in (and through) the church throughout all ages, world without end'.

That power is irresistible. I would therefore issue this warning once more. If you are indeed a child of God and a member of the church, a member of the body of Christ, let me warn you, in the light of this exalted and glorious teaching, that this body is going to be made perfect, and will be made perfect. Do not resist Him therefore, do not resist the ointments, the emollients, the gentle teaching which He gives in His instruction in the Word in various other ways. Because, believe me, if you become deeply stained with sin, He has some very powerful acids that He can use, and which He does use, in order to rid you of the sin! 'Whom the Lord loveth He chasteneth, and scourgeth every son whom He receiveth.' We are accustomed when we come to the Communion Table to remember what the Apostle says about this in 1 Corinthians 11:12 ff. 'Let every man', he says, 'examine himself.' The argument is this, that if we do examine ourselves and judge ourselves, we shall not be judged;

[178]

but if we fail to do so He will do it to us, He will do it for us. There is no question about this; this is quite categorical: 'Let a man examine himself, and so let him eat of that bread, and drink of that cup. He that eateth and drinketh unworthily' – which means in a careless manner, not thinking about what he is doing. Oh yes, he may think a little about Christianity on Sunday, but forget it for six days of the week, then come to a Communion Service because he is a church member. If you do it in that way, says the Apostle, beware: 'Let a man examine himself, and so let him eat of that bread, and drink of that cup. For he that eateth and drinketh unworthily, eateth and drinketh damnation to himself' – and 'damnation' means judgment – 'not discerning the Lord's body.' He does not understand what he is doing. 'For this cause' – because they do not examine themselves, because they do not realize that the church is the Bride of Christ and that He is going to make her perfect and glorified – 'for this cause many are weak and sickly among you, and many sleep'. 'Many are weak' means, never feeling quite well, they do not understand why. 'And many are sickly', that is to say, they are positively ill. 'For this cause' – because they do not examine themselves, the Lord has that other way of doing it. Read the biographies of the saints and you will find that many of them thank God, as they look back, for an illness which came to them. To me, one of the best examples of this is the case of the great Dr. Thomas Chalmers who would probably never have been an evangelical preacher if he had not had an illness that kept him on his back in bed for nearly twelve months. That was God's way of bringing him to see the truth fully. 'For this cause many are weak and many are sickly among you' – Yes – 'and many sleep' – which means that they are dead. It is a great mystery, I do not pretend to understand it, but the teaching of the Apostle is plain and clear. He says, 'If we would judge ourselves' – if we would examine ourselves and deal with ourselves and punish ourselves – 'we should not be judged. But when we are judged' – What does it mean? – 'we are chastened of the Lord, that we should not be condemned with the world.'

All that, being interpreted, means just what I am trying to say – that because the church is the Bride of Christ, and because His ambition for her makes Him look forward to that great day when she will be 'a glorious church, not having spot, or wrinkle, or any such thing', but she shall be 'holy and without blame before Him in love', He carries on His work to that end. And if we do not respond to Him, and yield to His endearments and to the manifestations of His tender love and wooing, I assert in His name, that He loves you so much that He will cleanse you, He will bring you there. He may have to apply to you the acid of 'weakness', or the acid of 'sickness' but it will be for your good. Do not misunderstand me. This does not mean that every time we are ill it is of necessity a chastisement. The Scripture does not say that; but it does say that it may be. That has often happened. You can read many instances of it in Scripture. Paul realized that the thorn in the flesh was given him in order to keep him humble lest he be exalted over-much. (2 Corinthians 12:7–10). There are foolish and glib people who say that it is never the Lord's will that a man should be ill. The Scripture teaches that 'the Lord chasteneth whom He loveth', and this is one of His ways – 'many are weak and many are sickly among you, and many sleep'. If you really are a child of God, be careful, be wary. Because you belong to the body of which He is the Head, He will cleanse, He will perfect you, He will have you to become that which He has destined for you.

That leaves us with one final question. When is all this going to happen? There seems to be no doubt about this. It must be a reference to the 'Second Coming' of our Lord Himself. It is when He will come and take the church to be with Himself. That is the teaching of the Scripture. 'I go to prepare a place for you. And if I go and prepare a place for you, I will come again, and receive you unto Myself; that where I am, there ye may be also'.

In the High Priestly prayer recorded in John 17 we have exactly the same teaching. Christ's will is that the church may see 'the glory which I had with Thee (the Father) before the foundation of the world'. That is what you and I, as Christians, are going to see. 'We shall see Him as He is'. He now has again the glory which He shared from eternity with the Father. He laid aside the signs of that glory when He was here on earth. That is why I never approve of any attempt to paint pictures of our Lord. It is pure imagination, and almost certainly wrong. There are no facts concerning His physical appearance. Scripture is silent at this point. He was here 'in the likeness of sinful flesh', and there is that suggestion in the 8th chapter of John's Gospel verse 57, that He looked much older than He was. He said of Himself: 'Before Abraham was, I am'. And they said, 'What is He talking about? He is not yet fifty years old'. He was about thirty-three years old but they chose the figure fifty. That

[180]

matters little – what does matter is that when He ascended to heaven the glory returned, and He is now in His glorified state. Paul had a glimpse of Him, on the road to Damascus, in all His glory. It was so wonderful that he fell blinded to the ground. But you and I are going to see it, to 'see Him as He is'. We shall need to be glorified before we can stand that sight; but it will most certainly happen to us. 'And I shall see Him face to face'. As the Bride of Christ we shall be there by His side sharing this glory.

When is this to be? It is when everything shall have been completed, when the fulness of the Gentiles, and of Israel, shall be saved and the church is complete and entire. There will not be a single person missing or lacking, not one. The devil cannot frustrate this; he is already a defeated foe. The Apostle always delights in saying this. He says it gloriously in the Epistle to the Philippians chapter 1, verse 6: 'Being confident of this very thing, that He which hath begun a good work in you will perform it until' – until when? – 'until the day of Jesus Christ'. That is the day, 'the day of the Lord', 'the day of Jesus Christ', 'the day of Christ', 'the crowning day (which) is coming by and by'. Or as he has put it at the end of the 3rd chapter of that Epistle: 'Our conversation is in heaven; from whence also we look for the Saviour, the Lord Jesus Christ: who' – when He comes – 'shall change our vile body, that it may be fashioned like unto His glorious body, according to the working whereby He is able even to subdue all things unto Himself.' Nothing can stop it! Again, the Apostle, in writing to the Romans in chapter 8 and in verses 22 and 23, says, 'We know that the whole creation groaneth and travaileth in pain together until now. And not only they, but ourselves also, which have the firstfruits of the Spirit, even we ourselves groan within ourselves, waiting for the adoption' – What is that? – 'to wit, the redemption' – the glorification – 'of our body'. That means getting rid of the spots and the stains and the wrinkles and every such thing, and being entire and glorious in His presence.

Have you noticed this in the 19th chapter of the Book of Revelation, verses 6 to 9?: 'And I heard as it were the voice of a great multitude, and as the voice of many waters, and as the voice of mighty thunderings, saying, Alleluia: for the Lord God omnipotent reigneth. Let us be glad and rejoice, and give honour to him; for the marriage of the Lamb is come, and his wife hath made herself ready. And to her was granted that she should be arrayed in fine linen,

[181]

clean and white: for the fine linen is the righteousness of saints. And he saith unto me, Write, Blessed are they which are called unto the marriage supper of the Lamb'. Oh, the privilege of being invited to the marriage supper of the Lamb, when He presents the Bride to Himself! She will be clothed with this garment of righteousness without, and within she will be perfect. Oh, the blessing of being present at that marvellous wedding feast! It is not surprising that Jude ends his short Epistle by saying, 'Now unto Him that is able to keep you from falling, and to present you faultless before the presence of His glory with exceeding joy, to the only wise God our Saviour, be glory and majesty, dominion and power, both now and for ever'.

How should we be feeling? We should feel exactly as any woman who becomes engaged to be married feels. We should be looking forward to the great day, and longing for it, and living for it. This should be at the centre of our lives to the exclusion of everything else. We should be animated by this, stimulated and moved by it, and ever looking forward to it – the wedding day, the ceremony, the friends looking on, the feasting, the wonder and the glory and the splendour of it all!

'That He might present her to Himself a glorious church, not having spot or wrinkle, or any such thing, but that she should be holy and without blemish'. He looking into her eyes, she looking into His eyes! That was our blessed Lord's object when He came on earth and lived and died and rose again. It is His objective for us. He died for us that we might come to that! He has separated us that we might come to that! He is cleansing us that we might come to that! He nourishes us that we might come to that! He cherishes us that we might come to that! May God give us grace to realize the privilege of being a member of the Christian church! May we also be given grace and strength and understanding so to realize something of that glory that awaits us that we shall set our affections on that, and not on things on the earth!

13
One Flesh

Ephesians 5:25–33

We are still considering the doctrine of Christ's relationship to the church. But it does not end even at what we have seen. We have to go further; and we shall find that the Apostle's doctrine rises to still greater heights. You would have thought that there could be nothing more exalted than that 27th verse where we are given a glimpse of what is awaiting us as the Bride of Christ, as members of the Christian church. But the doctrine goes even further; there is something still more wonderful, and almost incredible; and that is the extraordinary doctrine of the mystical union between Christ and the church. The Apostle's argument is that we do not truly understand what marriage means until we understand this doctrine of the mystical union of Christ and the church. We shall find that each of the doctrines helps to throw light upon the other. The mystical union between Christ and the church helps us to understand the union between husband and wife, and the union between husband and wife in turn gives a certain amount of light on the mystical union between Christ and the church. That is the wonderful thing about this whole statement. Human analogy and illustration help us to understand divine truth, but in the last analysis it is the understanding of divine truth that enables us to understand everything else; so the Apostle passes from one to the other.

We must therefore address ourselves to this exalted doctrine of the union between Christ and the church. We are all no doubt comforted by what the Apostle says in verse 32, 'This is a great mystery'. It is indeed a great mystery. Therefore we must approach it with care, and we must also approach it very prayerfully. It is certain that

[183]

apart from the anointing and unction which the Holy Spirit alone can give, we shall not be able to understand it at all. To the unregenerate, to the unconverted, to the world, this is sheer nonsense; and that is what the world says about it. Even to the Christian it is a great mystery. But, thank God, the use of the term 'mystery' in the New Testament never carries the idea that it is something which cannot be understood at all. 'Mystery' means something that is inaccessible to the unaided human mind. It does not matter how great that mind may be. The greatest brain in the world, the greatest philosopher, if he is an unregenerate man, is not merely a tyro, he is less than a babe, indeed he is dead in a spiritual sense. He has no understanding whatsoever of a subject like this. This is spiritual truth, and it is only understood in a spiritual manner. The best comment on all this is, once more, the First Epistle to the Corinthians chapter 2, verse 6 to the end of the chapter. It is not surprising therefore that such an elevated subject has been frequently misunderstood, and misunderstood in a very drastic manner.

Take, for instance, the teaching of the Roman Catholic church at this point. The Roman Catholic church translates the word which the Authorized Version renders as 'mystery' by the word 'sacrament'. They read, 'this is a great sacrament', and it is from this statement that they elaborate their doctrine that marriage is one of the seven sacraments. They speak about 'Seven Sacraments' – not merely the two which all Protestants recognize, namely, Baptism and the Lord's Supper – and of these marriage is one. Their supposed proof of that is this verse. On such a foundation they introduce their notion of marriage as a sacrament which therefore, of course, can only be performed by a priest. It is just one illustration of the way in which they elevate the priesthood and introduce a magical element into Christianity. It is all designed to do that. But it shows how the Scriptures can be perverted and misused and misappropriated in the interests of a controlling theory from which you start. If you start by exalting your church and the priesthood, then you have to hedge it round and about in every way you can – and that is what they proceed to do. 'Extreme unction' again is something that can only be administered by a priest, so that is a sacrament; and so on. All these things are designed to bolster up this purely artificial power of the priest. I am adverting to this simply to show how a statement like this can be misinterpreted. What shows, finally, how entirely and completely wrong that Roman Catholic interpretation is, is what the Apostle goes on to say in this selfsame verse – 'but I speak concerning Christ and the church'. That is the mystery to which he is referring. It casts its light upon human marriage between a man and a woman, but he is talking about 'Christ and the church'. So the real mystery is the relationship between Christ and the church. Hence the Roman Catholics are really committed to believing that the relationship between Christ and the church is a sacrament. But they do not say that, because it would be folly for them to do so. However, that is one of the ways in which this matter can be entirely misunderstood.

Rejecting the Romanist's view, let us look again at this phrase: 'This is a great mystery'. Paul means that it is a very profound matter; a matter which will call upon all your resources, and which shows the need of what he has already prayed for on behalf of these people in chapter 1 – 'That the eyes of your understanding might be enlightened' by the Holy Spirit. If we do not approach it thus, anointed by the Spirit, there are three main dangers that will confront us. The first is not to consider it at all. And that is the position, alas, of many Christian people. 'Ah', they say, 'this is a difficult matter', and because it is difficult they do not attempt to understand it, and rush on to the next statement. Surely there is no need for us to stay with that attitude. It is something which can never be defended, and must never be done. The mere fact that there are difficulties in the Scripture does not mean that we should by-pass them. They are there for our learning and instruction; and however difficult they may be, we must do our utmost to understand them and to grasp them. That is one of the reasons for the existence of the Christian church. That is why the Lord has given 'some, apostles; some, prophets; some, pastors; some, evangelists; some, teachers'; and so on. It is in order to instruct us in these things; and so that we may grapple with them. We must not say 'Ah, this is too difficult', and rush on to something else. You will never understand your own marriage, if you are married, unless you try to understand this. It was in order to help you to understand that the Apostle wrote this.

The second danger is so to deal with it as to do away with the mystery, or to detract from the mystery. There have been many, including commentators, who have done so. They have been so much afraid of this 'mystical union', and this teaching about it, that they have reduced it to a mere matter of general likeness, a mere

LIFE IN THE SPIRIT

unity of interests, and so on. But that is to take the 'mystery' right out of it. They say, 'This is just hyperbole, it is highly dramatic language used by the Apostle'. But that is to ignore the fact that Paul deliberately tells us that it is 'a great mystery'. We must not reduce the 'mystery', we must not make something ordinary of it. This is a danger that confronts us at many points in the Christian life, and in Christian teaching. It is the danger that confronts us in connection with our two sacraments – that in our fear of saying too much we say too little! We must avoid that danger.

The third danger is the danger of attempting to work out all this in too much detail. Deciding that it is our duty to face the matter and to try to understand it, and to work it out, we so work it out that there is no mystery left at all. Obviously that is equally wrong, because the Apostle himself says 'This is a great mystery'. That does not mean, I say, that we do not understand it at all, but it does mean that we do not understand it perfectly, that we do not understand it entirely, that there is still something that eludes us, something that leaves us gasping with astonishment and amazement.

Let us then try to avoid these particular pitfalls as we face this great mystery. This is a wonderful truth; and we rise here to those rarified heights which are to be found alone in the Scripture.

What is the Apostle's teaching about this mystical relationship between Christ and the church? We can start with something with which we are quite familiar, because we have met it before in this Epistle. The first thing he tells us is that the church is the 'body' of Christ: 'So ought men to love their own wives as their own bodies' (v. 28). Then he adds in verse 29: 'No man ever yet hated his own flesh; but nourisheth and cherisheth it, even as the Lord the church'. And then more particularly: 'We are members of His body'. He has already introduced this teaching at the end of chapter 1 and again in chapter 4, verse 16. But the Apostle is careful to remind us of this because he is anxious to bring out the principle of the intimate character of the relationship. It is the relationship between the head and the members of a body. What he is concerned to emphasize is that the relationship between husband and wife is not a mere external relationship. There is an external relationship, but much more than that. The essential characteristic of marriage is not simply that two people live together. That is only the beginning; much lies beyond; and there is something deeper here, something much more wonderful. The church, Paul says, is really a part of

[186]

Christ. As the members of the body are a part of the body, of which the head is chief part, so Christ is the Head of the church. As Paul puts it at the end of chapter 1, 'And hath put all things under His feet, and gave Him to be the Head over all things to the church, which is His body, the fulness of Him that filleth all in all'. And again, in the 4th chapter: 'Speaking the truth in love, may grow up into Him in all things, which is the Head, even Christ: from whom the whole body fitly joined together and compacted by that which every joint supplieth, according to the effectual working of the measure of every part, maketh increase of the body unto the edifying of itself in love'. We must hold on to that principle, as it is an essential preliminary to an understanding of the doctrine of the mystical union.

But that is only introduction. He goes further, and in verse 30 he adds, 'For we are members of His body' – then he makes this extraordinary addition – 'of His flesh, and of His bones'. He is talking about the relationship of the church to the Lord Jesus Christ. It is here that we really enter into the mystery. The notion of the church as the body of Christ, while difficult, is nothing like so difficult as this addition, 'of His flesh, and of His bones'. Some have tried to avoid this altogether by pointing out that in certain manuscripts this addition is not present; but it is generally agreed by all the best authorities that in all the best manuscripts this is present. So we cannot solve the problem in that fashion. And indeed the whole context, and the following quotation from Genesis 2, make it essential that we should keep it here, otherwise there is no point or purpose in the quotation. There, as I shall show, he is clearly referring to Genesis 2; and he is certainly doing the same here.

Here we enter into the very heart of this mystery. We must bear in mind that the Apostle's intent, his purpose, is still the same. There is the danger, if he just leaves it at saying that the church is the body of Christ, that we may still think of it in terms of some loose attachment. We must not, of course, do that, because anyone who knows anything about the body knows that it does not consist of a loose attachment of a number of parts. It cannot be repeated too frequently that the body does not consist of a number of fingers stuck on to a hand and a hand stuck on to a forearm, and so on. No! The essential thing about a body is the vital organic unity. And it is in order to emphasize, and to safeguard that principle that the Apostle

[187]

makes the addition, and says, 'We are members of His body, of His flesh, and of His bones'.

The only way to solve the problem, it seems to me, is to follow the hint that is given us by the Apostle himself, and go back to the statement which he quotes from the second chapter of the Book of Genesis, verse 23: 'And Adam said' – referring to the woman – 'This is now bone of my bones, and flesh of my flesh'. Here, again, is a statement that has been misinterpreted. There are those who say that the Apostle, in this 30th verse of this 5th chapter of Ephesians, is referring to the Incarnation, that it is just a round-about way of saying that when the Lord Jesus Christ came into this world He took upon Him human nature, that He took upon Him, in other words, our flesh and our bones. But such an interpretation is quite impossible. What the Apostle is saying is not that the Lord Jesus Christ, the second Person in the blessed Holy Trinity, has taken 'our' flesh and bones; what he says is that 'we' take His flesh and bones, that 'we are members of His body, of His flesh, and of His bones'. It is the other way round; so that is not the explanation.

Then there has been grievous misunderstanding of this in terms of the sacrament of the Lord's Supper. There are those who have said that when the Apostle writes 'We are members of His body, of His flesh, and of His bones', he is referring to our Lord's glorified body. The body which the Lord Jesus Christ took unto Himself has been glorified, and they say that we are literally parts and members of His glorified body. But surely there is one consideration that puts that out, once and for ever, namely that that glorified body is in heaven. That, therefore, cannot possibly apply to us. But even further, as I say, they have introduced the whole question of the Communion, of the Lord's Supper. The Roman Catholics say that there is no difficulty about this. Their teaching is that at the Communion table the priest performs a miracle, he turns a piece of bread into the very 'flesh and bones' of the Lord Jesus Christ. That is the doctrine of transubstantiation. What is on the plate looks like bread, but that is only the 'accident', the 'substance' has been changed. The whiteness remains, but what is offered to the communicant is now actually the body of Christ. So that as you eat you are eating 'His flesh and His bones', and so you become a part of Him. They drag in the teaching in the 6th chapter of John's Gospel in their attempt to support this.

Then the Lutheran doctrine, which is not transubstantiation, but what they call 'consubstantiation', comes to very much the same thing. They say that the bread is not actually changed into the body of Christ, but the glorified body of Christ enters into the bread, and is there with it. So you have the bread plus the glorified body of Christ, and you eat both.

It should surely be evident that this is merely to import something that is in no way suggested by the Apostle, either in the verse itself, or in the entire context. It is an attempt to explain the mystery in a manner which is not consistent with the context; and, in the last analysis, it almost does away with the mystery.

Surely if we follow the Apostle's own leading we shall arrive at the true explanation. He is obviously quoting Genesis 2:23: 'Adam said, This woman is now bone of my bones, and flesh of my flesh'. His analogy is clearly that of Adam and Eve, and Christ and the church. So it is right to say of the church that 'we are members of His body, of His flesh, and of His bones'.

But what does that suggest? We must go yet further into the mystery. Is not this like walking into some cave where you see the first chamber, and then see that there is another opening out of it? You go on into that and on, and on; and in the most central chamber there is the final treasure. What does the Apostle mean? That depends on the meaning of Genesis 2:23. The answer is, clearly, that the woman has been taken out of man. Have you noticed the exact wording of Genesis 2:23? 'Adam said, This is now bone of my bones, and flesh of my flesh: she shall be called Woman'. But why should she be called 'Woman'? The answer given is, 'because she was taken out of Man'. The true definition of a woman therefore is, one who has been taken out of man. That is the very meaning of the word 'woman'. Woman by definition, by origin, by name, is one who is taken out of man. But observe again the way in which this was done. 'And the Lord God said, it is not good that the man should be alone; I will make him an help meet for him' (verse 18). Again we are told at the end of verse 20, 'but for Adam there was not found an help meet for him'. The animals had been made, and animals are very wonderful, but not one of them is a help meet for man. There is an essential difference between man and the animal. Man is a special creation after all, he has not evolved out of the animals. The animal at its best is essentially different from the lowest type of man; he belongs to a different order, to a different realm altogether. Man is unique, he is made in the image of God. So though the animals are wonderful there was not one that could make a companion for man, the companion that man needs. So we go on, and read, 'And the Lord God caused a deep sleep to fall upon Adam, and he slept; and He took one of his ribs and closed up the flesh instead thereof; and the rib which the Lord God had taken from man, made He a woman'. Woman is taken out of man, out of his substance, out of 'his flesh', out of 'his bones'. God takes a part out of man, and of that He makes a woman. So what is woman? She is of the same substance as man, 'of his flesh, and of his bones'. God performed the operation. Man was put into a state of deep sleep, and then the operation was performed, the part was taken out, and out of that woman was made.

'This is a great mystery; but I speak concerning Christ and the church'. 'We are members of His body, of His flesh, and of His bones'. How? Woman was made at the beginning as the result of an operation which God performed upon man. How does the church come into being? As the result of an operation which God performed upon the Second Man, His only begotten, beloved Son on Calvary's hill. A deep sleep fell upon Adam. A deep sleep fell upon the Son of God, He gave up the ghost, He expired, and there in that operation the church was taken out. As the woman was taken out of Adam, so the church is taken out of Christ. The woman was taken out of the side of Adam; and it is from the Lord's bleeding, wounded side that the church comes. That is her origin; and so she is 'flesh of His flesh, and bone of His bones'. 'This is a great mystery'.

Had you realized that? It is not an accident that the Lord Jesus Christ is referred to in the New Testament as the 'Second Man' or as the 'Last Adam'. The Apostle teaches here that this is true also of Him in this respect. We normally think of our relationship to Him in an individual sense, and that is right. Take the teaching concerning the relationship of the Christian to the Lord Jesus Christ as found in Romans chapter 5, where you have again this same comparison between the first man and the Second Man; it tells us how we are all involved in the transgression of Adam, and how we are involved in the righteousness of Christ. As the one, so the other. There the emphasis is upon the personal. Here, it is in terms of the church as a whole, the communal relationship; and this is the great mysterious truth which Paul is teaching. As it is true to say of the woman, that she was taken out of the side of man, out of the very substance, 'his flesh and his bones', so the church is taken out of

Christ, and we are a part of Him, members of His body and of His very bones. He is the Last Adam, He is the Second Man. And as God operated on the first man to produce his bride, his help meet, so He has operated upon the Second Man to do the same thing in an infinitely more glorious manner.

But let us go on even further. We do so in fear and trembling; but let us go on. The Apostle is emphasizing that we are a part of Christ's very nature. Note that he uses the word 'himself' in the 28th verse: 'No man', he says, 'ever yet hated his own flesh, but nourisheth and cherisheth it, even as the Lord the church. So ought men to love their wives as their own bodies. He that loveth his wife loveth himself'. Still the same idea! The body is a part of the man, and therefore when he pays attention to his body he is paying attention to himself. He cannot divorce himself from himself. What he does for his body he is doing for himself; he does it because it is a part of himself. That is the relationship between Christ and the church. That does not mean that we are divine. We must be careful about that. We Christians are not gods, nor are we divine. But what it does mean is that the Lord Jesus Christ is the former and beginner of a new humanity. One humanity started in Adam, a new humanity started in the Lord Jesus Christ. We are sharers of that! We are partakers of that! That is why we find Peter saying in his Second Epistle, chapter 1, verse 4, that we are 'partakers of the divine nature.' We are partakers of this nature that the Mediator now has, having come through the Incarnation and having done all that He came to do. We derive our life, our being from Him, and we are truly parts of Him.

But we must take the final step, and go to verses 31 and 32: 'For this cause shall a man leave his father and mother, and shall be joined unto his wife, and they two shall be one flesh. This is a great mystery, but I speak concerning Christ and the church'. Here, again, we can only understand the Apostle's meaning by going back to the second chapter of Genesis. This verse is a direct quotation of Genesis 2:24. But what exactly does it mean? There are many who get frightened at this point and say: 'Ah, this is a great mystery and we must be careful that we do not press it too far'. So they say that the Apostle introduced the words, 'they two shall be one flesh', the quotation from Genesis 2:24, simply to round off his quotation. But the Apostle does not do that kind of thing; the Apostle does not quote unless he has an object and a purpose in quoting. They say,

[191]

'Of course, this patently has nothing to do with the Lord Jesus Christ and the church. Here, Paul is really just talking about husbands and wives; he is not talking about the church at this point'. But I cannot accept that, for Paul says 'This' – that which I have just been saying – 'is a great mystery, but I speak concerning Christ and the church'.

I believe that this expression concerning the 'one flesh' applies to the relationship between Christ and the church as it does to the relationship between the husband and the wife. But let us be careful, because this is a great mystery. I am not attempting or pretending to say that I understand it fully, but at the same time I do not want to detract from the mystery. I want to get hold of this teaching concerning this mystical relationship, this extraordinary unity, this oneness that Paul is talking about. The following seems to me to be the explanation. Go back to Genesis 2 and this is what you find. Adam was originally one, a perfect, a complete man. And yet there was a kind of lack, there was no help meet for him. So what we are told is that God performed the operation, and this man who had been one now begins to be two – Adam and Eve, the man and the woman. The woman was taken out of him, so she is a part of him; she was not created from nothing as man was. She was taken out of the man, and so she is a part of man. But it did not stop there – and this is where I see the point of this mystery. In one sense they were now two, but in another sense they were not two: 'For this cause shall a man leave his father and mother and shall be joined to his wife, and they two shall become one flesh'. That is the very essence of the mystery. There is a sense in which they are two, and there is a sense in which they are not two. We must never forget this unity, this one-ness, this idea of the 'one flesh'.

Let us rise then to the topmost peak of the mystery. Adam was incomplete without Eve: and the deficiency, the lack, was made up by the creation of Eve. So there is a sense in which we can say that Eve makes up the 'fulness' of Adam, makes up that which was lacking in Adam. And that is exactly what the Apostle says about the church in her relationship to Christ. Fortunately for us he has already said that in chapter 1, verse 23, which reads, 'Which is His body' – he is talking about the church – 'and gave him to be the Head over all things to the church, which is His body, the fulness of Him that filleth all in all'. The church is the 'fulness' of Christ. The church, he says, is that which 'makes up', as it were, this fulness of

Christ. And I suggest that here in chapter 5 he is just repeating that truth. As Adam and Eve became one flesh, and as Eve makes up, as it were, the fulness of Adam, so the church makes up the fulness of Christ. That is the meaning attached to the word 'fulness' every-where in the New Testament, as the authorities agree. Christ is not the fulness of the church, the church makes up His fulness, 'the fulness of Him that filleth all in all'.

We can look at the matter in this way. The Lord Jesus Christ, as the eternal Son of God, is perfect, complete and entire, and always has been from all eternity – 'in Him dwelleth all the fulness of the Godhead bodily'. He is and always has been co-equal and co-eternal with the Father. The whole fulness of the Godhead is in each of the Three Persons. There is no lack, there is nothing to make up, there is no fulness which is lacking. But as the Mediator, Christ is not full without the church. Now this is the mystery, the most glorious mystery of all. Jesus Christ as Mediator will not be full and complete and entire until every soul has been gathered in for whom He died – 'the fulness of the Gentiles' and 'all Israel'. It is only then that He will be full, only then will the fulness be complete.

This is the great mystery of salvation, and that is why we must be so careful. But the doctrine of salvation suggests this, that the blessed eternal Son of God, in order to save us, has put a limitation upon Himself. In taking unto Him human nature He took on a limitation. He remains God eternally – there is no limit on that, there is no lessening in His deity. It is a great mystery, and we must not try to understand it in an ultimate sense. It cannot be understood. But this is the teaching. There He is, One and unchangeable! Yes, but he became man, and He was subject to ignorance and infirmity when He was in this world, 'made in the likeness of sinful flesh'. And as the Mediator, I say, He will not be complete until the church is entire. He has a bride to whom He is to be joined, and they become 'one flesh'. When the Lord Jesus Christ returned to heaven He did not leave His body behind, He took it with Him. That human nature is in Him now, and always will be. He is still the second Person in the blessed Holy Trinity, but this human nature which you and I now have is there in Him, and we shall be in Him to all eternity. He has subjected Himself to something. I venture on what is almost a speculation, but the Apostle quotes these words: 'For this cause shall a man leave his father and mother and shall be joined unto his wife, and they two shall be one flesh'. I do not press the details but I say this – that the Lord Jesus Christ left the courts of glory and came into this world and on this earth for His Bride. There has been a 'leaving' in His case, as in the case of a man who leaves his father and mother that he may be joined to his wife. Yes, He left the courts of glory – as Charles Wesley reminds us –

> *He left His Father's throne above,*
> *So free, so infinite His grace!*

He left heaven and the courts of glory for the sake of His Bride. There was an awful moment when He cried out, 'My God, My God, why hast Thou forsaken Me?' For that moment He was separated from His Father. And why? Oh, that He might purchase and save this Bride of His, who now, as the result of that operation, is a part of His body, of His flesh, and of His bones.

This is, I say, the supreme mystery. There is nothing more wonderful, there is nothing more glorious than this. We are sharers of His human nature, we are joined to Him, and we shall be, throughout eternity. That is why we are told in the Scriptures that we shall be above the angels and 'judge' them. 'Know ye not', says Paul in 1 Corinthians 6, 'that the saints shall judge the world, that the saints shall judge angels?' Even angels! Why? Because we are raised above them; we are in the Son, we are a part of Him, joined to Him, 'one flesh' with Him. The church is the Bride of Christ, and as we think of this relationship we must always gaze into this mystery and realize that 'we are members of His body, of His flesh, and of His bones'. But above all let us realize what He did in order that we might become His. He left His Father's throne above, 'He humbled Himself', 'He made Himself of no reputation' – that is how He has loved the church! 'Husbands, love your wives, even as Christ also loved the church and gave Himself for it.'

14
The Bride's Privileges

Ephesians 5:25-33

We have been working our way through this great statement which is primarily designed for the edification of husbands, but which, as we have been seeing, has a glorious message for all Christian people. This is so because the Apostle in giving his message to the husband does so by using the comparison of the relationship between Christ and the church. That is the analogy that the husband is ever to bear in mind.

There is, however, one further thing for us to do before we come to the application of the teaching to the particular duties of husbands towards their wives. There is implicit in what the Apostle has been saying something further which will be of great importance when we come to the practical application, but which is also of inestimable value to us one by one as Christian people as we realize our relationship to the Lord Jesus Christ, and realize that together we are the Bride of Christ. Let me explain.

Because of all we have been considering it follows of necessity that the husband bestows certain things upon his Bride; and we are now going to look at what the Lord Jesus Christ as the Bridegroom of the Bride, which is the church, bestows upon her. As we do so we shall realize again the glorious privilege of being Christians and members of the Christian church. I am holding you to this truth because it is my increasing and profound conviction that the main problem, the main trouble, today is the failure of Christian people like ourselves to realize the privilege, and the dignity, of being members of the Christian church and of the body of Christ. I know, and I agree, that it is right to be concerned about the state of the world. We cannot be Christians without such a concern; but I cannot understand how anyone can be complacent about the state of the church. Surely the ultimate explanation of the state of the world is the state of the church. To me the saddest and the most grievous thing of all at the present time is the failure of Christian people to realize what the New Testament tells us about ourselves, and what it means to be members of the body of Christ. In a world that attaches such significance to honours and glories and position, is it not amazing that we can regard our membership of the church as we do? Many seem to regard it as almost a kind of dignity that they confer upon the church, instead of realizing that it is the highest and the most glorious privilege that anyone can ever have or know. Others regard their membership of the church as a task and as a duty, and are rather pleased with themselves if they perform any function. Now that betrays a complete failure to understand what it really means to be members of this body, which is the Bride of the Lord Jesus Christ Himself.

Let us therefore look at some of the things He bestows upon us, some of the things that are true of us as Christian people and members of the church. If the church but realized these things she would no longer be apologetic, and languishing, and drooping, and present such a miserable spectacle; she would be filled with a sense of pride and of joy and of glory.

What are the things He bestows upon us? The first is His life. We have already been looking at that truth, but I must mention it again in this connection. He gives us a part of His own life – we become sharers in His own life. That is what happens, is it not, when a man gets married? He was living his own life, but now he no longer lives his own life exclusively, his wife becomes a sharer in his life. As she is a part of him she is a sharer in his life and activity and everything that is true concerning him. The first thing a married man has to learn is that when he is confronted by various situations he now has to do something new. Before, the main problem for him was, How does this affect me, what is my reaction to this? But now he no longer stops at that. He now has to think also of how it will affect his wife. He no longer lives an isolated life, as it were, on his own; he has another to consider always who is a sharer of his life. Something may be acceptable to him, but there is somebody else to consider now.

I could elaborate on this; I could speak out of much pastoral experience of troubles and difficulties which I have had to deal with because husbands have forgotten just this very point. Let me give one illustration of it. I do so because it is one that I have often had to meet, and one concerning which I have often been misunderstood. But, taking that risk, I give it again in order to illustrate this point. A man has come to me and has said that he feels called to go to the foreign mission-field. Well, that is excellent. But then I have to ask a question – and I always do ask it if he is a married man – What does your wife say about it? Sometimes I have had to deal with men who do not seem to be concerned about that, and appear to regard the matter as if it were a purely personal decision. But it is not! A man has no right to isolate himself over a matter like that from his wife. Because the twain are one flesh, he has to consider his wife's views. We have already been dealing with the duties of wives towards their husbands. There is a great deal to be said on that side also; but the point I am establishing is that he is a very poor Christian who says, 'If I feel called to a particular work it does not matter what my wife says'. It does matter! That is a complete misunderstanding of this teaching.

But let us look at it from the other aspect, and realize that we are sharers of the life of the Lord Jesus Christ. It is a staggering thought, but we are entitled to say this, that we are ever in His mind; that in all His outlook we have our part and our place. We are 'in Christ', we are sharers of His life. The Apostle in writing to the Colossians uses this extraordinary phrase in the 3rd chapter verse 4, 'When Christ, who is our life, shall appear'. He is 'our life', which is another way of saying that we are sharers of His life. Now there is nothing beyond that! We were really looking at that when studying the statement that 'we are members of His body, of His flesh, and of His bones'. We are now looking at it from a slightly different angle; not so much from the angle of the mystical union, but from that of the Lord's own consciousness that He is giving of His life, sharing it, and that we are taken into it, and become part and parcel of His life.

But let us go on to show this in its various manifestations. One is that He bestows upon us His name. We take on ourselves His name because He gives us His name. We are called 'Christians', and that is the greatest truth about us. We are no longer what we were, we have changed our names. A woman when she gets married changes her name. How important that becomes in helping us to understand the teaching of the great Apostle in this fifth chapter of this Epistle to the Ephesians! What a lot it has to say also about this foolish modern movement called 'feminism'! When a woman gets married she gives up her name, she takes the name of her husband. That is biblical, and also the custom of the whole world. That teaches us the relationship between husband and wife. It is not the husband who changes his name, but the wife. There has been a striking illustration of this in recent times. I refer to it because I hope it will help to fix these truths in our mind. The whole nation knows what has happened in the case of Princess Margaret, how the name of her husband is always brought in when she is mentioned; and rightly so. It is unscriptural not to do so. It is the name of the husband that is taken, not the name of the wife. No matter who they are, this is the scriptural position.

But look at all this from our standpoint as members of the Christian church. Christ has put His name upon us. There is no greater compliment that can ever be paid us than that. That is the clearest expression of this married relationship. This is presented to us in many ways in the New Testament. 'There is no longer either Jew or Gentile, barbarian, Scythian, bond or free'. There used to be. Those were the names that we bore before. But no longer! We are now Christians, we have a new name. Or take the way in which this same Apostle puts it in his Second Letter to the Corinthians, chapter 5: 'Henceforth', he says, 'know we no man after the flesh'. 'I used to know people after the flesh', he says; 'I as a Jew used to say, "What is that man, is he a Jew? If not, he is a mere dog". But,' he says, 'I no longer think in those categories, I use new terms now. What I want to know is, "Is this man a Christian?" I do not care what his old name was; this is the name I am now interested in – "Christian!" Has he got the name of Christ on him?' So we realize that the Lord Jesus Christ bestows His name upon us. It is as real as this, says the Apostle again, in writing to the Galatians, 'I live; yet not I, but Christ liveth in me'. That is the idea. Paul is submerged in a sense, yet he goes on to say: 'The life I now live in the flesh I live by the faith of the Son of God, who loved me, and gave Himself for me'. What a wonderful statement that is of this married relationship! There is a sense in which the Christian's whole life is in the Husband, and yet he has not become lost altogether, he is still there – 'the life I now live in the flesh'.

There is the great mystery of the marriage relationship! But we

[198]

must hold on to this great fact that the name of the Lord Jesus Christ is upon us. What matters, and should matter, to every one of us is that we have changed our names. Here in the realm of the church the other names do not matter at all. It matters not what a man's name is, what his position or office is, what his ability is, what anything is. The one thing that matters about him now is that the name of Christ is on him. We are all one there, we are all together in Him. He has taken us to Himself – the church is the Bride of Christ. He says to us, in effect, 'Forget that old name, take my name on you; you belong to Me'. We find this in the Book of Revelation, chapter 3, verse 12: 'Him that overcometh will I make a pillar in the temple of My God, and he shall go no more out; and I will write upon him the name of My God, and the name of the city of My God, which is New Jerusalem, which cometh out of heaven from My God: and I will write upon him My new name'. That is it!

> *Write Thy new name upon my heart,*
> *Thy new best name of love.*

This is the astounding thing that happens to all who are Christians, all who are members of this body, which is the Bride of Christ. You have been given a new name by the Prince of glory, and wonder of wonders! it is His own name. There is no honour or glory greater than this. You are lost in a new name, and it is the highest name of all. We read that a day is coming when 'at the name of Jesus every knee shall bow, of things in heaven, and things on earth, and things under the earth' – and that is the name that is given to us who are constituted the Bride of Christ.

Then we see that out of that comes the fact that we are sharers in His dignity, in His great and glorious position. The Apostle has already said as much in chapter 2 where he has told us the amazing truth that 'He hath raised us up together (in Christ), and made us sit together in heavenly places in Christ Jesus'. That is true of us now. If we are Christians at all we are 'in Christ' and that means that we are 'seated with Him in the heavenly places'. Wherever the bridegroom is the bride is also, and the standing, the dignity, and the position that belong to him belong to her. It does not matter at all who she was; the moment she becomes his bride she shares all with him. And woe betide anyone who does not accord to her the position and the dignity! There is no greater insult that can be offered to the bridegroom than a refusal to honour his bride. This is the truth, says the New Testament, about the Christian. It is something that we are told repeatedly. One statement of it occurs in the 17th chapter of John's Gospel, verse 22, where our Lord says: 'And the glory which Thou gavest Me I have given them'. The glory, He says, which the Father had given Him He has given to His people. It is something that happens invariably in a marriage; the bride, being a part of the husband, and having his name on her, shares his whole position. 'The glory which Thou gavest Me I have given them'.

But take another statement of the matter. The Lord Jesus Christ said about Himself, 'I am the light of the world'. That is His claim, and there is no higher claim. The world is in darkness, He says, apart from Me. I am the only light that the world can ever receive, everything else is but an attempt of men to discover light; and they invariably fail. There is no light apart from Christ. But note what He says about us: 'Ye are the light of the world'. In other words, because He is what He is, and because of our relationship to Him, we likewise become the light of the world. It is very difficult for us to realize it, is it not? We are but a small number in this pagan land of ours, only ten in a hundred claiming to be Christians, and only half of those attending the house of God. So we are apologetic, and somewhat ashamed of ourselves. But the truth about us is this: We are the light of the world! It is the Lord Jesus Christ who said that. This dark, evil world knows no light, and has no light, apart from the light which you and I are disseminating in it.

But think of the matter from the aspect of our dignity, our glory – what He is, He makes us. This is inevitable because of the relationship. There are many other very wonderful statements of this. Listen to the Lord, again, in the Book of Revelation speaking to the church of the Laodiceans, of all people: 'To him that overcometh will I grant to sit with Me in My throne, even as I also overcame, and am set down with My Father in His throne'. Because the church is the Bride of Christ she is going to sit with Him in His throne. 'She is a commoner', you say. Yes, but that does not matter; she is married to the Prince, and she shares the throne with Him. That is the dignity, that is the privilege He confers upon us!

Then attend to this. The Apostle Paul in trying to teach the members of the church at Corinth something of this greatness and glory puts it thus in chapter 6 of the First Epistle, verse 2: 'Do ye not know that the saints shall judge the world?' Then: 'Know ye not that we shall judge angels?' That refers to you and me. Look at those miserable members of the church at Corinth. 'What is the matter with you?' asks the Apostle. 'Why are you quarrelling amongst yourselves? Why are you boasting of this man or that man or another man, and taking one another to the courts about disputes? Do you not realize that every one of you as a Christian is in such a relationship to Christ that you are going to judge the world, that you are going to judge the angels?' Here is the dignity that belongs to us.

Let me put it in this way. Think of the Christian in relationship to the angels. Had you realized that we are meant for a destiny which will put us above the angels? The angels are wonderful beings, they 'excel in strength'; but we are destined for a position which will be above that of the angels! The author of the Epistle to the Hebrews puts it thus: 'For unto the angels hath he not put in subjection the world to come, whereof we speak. But one in a certain place testified, saying, What is man, that Thou art mindful of him? or the Son of man, that Thou visitest him? Thou madest him a little lower than the angels; Thou crownedst him with glory and honour, and didst set him over the works of Thy hands: Thou hast put all things in subjection under his feet'. (Hebrews 2:5–8). 'But', says someone, 'I do not see all things put in subjection under man; what are you talking about?' 'O no', says the author of that Epistle, 'we do not yet see all things put under him. But we see Jesus, who was made a little lower than the angels for the suffering of death, crowned with glory and honour' (verse 9). These words mean, that you and I are going to be in that position. We already have it in the sight of God; we do not see it, but it is true of us now. We are above the angels because we are the Bride of Christ; and as He is above them in the heavenly places, we have that dignity and that greatness and that position even now.

That leads us to the next point, which is that we share not only in His life but in His privileges. The moment a woman becomes the bride of a man she shares his privileges. Whatever they are, she becomes partaker of them and sharer of them. The Apostle is saying here that this is true of the church. What do we share? We share the Father's love. There is a verse which in many ways is to me the most astounding verse in the whole Bible. It is the 23rd verse of the 17th chapter of John's Gospel. The Lord says, 'That the world may know that Thou hast sent Me, and hast loved them as Thou hast loved Me'. It is a statement to the effect that God the Father has loved us Christian people as He loves His own Son. What it means is that because of our relationship to Him we are in that relationship to God. Think of a man, without daughters, whose son has got married. He now says to the bride of his son: 'You are my daughter. I never had a daughter before, but you are my daughter.' And he regards her as such. She is one with his son, therefore he bestows his fatherly love upon her – 'that the world may know that Thou hast loved them, as Thou hast loved Me'. That is the privilege. It works out in this way – it gives us access to the Father. A father is ever ready to receive the bride of his son. She did not have that access to him before; there was no relationship; but the moment she becomes married to the son she has a right of access into the presence of the father. As the father is ready to receive the son, and to give the son privileges which he would not grant to his most trusted and favourite servants, so now he grants them to the bride because she is the wife of his son. Christian people, do we avail ourselves of this high privilege? Do we realize that we have a right of entry and of access into the presence of the Father? Though He is the Governor of the whole universe, if you have a need, remember that you have a right of entry to His presence. For His Son's sake He will not refuse you. Bride of Christ, He will always listen to you, He will always have time for you. There is no higher privilege than this. He loves us as He loves His Son, and He gives us this right of access and of entry into His holy presence.

Yet more, I am simply giving headings for you to think about and to meditate upon. We should spend much of our time with these points thinking about them. When you get on your knees to pray, do not start speaking immediately; stop and think. Think even before you get on your knees. Realize what you are doing; remember who you are, and because you are what you are, call to mind what is true of you, and the rights and privileges that are given you. Then go on to consider the possessions the Lord gives us. We are sharers in His possessions. The Apostle Paul in an extraordinary statement written to the church at Corinth says in effect: 'What are you troubling about? why are you divided amongst yourselves and jealous of one another, and envying one another? what is the matter with you? "All things are yours". Everything! I do not care what they are, says Paul, they are all yours. Why? "Because ye are Christ's, and Christ is God's".' Study that carefully in 1 Corinthians, at the end of chapter 4.

I ask again, Am I not right when I say that the real tragedy today is the failure of the church to realize the truth about herself? 'All things are yours' – everything! The cosmos is ours, in a sense, because we belong to Christ. The Apostle Paul was thrilled by this knowledge; and the test of our Christianity, the test of our spirituality, is as to whether we are moved and thrilled by these things. We may be having a hard time, we may be persecuted, we may be despised, people may be laughing at us because we are Christians. Do we know what we are to say to ourselves? We must say, 'Because we are children, we are therefore heirs; heirs of God and joint heirs with Christ'. (Romans 8:17). It matters little what the world may think or say – 'All things are yours', Christians are 'joint heirs with Christ'.

But I particularly like the way in which this is expressed by the author of the Epistle to the Hebrews in the 2nd chapter and verse 5. I have already quoted it, but I do so again: 'For unto the angels hath he not put in subjection the world to come, whereof we speak'. It is a pity that the A.V. translated it in that way. It is an awkward translation, it is an odd negative. 'For unto the angels hath he not put in subjection the world to come, of which we speak.' It means that 'He has not put the world to come, of which we speak, in subjection to angels, but to us'. What is this 'world to come' about which he is speaking? The 'world to come', of which he is speaking, is this old world in which you and I are living at this present time. Yes! but not as it is now. It is this same world when Christ shall have come back, and shall have destroyed all His enemies, and all evil, and every vestige and remains of evil; it is when the great burning shall have taken place, the great purification, the regeneration, when there shall be 'new heavens and a new earth wherein dwelleth righteousness'. That is the 'world to come' of which he is speaking. And this is a vital part of the essential Christian message. This world that we are in at this moment is only a passing world; this is not the real world, this is not the lasting world. What we see is the world as the result of what man has made it. We see the chaos that man has produced. The world itself, of course, is very interested in the visible and the present; and everybody is wondering what the latest conference is going to achieve – is there going to be disarmament, is war going to be banished, is everything going to be perfect for the rest of time? But that is all vain. This is an evil world, and evil and sin will go on manifesting themselves in it until God's appointed time of judgment shall arrive. But there is a 'world to come'; it is the New Jerusalem that will come down from heaven, this old world restored to all its pristine glory, this old world as God made it at the beginning, but yet more glorious. That will happen at Christ's second coming. He will dwell in it Himself, and His bride with Him. That is 'the world to come, of which we speak'. Who is going to live in that world, who is going to inherit that world? Well, says the Epistle, it is not the angels: 'For not unto the angels hath He subjected the world to come, of which we speak', but unto us. We are the heirs of this glory that is to come. Christian people, do you ever envisage that? do you ever remind yourself of that? You may be having a hard time striving against the world, the flesh, and the devil; you may be facing difficulties and obstacles. Turn away from that! do not look at that alone! 'While we look not at the things which are seen, but at the things which are not seen; for the things which are seen are temporal, but the things which are not seen are eternal'. (2 Corinthians 4:18). Lift up your heads, you share Christ's inheritance, His possessions! You have married Him – or rather, He has married you – and He puts these things into your hands. You are sharers of His possessions.

Let me again emphasize that we are sharers of His interests, His plans and His purposes. 'Co-workers together with God'. Do not think of your local church, or any other church in terms merely of yourself and what you are doing. The same applies to your denomination or movement. Rise above it, and consider His interests. I quote again, 'Ye are the light of the world'. The Lord has a purpose with respect to this world, and you and I are involved in, and sharers in that purpose. The husband tells his wife everything. She knows his every secret, his every desire, every ambition, every hope, every project that ever enters his mind. She is one with him. He tells her things that he would not say to anybody else; she shares everything, there is nothing kept back, nothing is hidden. Such is the relationship of husband and wife. It is also the relationship of Christ and the church; we are partners with Him in this business of saving men. Do you know that interest? Do you feel it, do you think about it, do you prize the privilege of being sharers in the secret? Do you feel something of the burden, and are you helping Him? That is what a Christian is for, that is what a wife is for – a help meet – and the church is the Bride of Christ. How often do you pray for the success of the preaching of the Gospel? To what extent are you concerned about the evangelistic message of the church? Do you think about it, do you feel you are a part of it, do you pray about it? A wife worthy of the name does not need to be exhorted to take an interest in her husband's affairs; she counts it her greatest privilege to be helping her husband; she is vitally interested in all he does, and in its success. The church is the Bride of Christ; He shares it all with us. Let us realize these things and rise to the dignity and privilege of it all.

But let me mention something which, to me, is one of the most fascinating and charming aspects of it all. The Lord not only shares His possessions, His interests, His plans and His purposes with us; He shares His servants with us. You may have been a Cinderella, the whole church was a Cinderella, in her rags, slaving and having a hard and a difficult life, doing all the chores for the other sisters. But Cinderella is married to the Prince; and what happens? Instead of having to slave in that way she now has her servants. Whose servants? His servants! Because she has become the bride of this Prince all his servants are her servants, and they minister to her as they do to him. Had you realized that this is true of us? Let us go back once more to the Epistle to the Hebrews, and to the first chapter. The writer is comparing and contrasting the Lord Jesus Christ with the angels, and this is how he expresses it: 'Unto which of the angels said He at any time, Sit on My right hand, until I make thine enemies thy footstool?' Then: 'Are they not all ministering spirits, sent forth to minister for them who shall be heirs of salvation?'

What it means is that because we are Christians the angels of God are our servants. That is how the Epistle describes an angel. An angel is a 'ministering spirit', who is sent forth to serve and to minister to us who are the heirs of the 'world to come' of which he is speaking. I fear that we neglect the ministry of angels; we do not think sufficiently about it. But whether we realize it or not, there are angels who are looking after us; they are round and about us. We do not see them, but that does not matter. We do not see the most important things; we only see the things that are visible. But we are surrounded by angels; and they are appointed to look after us and to minister to us – guardian angels. I do not pretend to understand it all; I know no more than the Bible tells me – but I do know this, that His servants, the angels, are my servants. They are surrounding us all, they are looking after us, and they are manipulating things for us in a way we cannot understand. And I further know that when we come to die they will carry us to our appointed place. It is the Lord Jesus Himself who taught that fact in the parable of Dives and Lazarus in Luke 16. We are told that the rich man died and was buried. But what happened to Lazarus? He was 'carried by the angels into Abraham's bosom'. Do we realize that the angels of God are ministering unto us because we are the Bride of the Son? From their origin they have ministered to Him, and they have waited upon Him; and because of the new relationship they are now our servants, ministering to us. May God give us grace to realize that we are surrounded by such ministries, and ministrations, and by such ministers! Nothing can finally harm us; they are there, sent by Him to look after us.

But remember that we are also sharers of His problems and of His troubles and of His sufferings. He said, 'If they have persecuted Me, they will also persecute you'. He spoke of hatred also. Do we share something of His problems? are we aware of this? 'My little children', says Paul to the Galatians, 'of whom I travail in birth again until Christ be formed in you'. He felt something of the pain. But he says in a still more striking manner in Colossians 1:24: 'Who now rejoice in my sufferings for you, and fill up that which is behind of the afflictions of Christ in my flesh for His body's sake, which is the church'. The Apostle Paul was so conscious of this relationship to the Lord Jesus Christ that he said that he was filling up in his own body something that remained of the 'sufferings of Christ'. A wife worthy of the name suffers whenever her husband suffers; she suffers in her heart as she sees him suffering; she shares it with him, she bears it with him. So did the Apostle Paul make up in his own body something of what remained of the sufferings of Christ as He works out His purpose in the world, the agony of the Son of God, that will continue until the 'crowning day' arrives. The Church is the Bride of Christ. Do we as parts and portions of the body know something of this agony, this suffering, the sufferings of the Head?

Finally, we share in all the glory of His prospects. I refer to 'the world to come' once more. 'When Christ, who is our life shall appear, then shall we appear with Him in glory.' (Colossians 3:4). 'A glorious church, not having spot, or wrinkle, or any such thing; but that she might be holy and without blemish' – when He comes in His glory. If we shall have already died, we shall come with Him; if we are still alive, we shall be changed and caught up to meet Him in the air. We shall share in everlasting glory with the Son of God. This is His special prayer to the Father (John 17:24): 'Father, I will that they also whom Thou hast given Me, be with Me where I am, that they may behold My glory, which Thou hast given Me'. 'The glory which Thou gavest Me, I have given them.' We shall share it with Him through all eternity. Is there anything that is comparable to this, to being members of the body of Christ, to being, as parts of the church, the Bride of Christ?

Shame on us for our weakness, our helplessness, our complaining, our lethargy, our half-envying the world and the so-called wonderful life it has, its joy and enjoyment so-called. It is a dying world; it is an evil world; it is under condemnation; and it is going to disappear. It is already 'passing away'. But you and I have this glory to look forward to, the glory that we shall share with the Lord Jesus Christ in that great day. The glory of that 'world to come' is indescribable; and we shall live and reign with Him in it.

Having taken the church as His Bride, He bestows all that upon her. His prospects are ours, His glory is ours, all things are ours. 'The meek shall inherit the earth'. We shall reign with Him over the whole universe, we shall judge angels. You and I! Such is the Christian! Such is the Christian church as the Bride of Christ!

15
The Husband's Duties

Ephesians 5 : 25–33

In considering this statement we have seen that there are two main themes. One is the theme of the relationship between the Lord Jesus Christ and the church, and the other is the relationship between the husband and the wife. The Apostle's teaching is that we can only truly understand the relationship of husband and wife as we understand the great doctrine of Christ and the church. We have therefore been considering the doctrine of Christ and the church first, and having done so we are now in a position to begin the application of that, particularly to the husbands, though, as you notice, the Apostle is careful at the end (v. 33) to consider it also from the aspect and the standpoint of the wife. The application of the doctrine is introduced by the terms 'even as' and 'so'. 'Husbands, love your wives *even as*' – and then at the end, 'Nevertheless let every one of you in particular *so* love his wife *even* as himself.' In other words, he is working out the comparison, which he has unfolded before us, of the relationship of Christ to the church in terms of the relationship of the husband to the wife.

As we come, then, to the application it seems to me that the best way of handling it is to divide it into two main sections. The first is that in which certain principles are taught with respect to husbands and their wives. Then, having laid down the general principles, we can move on to the second, which is the detailed practical application of the principles to the concrete situation.

The general principles, as I see them, are these. First, we must realize in connection with marriage, as indeed with everything else in the Christian life, that the secret of success is to think and to understand. That is surely obvious, on the very surface of the passage. Nothing happens automatically in the Christian life. That is a very profound principle, for I believe that most of our troubles arise from the fact that we tend to assume that they do happen automatically. We persist in holding on to a semi-magical notion of regeneration which teaches that, because of what has happened to us, the rest of the story is, quite simply, 'they all lived happily ever after'. But of course we know that that is not true. There are problems in the Christian life; and it is because so many do not realize that it is not something that works automatically, that they get into trouble and into difficulties. Obviously the antidote to that is to think, to have an understanding, to reason the thing out thoroughly. The world does not do that. The trouble with the world, ultimately, according to the teaching of the Bible, is that it does not think. If only people thought, most of their problems would be solved.

Take the problem of war for instance. War is something which is inherently ridiculous; it is insane. Why then do people fight? The answer is, because they do not think. They act instinctively, they are governed by primitive instincts such as desire and greed, anger, and so on; and they hit before they think. If only they all stopped to think, there would be no more war. The fallacy of the humanist is, of course, that he believes that all you have to do therefore is to tell people to think. But as long as they are sinners they will not think. These elemental forces are so much stronger than the rational forces that 'man in sin' is always irrational.

When we become Christians we still need to enforce this self-same principle. Even the Christian does not think automatically; he has to be taught to think – hence these New Testament epistles. Why were they ever written? If a man who becomes a Christian automatically does the right thing, why did the Apostle ever have to write these epistles? Or if you can receive your sanctification as one act, one blessing, why were these epistles ever written? Here they are, full of reason, full of argument, full of demonstrations, full of analogies and comparisons. Why? In order to teach us how to think, in order to teach us how to work these things out, and how to gain understanding.

Thinking is essential, as the Apostle shows, in connection with this whole subject of marriage. The world views marriage in the following way. It more or less first of all takes certain great things for granted. It relies upon what it calls 'love', it relies upon

[209]

feelings. Two people say that they have 'fallen in love' with each another, and on the strength of that they get married. They do not stop to think and to ask questions; to do so is very exceptional. They are moved and animated and carried away by the feeling that everything is bound to go well, that their happiness is certain to last and can never fail. All this is encouraged by the popular literature and by the films shown in cinemas and in the home on the television set. But then you read the newspapers and their reports and you find that it does fail. Why does it fail? The answer is, because they have never thought the matter through; and therefore it cannot stand up to the tests and the stresses and the strains that must inevitably come as life is lived from day to day with its weary round and its physical tiredness and the many other things that produce difficulties. And it is because such people have never thought the thing through that they have nothing to fall back upon. They have acted on a feeling, on an impulse; they have acted emotionally. The mind has scarcely come in at all, with the result that when they are confronted by difficulties they have no arguments to fall back upon. They do not know what to do; everything seems to have gone; and so they panic and sue for a divorce immediately; and many repeat the same process time and again. The whole cause of the trouble is an absence of understanding, a lack of thought.

When you consider the Christian position you find the main difference to be this – that the Christian is exhorted to think and to understand, and is given a basis on which he can do so. That is the meaning and purpose of this teaching which is provided for us; so we are left without excuse if we neglect it. The world has no such teaching, but we are no longer in that position. So the first thing we are reminded of by this paragraph is that we must think. We are even told how to do so, and it is put before us in detail. That is the first principle.

The second principle is that as Christians our conception of marriage must be positive. The danger is that we should think of marriage amongst Christians as essentially the same as it is with everybody else, the only difference being that these two people happen to be Christians whereas the others are not. Now if that is still our conception of marriage then we have considered this great paragraph entirely in vain. Christian marriage, the Christian view of marriage, is something that is essentially different from all other

[210]

views. That is, surely, what has been emerging as we have worked our way through this paragraph.

Here we get a view of marriage which is not possible but within the Christian faith; it is lifted up to the position of the relationship between the Lord Jesus Christ and the church. So the Christian's attitude towards marriage is always a positive one, and he should always be straining after this ideal. The Christian's view must not be negative in the sense that, because certain new factors have entered in, therefore this marriage ought to last, whereas the other one is not likely to do so. That is purely negative. It is not merely that we avoid certain things that are true of the others; we must have this ideal, positive conception of marriage. It is something that we must always think of in terms of the relationship of the Lord Jesus Christ and the church. We have to learn to test ourselves constantly by asking the question: Does my married life really correspond to that relationship? Is it manifesting it? Is it being governed by it? In other words, in the Christian position we do not stop thinking about these things when we have been married a few months. We go on thinking, and we think more and more, and the more Christian we become and the more we grow in grace, the more we think about our marriage, and the more we are concerned that it should conform to this heavenly pattern, to this glorious ideal of the relationship between the Lord Jesus Christ and the church. This is something which it is difficult to put into words. What I am trying to convey is that the great difference between the marriage of Christians and the marriage of non-Christians should be that in the case of the Christians the marriage becomes progressively more wonderful, more glorious, as it conforms to, and attains to the ideal increasingly. We all, surely, see the significance of that as we apply it to what is so commonly true of marriage, not only among non-Christians but, alas, among Christians also. The Christian conception of marriage is one which continues to grow and develop and increase.

My third and last general principle is one that has come out in the whole of the exposition – that the real cause of failure, ultimately, in marriage is always self, and the various manifestations of self. Of course that is the cause of trouble everywhere and in every realm. Self and selfishness are the greatest disrupting forces in the world. All the major problems confronting the world, whether you look at the matter from the standpoint of nations and statesmen, or from the standpoint of industry and social conditions, or from any other standpoint – all these troubles ultimately come back to self, to 'my rights', to 'what I want', and to 'who is he'? or 'who is she'? Self, with its horrid manifestations, always leads to trouble, because if two 'selfs' come into opposition there is bound to be a clash. Self always wants everything for it-self. That is true of my self, but it is equally true of your self. You at once have two autonomous powers, each deriving from self, and a clash is inevitable. Such clashes occur at every level, from two people right up to great communities and empires and nations.

The apostle's teaching in the verses under consideration is designed to show us how to avoid the calamities that result from self. That is why I was at such pains to emphasize verse 21 before we began to consider the question of marriage. It is the key to the entire paragraph – 'Submitting yourselves one to another in the fear of God'. That is the basic principle, and it is to be true of all members of the Christian church. Whether married or unmarried, we are all to be submitting ourselves one to the other in the fear of God. Then the Apostle goes on to apply the principle to the particular case of man and woman, husband and wife, and he has made it so plain and clear that surely no-one can miss it. What is the essential thing about marriage? He says, it is this unity – these two, these twain, have become one flesh. So you must stop thinking of them as two, they have become one. Therefore any tendency to assert self at once conflicts with the fundamental conception of marriage. In marriage, says the Apostle, it should be unthinkable for such a conflict to arise, for to think of these two as two is to deny the basic principle of marriage, which is that they are one. 'These two shall be one flesh'. The wife is 'the body' of the husband, even as the church is the body of Christ – and so on. So here we have, above everywhere else, the final denunciation of self and all its horrid manifestations; and we are shown the one and only way whereby we can finally be delivered from it.

Those are the three general principles which, in marriage, underlie the practical application of the doctrine of the relationship of the Lord Jesus Christ to the church. Now the husband is to be governed by these principles. How does this work out in practice? First of all, the husband must realize that his wife is a part of himself. He will not feel this instinctively; he has to be taught it; and the Bible in all its parts teaches it. In other words, the husband must understand that he and his wife are not two: they are one. The Apostle keeps on repeating that: 'So ought men to love their wives as their own bodies'. 'He that loveth his wife loveth himself'; 'they two shall be one flesh'. 'We are members of His body, of His flesh, and of His bones'. That is all true of our relationship to the Lord, it is true also in this other relationship.

I would therefore put it in this way, that it is not sufficient for us even to regard our wives as partners. They are partners, but they are more than partners. You can have two men in business who are partners, but that is not the analogy. The analogy goes higher than that. It is not a question of partnership, though it includes that idea. There is another phrase that is often used – at least, it used to be common – which puts it so much better, and which seems to me to be an unconscious statement of the Christian teaching. It is the expression used by men when they refer to their wives as 'my better half'. Now that is exactly right. She is not a partner, she is the other half of the man. 'They two shall be one flesh'. 'My better half'. The very word 'half' puts the whole case which the Apostle elaborates here. We are not dealing with two units, two entities, but dealing with two halves of one – 'They two shall be one flesh'. Therefore, in the light of this, the husband must no longer think singly or individually. That should be quite impossible in marriage, says the Apostle, because, 'He that loveth his wife loveth himself'. He is in a sense not loving somebody else, he is loving himself. Such is the difference that marriage makes.

On the practical level, therefore, the whole of the husband's thinking must include his wife also. He must never think of himself in isolation or in detachment. The moment he does so he has broken the most fundamental principle of marriage. Everybody sees it when it happens on the physical level, but the real damage is done before that, on the intellectual and the spiritual level. In a sense, the moment a man thinks of himself in isolation he has broken the marriage. And he has no right to do that! There is a sense in which he cannot do it, because the wife is a part of himself. But if it happens he is certain to inflict grievous damage on his wife; and it is a damage in which he himself will be involved because she is a part of him. He is therefore even acting against himself, did he but realize it. His thinking, therefore, must never be personal in the sense of being individualistic. He is only the half, and what he does involves of necessity the other half. The same applies to his desires. He must never have any desire for himself alone. He is no longer one man, he is no longer free in that sense; his wife is involved in all his desires. It is his business therefore to see that he is always fully alive to these considerations. He must never think of his wife, in other words, as an addition. Still less – I am sorry that I have to use such an expression – as an encumbrance; but there are many who do so.

To sum it up, this is a great commandment to married men never to be selfish. Neither must the wife be selfish, of course. Everything applies on the other side, but here we are dealing particularly with husbands. We have already seen that the wife is to submit herself. In doing so she has acted on the same principle; this is now the husband's side of the matter. He must therefore deliberately remind himself constantly of what is true of him in this married state, and that must govern and control all his thinking, all his wishing, all his desiring, indeed the totality of his life and activity.

But we can go further and put this more strongly. Verse 28 closes with the words, 'He that loveth his wife loveth himself'; but we remember that the Apostle, in describing the relationship between the Lord and the church, has used the analogy of the body. 'So', he further says, in the same verse, 'So ought men to love their wives as their own bodies'. Then he elaborates it in verse 29: 'For no man ever yet hated his own flesh; but nourisheth and cherisheth it, even as the Lord the church'. Here, then, is the teaching – that we not only have to realize that the husband and wife are one, but the husband must realize that the wife is actually a part of himself according to this analogy of the body. A man's attitude to his wife, says the Apostle, should be his attitude, as it were, to his body. That is the analogy – and it is more than an analogy. We have already considered the matter as it is taught at the end of Genesis chapter 2. The woman was originally taken out of the man. There we have the proof of the fact that she is a part of the man, and that describes the characteristic of the unity. The man therefore is told this: 'So ought men to love their wives as their own body'. Now that little word 'as' is a most important and vital one, because we can easily misunderstand it. Paul does not say, 'So ought men to love their wives in the same way as they love their bodies'. That is not the meaning. The meaning is, 'So ought men to love their wives because they are their own bodies'.

A man loves his wife as his body – that is what he is saying. Not 'as' he loves his body so must he love his wife. No! a man must love his wife as his body, as a part of himself. As Eve was a part of Adam, taken out of his side, so the wife is to the man, because she is a part of him.

I am stressing this for the reason which the Apostle brings out clearly, namely, to show that there is this element of indissolubility about marriage, which, as I understand the biblical teaching, can only be broken by adultery. But what we are concerned to say now, is that the Apostle puts it in this form in order that a husband may see that he cannot detach himself from his wife. You cannot detach yourself from your body, so you cannot detach yourself from your wife. She is a part of you, says the Apostle, so remember that always. You cannot live in isolation, you cannot live in detachment. If you realize that, there will be no danger of your thinking in detachment, no danger of your wishing and willing and desiring any detachment. Still less can there be any antagonism or hatred. Notice how he puts it: 'No man', he says, to ridicule the thing, 'no man ever yet hated his own flesh but nourisheth and cherisheth it, even as the Lord the church'. So any element of hatred between husband and wife is sheer madness; it shows that the man has no conception at all as to what marriage means. 'No man hated his own flesh' – but his wife is his own flesh, she is his body; so he is to love his wife as his own body.

What does this lead to in practice? Here I come to very detailed teaching which is needed by all, Christian people as well as others. God knows, we all have failed; we all have sinned by failing to understand this teaching and to apply it in detail. The principle is that the wife is, as it were, the body of the man. So what his body is to his personality his wife should be to him. Out of that comes the Apostle's detailed teaching. How is a man to treat his wife? Let me give some negatives first. He is not to abuse her. It is possible for a man to abuse his body, and many men do abuse their bodies – by eating too much, by drinking too much, and in various other ways. That is to abuse the body, to maltreat it, to be unkind to it. Now, says the Apostle, a man who does that is a fool, because if a man maltreats his body, and abuses it, he himself is going to suffer. You cannot detach yourself from your body; and if you think you can, and abuse your body, you will be the one to suffer. Your mind will suffer, your heart will suffer, the whole of your life will suffer. You may say, 'I do not care about my body, I am living a life of the intellect'; but if you keep on doing that you will soon find that you no longer have the intellect that you once had, and you will not be able to think as you once did. If you abuse your body, you are the one who is going to suffer. Not only the body, but you yourself will suffer as well. It is exactly the same in the married relationship. If a man abuses his wife he will suffer as well as the wife. So, apart from the inherent wrongfulness, the man is a fool. If a man abuses his wife there is going to be a breakdown not only in the wife but also in the man, and in the relationship between the two. Surely this is what is happening so commonly in the world today. It should be unthinkable that a Christian man should abuse his wife.

But not only should the husband not abuse his wife, in the second place, he should not neglect her. Come back again to the analogy of the body. A man can neglect his body. It often happens, and again it always leads to trouble. To neglect the body is bad, it is foolish, it is wrong. Man has been so constituted that he is body, mind and spirit, and the three are in intimate relationship one with another. We are all surely aware of this. Take an example in terms of the frailty of the body. If I am suffering from laryngitis I cannot preach, though I may want to do so. I may be full of ideas, and of a desire to preach, but if my throat is inflamed I cannot speak. And it is so with the whole of the body. If you neglect the body you yourself will suffer for it. Many a man has done that, many a scholar has done that, and through neglect of the body his work has suffered. That is because of the essential unity between these parts of our personalities.

It is exactly the same in the married relationship, says the Apostle. How much trouble is caused in the realm of marriage simply because of neglect! Very recently there has been evidence in the papers by medical men who have reported that large numbers of wives today have been driven to chain smoking. Why? Simply because they have been neglected by their husbands. The husbands spend their nights out at sports, or in their public house, or playing games with their friends; and the poor wife is left at home with the children and the work. The husband comes home at night just in time to go to bed and to sleep; and he gets up and goes out in the morning. Neglect of the wife is leading to these nervous conditions that reveal themselves in excessive smoking and other manifestations of nervous tension. It is lamentable that a man should get married and then proceed to neglect his wife. In other words, here is a man who has married, but who in essential matters goes on living as if he were still a bachelor. He is still living his own detached life, he still spends his time with his men friends.

I could elaborate on this very easily, but the facts are so familiar that it is unnecessary. But I have a feeling that I detect a tendency even in Christian circles, and even in evangelical circles, to forget this particular point. A married man must no longer act as if he were a single man; his wife should be involved in everything. I recently received an invitation to a social occasion in connection with some evangelical organization; but the invitation was addressed to me only, and not to my wife also. I automatically refused it; as I always do when that kind of thing happens. This was an instance of an evangelical organization that is obviously not thinking clearly about these matters. I venture to lay it down as a rule that a Christian man should not accept an invitation to a social occasion without his wife. There is irreparable damage done to many marriages because men meet alone in their clubs without their wives. That is wrong, because it is a denial of first principles. Man and wife should do things together. Of course, the man in his business has to be alone, and there are other occasions when he has to be alone; but if it is a social occasion, something into which a wife can enter, she should enter, and it is the business of the husband to see to it that she does enter. I suggest that all Christian husbands should automatically refuse every such invitation which comes to them alone and does not include their wives.

But there is another aspect of this matter that at times causes me great concern. I am constantly hearing of what sometimes has been called 'evangelical widows'. The expression means that the husband of that particular type of woman is a man who is out every night at some meeting or other. His explanation, indeed his argument, is that he is engaged in good Christian work; but he seems to forget that he is a married man. At the other extreme, of course, there is the kind of Christian who does nothing, but who just indulges himself and his laziness, and spends all his time at home. Both extremes are wrong always; but at the moment I am condemning this particular extreme – the case of the man who is so busy with Christian work that he neglects his wife. I have known many cases of this. I was told of one recently in the North of

England – the case of a man who was out speaking at meetings, organizing this and that, every night. The man who told me confessed that he had been tending to do the same thing himself, but that suddenly he had been awakened when he had met the wife of this other man about whom everybody was talking. He said that the poor little woman appeared like a slave; she looked exhausted, weary, tired, neglected and unhappy, and sick at heart. The conduct of such a husband is grievously sinful. Though it is done in the name of active Christian work, a man cannot and must not contract out of his married relationship in that way, because the wife is a part of him – his 'better half', not his slave. Christian husbands must therefore examine themselves in this matter. A home is not a dormitory where a man returns to sleep. No! there is to be this active, ideal, positive relationship; and we must ever be holding it in the forefront of our mind. A man therefore must seek wisdom from God to know how to divide himself up in this respect. But I care not what a man is; if he is a married man, he must not behave as a single man, even in connection with Christian work, because in so doing he is denying the very teaching of the Gospel which he claims to be preaching. There can be untold selfishness just at that point. This generally happens, I know, as the result of nothing worse than thoughtlessness; but thoughtlessness generally leads to selfishness. In any case a Christian should not be guilty of thoughtlessness.

So I move on to the third practical outworking of the teaching. The husband must not abuse his wife, he must not neglect his wife, and, thirdly, he must never take her for granted. The positive element must always be there. A man's wife is not just his housekeeper; there is this positive element. How can that best be brought out? Let me take the Apostle's own terms. He puts it like this: 'So ought men to love their wives as their own bodies. He that loveth his wife loveth himself. No man ever yet hated his own flesh; but' – What? 'Nourisheth and cherisheth it even as the Lord the church'. You remember how, when we considered these words, we were amazed and staggered at the way in which the Lord nourishes and cherishes us. But that is the way in which a husband should behave towards his wife. 'Nourisheth and cherisheth'. Again, you cannot do this without thinking.

Once more, this can be worked out in terms of the analogy that a man does not hate his own body, but nourishes it and cherishes it.

How does he do so? We can divide it up simply thus: First of all, there is the question of diet. A man has to think about his diet, about his food. He has to take sufficient nourishment, he has to take it regularly, and so on. All that must be worked out in terms of husband and wife. The man should be thinking of what will help his wife, what will strengthen his wife. As we take our food we not only think in terms of calories, or protein, fat, and carbo-hydrate; we are not purely scientific, are we? Another element comes into this question of food. We are influenced also by what appeals to the palate, by what gives us pleasure and enjoyment. So ought the husband to treat his wife. He should be thinking of what pleases her, what gives her pleasure, what she likes, what she enjoys. Of course, before he got married he went out of his way to do this; but then after he gets married he often stops doing so. Is not that the difficulty? Very well, says the Apostle, you must not stop, you must go on thinking; and as you are a Christian, you should engage in thinking more and more, not less and less. That is his argument. Are we not all condemned? But this is the apostolic teaching, the New Testament teaching. Diet – consider her whole personality and her soul. There has to be this active thought about the development of the wife, and her life, in this amazing relationship which God Himself has established.

Again, there is the question of exercise. The analogy of the body suggests that at once. Exercise for the body is essential; exercise is equally essential in the married relationship. It can mean as simple a thing as this – just talking. Alas, I have known trouble in mar-riages so often, simply because of an absence of conversation. We all know how much there is to be said by way of excuse. A man is tired, he has been at his work or his office all day, and he comes home weary and tired, and wants rest and peace. Yes, but the same thing is also true of his wife, with the difference that perhaps she has been alone all day, or only had the society of little children. Whether we feel like it or not we must talk. The wife needs exer-cise in this sense. Tell her about your business, about your worries, about your affairs; bring her into it. She is your body, she is a part of you, so allow her to speak concerning it. Consult her, let her bring her understanding to bear. She is a part of your life, so bring her into the whole of your life. Make yourself talk. In other words, one has to force oneself to think. I repeat once more that I know all the excuses, and how difficult it often can be; but let me put it like this – I think it is a fair argument. This man was equally tired and working equally hard before he got married; but in the days before marriage, whatever he had been doing, he was most anxious to talk to his fiancée and to bring her into everything. Why should that stop when they get married? It should not stop, says the Apostle. The husband and wife are one. Look at her, and consider her as you do your body, and remember this element of exercise. Bring her into everything deliberately. It will be wonderful for her, for her development; and it will be good for you yourself, because the whole marriage will grow and develop as you do so.

And that brings us to the fourth point, which is the element of protection. Here is this body, it needs food, it needs exercise; but in addition every man has to learn to understand his own body. The Apostle works out the argument. The Apostle Peter, you remember, puts it like this. He tells the husband to remember that his wife is 'the weaker vessel'. This means that these bodies of ours are subject to certain things. We are all different even in a physical sense. Some of us are subject, perhaps, to feeling the cold, or subject to chills in a way that does not seem to worry other men. Some of us are so constituted that we have these minor problems; and we are subject to odd infections and various other things that come to try us. What does a wise man do? He takes great care about such things; he puts on a heavy overcoat in winter, he may put on a scarf; and he refrains from doing certain things. He is protecting himself and his weak constitution against some of the hazards that come to meet us in life. 'So ought men to love their wives'. Have you discovered that your wife has some peculiar temperamental weakness? Have you discovered that she has certain special characteristics? Is she nervous and apprehensive; or is she too outspoken? It does not matter what it is in particular; she has certain characteristics which are, in a sense, weaknesses. What is your reaction to them? Are you irritated, or annoyed? And do you tend to condemn them and to dismiss them? Act as you do with your body, says the Apostle. Protect her against them, guard her against them. If your wife happens to have been born with that worrying temperament, well, save her from it, protect her. Do everything you can to safeguard her from the weaknesses and the infirmities and the frailties; as you do so for your body, do so for your wife.

Then, of course, there are great infections that come – a wave of influenza, fevers, things that kill people by the thousand. Corresponding things come also in the married life – trials, troubles, tribulations, which are going to test the marriage to the very limit.

What do we do about these? Once more, what do you do with your body when you get that kind of illness, when you get that attack of influenza with a raging temperature? The answer is that you put yourself to bed, with a hot-water bottle; and you put yourself on the appropriate diet, and so on. You do everything you can to treat the fever and to help your body to resist it. 'So ought men to love their wives as their own bodies'. If there is some peculiar, exceptional trial or anxiety or problem, something that tests your wife to the uttermost, then, I say, the husband is to go out of his way to protect his wife and to help her and aid her. She is 'the weaker vessel'.

That brings us to the last point. You try to protect your body against infections by having various inoculations. Apply all that to the married state. Do everything you can to build up the resistance, to prepare your wife to face the hazards of life. You have to build her up. Do not do everything yourself, as it were; but build her up so that she will be able to act also; so that if you are taken away by death she is not left stranded. We have to think out all these things in detail exactly as with the care of the body. And if an illness comes, take extra care, give the appropriate medicaments, go out of your way to do those extra things which will promote and produce the restoration of health and vigour and happiness.

We leave it at that. But, there, we have been looking at one big principle which is most important. A man has to love his wife 'even as' – because she is – his own body. 'No man ever yet hated his own flesh; but nourisheth and cherisheth it, even as the Lord the church'. 'Husbands, love your wives, even as Christ also loved the church'.

16
Transformed Relationships

Ephesians 5:25–33

We come to our final consideration of this most important and extraordinary statement. The Apostle is dealing primarily with the duty of husbands towards their wives, though in the last verse, you notice, he again reverts to the duty of wives towards their husbands, in order that he may present his teaching concerning marriage as a whole and in a complete form. In applying all this we have seen that the great thing is to understand the teaching. The Christian, of all people, should be one who thinks and reasons, who employs his mind. There is nothing magical about the Christian life. The great act of regeneration is the operation of God, but the moment we receive life we are able to think and to reason and to use our understanding. So all these New Testament Epistles are addressed to the understanding. At the beginning of this very Epistle the Apostle has prayed 'that the eyes of your understanding might be enlightened' by the Holy Spirit. So we have found that what the Apostle does here is to set out this great doctrine of Christ and the church and then say, 'Even so, just like that'.

There are a few practical points which must be dealt with in order that our exposition may be complete. There are certain practical injunctions which the Apostle gives here, and they are all related to this great analogy which he uses. The great vital principle is that unity. What we have to grasp is the essential unity between the husband and wife – 'these two shall be made (or become) one flesh'. This unity is comparable to the unity between a man and his own body, and also to the mystical union between Christ and the church.

[222]

Unity is the central principle in marriage; and it is because so many people in this modern world have never had any conception of what is involved in marriage, from the standpoint of unity, that they are riding so loosely to it and breaking their vows and pledges, so much so that divorce has become one of the major problems of our age. They have never caught sight of this unity; they still think in terms of their individuality, and so you have two people asserting their rights, and therefore you get clashes and discord and separation. The answer to all that, says Paul, is to understand this great principle of unity.

The Apostle has worked that out in terms of the body, but now he puts it very explicitly by reminding us again of what is said in the second chapter of Genesis in connection with the making of Eve out of Adam, that Adam might have an 'help meet'. The moment God made Eve, in order that the man and the woman might enter into this married state, the statement was made that a man should leave his father and mother and should be joined unto his wife, and 'they shall be one flesh'. The Apostle quotes the very words in verse 21: 'For this cause shall a man leave his father and mother, and shall be joined unto his wife, and they two shall be one flesh'. This is a command which is given to the man who is becoming a husband. He has to leave his father and mother. Why has he to do so? Because of this new unity that is coming into being between him and his wife. 'For this cause' says the Apostle. What is that cause? He has just told us – 'We are members of his body, of his flesh, and of his bones'. That is the relationship of husband and wife, and because of that – 'for this cause' – a man must leave his father and mother in order that he may thus be joined to his wife.

This is a most important point. It is, in a way, the final proof of the unity that exists in true marriage, and it is an external indication of the unity. The Apostle is saying, in other words, that when a man gets married he enters into a new unity that breaks former relationships. He is no longer to be bound and held by the former relationships because he is entering into a new and into a more intimate relationship of unity. Until he got married the man's chief loyalty was to his father and mother; but that is no longer the case; he has now to 'leave his father and mother' and enter into this new relationship. That is a staggering statement, especially in view of the fact that there is so much teaching in the Scripture

[223]

about the relationship of parents and children. The family is the fundamental unit in life, and so the Apostle will go on in the next chapter to say, 'Children, obey your parents in the Lord; for this is right'. But that statement must be taken in the light of this, that when a man gets married he is no longer a child in that sense. He leaves his father and mother, he is now entering into a new unity. He comes out of where he was in order that he may enter into this new unity, this new relationship. He is now the head of a new unit, the head of a new family.

It is very largely at this point that tensions tend to arise most acutely, and difficulties occur, in the married relationship. Obviously in all these matters the biblical statements must be taken in their context, and with reason. We must never become legalistic about these things. Take this statement about a man 'leaving his father and mother'. That does not mean, obviously, that he should never have anything to do with them again. The term is 'let him leave', so we must consider the meaning of 'to leave'. It is a very practical matter, of course, but the important thing is the spiritual understanding of what is involved. Sometimes this is treated, as I say, in a legalistic way, and people become harsh and almost unkind to the father and the mother. That is not the Apostle's teaching. But he is concerned about the principle, and this is the thing to which we must pay chief attention. In practice it means that this man has to regard himself henceforth, not primarily as a child of his parents, but as the husband of his wife. All his life he has been regarding himself as the child of his parents, and rightly so. 'Honour thy father and thy mother' is one of the Ten Commandments. But now he has to make a great mental adjustment; he has to think matters through, to assume new responsibilities, and to begin to live in a new way. He is no longer in a position of subservience, he now has become the head of a new family. He must regard himself as such, and he must comport himself as such. The leaving of the father and the mother in reality means this, that he must not allow his father and mother to control him as they have always done hitherto. This is the point at which difficulties arise. For twenty, twenty-five, thirty years, that old relationship has been in existence – father and mother, child. It has become a habit, and one thinks instinctively along those lines. But now this man is married. It is difficult for him – it is even more difficult perhaps for his father and mother – to realize the new situation that has come into being; but the teaching here is that the man must leave his father and mother that he may be joined to his wife. He has to assert and to safeguard his new status, and, as I say, defend it against any interference on the part of his parents. And in his own behaviour, he must no longer act simply and only as he did before, because he is now joined to his wife. He is no longer what he was before. He is what he was before – plus, and that plus creates the difference between the old and the new relationship.

Such is the meaning of this expression, 'leave his father and mother'; he has to assert the new position which has come into being as the result of his marriage. And, of course, when you look at it from the standpoint of the father and mother the situation should be equally clear. They must re-adjust themselves even as their son does. They have to realize that their son's first loyalty now is to his wife, and that he is a very poor specimen of manhood, a very poor husband, and, ultimately, a very poor son if he fails to show that loyalty. They must not interfere in this new married life. They have always commanded their son in the past in various ways, and it was right that they should do so. They must not do so any longer; they must recognize that something entirely new has emerged, and that they must not think of their son any longer simply as their son. He is now married, a new unity has been created, and whatever they do to him they do to his wife at the same time. So obviously they cannot treat him as they treated him formerly. All that is included in this idea of a man leaving his father and his mother in order that he may become joined to his wife. It is really the essence of the Apostle's teaching about marriage that all parties involved have to realize that a new unity has come into being. It was not there before, but it is there now. The new husband has to realize that he is not what he was; the new wife has to realize that she also is not what she was in her relationship to her parents. The parents on both sides have to realize that they are not what they were before. Everything is different. There has to be a re-adjustment all along the line because of the new unity that has come into existence as the result of a marriage. 'For this cause shall a man leave his father and mother.'

According to biblical teaching there is nothing more drastic that can happen than this double action – 'leaving' and 'joining'. The family is the fundamental unit of our earthly life, yet though the man is still the son of his parents, and though, of course, he still belongs in that general sense to his family, the important thing about him is that he is now the head of a new family, and he must be treated with the dignity that corresponds to the new status. He must think of himself in this way; he must not revert to thinking of himself as he was before; and he must not allow his parents to think of him in that way. 'A man shall leave his father and his mother, and shall be joined unto his wife, and they two shall be one flesh'. The moment we realize this, marriage becomes one of the most momentous, indeed the most momentous thing that ever happens in life. Hence, when you are at a marriage service you should realize that this new unity is coming into being, and that you have to re-adjust your thinking, and henceforth think of the bride and the bridegroom in this new relationship. This new married state now has precedence over every other human relationship. A man leaves his father and mother; so does his wife; and it is as this principle is grasped and put into operation that you get the ideal married state that is outlined here, and you see the difference between Christian and non-Christian marriage. That, then, is the first practical injunction that the Apostle gives us.

The second is – 'Nevertheless let every one of you in particular so love his wife, even as himself'. In a sense we have already dealt with the point which the Apostle is making, as we were dealing with the man in his relationship to his body, and in regard to his thoughts about his wife. The best comment on the matter is that found in the Epistle to the Colossians, chapter three, verse nineteen, where the Apostle says, 'Husbands, love your wives, and be not bitter against them'. The negative there helps us to understand the positive in this last verse in the fifth chapter of the Epistle to the Ephesians. The great danger obviously is for the husband to domineer. The emphasis is upon the fact that he is the head, he is the leader, he is in the position of responsibility. That is how God established it at the beginning. So the danger confronting the man always, as the Apostle puts it there, is 'to be bitter', which means 'to be harsh'. The antidote is, 'Husbands, let every one of you in particular so love his wife, even as himself'. You are not harsh to yourself, therefore, do not be harsh to your wife, do not be crushing, do not be domineering.

This statement, when it was written by the Apostle, was one of the most astounding that had ever been put on paper. When we read of the pagan view of marriage, and especially the typical attitude of husbands towards wives – and, indeed, not only pagan, but also what you read of in the Old Testament – we see how revolutionary and transforming the teaching is. Wives were virtually nothing but slaves. The whole notion of polygamy conveys that idea. There is the heroic illustration of women rebelling against that view in the first chapter of the book of Esther, in the case of Vashti, the wife of Ahasuerus. But that was very exceptional. The whole notion was really one of slavery, and so husbands were generally guilty of this harshness, this domineering attitude. The wife was but a vassal, a chattel, as it were. But at once when the Christian message comes in the whole idea is entirely transformed and changed. It is in matters like this that the Christian faith staggered and conquered the ancient world in the first century. Nothing like this had ever been taught before. It was partly as the result of Christian people living this new kind of life that the Gospel of our Lord and Saviour spread in that ancient world. This is how Christians testify to the truth of the Gospel. The idea that Christians testify by getting up and speaking in a meeting is not found much in the New Testament, if at all. The testimony was borne in their ordinary daily lives. For a man to speak kindly and affectionately to his wife was something that was almost unheard of; and it was as they saw this that people began to ask, What is this? And especially when they saw it in a man who had been very different as a pagan. A new tenderness had come into human life.

True marriage is an illustration of the New Testament teaching about love; it is what you find in 1 Corinthians 13 being put into practice in the married relationship. It was introduced in the eighteenth verse, which is the key to it all: 'Be not drunk with wine, wherein is excess; but be filled with the Spirit'. If you are filled with the Spirit you will be different in every realm and relationship. The Apostle is here giving us one illustration of it – the home. That is the place where it should be seen if anywhere; that is the place to judge a man and a woman – in the home, what they are there. Now, says the Apostle, let it be known in the home that you are filled with the Spirit, so that anybody who comes to visit you will be staggered, will be taken aback by this, and ask, What is this? There is no greater recommendation to the truth and power of the Christian faith than a Christian husband and wife, a Christian marriage, and a Christian home. That helped to revolutionize the ancient world. Remember, then, the second injunction given to the husband. He is given this position of dignity and of leadership and of headship; and if he understands what it means he will never abuse it, he will never misuse it, by being harsh or dictatorial or unkind or unfair. To be guilty of such behaviour is a denial of the marriage principle, and means that there is an absence of the Spirit.

But let us look at the other side. The third injunction is, 'and the wife see that she reverence her husband'. The Apostle used a very striking word here. It is rightly translated in the Authorized Version as 'reverence'; but the word really means 'fear'. 'And the wife see that she fears her husband'. But we must remember that there are different types of fear. There is a fear, as John reminds us in his first Epistle (chapter 4) 'that hath torment'. That is not the fear the Apostle speaks of here; he speaks of 'reverential' fear. What it really means is 'deference'. 'Wives, see that you treat your husbands with deference', 'with reverential obedience'. Here, again, is an idea the Apostle has already introduced when he was dealing with the wives. He says, 'Wives, submit yourselves unto your own husbands, as unto the Lord. For the husband is the head of the wife, even as Christ is the head of the church: and he is the saviour of the body. Therefore as the church is subject unto Christ, so let the wives be to their own husbands in everything.' He comes back to it again here, 'Let the wife see that she treats her husband with due deference, with reverential obedience'.

Perhaps the best commentary on this is found in the first Epistle of Peter, chapter 3 and verse 6, where Peter is in his own way dealing with exactly the same subject. Peter goes back to the great example and pattern of this particular teaching. He puts it in this form: 'Likewise, ye wives, be in subjection to your own husbands' – the same idea, 'deference' – 'that if any obey not the Word, they also may without the Word be won by the conversation of the wives'. Peter here introduces a slightly different matter, to which I will refer in a moment. However, in order to impress this upon the wives, he proceeds to say, 'For after this manner in the old time the holy women also, who trusted in God, adorned themselves, being in subjection unto their own husbands'. Then in the sixth verse, 'Even as Sara obeyed Abraham, calling him lord: whose daughters ye are, as long as ye do well, and are not afraid with any amazement'. Being interpreted, it means something

[228]

like this. The wife is to treat her husband with deference; in other words, she is to recognize this biblical and Christian view of marriage, she is to regard the husband as her head, the head of this new unit. They are both one, but there is a head to the unit, as there is a head to our body, as Christ is the Head of the church. As the husband is the head, the wife is to treat him with the deference that is becoming in one who realizes that relationship. So what it means for the wife is that the deference which she formerly paid primarily to her parents she is now to pay to her husband. Such is the meaning of the injunction in Psalm 45, verse 10, which puts it like this: 'Forget also thine own people, and thy father's house'. That was addressed prophetically to the Christian church; that is what she is to do when she becomes joined to her heavenly Bridegroom; but it is also applicable to the case of the wife in the marriage relationship. 'Forget thine own people, and thy father's house'. As the man is commanded to leave his father and his mother, the wife is to forget her own people and her father's house. I repeat again, that you have to use common sense in interpreting words such as these. She is not to forget in an absolute sense, but she is to forget in this sense, that she is no longer to be controlled by her parents. The man is not to be controlled by his parents, and the wife is not to be controlled by her parents.

It may occur to someone to ask this question: Why, in connection with the plain teaching about marriage, are we told that the man is to leave his father and mother and to be joined unto his wife, while there is no corresponding statement about the woman either in Genesis chapter 2, or in Ephesians chapter 5? The answer, it seems to me, is quite simple. The woman is always in this position of paying deference. The man was in this position until he got married; but from that point onwards he becomes the head. The women pays deference to her parents; she gets married, and now she pays deference to her husband. She is always in the position of paying the deference, she is never the head. But the man who formerly was a child and a son and paid deference now becomes the head and receives this deference from his wife. As we work these things out in detail, is it not obvious that it is because people have no conception of this teaching that there is so much trouble in marriages, and so many breakdowns?

There is nothing that is so fatal to a marriage as that either partner should be paying deference to a third party. In so doing they are breaking the unity, they are failing to realize the fact of this new unit and the headship of the man in the new unit. So the wife must see to it that she pays this reverential deference to her husband. She has to make a mental and spiritual adjustment as had her husband also in his case. She does not receive her instructions any longer from parents; she does not submit herself to them, she submits herself to her husband. She still maintains the relationship of daughter, of course; but she must see to it that her own attitude is right, and that the attitude of her father and mother is right. So often there is failure at this point on the one side or the other. The man who gets married becomes absorbed into his wife's family, or the wife becomes absorbed into her husband's family. That is wrong on both sides and should never be allowed to happen. This is a new family. The relationships of love should be maintained with the parents on both sides, but never in terms of deference and of submission. And the essence, the whole secret of Christian marriage, and of a happy married life is, that the man and the woman who get married realize this at the beginning, and act upon it, and stand to it at all costs. If there is interference by the parents on either side they are guilty of sin, and of failure to understand and to live according to the biblical teaching concerning marriage. 'Let the wife see that she reverence her husband'. That is the great adjustment she makes. She submits to him. She must not compete with him, she must not strive with him; she must recognize that the essence of marriage is that she pays this deference to him.

There is an odd phrase used by the Apostle Peter, which we must glance at for a moment: 'Even as Sara' he says, 'obeyed Abraham, calling him lord'. Have you been interested in the change of fashion with respect to this matter? One can read about people in the eighteenth century and notice how the wife habitually referred to her husband as Mr. So-and-so. You may smile at that, you may ridicule it, and I will agree with you; but I am quite sure that we have gone too far to the opposite extreme. There is a right balance in these matters. Sara called Abraham 'lord', and thereby she recognized the biblical principle. Then we read, 'whose daughters ye are, as long as ye do well, and are not afraid with any amazement'. The meaning is this: Christian wives are to pay deference to their husbands, and Peter tells them that they should do so in spite of what the pagan women round about them might say. Here was something new, it was rare, it was exceptional, and of course it created a great stir. When the pagan women, who were restless and rebellious – and rightly so – saw a woman behaving in this manner, offering and paying this deference to her husband, many of them would attack her, and persecute her. What Peter is saying is this: Go on doing it because it is right; do not let them frighten you, do not let their persecution make the slightest difference to you. Let them insult you as much as they like; take no notice of them. Do not be afraid with any amazement. And indeed, even if *the husband* misunderstands it and abuses it, go on doing it, says the Apostle; 'Do not be afraid with any amazement'. Do what is right. Do not be worried at what other people may say. This twentieth-century pagan world in which we are living says the same thing still; Christian wives will be told that they are being foolish, that they are denying their rights as women. Do not pay any attention, says Peter, let the people of the world say what they will. What do they understand? They have not got Christian minds, they are not filled with the Spirit. Realize always that you are meant to do that which is right, that which is good; and do not be frightened, do not be put off, do not allow them to interfere with your conduct and your behaviour. Such, then is the Apostle's last injunction. We cannot but comment on the wonderful balance which is ever preserved in the Scriptures.

The Apostle sums it all up in verse 33, 'Nevertheless, let every one of you in particular so love his wife even as himself, and the wife see that she reverence her husband'. As long as they both do that there is no risk of dispute about 'rights' or about 'my position', or 'my status'. Here is a man given headship; yes, but because he loves his wife as himself he never abuses his position. And here is a woman submitting herself to this great and glorious ideal. She need never be afraid that she will be taken advantage of, or that she will be trodden upon. Husband and wife are both dealt with, and the balance is perfect and entire. We realize, of course, that the Apostle Paul in this statement is writing on the assumption that both the husband and the wife are Christians. The Apostle Peter, as we saw, in his first Epistle, chapter 3, was writing partly on the assumption that the husband might not be a Christian; but everything we have here is on the assumption that both the partners are Christians. And as the Apostle does not treat anything else I have refrained from doing so. This is how a Christian man and a Christian woman become married and become this new unit – and I would repeat again that there is no more wonderful way of testifying to the difference it makes to be a Christian than just this.

Surely one of the greatest needs in this modern world of ours is found at this precise point. Most people are troubled about the discord between nations. That is right, and it is also right that we should be deeply concerned about the clashes within nations. People are giving their opinions, and talking boldly, and condemning this side and that side. But when you get to know something about the private lives of some of the people who are most eloquent in that respect, you will find that, in their own married lives, they are doing exactly the same things that they are condemning! How ridiculous it is! One great difference between Christianity and Secularism is that Secularism is always talking about generalities, and the individual is forgotten. Christianity realizes that the mass, the nation, is nothing after all but a collection of individuals. I have very little interest in what a statesman has to say if he does not carry out his principles in his own personal life. What right has he to talk about the sanctity of International Contracts, and to say what people should do and not do in groups, if he is not carrying out in his own private life the precepts he gives to men and women in their various spheres? It is as individuals are put right that a nation is put right. The most glorious epochs in the history of this country have followed times when a personal Gospel has been preached, and when a large number of individuals have become Christians. It is only then that we have begun to approximate to a Christian nation. But it is no use telling people to employ Christian principles in their conduct if they are not Christians themselves, and if they do not understand the Christian faith in a personal sense. That is my answer to those who criticize evangelical preaching and biblical exposition, saying, 'I thought you would have had something to say about disarmament conferences, or about what is happening in South Africa, and here you are talking about husbands and wives. I wanted to know how to solve the great world problems'. I trust that by now it is clear that it is evangelical preaching alone which really deals with these big problems, all else is but talk. You can organize marches and make your protests. It all comes to nothing, and makes not the slightest difference to anyone. But if you have a large number of individual Christians in a nation, or in the world, then and only then can you begin to expect Christian conduct on the international and national level. I do not listen to a man who tells me how to solve the world's problems if he cannot solve his own personal problems. If a man's home is in a state of discord, his opinions about the state of the nation or the state of the world are purely theoretical. We can all talk, but the problem is how to apply Christian doctrine in practical living. And it is precisely at this point that you must be 'filled with the Spirit'.

In the light, then, of the several principles which have emerged, we can draw certain conclusions about Christian marriage. First, the importance of 2 Corinthians 6:14: 'Be ye not unequally yoked together with unbelievers'. Having understood something about the true nature of marriage, and of Christian marriage in particular, is it not an obvious deduction? A Christian should not marry a non-Christian; if he does he is asking for trouble. You cannot get the two sides, the balance indicated in this last verse, unless the two partners are Christians. 'Be not unequally yoked together with unbelievers'.

Secondly, there is only one thing that really breaks marriage, and that is, adultery. 'The two shall be one flesh', and it is only when that 'one flesh' is broken that the marriage is broken. According to the biblical teaching – and you will find it in the Sermon on the Mount and elsewhere – there is no cause for divorce and the breaking of a marriage apart from adultery. That is a cause, because it breaks the 'one flesh'.

Thirdly and lastly, the supreme thing always is to consider our Lord Jesus Christ. If a husband and a wife are together considering Him, you need have no worry about their relationship to each other. Our human relationships and affections and loves are cemented by our common love to Him. If both are living to Him and His glory and His praise, if both have got uppermost in their minds the analogy of Christ and the church, and what He has done for the church that she might be redeemed, and that they, as individuals, might become the children of God – if they are overwhelmed by that thought and governed by it, there will be no danger of their personal relationship meeting with disaster. The headship of the husband will be the same kind of headship as the Headship of Christ over the church. He gave Himself for her; He died for her; He nourishes and cherishes her life, He lives for her, He intercedes for her, His concern is that she may be glorious and spotless and blameless, without spot, or wrinkle, or any such thing. That is the secret – that we are ever to be looking unto Him and realizing that marriage is but a pale reflection of the relationship between Christ and His church. So the principle of success in marriage is this: 'Let this mind be in you which was also in Christ Jesus'. 'Husbands, let every one of you in particular so love his wife even as himself, and the wife see that she reverence her husband'. 'Husbands, love your wives, even as Christ also loved the church, and gave Himself for it'. Thank God we are brought into a new life, we are given a new power, and everything is changed – 'old things are passed away, behold, all things are become new'. All the relationships of life are transfigured and transformed, are elevated and uplifted, and we are enabled to live after the pattern and the example of the Son of God.

HOME

Ephesians 6:1–4

1 *Children, obey your parents in the Lord: for this is right.*
2 *Honour thy father and mother; which is the first
commandment with promise;*
3 *That it may be well with thee, and thou mayest live long
on the earth.*
4 *And, ye fathers, provoke not your children to wrath: but
bring them up in the nurture and admonition of the Lord.*

17
Submissive Children
Ephesians 6:1-4

We come, here, not only to the beginning of a new chapter in Paul's Epistle to the Ephesians, but also to a new sub-section, and a new subject – the relationship of children and parents. As we do so it is very important for us to bear in mind that this is only a further illustration of the great principle which the Apostle has laid down in the previous chapter, and which he works out in terms of our varied human relationships.

That principle is stated in the eighteenth verse of the fifth chapter, 'And be not drunk with wine, wherein is excess; but be filled with the Spirit'. That is the key – and all he says from there on is but an illustration of how the life of Christian man or woman, who is filled with the Spirit, is lived in various respects. Another subsidiary general principle was stated in the twenty-first verse, 'Submitting yourselves one to another in the fear of God'. In other words we have to bear in mind that the Apostle is contending that the Christian life is an entirely new life, altogether different from the 'natural' life even at its very best. He was primarily concerned to contrast this new life with the old pagan life which these people had been living before their conversion; and it is virtually the difference between a man who is drunk and a man who is filled with the Spirit of God. I remind you of this in order to emphasize that what we have here is not mere ethics or morality; this is the application of Christian doctrine and Christian truth.

Having worked out his principle in terms of husbands and wives the Apostle now proceeds to do the same in terms of the

[237]

relationships within the family, especially that between parents and children, and children and parents. All will agree that this is a tremendously important subject at this present time. We are living in a world which is witnessing an alarming breakdown in the matter of discipline. Lawlessness is rampant, there is a breakdown in discipline in all these fundamental units of life – in marriage and in home relationships. A spirit of lawlessness is abroad, and things which were once more or less taken for granted are not only being queried and questioned but are being ridiculed and dismissed. There is no question but that we are living in an age when there is a ferment of evil working actively in the whole of society. We can go further – and I am simply saying something that all observers of life are agreed about, whether they are Christians or not – and say that in many ways we are face to face with a total collapse and breakdown of what is called 'civilization' and society. And there is no respect in which this is more evident and obvious than in this matter of the relationship of parents and children. I know that much of what we are witnessing is probably a reaction from something that was far too common, unfortunately, at the end of the Victorian era and in the early years of this present century. I shall have more to say about that later, but I mention it now in passing in order to set out this problem clearly. There is no doubt a reaction against the stern, legalistic and almost cruel Victorian type of father. I am not excusing the present position, but it is important that we should understand it and try to trace its origin. But whatever the cause there is no doubt that it is part and parcel of this collapse in the whole matter of discipline and law and order.

The Bible in its teaching and in its history tells us that this is something that always happens at a time of irreligion, at a time of godlessness. For instance we have a notable example in what the Apostle Paul says about the world in the Epistle to the Romans in the second half of the first chapter from verse 18 to the end. There he gives an appalling description of the state of the world at the time when our Lord came into it. It was a state of sheer lawlessness. And in the various manifestations of that lawlessness which he lists, he includes this very matter we are now considering. First he says, 'God gave them over to a reprobate mind, to do those things which are not convenient' (verse 28). Then follows the description – 'Being filled with all unrighteousness, fornication, wickedness, covetousness, maliciousness; full of envy, murder, debate, deceit, malignity; whisperers, backbiters, haters of God, despiteful, proud, boasters, inventors of evil things, disobedient to parents, without understanding, covenant-breakers, without natural affection, implacable, unmerciful . . . .' In that horrible list Paul includes this idea of being disobedient to parents. Again, in the second Epistle to Timothy, probably the last letter he ever wrote, we find him saying in the third chapter, verse 2: 'In the last days perilous times shall come'. Then he states the characteristics of such times: 'For men shall be lovers of their own selves, covetous, boasters, proud, blasphemers, disobedient to parents, unthankful, unholy, without natural affection', – that has gone – 'trucebreakers, false accusers, incontinent, fierce, despisers of those that are good, traitors, heady, highminded, lovers of pleasures more than lovers of God'.

In both instances the Apostle reminds us that at a time of apostasy, at a time of gross godlessness and irreligion, when the very foundations are shaking, one of the most striking manifestations of the lawlessness is, 'disobedient to parents'. So it is not at all surprising that he should call attention to it here, as he gives us illustrations of how the life that is 'filled with the Spirit' of God manifests itself. When will the civil authorities learn and realize that there is an indissoluble connection between godlessness and a lack of morality and decent behaviour? There is an order in these matters. 'The wrath of God is revealed from heaven', says the Apostle in Romans 1:18, 'against all ungodliness and unrighteousness of men'. If you have ungodliness you will always have unrighteousness. But the tragedy is that the civil authorities – irrespective of which political party is in power – all seem to be governed by modern psychology rather than by the Scriptures. They all are convinced that they can deal with unrighteousness directly, in and by itself. But that is impossible. Unrighteousness is always the result of ungodliness; and the only hope of getting back any measure of righteousness into life is to have a revival of godliness. That is precisely what the Apostle is saying to the Ephesians and to ourselves. The best and the most moral periods in the history of this country, and every other country, have always been those periods which have followed mighty religious awakenings. This problem of lawlessness and lack of discipline, the problem of children and of youth, was just not present fifty years ago as it is today. Why? Because the great tradition of the

Evangelical Awakening of the 18th century was still operating. But as that has gone, these terrible moral and social problems are coming back, as the Apostle teaches us, and as they have always come back throughout the running centuries.

Present conditions therefore demand that we should look at the Apostle's statement. I believe that Christian parents and children, Christian families, have a unique opportunity of witnessing to the world at this present time by just being different. We can be true evangelists by showing this discipline, this law and order, this true relationship between parents and children. We may be the means under God's hand of bringing many to a knowledge of the Truth. Let us therefore think of it in that way.

But there is a second reason why we all need this teaching, for according to the Scriptures it is not only needed by those who are not Christians in the way I have been indicating, but Christian people also need this exhortation because the devil often comes in at this point in a most subtle manner and tries to side-track us. In the fifteenth chapter of Matthew's Gospel our Lord takes up this point with the religious people of His day, because they were in a very subtle way evading one of the plain injunctions of the Ten Commandments. The Ten Commandments told them to honour their parents, to respect them and to care for them; but what was happening was that some of those people, who claimed to be ultra-religious, instead of doing what the Commandment told them to do, said in effect, 'Ah, I have dedicated this money which I have, to the Lord; I therefore cannot look after you, my parents'. This is how He puts it: 'Ye say, Whosoever shall say to his father or mother, It is a gift, by whatsoever thou mightest be profited by me; and honour not his father or his mother, he shall be free'. They were saying, 'This is Corban, this is dedicated to the Lord. Of course I would like to look after you and help you, and so on, but this has been dedicated to the Lord'. In this way they were neglecting their parents and their duties towards them.

That was a very subtle danger, and it is a danger that is still present with us. There are young people who are doing great harm to the Christian cause today through being deluded by Satan at this very point. They are being rude to their parents, and what is still more serious, they are rude to their parents in terms of their Christian ideas and their Christian service. Thus they are a stumblingblock to their own un-converted parents. Such Christians cannot see that we do not put these great Commandments on one side when we become Christians, but that, rather, we should live them out and exemplify them more than we have ever done before.

Let us, then, in the light of these things notice how the Apostle states the matter. He starts – using the same principle as he used in the case of the married relationship – with the children. That is to say, he starts with those who are under obedience, those who are to be subject. He started with the wives, and then went on to the husbands. Here he starts with the children and then goes on to the parents. He does so because he is illustrating this fundamental point, 'Submitting yourselves one to another in the fear of the Lord'. The injunction is, 'Children, obey your parents'. And then he reminds them of the Commandment, 'Honour thy father and mother'. In passing we note the interesting point that here, once again, we have something that differentiates Christianity from paganism. The pagans, in these matters did not link the mother with the father, but spoke of the father only. But the Christian position, as indeed the Jewish position, as given by God to Moses, puts the mother with the father. The injunction is that children are to obey their parents, and the word 'obey' means not only to listen to, but to listen as realizing that you are under authority, to listen 'under'. You are looking up for a commandment, and you not only listen, but you recognize your position of subservience and you proceed to put it into practice.

But it is most important that this should be governed and controlled by the accompanying idea, that of 'honouring'. 'Honour thy father and mother'. That means 'respect', 'reverence'. This is an essential part of the Commandment. Children are not to give a mechanical and a grudging obedience. That is quite wrong; that is to observe the letter but not the spirit. That is what our Lord condemned so strongly in the Pharisees. No, they are to observe the spirit as well as the letter of the law. Children are to reverence and to respect their parents, they are to realize the position as it obtains between them, and they are to rejoice in it. They are to regard it as a great privilege, and therefore they must go out of their way always to show this reverence and respect in their every action.

The Apostle's appeal implies that Christian children should be an entire contrast to godless children who generally show lack of reverence for parents and ask 'Who are they?' 'Why should I listen?' They regard their parents as 'back numbers' and speak of them disrespectfully. They assert themselves and their own rights and their 'modernism' in this whole matter of conduct. That was happening in the pagan society out of which these Ephesians had come, as it is happening in the pagan society that is round and about us at this present time. We read constantly in the newspapers of how this lawlessness is coming in, and how children, so it is worded, 'are maturing at an earlier age'. There is no such thing, of course. Physiology does not change. What is changing is the mentality and the outlook leading to aggressiveness, and a failure to be governed by biblical principles and biblical teaching. One hears of this on all hands – young people speaking disrespectfully to their parents, looking disrespectfully at them, flouting everything that they tell them, and asserting themselves and their own rights. It is one of the most ugly manifestations of the sinfulness and the lawlessness of this present age. Now, over and against all such behaviour, the Apostle says, 'Children, obey your parents; honour your father and mother, treat them with respect and reverence, show that you realize your position and what it means'.

But let us look at the Apostle's reasons for giving the injunction. The first is – and I am taking them in this particular order for a reason which will emerge later – 'For this is right'. By this he means: It is righteous, it is something which is essentially right and good in and of itself. Are you surprised that the Apostle puts it like that? There are certain Christian people – they generally claim for themselves an unusual degree of spirituality – who always object to this kind of reasoning. They say, 'I no longer think along the natural level; I am a Christian now'. But the great Apostle did not speak in that way. He says, 'Children, obey your parents'. Why should I obey my parents? says someone. His first answer is, 'It is right'; this is a righteous thing to do. The Christian does not despise that level, he starts with the natural level.

What Paul means by 'right', in other words, is this; he is going back to the whole order of creation laid down at the very beginning, away back in the Book of Genesis. We have already seen that in dealing with husbands and wives he did exactly the same thing; he went back and he quoted from the second chapter of Genesis: 'For this cause shall a man leave his father and mother and shall be joined unto his wife, and they two shall be one flesh'.

He did not hesitate, in dealing with the married relationship, to say in effect, 'I am only asking you to do what is foundational, what is natural, what has obtained from the very beginning as regards man and woman, husband and wife'. And now, he tells us that, with regard to this question of children, the principle is there at the beginning, it has always been so, it is a part of the order of nature, it is a part of the basic rule of life. This is something you find not only among human beings, it operates even among the animals. In the animal world, the mother cares for the young off-spring that has just been born, looks after it, feeds it, protects it. Not only that, she teaches it how to do various things – she teaches a little bird how to use its wings, a little animal how to walk and to stumble and to struggle along. This is the order of nature. The young creature in its weakness and ignorance needs the protection and the guidance and the help and the instruction which is given by the parent. So, says the Apostle, 'Obey your parents . . . for this is right'. Christians are not divorced from a natural order found everywhere in creation.

It is a regrettable thing that this needs to be said to Christians at all. How does it become possible that people can deviate at any point from something that is so patently obvious and belongs to the very order and course of nature? Even the wisdom of the world recognizes this. There are people around us who are not Christians at all but they are firm believers in discipline and order. Why? Because the whole of life and the whole of nature indicates this. For an offspring to be rebellious against the parents and to refuse to listen and to obey is something ridiculous and foolish. We see animals doing it sometimes and we are amused at them. But how much more ridiculous it is when that kind of thing is done by a human being! It is unnatural for children not to obey their parents; they are violating something that is clearly a part of the whole warp and woof of human nature, seen everywhere, from top to bottom. Life has been planned on this basis. And if it were not, of course, life would soon become chaotic and it would end its own existence.

'This is right!' There is something about this aspect of the teaching of the New Testament which seems to me to be very wonderful. It shows that you must not divide the Old Testament from the New Testament. There is nothing which displays more ignorance than for a Christian to say, 'Of course, being a Christian now, I am not interested in the Old Testament'. That is entirely wrong because, as the Apostle reminds us here, it is the God who created at the beginning who is the God who saves. It is one God from beginning to end. God made male and female, parents and children, right through the whole of nature. He did it in that way, and life is to work along these principles. So the Apostle starts his exhortation by virtually saying: 'This is right, this is basic, this is fundamental, this is part of the order of nature. Do not go back on that; if you do you are denying your Christianity, you are denying the God who established life after this fashion and made it work according to these principles. Obedience is right'.

But having spoken thus the Apostle proceeds to his second point. This is not only right, he says, this is also 'the first commandment with promise'. 'Honour thy father and thy mother; which is the first commandment with promise'. He means that the honouring of parents is not only essentially right, but that it is actually one of the things that God pin-pointed in the Ten Commandments. This is the fifth commandment, 'Honour thy father and thy mother'. Here again is an interesting point. In a sense there was nothing new in the Ten Commandments. Why then were they ever given? For this reason, that mankind, the children of Israel included, in its sin and its folly had forgotten and strayed away from these fundamental laws of God pertaining to the whole of life. So God, as it were, said, 'I am going to state them again one by one; I am going to write them and underline them so that people shall see them clearly'. It had always been wrong to be disobedient to parents; it had always been wrong to steal and to commit adultery. Those laws did not start at the giving of the Ten Commandments. What the Ten Commandments were designed to do was to impress them upon the minds of people, to state them clearly and to say, 'These are the things you must observe'. The first commandment with promise, the fifth commandment in the Decalogue! God has gone out of His way to call attention to this very thing.

What does the Apostle mean by the expression 'First commandment with promise?' This is a difficult point and we cannot be quite final in our answer. It obviously does not mean that this is the first commandment which has a promise attached to it, for it will be noticed that none of the other commandments have a promise attached to them at all. If it were true to say that com-

[244]

mandments 6, 7, 8, 9 and 10 had promises attached to them, then it could be said, 'Paul means of course that this is the "first" of the commandments to which he attaches a promise'. But there is not a promise attached to the others, so it cannot bear that meaning. What then does it mean? It may mean that here in this fifth commandment we begin to have instruction with respect to our relationships to one another. Until then it has been our relationship to God, His name, His day, and so on. But here He turns to our relationships with one another; so it may be the first in that sense. Over and above that, however, it may mean that it is the first commandment, not so much in order as in rank, that God was anxious to impress this upon the minds of the children of Israel to such an extent that He added this promise in order to enforce it. First, as it were, in rank, first in importance! Not that ultimately any one of these is more important than the others, for they are all important. Nevertheless there is a relative importance, and I would therefore view it like this, that this is one of those laws which, when neglected, leads to the collapse of society. Whether we like it or not, a breakdown in home-life will eventually lead to a breakdown everywhere. This is, surely, the most menacing and dangerous aspect of the state of society at this present time. Once the family idea, the family unit, the family life is broken up – once that goes, soon you will have no other allegiance. It is the most serious thing of all. And that is perhaps the reason why God attached this promise to it.

But I believe that there is even a further suggestion here. There is something about this relationship of children to parents which is unique in this sense, that it points to a yet higher relationship. After all, God is our Father. That is the term He Himself uses; that is the term our Lord uses in His model prayer – 'Our Father, which art in heaven'. The earthly father therefore is, as it were, a reminder of that other Father, the heavenly Father. In the relationship of children to parents we have a picture of the relationship of all mankind originally to God. We are all 'children' face to face with God. He is our Father, 'We are all His offspring' (Acts 17, 28). So in a very wonderful way the relationship between the parent and the child is a replica and a picture, a portrayal, a preaching of this whole relationship that subsists especially between those who are Christian and God Himself. In the third chapter of this Epistle there is a reference to the matter in the fourteenth and fifteenth verses. The Apostle says, 'For this cause I bow my knees unto the Father of our Lord Jesus Christ, of whom the whole family in heaven and earth is named'. Some say that the translation here should be, 'God is the Father of all fathers'. Whether that is so or not, there is at any rate this suggestion, that the whole relationship of father and child should always remind us of our relationship to God. In that sense this particular relationship is unique. That is not true of the relationship of husband and wife which, as we have seen, reminds us of Christ and the church. But this relationship reminds us of God Himself as Father and ourselves as children. There is something very sacred about the family, about this relationship between parents and children; and God, as it were, has told us so in the Ten Commandments. When He came to lay down this commandment, 'Honour thy father and mother', He attached a promise to it.

What promise? 'That it may be well with thee, and that thou mayest live long on the earth'. There can be no doubt that, as the promise was originally given to the children of Israel, it meant the following: 'If you want to go on living in this land of promise to which I am leading you, observe these commandments, this one in particular. If you want to have a time of blessedness and happiness is that promised land, if you want to go on living there under my blessing, observe these commandments, especially this one'. There is no doubt that that was the original promise.

But now the Apostle generalizes the promise because he is dealing here with Gentiles as well as Jews who had become Christians. So he says in effect, 'Now if you want everything to be well with you, and if you want to live a long and a full life on the earth, honour your father and mother'. Does that mean that, if I am a dutiful son or daughter, I am of necessity going to live to great age? No, that does not follow. But the promise certainly means this, that if you want to live a blessed life, a full life under the benediction of God, observe this commandment. He may choose to keep you for a long time on this earth as an example and illustration. But however old you may be when you leave this world, you will know that you are under the blessing, and the good hand, of God. We must not regard these things in a mechanical manner. What it is meant to convey is that God is very well pleased with people who observe this commandment, and that if we set ourselves to observe these commandments, and this one in

[246]

particular, for the right reason, then God will look down with pleasure upon us, and will smile upon us and bless us. Thank God for such a promise!

That brings us to the third and last point. You notice how the Apostle puts it: 'Children, obey your parents. Honour thy father and mother'. Nature dictates it, but not only nature, the Law dictates it. But we must go beyond that to – Grace! This is the order – Nature, Law, Grace. 'Children, obey your parents "in the Lord"'. It is important that we should attach that phrase 'in the Lord' to the right word. It does not mean 'Children, obey your parents in the Lord'. It is, rather, 'Children, obey in the Lord your parents'. In other words, the Apostle is repeating the very thing he said in the case of husbands and wives. 'Wives, submit yourselves unto your own husbands *as unto the Lord*'. 'Husbands, love your wives, *even as Christ also loved the church*'. When we come to his words about servants we shall find him saying, 'Servants, be obedient to them that are your masters according to the flesh *as unto Christ*'. That is what *in the Lord* means. In other words, this is the supreme reason. We are to obey our parents and honour them and respect them because it is a part of our obedience to our Lord and Saviour Jesus Christ. Ultimately that is why we are to do it. Nature dictates it, Law has emphasized it, but as Christians we have this further reason, this great and mighty reason – He asks us to do it; it is His commandment; it is one of the ways in which we show our relationship to Him and our obedience to Him. 'Children, obey your parents *as unto the Lord*'. There are these subsidiary reasons, but you must not stop at them, but obey the command for Christ's sake.

Here again let me emphasize the point that this is highly typical of the New Testament teaching. Christianity never does away with nature. Do not misunderstand me; I am not saying 'fallen nature'. I am saying 'nature', that which God originally created and ordained. Christianity never contradicts nature in that sense. There were people early in the Christian era who thought that it did so even in the married relationship. Paul had to write the seventh chapter of 1 Corinthians for that reason. Some at Corinth were arguing in this way: 'I have become a Christian, my wife has not done so. Well then, because I am a Christian and she is not, I will leave her'. And wives were saying the same. But that is wrong, says Paul. Christianity never calls upon us to deny or to

[247]

go against nature; we are never meant to be unnatural. What Christianity does is to lift up and sanctify the natural.

The same is true of the Law. Christianity does not do away with the Law as a portrayal of life. What it does is to add grace to it, enabling us to carry out the Law. 'Children, honour thy father and mother'. The Law gave that command, Christianity does the same; but it gives us this greater reason for obeying it, it gives us an insight and an understanding into it. We who are Christians realize that we are doing it 'as unto the Lord', the Lord who came from heaven. He came from heaven to honour His Father's Law. He kept the Law, He lived according to the Law. And He has redeemed us that we might be 'a peculiar people, zealous of good works', that we might 'fulfil' the Law. He gave Himself for us, 'that the righteousness of the Law might be fulfilled in us, who walk not after the flesh, but after the Spirit' (Romans 8:4). Grace raises the commandment to the highest level, and we are to obey our parents, and to honour them, and to respect them in order to please our Lord and Saviour who is looking down upon us. The Apostle has said this already in the third chapter, in verse 10: 'To the intent that now unto the principalities and powers in the heavenly places might be known *by the church* the manifold wisdom of God'. Do you realize that as the angels and principalities and powers look down upon us Christian people, and see us exemplifying these things in our daily lives, they are amazed that He, the Son, has ever been able to make such people of us, that we can live according to the commandments of God in a sinful world such as this?

Do it 'as unto the Lord'. Obey your father and mother 'in the Lord'. That is the finest and greatest inducement of all. It gives Him pleasure; it is a proof of what He said; we are substantiating His teaching. He said He had come into the world to redeem us, to wash away our sins, to give us a new nature, to make us new men and women. Well, says the Apostle, prove it, show it in practice. Children, show it by obeying your parents; you will be unlike all other children; you will be unlike those arrogant, aggressive, proud, boastful, evil-speaking children that are round about you at the present time. Show that you are different, show that the Spirit of God is in you, show that you belong to Christ. You have a wonderful opportunity; and it will give Him great joy and great pleasure.

[248]

But let us go even further. 'Children, obey your parents', for this reason also, that when He was in this world He did so. This is what I find in Luke 2:51: 'And He went down with them, and came to Nazareth, and was subject unto them'. The words refer to the Lord Jesus at the age of twelve. He had been up to Jersualem with Joseph and Mary. They were making their return journey, and they had travelled for a day before they discovered that He was not in the company. They went back and found Him in the Temple reasoning and debating and arguing with the doctors of the Law, and confuting and confounding them. They were staggered and amazed. And He said, 'Wist ye not that I must be about my Father's business?' He had this dawning realization at the age of twelve. But then we are told that He went back with them to Nazareth – 'He went down with them, and came to Nazareth, and was subject unto them'. The Son of God incarnate submitting Himself to Joseph and Mary! Though He had this consciousness within Him that He was in this world about His Father's business, He humbled Himself and was obedient unto His parents. Let us look at Him, let us realize that He was doing it primarily to please His Father in heaven, that He might fulfil His Law in every respect and leave us an example that we might follow in His steps.

There, then, you have the reasons for this injunction, and surely there is no more to be said. It is right. Nature dictates it. It is established by God's Law, underwritten, underlined. It pleases the Lord. Obedience is proof that you are like Him, for you are doing what He Himself did when He was here in this sinful, evil world. May God enlighten us one by one to the importance of observing this injunction!

We shall see that the Apostle goes on as he always does. He has a balanced teaching, so he has a word to say to parents also. What we have said can be misunderstood. If parents stop at this they are guilty of grievous misunderstanding. Paul has not finished; there is a word for parents still to come. But so far this is the word to the children. And as we read it in the light of what he says to parents, we shall be able, perhaps, to deal with some of the problems confronting certain children, whatever their age, who may have parents who are not Christians, and who are wondering what they should do. May God give us all grace to heed this injunction!

18
Unbelieving Parents

Ephesians 6:1–4

We have seen that this subject of parents and their children, which is always important, is unusually so at this present time. And it is important for all of us. It not only concerns children as such, and young people; and not only parents who have children; this is a subject that belongs and applies to all. There is something rather pathetic in the fact that certain Christian people seem to divorce themselves from these matters. I have heard of some, for instance, who have a feeling that the subject of husbands and wives has nothing to do with them because they are not married. That is most regrettable because, whether married or not, whether parents or not, Christians should be interested in principles of truth. Moreover if you are not married yourself you may have a married friend who may be in trouble about his or her married life; so if you are to function as a Christian you must be able to help such a person. To do so you must know how to help, and you can only discover how to help by understanding the Scriptural teaching. No-one should sit back therefore, and feel that this has nothing to do with him or her. You may be unmarried, or you may be married but without children, but you should have sympathy with and compassion for parents at the present time in this difficult modern world. It is your duty and business to help them and to assist them. These particular injunctions are not only for particular people, they are for all of us.

But, over and above that, we should all be interested in the opening out of divine truth and in observing how God in His infinite kindness and wisdom and condescension comes to meet us

[250]

in our various situations as we travel through this world. The civil authorities themselves recognize the importance of the whole problem at the present time. An important Commission on the whole question of education has stated recently that one of the most urgent problems confronting this country today is the breakdown in home and in family life. We are looking therefore at something on which the whole future of society, and of this country, may well depend. Of all people it is we who are Christians who should be giving urgent attention to these matters in order that we may set an example to others and show them how to live as children and parents, and how family and home life should be conducted.

So far we have been looking at the position only from the standpoint of the children, and the injunction that comes to them is that they are to obey their parents. But now in the fourth verse the Apostle puts before us the other side. 'And ye fathers', he says, 'provoke not your children to wrath'. It is not that this addition neutralizes what the Apostle has been saying about the children; it is given, rather, to safeguard it, and to remove every hindrance that may be in the path of children in giving obedience to their parents. It is another notable illustration of the balance and the fairness of the Scriptures. How can anybody face to face with this perfect balance, this fairness, this putting of the two sides together always, deny that this is the inspired Word of God. We have seen its divine character in the case of husbands and wives, and here we find it again in the case of parents and children; and we shall find it later in the case of masters and servants.

The obedience required of the children must be yielded to every kind of parent. There are parents who are guilty of provoking their children to wrath. Now let us be clear that the Apostle's teaching is that the children are to obey even such parents. It is a general statement. The command is to be obeyed without regard of the character of the parents, and it applies even in the case of non-Christian parents.

I want to examine this aspect of the matter carefully because I can say truthfully out of a long pastoral experience that this is one of the commonest problems I have had to deal with, as people have come and spoken to me about the difficulties in their personal lives. You remember what our Lord said in Matthew 10:34: 'Think not that I am come to send peace on earth: I came not to send peace, but a sword'. He said that His teaching was not going to smooth things over, but rather to create division, dividing father and son, mother and daughter, and so on; the reason being that, when a person becomes a Christian, there is such a profound change that it immediately has its effects in all spheres. And there is no realm where this is felt more acutely than in that of the most intimate and most personal relationships; for the moment a person becomes a Christian he or she realizes that the final allegiance is to God and to the Lord Jesus Christ. That inevitably has its effect upon every other form of allegiance. So our Lord says that He is going to be a cause of division – 'A man's foes shall be those of his own household'. You need to be prepared, He says, for these possibilities, and in actual practice this does prove to be the case.

The problem that arises acutely and frequently is that of children who have become Christians whose parents have not become Christians. A state of tension arises immediately. What are these children to do? How are they to behave? I am simply emphasizing that the Apostle says that these children, young people – the term 'children' must not be thought of purely in terms of age – are to obey the commandment. What he is saying is, 'Children, obey your parents whether they are Christians or non-Christians, no matter what they are like'. It is a general statement, and a general injunction; but unfortunately it is a point at which very much unconscious harm is often done by many young Christians. There is, perhaps, more failure just at this point than at any other. How are these children to conduct themselves with regard to their non-Christian parents? That is the problem. Unconsciously such children often do much harm through a failure to understand the biblical teaching at this point, and through a lack of balance in their whole outlook. Often they are the cause of antagonizing their own parents from the Christian faith. It is therefore a most important matter.

There is only one qualification which must be added to this general injunction, 'Children, obey your parents' and that one qualification is where our relationship to God is involved in a vital sense. I weigh my words with particular care at this point. If your parents are trying to prohibit you from worshipping God, and giving Him obedience, in that case you do not obey your parents. If they are deliberately inciting you, or trying to compel you, to sin, to acts of sin, again you must refuse. But that is the only qualification. Short of that (and I emphasize this) we must go to the extreme limit; and even in this matter, where we have to face the question as to whether they are standing between us and our relationship to God, we must again go to the extreme limit of conciliation and of concession.

It is just there, I find in pastoral experience, that most people get into difficulties. I mean that as Christians they take a stand on what I would regard as completely unimportant details. Of course that is very natural. We are all by nature people of extremes; and having become Christians we know exactly how we should live. Our great danger at that point – and the devil undoubtedly comes in – is to stand on utterly ridiculous points which really are quite immaterial, and which do not affect our Christian position at all.

Let me give you an illustration. It often comes up, I find, over the question of a marriage service, or the whole question of marriage. Two Christian young people decide to get married, and the parents in both instances are not Christians. The two young Christians are most anxious that this should be an excellent example of Christian marriage and they intend to invite their Christian friends to it. But, of course, the parents have to be present also – these non-Christian parents on both sides – and also some of their friends and relations who are not Christian. I have found so often that the tendency of these excellent young Christian people is to take a stand on matters of details in the service which do not matter, and thereby do much more harm than good. In other words, they say that everything must be exclusively Christian; and they tend to press that to such a point that it becomes an offence to the non-Christians who are present. It is just there, I feel, that they fail to exercise the judgment and the balance found in the Scriptures. Of course there has to be a Christian service, but there are many other incidental matters in the arrangements which seem to me to be matters of sheer indifference. If we are to be truly Christian we are to make concessions at that point as much as we can, and do everything possible to make it easy for the others, hoping that when they see what a Christian marriage really is they will be attracted to the faith. But if we take a rigid stand and will not make any concession on any point or detail, and insist that it has to be done in our way – in other words, if we are more concerned about impressing our Christian friends than in helping our

unbelieving parents – then we are not fulfilling this apostolic injunction about obeying our parents. That is what I mean by
standing only on matters which are really vital, and not merely on
unimportant and incidental details.

Furthermore, it is important that when we do take a stand we
should do so in the right spirit. If we are standing on some
Christian principle we must never do so in a contemptuous or impatient manner. Still less must we ever do so in an arrogant
manner, or in a censorious manner. We betray ourselves very often
in the way in which we say things. I have noticed that people who
are guilty of this failure often reveal their wrong attitude even as
they discuss the wedding arrangements with me. They say to me
with a smile and a smirk on their faces, 'Of course my parents are
not Christians'; and dismiss them like that. The moment a person
speaks in that way I know that he or she is already in the wrong.
Any stand that such a person may take on Christian grounds is
almost certain to be useless, and it is liable to do much more harm
than good. If your parents are not Christians you should not speak
about them in that way, you must not dismiss them, you must not
speak with contempt about them. You should be heart-broken
because of them, and therefore you should speak of them with
grief, with sorrow. But I find that far too often there is glibness
and a hardness that are not Christian.

Such 'children' are not obeying their parents, they are not
honouring their father and mother. You have to honour your
father and mother whether they are Christians or not; that is the
injunction. It is often difficult, but this is the injunction; and I
repeat that there is only one limit, namely, the point at which they
try, definitely and deliberately, to prevent your worshipping God
and serving Him, or try to lead you deliberately into the com-
mittal of sin. The spirit in which we act at that point is of vital
importance; and whenever we reach the stage at which we really
have to stand and disobey, we should do so in such a manner as to
give the impression that it grieves us, and hurts us, that we are
sorry, and that it is a most dreadful decision. For a child to have to
stand against a parent is one of the most solemn and serious things
we can ever be called upon to do in this life; so whenever it is done
in the name of Christ and of God it should be done with a broken
heart. We must not fail to give our parents the impression that it is
hurting us and causing us grief and costing us much, that we

would cut off our right hand in order to avoid it; but that we have no choice in the matter.

If it is done in that way it may well be used of God to influence them; but if it is done arrogantly, contemptuously and censoriously it will certainly do harm. It will be of no value at all, it will drive people away from Christ, it will make them feel and say, 'These children, since they have become Christians, are opinionated, are know-alls, are hard and rigid and legalistic'. It will set up a terrible barrier between them and their coming to a knowledge of God and of our Lord and Saviour. Any stand we feel compelled to take should always be done with a broken heart, with a spirit that is bowed and humbled. We should give the impression that our very hearts are bleeding as we are compelled by this marvellous thing which God has done to us to have to oppose our parents. We must always think of it in that way.

Let me give some reasons why we should do so in order that we all may be helped and guided whenever we find ourselves in such a position. Why is it that the Christian should behave in the manner I have been indicating, both negatively and positively? The answer is, because the Christian child should be the best type of child in the world. That is a general statement, a universal statement. Whatever the Christian does he should always be doing it at its very best. I lay that down as a general proposition. The Christian child should be a better child than any other child, the Christian husband a better husband, the Christian wife a better wife, the Christian family the best type of family in the whole world, the Christian businessman the best businessman conceivable, the professional man the best man in the profession. I do not mean from the standpoint of ability, but from all other aspects. Everything the Christian does should be done with all his might, and with a thoroughness and with an understanding which nobody else is capable of. That of course is the background to all these detailed injunctions which we are studying. The Christian, remember, is a man who is filled with the Spirit: 'Be not drunk with wine, wherein is excess, but be filled with the Spirit'. Now when any child is 'filled with the Spirit', by definition that child will be an exemplary child, a better child altogether than one of whom this is not true.

To what, then, does that lead? To the conclusion that Christian children should be the best children in the world because they alone have a real and a true understanding of this relationship.

[255]

There is a breakdown in family and home life today because both sides, parents and children, do not understand the meaning of these things. They know nothing about the relationship of parents and children from the biblical angle. They cannot see these things 'in the Lord' as we are to see them; but because we are 'in the Lord' we have a new understanding about these things. We see that this relationship of parent and child is a reflection and a picture of the relationship of God and the Christian who is His child. So we have this exalted, elevated notion of parenthood and of the relationship of the children to their parents. It is because the Christian child alone has an understanding of these matters, and of this relationship, that he or she should always excel others in practice. As Christians we do not act automatically. The Christian always knows why he does anything. He has his reasons, he has these explanations and expositions of Scripture; so he understands the situation.

Then it is the Christian alone who has the right spirit – 'Be filled with the Spirit'. The whole problem in these matters is ultimately one of spirit. The modern attitude is, 'Why should I listen to my parents. Who are they? Back numbers, out of date in any case! What do they understand?' That is the spirit that is causing so much trouble today. The parents, on the other hand, are guilty of the same failure in spirit. 'These children are a nuisance', they often say. 'We like to be going out in the evenings as we used to, but the children have arrived and we can no longer do so.' The spirit is already wrong, and that is why there are so many failures. These problems are all matters of 'the spirit', and that is why the pathetic politicians and statesmen, with their Acts of Parliament, are not even beginning to see the nature of the problem with which they are dealing. You cannot legislate about these matters; it is a matter of the spirit.

It is very important that the Christian child should have the right spirit in these matters; and the last thing he must be guilty of is a selfish spirit. I have referred to that earlier. Here is this very delicate position. These Christian young people are about to be married, and there are these non-Christian parents. The temptation that comes to these young Christians is, 'I must insist upon this and that; I am a Christian, I understand, and therefore it must be done as I say'. The spirit is already wrong. Your desire is to do what you regard as right: but what of these others? 'Conscience, I say, not thine own, but of the other also'. 'All things are lawful, but all things are not expedient'. What about the weaker brother? What about the one who is not Christian at all? Do you not give them any thought? Are you simply concerned that everything should be done in such a way that you emerge absolutely right, and have kept the letter of the law in every detail? That is the essence of Pharisaism! That is the spirit that 'tithes mint and rue and all manner of herbs, and forgets the weightier matters of the law, such as love and mercy'. May God grant us wisdom in these matters! I have seen so much harm done to the cause of Christ by failure at this point that I am giving it special emphasis. We must never act in a selfish, self-righteous spirit.

But let me add something further. The Christian is in an exceptionally advantageous position in these matters because as a Christian he should have an understanding of the difficulties of his parents. Take the case of non-Christian children coming into conflict with the opinion and the will of non-Christian parents. What happens? Immediately, it is a clash of personalities, a clash of the wills, and neither side has any understanding of the other. The child says, 'The parents have no right to say this'; and the parents look at their children and say, 'These children are impossible and altogether wrong'. Both sides are standing rigidly without any attempt to understand the opposing viewpoint. But that should never be true of the Christian. He has this great advantage over the non-Christian; as a Christian he should know why his parents cannot understand him and why they are behaving as they do. He does not merely regard them as difficult parents, he is not merely interested in their personalities. Instead, as a Christian he says, 'Of course they cannot help it, in a sense; it is very sad, it is very tragic, but I must not be annoyed with them, because they cannot possibly see it from the Christian position. They are not Christians, and for me to expect them to take the Christian view when they are not Christians is to ask them to do the impossible. I myself was once in that position, I was just as blind. Thank God, my eyes have been opened and I now see the right way; but they do not, therefore I must be sympathetic towards them, I must be patient, I must be understanding. I must make every concession I can, I must go as far as I can to meet them and to help them and to placate them.' Such is the advantage enjoyed by the Christian. 'Children, obey your parents, in the Lord'; you have this understanding. Do not merely stand as one personality against another personality; see that it is the blindness of sin that is causing the trouble. Do not look at them simply as parents who are against you; see, rather, the sin that is coming in and causing the division. That is what our Lord meant in His teaching about 'bringing a sword' and causing this kind of division. We must not be surprised at it, but we must not react violently to it. We must approach it all in a spirit of understanding and of sympathy.

That leads to my last reason. Whatever you and I may do as Christians, whatever we may do as Christian children, whenever we may come up against this clash, this division, and feel that we are compelled even to say 'No' to our parents, we must be always sure that what is uppermost in our minds at that point is a concern for the souls of our parents. 'Honour thy father and mother'. The fact that you have now become Christians, and that they are not Christians, does not mean that you look down on them and treat them with contempt and disdain, and dismiss them. You are to honour them, and you can honour them most of all by being concerned about their souls. If as Christian people we do not have a concern in our spirits and in our hearts about the souls of those who are related to us in this most intimate relationship, then we are not obeying our parents, we are not 'honouring our father and mother' in the way the Scriptures indicate.

Let us therefore safeguard ourselves by these considerations from the glib, superficial, mechanical kind of behaviour that is so often recommended to us, if not actually imposed upon us, by well-meaning but ignorant Christian people. There are many such. They say, 'Now you are converted, this is what you do now', and they almost encourage you to turn against your own parents. Never allow them to do so. These fundamental rules and laws abide and remain. The only division that is legitimate is the one that is caused by Christ Himself. We must never create divisions; we must do our utmost to avoid them, and must go to the uttermost limit to avoid them. The only lawful division is that inevitable, tremendous division that is made by the sword of the Spirit wielded by the Son of God Himself, our Lord and Saviour Jesus Christ. We must never be difficult, we must never stand on irrelevant details; we must never do anything that causes division. The only division that is inevitable and allowable is that which is produced by the sword which our Lord said He had come to bring (Matthew 10:34–38).

We now turn our attention to the parents. 'Fathers,' says the Apostle – 'Ye fathers, provoke not your children to wrath'. Notice that he mentions the fathers only. He has just quoted the words of the Law – 'Honour thy father and mother' – but now he singles out the fathers because the whole of his teaching has been, as we have seen, that the father is the one who is in the position of authority. That is what we always find in the Old Testament; that is how God has always taught people to behave; so he naturally addresses this particular injunction to the fathers. But the injunction is not to be confined to the fathers; it includes the mothers also; and at a time like the present we have reached a position in which the order almost has to be reversed! We are living in a kind of matriarchal society where fathers, alas, and husbands, have so abdicated their position in the home that almost everything is being left to the mothers. We have to realize therefore that what is said here to the fathers applies equally to the mothers. It applies to the one who is in the position of having to exercise discipline. In other words, what we are introduced to here in this fourth verse, and it is involved in the previous verse, is the whole problem of discipline.

We must examine this subject carefully, and it is of course a very extensive one. There is no subject, I would say once more, that is of such urgent importance in this country, and in every other country, as this whole problem of discipline. We are witnessing a breakdown in society, and it is mainly in connection with this matter of discipline. We have it in the home, we have it in the schools, we have it in industry; it is everywhere. The problem confronting society today in every walk of life is ultimately the problem of discipline. Responsibility, relationships, how life is to be conducted, how life is to proceed! The whole future of civilization, it seems to me, rests upon this. It is not the primary business of preaching to deal with political and social questions, though we can throw a most important light upon them.

We are told that the most important division in the world today is that brought about by the 'Iron Curtain'. In view of that, I venture on this assertion, this prophecy: If the West goes down and is defeated, it will be for one reason only, internal rot. There is no problem of discipline on the other side because there is a dictatorship there, and therefore they will have efficiency. We do not believe in dictatorship; therefore there is nothing more important for us than the problem of discipline. If we continue to spend our lives in jollification, doing less and less work, demanding more and more money, more and more pleasure and so-called happiness, more and more indulgence of the lusts of the flesh, with a refusal to accept our responsibilities, there is but one inevitable result – complete and abject failure. Why did the Goths and the Vandals and other barbarians conquer the ancient Roman Empire? Was it by superior military power? Of course not! Historians know that there is only one answer; the fall of Rome came by reason of the spirit of indulgence that had invaded the Roman world – the games, the pleasures, the baths. The moral rot that had entered into the heart of the Roman Empire was the cause of Rome's 'decline and fall'. It was not superior power from the outside, but internal rot that was Rome's ruination. And the really alarming fact today is that we are witnessing a similar declension in this, and most other Western countries. This slackness, this indiscipline, the whole outlook and spirit is characteristic of a period of decadence. The pleasure mania, the sports mania, the drink and drug mania have gripped the masses. This is the essential problem, this sheer absence of discipline and of order and of true notions of government!

These matters, it seems to me, are raised very clearly by what the Apostle tells us here, I shall proceed to present these further to view, and to show how the Scripture enlightens us in regard to them. But before doing so, let me mention something that will assist and stimulate your whole process of thinking. One of our problems today is that we no longer do our own thinking. Newspapers do it for us, the people interviewed on Radio and Television do it for us, and we sit back and listen. That is one of the manifestations of the breakdown of self-discipline. We must learn to discipline our minds. So I will give two quotations of Scripture, one on the one side, and one on the other side of this whole position. The problem of discipline lies between the two. Here is the limit on one side: 'He that spareth his rod hateth his son' (Proverbs 13:24). The other is, 'Fathers, provoke not your children to wrath'. The whole problem of discipline lies between those two limits, and they are both found in the Scriptures. Work the problem out in the Scriptures, try to get at the great Scriptural principles that govern this vital, this urgent matter, this greatest problem confronting all the Western nations, if not also others, at this hour. All our problems result from our going to one extreme or the other. That is never found in Scripture. What characterizes the teaching of the Scriptures always and everywhere is their perfect balance, a fairness that never fails, the extraordinary way in which grace and law are divinely blended. We shall consider these matters in detail.

19
Discipline and the Modern Mind
Ephesians 6:1-4

We continue our study of what is one of the basic and fundamental matters concerning the whole of life and of conduct. It is
a problem not only for Christian people, but for the whole of
society. What particularly affects us who are Christian is this, that
we are set, as the Scriptures remind us, as 'lights in the world', as
'the salt' of society, and like 'a city set upon a hill'. There is no
hope for the world apart from the light which comes to it from
the Christian teaching. It is therefore doubly important that as
Christian people we should be careful to observe and to understand the apostolic teaching. It is for us to give an example to
the whole world as to how life is to be truly lived. And we have
a unique opportunity, I feel, at such a time as this for showing the
Christian, biblical, balanced view concerning this vexed problem
of discipline.

This urgent problem is not confined, of course, to the problem
of children. The same principle is involved in the modern attitude
to crime and to war and to punishment in every shape and form;
it is a part of that same larger and general problem. But here we are
looking at it in particular as it affects the discipline of children and
the discipline of the home. We have seen that there are two fundamental statements which seem to govern any true thinking about
this question of discipline. On the one hand you have the familiar
statement 'Spare the rod and spoil the child', or the other forms of
that statement which are found at various points in the Book of
Proverbs and in the Old Testament 'Wisdom' literature. That is
one side. The other side is, 'Fathers, provoke not your children to

wrath'. There are the two fundamental positions. Within the ellipse between these two foci we shall find the biblical doctrine concerning this subject.

We shall look at it first of all in general. What strikes us at once is the great change that has taken place during the present century with regard to this whole problem of discipline, and especially during the last thirty years or so. But it has been going on during the whole of this century. There has been a complete revolution in the attitude of people towards this matter. Formerly we had what people today like to call derisively the Victorian outlook with regard to this matter of discipline. Let us admit quite readily and frankly that there is no question at all but that that was excessive. It was repressive, it was often brutal, indeed it can be said that sometimes it was even inhuman. The Victorian father, the Victorian grandfather, is a well-known and a well-recognized type. There was an element – indeed a considerable element – of the tyrant in their conception of fatherhood and of family discipline. The children were ruled severely and sternly, and the saying was, 'Children are to be seen and not heard'. That idea was certainly put into operation. Children were not allowed to express their opinion, they were frequently not allowed to ask questions; they were told what to do, and they had to do it; and if they refused they were punished with very great severity. We need not spend our time with this; it has been attacked and ridiculed and caricatured so much that everybody, surely, is familiar with that picture. Most of us probably are not old enough to remember it in actual practice, except those who are beyond, say, the age of sixty; but we are all familiar with the general picture and idea. That was the position about a hundred years ago and it continued more or less until the first world war.

But since then there has been an entire change; and today we are confronted by a position which is almost its exact opposite, for now we are tending to do away with discipline altogether. It is, as I have said, a part of a general attitude towards war, towards crime, towards punishment as a whole, and especially corporal and capital punishment. A new climate of opinion has come in, which in toto rejects the ideas that constituted the Victorian outlook. Indeed we can describe it as a general opposition to the whole idea of justice, and of righteousness, of wrath and of punishment. These terms are all abominated and are hated. In general, the modern man dislikes them radically. We find this exemplified in our news-papers, in observable tendencies in Acts of Parliament, and in the changes that have been introduced increasingly. These great terms – right, truth, justice, righteousness – are rarely heard. The much-used words of today are peace, happiness, enjoyment, ease, toler-ance. The modern man has revolted against the great terms that have always characterized the heroic ages in man's history, but that is very largely a reaction against the severities of the Victorian age.

What makes the position so serious is that this attitude is generally presented in terms of Christianity, and especially in terms of the New Testament teaching, and this, in particular, as contrasted with the Old Testament teaching. The case is often put thus, 'Of course the trouble with those Victorians was, as it was with the Puritans, that they lived in the Old Testament, they worshipped the God of the Old Testament. But', they add, 'of course we no longer believe that; theirs was only a tribal God; that is not the God of the Christian, that is not the "Father" of Jesus'. They claim that these modern ideas concerning discipline are based upon the New Testament, and that they have the true New Testament conception of God. They are therefore not interested, they say, in justice and righteousness, wrath and punishment. Nothing matters but love and understanding.

This is the point at which it all becomes so serious. And it is interesting to notice that men who do not even claim to be Christians are saying this kind of thing. You can even read state-ments in books and articles and journals which do not hesitate to assert that the Christian position is generally being put today, not by the church, but by some of the popular infidel writers, who are openly and frankly not Christian at all. We are told that the Christian case is going by default, that the church is not putting it forward, and that Christianity is really being presented today by men who are outside the church. It is said that they are giving the true exposition of the New Testament teaching as over against the Old Testament teaching. There exists this curious alliance of some people who call themselves Christians, and others who openly assert that they are not Christians; but together they agree that Christianity and the New Testament teach this modern view with regard to discipline, and that they therefore have departed from the former Victorian view, and particularly the Old Testa-ment view.

Summing it up, we can say that the basic idea underlying this view is that human nature is essentially good. That is the fundamental philosophy. What is needed therefore is to draw out, to encourage, and to develop the child's personality. So there must be no repelling, no control; there must be no punishing, and no administering of correction because that tends to be repressive. That being the controlling principle, it naturally works out all along the line in every department of life.

Take, for instance, teaching methods. This is surely one of the most urgent matters confronting this country today. Teaching methods during the last twenty years or so have been determined almost entirely by this new outlook, by this new psychology which regards human nature as essentially good. The idea is that you must not compel or coerce the child. One of the first to describe this teaching was a Dr. Maria Montessori whose method of teaching roughly came to this, that you should allow children to decide for themselves, and choose for themselves, what they want to learn. Before her days, of course, there had been a compulsory method of teaching the three Rs and you had to use it whether you wanted to or not. Children had to learn multiplication tables, and much else, by heart. It was done mechanically, there was no attempt to make it interesting to the children. They were simply told that they had to learn their Alphabet, their Tables, and their Grammar. All was drummed into them, and they had to repeat it mechanically until they knew it by memory and could repeat it by rote. Now all that, we are told, is quite wrong because it did not develop the child's personality. Teaching must be made interesting, and everything must be explained to him. He must not learn in a mechanical manner, but must understand what he is learning; so the explanations are given. The old method has been discarded in terms of this new view of human nature, this whole attitude towards life which claims to be Christian. Thus in the matter of educational theory and method there has been this profound revolution. By now we are beginning to discover some of its results. You find industrialists and others complaining that many who apply for posts as clerks and typists can no longer spell or do simple arithmetic. But my concern is not with the practical and economic results but with the underlying principles.

Again, with respect to the question of punishment, this too has very largely become a thing of the past. We are told that you must not punish; you must appeal to children, show them the wrong, set them a good example, and then reward them positively. We must grant, of course, that there is a measure of truth in all this, but the danger is that men usually go from one extreme to the other, and by today the whole notion of punishment has largely vanished. Indeed there are some who would press this notion so far as to say that you should never punish a child. Some even say that the thing to do if a child does anything wrong is take the punishment upon yourself, and thereby you will shame the child, and lead him to give up his wrong and evil practice. I remember very well some thirty years ago a man who literally put this into practice in his own family. He had a child, who, like every other child, was given occasionally to disobedience and to doing wrong things; but this man having got hold of this new theory, decided that he would no longer punish the child in any shape or form, but take the punishment on himself. For instance, instead of punishing the child, he, the father, would not eat his supper on the night of the offence. The experiment, I must add, did not last long. In the interests of his own health he soon had to return to the old method!

That is a typical illustration of the modern attitude. Human nature, it is claimed, is essentially good, and you have but to appeal to that which is best and highest in it. You need never punish, you need never restrain, you need never exercise discipline. You have but to state the ideal, and suffer in yourself the punishment of wrong-doing in others, and the offenders will respond. People of this type believed that if you acted in that way with Hitler there would be no war; you could change Hitler if you just went and spoke nicely and kindly to him, and showed him how you were ready to suffer. There was a very popular preacher in London before the second world war who actually proposed that he and a few others should go and stand between the armies of Japan and China that were fighting at that time. They did not actually do it, but they were quite convinced that if they but went and stood there between the rival armies, and sacrificed themselves, the war would end at once.

All this, I repeat, is based upon the notion that human nature is essentially good; so you have only to appeal to it. You will never need to resort to punishment. And if you do punish at all, it must never be corporal, and it must never be punitive; if there is any sort of punishment, we are told, it must be reformatory. This is an interesting point. The new notion is that the business of punish-ment – if as much as this can be said in its favour – is to reform, not to exercise retribution. We are told that we must always be posi-tive, that we must always be aiming at building up a new type of personality and of character. How does it work out? Take the question of prisons. The modern notion is that the business of prisons is not to punish offenders but to reform them. So we are being told increasingly that what is needed in prisons is the aboli-tion of restrictions and punishments. We must abolish the 'cat' and every form of corporal punishment, and the prisons must be manned by psychiatrists. A prison is a place in which a man should receive psychological and psychiatric treatment. You must not punish the prisoner for what he has done because essentially he is a good man. What you must do is to build up the goodness that is in him, and to draw it out. Show him the evil and wrong of certain of his own ideas, and of what he has been doing against society, and he will soon come to acknowledge his errors and to forsake them. The great need is to build up 'the other side'. And so by means of psychiatric treatment you will be reforming the man and building up his character and personality.

Such is the controlling idea today with regard to the treatment of crime and its punishment. Capital punishment has been aboli-shed, all forms of corporal punishment must be abolished, indeed any kind of severity must be abolished; the whole emphasis is on this treatment by psychiatry – the psychological approach, the building up, the working on this positive something that is there in human nature! And, of course, the same idea comes into the handling of children. The whole tendency today, if a child does not behave himself in school as he should, is to send him to a child psychiatrist; everybody must be treated psychologically. Essen-tially they are all good; therefore you must never punish. The rod, the cane, must be scrapped. What is needed is to draw out this inherent hidden good. So when the teacher fails to maintain discipline the child is sent off to the psychiatrist, the child psycho-logist, for investigation, and the prescribing of the appropriate treatment.

The point I am making is that all this is being done in the name of Christianity, and with the plea that it is New Testament as against Old Testament. This, we are told, is the approach of Christ towards these matters. In many senses, therefore, the whole

Christian position is involved at this point, and the whole future of the church. Here is a view that infidels are advocating and supporting – as well they might – but it is being done in the name of Christianity and of the New Testament.

Let us examine this question further. What is the biblical, the Christian teaching with regard to this matter? I do not hesitate to assert that the biblical and Christian attitude towards these two extremes is that they are both wrong; that the Victorian position was wrong, and that the modern position is wrong, even more so. But we are concerned especially with the present and the prevailing argument. I shall return later to the Victorian notion, which can be dealt with in terms of this exhortation 'Ye fathers, provoke not your children to wrath'; for that is exactly what they did; and this modern attitude is so much reaction to that. But let us look at the modern position first.

My first reason for asserting that, from the biblical and Christian standpoint, this modern notion with regard to the problem of discipline is completely wrong, is that the opposite of a wrong type of discipline is surely not to have no discipline at all. Yet that is what is happening today. The Victorians, we are told, were wrong; so let there be literally no discipline at all, no punishment; allow the child to do as he likes, and almost everyone else to do as he likes. There is a fundamental fallacy here. The opposite of wrong discipline is not the absence of discipline, but right discipline, true discipline. That is what we find here in Ephesians chapter 6. 'Children, obey your parents in the Lord', and 'Ye fathers, provoke not your children to wrath'. Discipline them, yes, but do not let it be a wrong discipline; let it be the right sort of discipline. 'Do not provoke them to wrath, but bring them up in the nurture and admonition of the Lord'. Now that is true discipline. But the tragedy of today, with its superficial thinking, is to assume that the opposite of wrong discipline is no discipline at all. That is a complete fallacy from the standpoint of mere thought and philosophy, if from no other standpoint.

Or let me put the matter in another way. Any position which says 'law only' or which says 'grace only' is of necessity wrong, because in the Bible you have 'law' and 'grace'. It is not 'law or grace', it is 'law and grace'. There was grace in the Old Testament Law. All the burnt offerings and sacrifices are indicative of that. It was God who ordered them. Let no one ever say that there was no grace in the Law of God as given to Moses and the children of Israel. It is ultimately based on grace, it is Law with grace in it. And on the other hand we must never say that grace means lawlessness; that is Antinomianism, which is everywhere condemned in the New Testament. There were some early Christians who said, 'Ah, we are no longer under Law, we are under grace; that means that what we do does not matter. Because we are no longer under Law but are under grace, let us sin that grace may abound! Let us do what we like, it does not matter. God is love, we are forgiven, we are in Christ, we are born again, so let us do anything we like'. These false deductions are dealt with in the Epistles to the Romans and to the Corinthians and to the Thessalonians, and also in the first three chapters of the Book of Revelation. It is a tragic fallacy to think that when you have grace there is no element of law at all, but that it is a kind of licence. That is a contradiction of the biblical teaching concerning both law and grace. There is grace in law, there is law in grace. We are not 'without law' as Christians, says Paul, 'but we are under law to Christ' (1 Corinthians 9:21).

Of course there is discipline! In fact the Christian ought to be much more disciplined than the man who is under the Law, because he sees its meaning more clearly, and he has greater power. He has a truer understanding, and should therefore live a better and a more disciplined life. There is not less discipline in the New Testament than in the Old; there is more, and at a deeper level. And in any case, as the Apostle Paul teaches in writing to the Galatians, you must not dismiss the Law, for the Law was 'our schoolmaster to bring us to Christ' (3:24). Do not set up these things as opposites. The Law was given by God in order that men might be shut up and shut in, as it were, to Christ, who was to come, who was to give them this great salvation. I assert, therefore, that this modern idea completely misunderstands both law and grace. It is a complete muddle, it is utter confusion; indeed it is not biblical at all. It is nothing but human philosophy, human psychology. It uses Christian terms but it really evacuates such terms of their real meaning.

Thirdly, the modern teaching – and this is one of the serious things concerning it – displays a complete misunderstanding of the biblical doctrine of God. This is the desperately serious thing. Modern man does not take his picture of God from the Bible; he takes it from his own brain and heart. He does not believe in 'revelation'. That is why he began the so-called Higher-criticism of the Bible about one and a half centuries ago. Man has been creating a god in his own image, a god who must be the exact antithesis of the Victorian father. I am quoting the description from an eminent writer of the present century. 'Do you not see', he writes, 'that the God of the Old Testament is your Victorian father; and that that is all wrong?' So the Old Testament is virtually shed. 'The God we believe in', men say, 'is the God and Father of our Lord Jesus Christ'. But the Lord Jesus Christ believed in the God of the Old Testament. He said, 'Think not that I am come to destroy the law, or the prophets: I am not come to destroy, but to fulfil'. He believed in the God who gave a revelation of Himself to Moses on the mount, and in the Ten Commandments. Our Lord believed and accepted all the Old Testament teaching.

The moderns have no right to claim that the new line is Christ's. It is not His teaching; it is their own teaching. The God who has revealed Himself to us through the Bible is a God who is holy. It is the New Testament as well as the Old that tells us that we must 'approach God with reverence and godly fear, for our God is a consuming fire' (Hebrews 12:29, quoting Deuteronomy 4:24). Indeed the New Testament teaches that in the Old Testament we are given only a dim notion of the holiness, the majesty and the glory and the greatness of God. There, it was only an external representation. God is infinitely holy. 'God is light, and in Him is no darkness at all'. God is righteous, God is always just. God is love, I know, but God is also all these other things; and there is no contradiction in them. They are all one, and they are all present at the same time, and in eternal power and fulness, in the Godhead. That is the revelation of the Scripture. And the notion that God is One who can wink at sin and pretend that He has not seen it, and cover it over and forgive every offender, and never feel any wrath, and never punish is, I say, not only to deny the Old Testament, but to deny the New Testament also. It is the Lord Jesus Christ who spoke about the place 'where their worm dieth not, and the fire is not quenched'. It is He who tells us about the division of the sheep from the goats; it is He who says to certain men, 'Depart from me. I never knew you'; 'depart unto the place prepared for the devil and his angels'. Nothing could be more monstrous than that this modern teaching should masquerade in the name of the New Testament and of the Lord Jesus Christ. It is a denial of the biblical doctrine of God, as found in both Testaments. God is a holy God, a just God, a righteous God, who has made it plain that He will punish sin and transgression, and who has done so in history many times. He punished His own children of Israel for their transgressions; He sent them into captivity; He raised up the Assyrians and the Chaldeans as His instrument of chastisement of them. The Apostle Paul teaches explicitly in the Epistle to the Romans (1:18–32), that God punishes sin, and does so sometimes by abandoning the world to its own evil and iniquity. And it is becoming increasingly clear that He is doing so at this present hour, but that men blinded by modern psychology cannot see it, for they do not understand the biblical truth about God.

Why is the world in such trouble? Why are we all, as it were, trembling as to what is going to happen next? Why are we all alarmed about these terrible new armaments and the possibility of an atomic war? The explanation, I suggest, is that God is punishing us by abandoning us to ourselves, because we have refused to submit to Him and to His holy and righteous laws. Our departure from the biblical teaching concerning God, and as a consequence of that, from the whole revealed truth concerning discipline and government and order, has resulted in the very punishment to which men are so blind.

In the fourth place there is a complete failure to realize what sin has done to man. The modern notions that man is fundamentally and essentially good, and that, if only the good is drawn out, everything will be right; that you have only to make an appeal, and never punish, but simply take the suffering upon yourself, that offenders will be so moved by it, and so broken down by the moral appeal that you are putting to them, that they will stop doing wrong and begin to behave well – all these notions, I say, are the consequence of the rejection of the biblical doctrine of sin. The simple answer to them is that man's nature is evil, that as the result of the Fall he is altogether evil. He is a rebel, he is lawless, he is governed by wrong forces, and therefore he is impervious to all appeals that may come to him.

The modern world is proving it by bitter experience. The modern method has been tried now for a number of years. But what of the results? Mounting problems – juvenile delinquency, disorder in the home, theft, violence, murders, robbery and the whole of modern society in confusion! The new theory has been given a good trial for thirty years and more, and the resulting problems are mounting up from week to week and almost from day to day. But nothing else is to be expected! Man is not fundamentally good. 'All the imaginations of the thoughts of his heart are only evil continually', as we are told they were in the days before the Flood. (Genesis 6:5). Man is not a good creature who only needs a little encouragement; his nature is twisted and perverted and vile. He is a rebel, he hates the light, he loves the darkness, he is a creature of lust and passion. And it is the failure to recognize this that is responsible for this modern disastrous notion.

But in the fifth place, there is also a complete misunderstanding of the doctrine of the atonement and of redemption, and of the cardinal doctrine of regeneration. I still have to meet a pacifist who understands the doctrine of the atonement! I still have to meet the man who holds the modern view about discipline and punishment who understands the doctrine of the atonement. The biblical doctrine of the atonement tells us that, on the Cross of Calvary, the just and holy and righteous God was punishing sin in the person of His own Son, that He might 'be just, and the Justifier of him that believeth in Jesus' (Romans 3:25 & 26). 'God hath laid on Him the iniquity of us all' (Isaiah 53:6). 'God hath made Him to be sin for us who knew no sin, that we might be made the righteousness of God in Him' (2 Corinthians 5:21). 'By His stripes we are healed' (1 Peter 2:24). 'It hath pleased the Lord to bruise Him' (Isaiah 53:10). The justice and the righteousness of God demanded this, the wrath of God upon sin insisted upon this. But this is where we see truly the love of God, that it is so great that the wrath is poured out even on His own Son in all His innocence, in order that you and I might be rescued and delivered. But the moderns do not understand or believe in atonement. They see nothing but sentimentality in the Cross; they see cruel soldiers putting to death the Son of God who nevertheless smiles upon them and says, 'I still forgive you though you have done this to me'.

That is what they say; but the Bible does not teach that. It is full of teaching concerning burnt offerings and sacrifices, of the necessity for the shedding of sacrificial blood, and that 'without shedding of blood there is no remission (of sins)' (Hebrew 9:22). That is the teaching of the Old Testament and the New, and this modern idea is a complete denial of it. Punishment is taught everywhere; and you see it supremely on the Cross on Calvary's hill.

Or take the doctrine of regeneration. If man is essentially good he does not need to be 'born again', he does not need regeneration. But regeneration is a central doctrine in the Bible; our only hope is that we be made 'partakers of the divine nature'. Thus this new teaching is a denial of the fundamental biblical doctrines, and yet it comes and masquerades in the name of Christianity. The biblical teaching is that until a man comes 'under grace' he has to be kept 'under law', that sin and evil must be kept within bounds. And God has done that! Who has appointed magistrates? God! Read Romans 13. 'The magistrate', we are told there, 'beareth not the sword in vain'. Who has appointed kings and governors? God! Who has appointed States? God! To keep sin and evil within bounds. If He had not done so the world would have putrified to nothing centuries ago. God has instituted law because of man's sinful nature, and in order that man may be restrained and kept from evil until he comes 'under grace'. It is God who, in the days of Moses, gave the Law, and He gave it for that reason. And obviously if a law is to be effective it must have sanctions. There is no value in having a law, if, when a man is arrested in enforcement of the law, you immediately tell him, 'Well, do not feel troubled, we have arrested you, but there is no punishment'. Would that be effective?

There is surely a contemporary illustration that ought to satisfy our minds with regard to this matter. Consider the slaughter that is taking place on the roads. What is being done about it? The authorities are making appeals, issuing statements, bringing in new regulations, getting the radio and the television to keep on repeating warnings, especially before Easter and Christmas. But do they have any effect? Very little! Why? Because man is a rebel, because he is naturally lawless. There is only one way in which the State can deal with this problem, and that is, by the punishment of offenders. That is the only language they can understand. Man in sin never has understood any other language. Go to him in a spirit of sweet reasonableness and he will take advantage of you. The British government tried that method with Hitler; we called it appeasement. If we can see that it was wrong there, why cannot we see that it is wrong with all other individuals? There is no purpose in making appeals in terms of sweet reasonableness to men who are evil and governed by lust and passion.

The biblical teaching is that such people are to be punished, and are to feel their punishment. If they will not listen to the law, then the sanctions of the law are to be applied. God, when He gave His Law, accompanied it by the sanctions which were to be applied following transgression. When the Law was broken the sanctions were carried out. God does not give a Law and say that disobedience to its requirements does not matter. God carries out His Law. And as you look at the history of this country, not to look further afield, you will always find that the most disciplined and the most glorious periods in that history have been the periods that have followed a religious reformation. Look at the Elizabethan period following the Protestant Reformation, when men brought the Bible back – Old Testament and New Testament – and put it into practice, and enforced their laws. The Elizabethan period, the Cromwellian period, and the period following the Evangelical Awakening of the eighteenth century all illustrate the biblical principle. The biblical teaching is that because man is a fallen creature, because he is a sinner and a rebel, because he is a creature of lust and passion, and governed by them, he must be forcibly restrained, he must be kept in order. The principle applies alike to children and to adults who are guilty of misdemeanour and crime and a departure from the law of the land and from the Law of God. Try any other method and you will have a return to chaos, as we are already beginning to experience. The biblical teaching, founded upon the character and being of God, and recognizing that man is in a state of sin, requires that law must be enforced, in order that men may be brought to see and to know God; next that they may be brought into grace; so that finally they may be brought to own and obey the higher law under which they delight in pleasing God and honouring and keeping His holy commandments.

We must start therefore with this principle that the biblical teaching everywhere is that there must be discipline, there must be punishment. But then that leaves us with this question: How, exactly, is that punishment to be meted out, and particularly in the Christian home? And it is there that our text is so important. You must exercise discipline, but you must not 'provoke your children

[274]

to wrath'. There is a wrong way of exercising discipline as well as a right way, and what we shall be concerned about further is to discover the right, the true, the biblical method of exercising the discipline which is commanded us by the holy Law of God. The modern notion, although it often claims the name of Christ, is a denial of all the basic and fundamental doctrines of the Christian faith. It is not surprising that infidels are advocating it very loudly with respect to capital punishment, to war, to education, to prison reform, and much else. It is not surprising, I say, that they are advocating it, because we do not expect Christian and biblical understanding of them. But a Christian should and must understand.

20

Balanced Discipline

Ephesians 6:1–4

We come now to the question of the administration of discipline. The Apostle deals with that, in particular, in this fourth verse. There is no question about the need of discipline, and that it must be enforced. But how is that to be done? It is here that a great deal of confusion has often arisen. We have agreed already that beyond question our Victorian grandfathers were guilty of error at this point, and that they frequently did not exercise discipline in the right and the biblical way and manner. We see also that what we have today is largely a violent reaction against that. That does not justify the present position, but it does help us to understand it. What is important is that we must not fall into the error of reverting again from the present position to that other extreme which was equally wrong. And here, if we but follow the Scripture we shall have a balanced view. Discipline is essential and must be enforced; but the Apostle exhorts us to be very careful as to how we exercise it, because we can do more harm than good if we do not do it in the right way.

In general, of course, there is very little need of this teaching at the present time, because, as I have been indicating, the trouble today is that people do not believe in discipline at all. There is little need, therefore, to tell them not to exercise discipline in the wrong way. We have to urge the modern man to recognize the need of discipline and to put it into practice. But in the realm of the church – and perhaps in the realm of evangelical Christians in particular, and especially in the U.S.A. – what the Apostle says in this fourth verse will be needed more and more. That need arises in this way. The ever-present danger is to react too violently. It is always wrong when our attitude is determined by another attitude which we regard as wrong. Our view should never result from a merely negative reaction. This principle is true not only with respect to this particular subject, but in many realms and departments of life. Far too often we allow our attitude to be governed and determined by something that is wrong. Let me give one present-day illustration of this tendency. There are Christians in certain parts of the world who are reacting so violently to a wrong kind of fundamentalism at the present time that they are almost losing their hold of essential Christian doctrine. It is their annoyance with something that is wrong that determines their position. That is always wrong. Our position must always be determined positively by the Scriptures. We must not merely be reactionaries. And in this particular matter of discipline in the home, and of children, there is a very real danger that good evangelical Christians, having seen clearly that the modern attitude is entirely and utterly wrong, and being determined not to accept it, may go to the other extreme and revert to the old Victorian idea. They therefore need the exhortation which we find in these verses of our Epistle.

The Apostle divides his teaching into two sections, the negative and the positive. This problem he says is not confined to the children; the fathers, the parents, have also to be careful. Negatively, he tells them, 'Provoke not your children to wrath'. Positively, he says, 'But bring them up in the nurture and the admonition of the Lord'. As long as we remember both aspects all will be well.

We start with the negative, 'Provoke not your children to wrath'. These words can be translated, 'Do not exasperate your children, do not irritate your children, do not provoke your children to become resentful'. That is always a very real danger when we exercise discipline. And if we become guilty of it we shall do much more harm than good. We shall not have succeeded in disciplining our children, we shall simply have produced such a violent reaction in them, so much wrath and resentment, that the position will be worse, almost, than if we had not exercised any discipline at all. But as we have seen, both extremes are altogether wrong. In other words we must exercise this discipline in such a manner that we do not irritate our children or provoke them to a sinful resentment. We are required to keep the balance.

How is this to be done? How is such discipline to be exercised by parents? And not by parents only, but by school-teachers, or anyone who is in the position of having charge and control of those who are younger than themselves. Once more we must go back to chapter 5, verse 18. 'Be not drunk with wine wherein is excess, but be filled with the Spirit'. That is always the key. We saw when we were dealing with that verse that the life lived in the Spirit, the life of a man who is filled with the Spirit, is characterized always by two main things – power and control. It is a disciplined power. Remember how Paul puts it in writing to Timothy. 'God', he says, 'hath not given us the spirit of fear, but of power, and of love and of a sound mind (discipline)' (2 Timothy 1:8). Not uncontrolled power, but power controlled by love and a sound mind, discipline! That is always the characteristic of the life of a man who is 'filled with the Spirit'.

In other words, the Christian is entirely unlike the man who is under the influence of wine, the man who is besotted with wine. There is always excess in that case and the man reacts violently. You can easily irritate a drunken man and provoke him to a violent reaction. He lacks balance, he has no judgment, he takes great offence at a triviality, and on the other hand is much too pleased about something which in itself is trivial. He is invariably guilty of excessive reaction. But the Christian, says the Apostle, is always to manifest the antithesis of that type of behaviour.

How, then, am I to exercise this discipline? 'Provoke not your children to wrath.' This is to be the first principle governing our action. We are incapable of exercising true discipline unless we are first able to exercise self-control, and discipline our own tempers. The trouble with a man who is 'drunk with wine' is that he cannot control himself; he is being controlled by his instincts and passions and lower nature. Alcohol puts out of action the higher centres of the brain, including the sense of control. It is one of those depressant drugs that knocks out the finer discriminating abilities of the brain, the highest centres of all, with the result that the instinctual, the elemental elements come out. That is what happens to the man who is drunk with wine, hence his excess and lack of control. But Christians are to be filled with the Spirit, and people who are filled with the Spirit are always characterized by control. When you are disciplining a child you should have first controlled yourself. If you try to discipline your child when you are in a temper, it is certain that you will do more harm than good. What right have you to say to your child that he needs discipline when you obviously need it yourself? Self-control, control of temper is an essential pre-requisite in the control of others. But that is the trouble, is it not? We see it on the streets, everywhere. We see parents administering chastisement in a rage, often trembling in a temper. They have no self-control, and the result is that the child is exasperated. So the very first principle is that we must start with ourselves. We must be certain that we are in control of ourselves, that we are cool. Whatever may have happened, whatever the provocation, we must not react with the violence similar to that of the man who is drunk; there must be this personal discipline, this self-control that enables a man to look at the situation objectively, and to deal with it in a balanced and controlled manner. How important this is! The nations need to learn this very lesson. Their conferences break down because men behave like children or worse; they cannot control themselves, they react violently. This 'drunken' condition, these violent reactions, are a cause of war. They are the chief causes of all the breakdowns in life – in marriage, in the home, and in every other sphere. But nowhere is this lesson more important than in the realm of disciplining our children.

The second principle arises, in a sense, out of the first. If a parent is to exercise this discipline in the right way he must never be capricious. There is nothing more irritating to the one who is undergoing discipline than a feeling that the person who is administering it is capricious and uncertain. There is nothing more annoying to a child than the kind of parent whose moods and actions you can never predict, who is changeable, whose condition is always uncertain. There is no worse type of parent than he who one day, in a kindly mood, is indulgent and allows the child to do almost anything it likes, but who the next day flares up in a rage if the child does scarcely anything at all. That makes life impossible for the child. Capriciousness in the parent is again indicative of this 'drunk with wine' condition. The reactions of a drunken man are unpredictable; you cannot tell whether he is going to be in a genial mood or in a bad temper, he is not governed by reason, there is no control, there is no balance. Such a parent, I say again, fails to exercise a true and helpful discipline, and the position of the child becomes impossible. He is provoked and irritated to wrath, and has no respect for such a parent.

I am referring not only to temperamental reactions, but to conduct also. The parent who is not consistent in his conduct cannot truly exercise discipline in the case of the child. A parent who does one thing today, and the contrary thing tomorrow, is not capable of sound discipline. There must be consistency, not only in the reaction but also in the conduct and the behaviour of the parent; there must be a pattern about the life of the parent, for the child is always observing and watching. But if he observes that the parent is erratic and himself does the very thing that he forbids the child to do, again you cannot expect the child to benefit from any discipline administered by such a parent. There must be nothing erratic, capricious, uncertain or changeable in the parents if they are to exercise discipline.

Another most important principle is that the parents must never be unreasonable or unwilling to hear the child's case. There is nothing that so annoys the one who is being disciplined as the feeling that the whole procedure is utterly unreasonable. In other words, it is a thoroughly bad parent who will not take any circumstances into consideration at all, or who will not listen to any conceivable explanation. Some fathers and mothers, in the desire to exercise discipline, are liable to become utterly unreasonable, and they themselves may be very much at fault. The report they have received concerning the child may be wrong, or there may have been peculiar circumstances of which they are ignorant; but the child is not even allowed to state the position, or to give any kind of explanation. Of course one realizes that advantage can be taken of this by the child. All I am saying is that we must never be unreasonable. Let the explanation be given by the child, and if it is not a true reason, then you can chastise for that also as well as for the particular act which constitutes the offence. But to refuse to listen, to prohibit any kind of reply, is inexcusable.

We are all clear about this principle when we see a State behaving in a wrong way. We do not like a police State, we are proud of the Habeas Corpus Act in this country, which says that it is a grievous wrong to keep a man in prison without giving him a trial. We wax eloquent about this, but very often in our homes we do exactly the same thing. The child is not given any opportunity at all to state his case, reason does not come into the situation for a moment, we refuse to grant even the possibility that there might be some explanation that we have not heard of hitherto. Such conduct is always wrong; that is to provoke our children to wrath. It is certain to exasperate and irritate them into a condition of rebellion and of antagonism.

But there is another principle to be considered – the parent must never be selfish. 'Parents, provoke not your children to wrath.' This happens sometimes because parents are guilty of just plain selfishness. My charge applies to persons who do not recognize that the child has his own life and personality, and who seem to think that children are entirely for their pleasure, or for their use. They have an essentially wrong notion of parenthood and what it means. They do not realize that we are but guardians and custodians of these lives that are given to us, that we do not possess them, that they do not 'belong' to us, that they are not 'goods' or chattels, that we have no absolute right over them. But there are many parents who behave as if they had such a right of ownership; and the personality of the child receives no recognition. There is nothing more deplorable or reprehensible than a domineering parent. I am referring to the kind of parent who imposes his or her personality upon the child, and who is always crushing the child's personality; the type of parent who demands everything and who expects everything from the child. It is generally referred to as possessiveness. This is a most cruel attitude, and alas, it can persist into adult life.

Some of the greatest tragedies I have encountered in my pastoral experience have been due to this very thing. I know many people whose lives have been entirely ruined by selfish, possessive, domineering parents. I know many men and women who have never married for this reason. They were made to feel that they were well-nigh criminals because they even thought of leaving father or mother; their whole life was to be lived for the parents. For what had they come into the world if not for this? They were not allowed to have an independent life of their own, or to develop their own personality; a domineering father or mother had crushed out the life and the individuality and the personality of the son or daughter. That is not discipline; it is tyranny of the foulest type, and a contradiction of the plain teaching of Scripture. It is utterly inexcusable, and while it crushes the personality of the child it breeds resentment. How can it fail to do so? Let us make sure that we are entirely free from that. 'Be not drunk with wine, wherein is excess.' The drunkard thinks of no one but himself, his one concern is his own satisfaction. If he thought of others he would never be drunk, because he knows that he brings suffering upon them. Drunkenness is a manifestation of selfishness, it is sheer selfish indulgence. We must not be guilty of that spirit in any respect, and particularly in this most delicate relationship of parents and children.

Yet again: Punishment, discipline, must never be administered in a mechanical manner. There are people who believe in discipline for its own sake. That is not the biblical teaching, but the philosophy of the Sergeant Major. There is nothing to be said for it, it is unintelligent! That is the horrible thing about such discipline. In the Army and other armed Services it is unintelligent; it is done by numbers, personality is not considered at all. It may be necessary there, but when it comes into the realm of the home it, too, is something which is quite inexcusable. In other words, in order to administer discipline in the right and true way there must always be a reason for it; it is not to be applied in a mechanical manner. It must always be intelligent; there must always be a reason for it, and that reason should always be made plain and clear. It must never be thought of in terms of pressing a button and expecting an inevitable result to follow. That is not true discipline; it is not even human. That belongs to the realm of mechanics. But true discipline is always based on understanding; it has something to say for itself; it has an explanation to give.

Notice that all along we are finding it necessary to strike a balance. In criticizing the modern view which does not recognize discipline at all, we noted that it starts on the assumption that all you have to do is to give explanations, and make appeals, and all will be well. We saw clearly that that is not true in either theory or practice; but it is equally wrong to swing over to the other extreme and say, 'This has to be done because I say so. There is to be no questioning and there will be no explanation'. A Christian, balanced discipline is never mechanical; it is always living, it is always personal, it is always understanding, and above all it is always highly intelligent. It knows what it is doing, and it is never guilty of excess. It has not lost control of itself, it is not a kind of cataract pouring forth in an uncontrolled and violent manner.

There is always this intelligent and understanding element at the very heart and centre of true discipline.

That leads inevitably to the sixth principle. Discipline must never be too severe. Here is perhaps the danger that confronts many good parents at the present time as they see the utter lawlessness about them, and as they rightly bemoan it and condemn it. Their danger is to be so deeply influenced by their revulsions as to go right over to this other extreme and to become much too severe. The opposite of no discipline at all is not cruelty, it is balanced discipline, it is controlled discipline. An ancient adage supplies a fundamental rule and law about this whole matter. It is that 'the punishment should fit the crime'. In other words, we must be careful that we do not administer the maximum punishment for all offences, great or small. This is simply to say again that it must not be mechanical; for if the punishment meted out is disproportionate to the misdemeanour, the crime, or whatever it is, it cannot possibly do good. It will inevitably give the one who is punished a sense of injustice, a feeling that the punishment is so severe, so out of proportion to what was done that it constitutes an act of violence, not one of sane chastisement. That inevitably produces this 'wrath' of which the Apostle speaks. The child is irritated, he feels it is unreasonable. Though perhaps he is prepared to admit a measure of guilt he is quite sure that it was not as bad as all that. To put it in another way, we must never humiliate another person. If in punishing or administering discipline or correction, we are ever guilty of humiliating the child, it is clear that we ourselves need to be disciplined. Never humiliate! Certainly punish if punishment is called for, but let it be a reasonable punishment based upon understanding. And never do it in such a way that the child feels that he is being trampled upon and being utterly humiliated in your presence, and still more, in the presence of others.

All this, I well know, can prove very difficult; but if we are 'filled with the Spirit' we shall have sound judgment in these matters. We shall learn that our administering of discipline must never be merely a means of giving relief to our own feelings. That is always wrong; and we must never allow ourselves to be governed by a delight in punishing; nor, as I have stressed, must we trample upon the personality and the life of the individual with whom we are dealing. The Spirit warns us to be extremely careful at this point. The moment personalities are left out, and this rigid, hard and harsh idea of punishment comes in, we are guilty of the very things against which Paul warns us. We are indeed provoking and irritating our children to wrath and we are making rebels of them. We are losing their respect, we make them feel they are hardly done by; a sense of injustice rankles within them, and they feel that we are being cruel. That benefits neither one party nor the other, and so we must never attempt discipline in that way.

So we come to what is in many ways the last of our negatives. We must never fail to recognize growth and development in the child. This is another alarming parental defect which, thank God, one does not see now so often as formerly. But there are still some parents who continue to regard their children all their lives as if they had never outgrown their childhood. The children may be twenty-five but they still treat them as if they were five. They do not recognize that this person, this individual, this child whom God has given them in His grace, is one that is growing and developing and maturing. They do not recognize that the child's personality is blossoming forth, that knowledge is being gained, that experience is being widened, and that the child is developing even as they themselves have done. This is of particular importance at the stage of adolescence; hence one of the major social problems of today is the handling and the treatment of the adolescent. It is the problem of the Sunday schools as well as the day schools. Sunday school teachers testify that they have little difficulty until children come to adolescence, but that then they tend to lose them. Parents find the same thing. This period of adolescence is notoriously the most difficult age through which we all have to pass, and it therefore needs special grace and understanding, and the most careful handling.

As parents we must never be guilty of failing to recognize this factor, and we have to adjust ourselves to it. Because you are able to dominate your child, say up to the age of nine or ten years, you must not say 'I am going to continue to do this, come what may. His will must be broken by mine. I care not what he may feel or what he understands, children know very little, so I shall continue to impose my will on him'. To think and to act in that way means you are certain to provoke your child to wrath, and thereby do him great harm. You will do the child psychological harm, you may even do him physical harm. You will create in him various types of psychosomatic illnesses which are so common at the present time. This kind of behaviour on the part of parents is prolific in the production of such effects and results. We must never be guilty of that.

*

'How do I avoid all these evils?' you ask. One good rule is that we should never foist our views upon our children. Up to a certain age it is right and good to teach them certain things and insist upon them, and there will be no difficulty about that if done properly. They should even enjoy it. But shortly they come to an age when they begin to hear other views and ideas from their friends, probably in school or other associations. Now a crisis begins to develop. The parents' whole instinct, very rightly, is to protect the child, but it can be done in such a way as, again, to do more harm than good. If you give the impression to the child that he has to believe these things simply because you believe them, and because your parents did so, you will inevitably create a reaction. It is unscriptural to do so. And not only is it unscriptural, but it betrays a dismal lack of understanding of the New Testament doctrine of regeneration.

An important principle arises at this point which applies not only in this realm but in many other realms. I am constantly having to tell people who have become Christian and whose loved ones are not Christian, to be careful. They themselves have come to see the Christian truth, and they cannot understand why this other member of the family – husband, wife, father, mother, or child – fails to do so. Their whole tendency is to be impatient with them and to dragoon them into the Christian faith, to foist their belief upon them. This must on no account be done. If the person in question is not regenerate he or she cannot exercise faith. We need to be 'quickened' before we can believe. When one is 'dead in trespasses and sins' one cannot believe; so you cannot foist faith on others. They do not see it, they do not understand it. 'The natural man receiveth not the things of the Spirit of God, for they are foolishness unto him; neither can he know them, for they are spiritually discerned' (1 Corinthians 2:14). Many parents have fallen into this error just at this point. They have tried to dragoon their children in the adolescent stage into the Christian faith; they have tried to foist their views on them, they have tried to compel them to say things that they do not really believe. This method is always wrong.

'Well, what can one do?' I shall be asked. Our business is to try to win them, to try to show them the excellence and the reasonableness of what we are and of what we believe. We must be very patient with them, and bear with their difficulties. They have their difficulties, though to you they are nothing. But to them they are very real. The whole art of exercising discipline is to recognize this other personality all the time. You must put yourself into his place, as it were, and with real sympathy and love and understanding try to help him. If the children refuse and reject your efforts, do not react violently, but give the impression that you are very sorry, that you are very grieved for their sakes, and that you feel they are missing something most precious. And at the same time you must make as many concessions as you can. You must not be hard and rigid, you must not refuse everything automatically without any reason, simply because you are the parent, and this is your method and manner. On the contrary, you must be concerned to make every legitimate concession that you can, to go as far as you can in the matter of concession, thereby showing that you are paying respect to the personality and to the individuality of the child. That in and of itself is always good and right, and it will always result in good.

Let me summarize my argument. Discipline must always be exercised in love, and if you cannot exercise it in love do not attempt it at all. In that case you need to deal with yourself first. The Apostle has already told us to speak the truth in love in a more general sense; but exactly the same applies here. Speak the truth, but in love. It is precisely the same with discipline; it must be governed and controlled by love. 'Be not drunk with wine, wherein is excess, but be filled with the Spirit'. What is 'the fruit of the Spirit'? 'Love, joy, peace, longsuffering, gentleness, goodness, meekness, faith and temperance.' If, as parents, we are 'filled with the Spirit', and produce such fruit, discipline will be a very small problem as far as we are concerned. 'Love, joy, peace, longsuffering' – always in love, always for the child's good. The object of discipline is not to keep up your standard, or to say 'I have decided that this is how it should be, and therefore it shall be so'. You must not think of yourself primarily, but of the child. The child's good is to be your controlling motive. You must have a right view of parenthood and regard the child as a life given to you by God. What for? To keep to yourself, and to mould to your pattern, to impose your personality upon it? Not at all! But put into your care and charge by God in order that his soul may ultimately come to know Him and to know the Lord Jesus Christ. The child is as much an entity as you are yourself, given, sent by God into this world even as you were. So you must look even at your own children primarily as souls, and not as you look at an animal that you happen to possess, or certain goods that you possess. This is a soul given to you by God, and you are to act as its guardian and custodian.

Finally, discipline must always be exercised in such a way as to lead children to respect their parents. They will not always understand, and they will probably feel at times that they do not deserve punishment. But if we are 'filled with the Spirit', the effect of our disciplining them will be that they will love us and respect us; and a day will come when they will thank us for having done it. Even when they want to defend themselves there will be something within them that tells them that we are right. They will have a fundamental respect for our characters. They are watching our lives; they see the discipline and the control we exercise over ourselves, and they will see that what we do to them is not something capricious, that we are not merely giving vent to our own feelings and getting relief. They will always know that we love them, that we are concerned about their well-being and their benefit in this sinful, evil world: and so there will be this underlying respect and admiration and liking and love.

'And ye fathers, provoke not your children to wrath.' What a tremendous thing life is! How wonderful are all these relationships – husband, wife, parents, children! We see people in the world about us rushing into marriage and rushing out of marriage. As for the children, so many of them have no conception of what parenthood really means! Children to many are but a nuisance, over-fondled at one time, too severely punished at another; often left alone in their homes while the parents go out to 'enjoy' themselves; sent off to residential schools so that the parents may have their freedom! How little thought is given to the child, to his suffering, to the strain upon his sensitive nature! The tragedy of it all is that the lives of such people are not governed by the New Testament teaching; they are not 'filled with the Spirit'; they do not treat their children as God in His infinite love and kindness and compassion has treated us. What if God dealt with us as we often deal with our children! O the longsuffering of God! O the patience of God! O the amazing way in which He bears with our evil manners as He did with those of the children of Israel of old! There is nothing more amazing to me than the patience of God, and His longsuffering toward us. I say to Christian people, and all who are in any way responsible for the discipline of children and of young people, 'Let this mind be in you which was also in Christ Jesus'. And let the same love be in us also, lest we 'provoke our children to wrath' and thereby involve them and ourselves in all the evil consequences of our failure.

21

Godly Upbringing

Ephesians 6:1–4

We have seen that the Apostle's exhortation to the parents has two sides. There is the negative side which tells us that we must not do anything to exasperate our children, must not irritate them, must not provoke them; and then the positive side: 'Bring them up in the nurture and admonition of the Lord'. So we turn now to this positive side of the Apostle's injunction.

The very way in which Paul puts his exhortation is interesting – 'Bring them up', he says, and that is but another way of saying, 'Rear, nourish them to maturity'. In other words, the first thing that parents have to do is to realize their responsibility for the children. As we have emphasized, they are not our property, they do not ultimately belong to us, they are given to us by God for a while. For what purpose? Not that we may get what we want out of them, and use them simply to please ourselves, or to gratify our own desires. No, our business is to realize that they have to be 'reared', 'brought up', 'nurtured', 'prepared' not only for living their life in this world, but especially for the establishment of a right relationship of their souls to God. These injunctions remind us of the greatness of life; and there is nothing more sad and tragic about the world today than the failure of the masses of the people to realize its greatness.

What a tremendous thing it is that we should exist and live as individuals! And when we consider the realm of the home and the family it becomes yet more wonderful. What a great conception the Apostle's teaching gives us of parenthood and its function! He tells us that we are given these children in order that we may bring

[289]

them up and rear them and train them in the way they should go. The newspapers are constantly reminding us of the care and the attention which people give to rearing various types of animals. It is not an easy thing to train an animal, whether it is a horse or a dog or any other. It demands much time and attention. The diet has to be considered, the exercises have to be planned, suitable bedding has to be provided; the animal has to be protected from various hazards; and so on. People pay large sums of money, spend a good deal of time, and give much thought to the bringing up and rearing of an animal that it may become a prize-winner in a show. But sometimes one is given the impression that very little time and care, attention and thought, are given to the rearing of children. That is one reason why the world is as it is today, and why we are confronted by acute social problems at this present time. If people but gave as much thought to the rearing of their children as they do to the rearing of animals and flowers, the situation would be very different. They read books and listen to talks about these other matters, and want to know exactly what they have to do. But how much time is given to the consideration of this great question of rearing children? It is taken for granted, done anyhow, and the consequences are painfully obvious.

If we are to carry out the Apostle's injunction, therefore, we must sit back for a moment, and consider what we have to do. When the child comes we must say to ourselves, We are the guardians and the custodians of this soul. What a dread responsibility! In business and in professions men are well aware of the great responsibility that rests upon them in the decisions they have to take. But are they aware of the infinitely greater responsibility they bear with respect to their own children? Do they give even the same amount of thought and attention and time to it, not to say more? Does it weigh as heavily upon them as the responsibility which they feel in these other realms? The Apostle urges us to regard this as the greatest business in life, the greatest matter which we ever have to handle and transact.

The Apostle does not stop at that: ' . . . bring them up', he says, 'in the nurture and admonition of the Lord'. The two words he uses are full of interest. The difference between them is, that the first, 'nurture', is more general than the second. It is the totality of nurturing, rearing, bringing up the child. It includes, therefore, general discipline. And, as all the authorities are agreed in pointing out, its emphasis is upon actions. The second word, 'admonition', has reference rather to words which are spoken. 'Nurture' is the more general term and includes everything that we do for the children. It includes the whole process in general of the cultivation of the mind and the spirit, the morals and the moral behaviour, the whole personality of the child. That is our task. It is to look upon the child and care for it, and guard it. We have already met this same term when we were dealing with the relationship of husbands and wives, where we were told that the Lord Himself 'nourisheth and cherisheth' the church. 'No man ever yet hated his own flesh, but nourisheth and cherisheth it, even as the Lord the church'. Here we are told to do the same with respect to our children.

The word 'admonition' carries much the same meaning, except that it puts greater emphasis upon speech. Thus there are two aspects of this matter. First we have to deal with general conduct and behaviour, the things we have to do by actions. Then, in addition, there are certain admonitions that should be addressed to the child, words of exhortation, words of encouragement, words of reproof, words of blame. Paul's term includes all these, indeed everything we say to the children in actual words when we are defining positions and indicating what is right or wrong, encouraging, exhorting, and so on. Such is the meaning of the word 'admonition'.

Children are to be reared in 'the nurture and the admonition' – and then the most important addition of all – 'of the Lord': 'the nurture and admonition of the Lord'. This is where Christian parents, engaged in their duty towards their children, are in an entirely different category from all other parents. In other words, this appeal to Christian parents is not simply to exhort them to bring up their children in terms of general morality or good manners or commendable behaviour in general. That, of course, is included; everyone should be doing it; non-Christian parents should be doing it. They should be concerned about good manners, good general behaviour, an avoidance of evil; they should teach their children to be honest, dutiful, respectful, and all these various things. That is but common morality, and Christianity has not started at that point. Even pagan writers interested in the good ordering of society have always exhorted their fellow-men to teach such principles. Society cannot continue without a modicum of discipline and of law and order, at every level, and at every age. But the Apostle is not referring to that only; he says that the children of Christians are to be brought up 'in the nurture and admonition of the Lord'.

It is at this point that the peculiar and specific Christian thinking and teaching enter. In the forefront of the minds of Christian parents must ever be the thought that the children are to be brought up in the knowledge of the Lord Jesus Christ as Saviour and as Lord. That is the peculiar task to which Christian parents alone are called. This is not only their supreme task; their greatest desire and ambition for their children should be that they should come to know the Lord Jesus Christ as their Saviour and as their Lord. Is that our main ambition for our children? Does that come first? – that they may come to 'know Him whom to know is life eternal', that they may know Him as their Saviour and that they may follow Him as their Lord? 'In the nurture and the admonition of the Lord!' These, then, are the terms the Apostle uses.

We now come to the practical question as to how this is to be done. Here, again, is a matter that needs our most urgent attention. In the Bible itself there is a great deal of emphasis laid upon child training. Take, for instance, words found in the sixth chapter of Deuteronomy. Moses has reached the end of his life, and the children of Israel are shortly to enter the promised land. He reminds them of the Law of God and tells them how they are to live when they enter into the land of their inheritance. And among other things he is very careful to tell them that they have to teach their children the Law. It is not enough that they know it and observe it themselves, they must pass on their knowledge. The children must be taught it, and must never forget it. So he repeats the injunction twice in that one chapter. It occurs again in chapter 11 of Deuteronomy, and frequently here and there throughout the Old Testament. It is found in the New Testament similarly.

It is very interesting to observe in the long history of the Christian church how this particular matter always reappears and receives great prominence at every period of revival and re-awakening. The Protestant Reformers were concerned about it, and the instruction of children in moral and spiritual matters was given great prominence. The Puritans gave it still greater prominence, and the leaders of the Evangelical Awakening of two hundred years ago also did the same. Books have been written about this matter and many sermons preached about it.

This happens, of course, because when people become Christian it affects the whole of their lives. It is not merely something individual and personal; it affects the marriage relationship, and so there are far fewer divorces among Christian people than among non-Christian people. It also affects the life of the family; it affects the children, it affects the home, it affects every department of human life. The greatest epochs in the history of this country, and of other countries, have always been the years which have followed a religious awakening, a revival of true religion. The moral tone of the whole of society has been raised; even those who have not become Christian have been influenced and affected by it.

In other words, there is no hope of dealing with the moral problems of society except in terms of the Gospel of Christ. Right will never be established apart from godliness; but when people become godly they proceed to apply their principles all along the line, and righteousness is seen in the nation at large. But, unfortunately, we have to face the fact that for some reason this aspect of the matter has been sadly neglected in this present century. It is a part of the breakdown that we have been considering in life and morals and the family, the home and other aspects of life. It is a part of the mad rush in which we are all living, and by which we are all influenced so much. For one reason or another the family does not count as it used to do; it is not the centre and the unit that it was formerly. The whole idea of family life has somehow been declining; and this, alas, is partly true in Christian circles also. The family's central importance that is found in the Bible and in all the great periods to which we have referred seems to have disappeared. It is no longer being given the attention and the prominence that it once received. That makes it all the more important for us to discover the principles that should govern us in this respect.

First and foremost, the bringing up of children 'in the nurture and admonition of the Lord' is something which is to be done in the home and by the parents. This is the emphasis throughout the Bible. It is not something that is to be handed over to the school, however good the school may be. It is the duty of parents, their primary and most essential duty. It is their responsibility, and they are not to hand over this responsibility to another. I emphasize this because we are all well aware of what has been happening increasingly during this present century. More and more, parents have been transferring their responsibilities and their duties to the schools.

I regard this as a most serious matter. There is no more important influence in the life of a child than the influence of the home. The home is the fundamental unit of society, and children are born into a home, into a family. There you have the circle that is to be the chief influence in their lives. There is no question about that. It is the biblical teaching everywhere; and it is always in so-called civilizations where ideas concerning the home begin to deteriorate that society ultimately disintegrates. It thus becomes the business of Christian people to consider and re-consider very carefully the whole question of boarding schools, as to whether it is right to send children to some kind of institutional life, where they spend half of each year or more away from the home and its special peculiar influence. Can that be reconciled with the biblical teaching? The question is urgent because this has become more or less the custom and the practice of virtually all evangelical Christians who can afford to do so.

The teaching of the Scripture is that the child's welfare, the child's soul, should always be the primary consideration; and all matters of prestige – not to use any other term – and all matters of ambition should be put severely aside. Anything that militates against the child's soul, and its knowledge of God and the Lord Jesus Christ, should be rejected. The first consideration invariably should be the soul and its relationship to God. However good the education offered by a boarding school may be, if it militates against the welfare of the soul it must be put on one side. To promote that welfare is the essential element in 'the nurture and admonition of the Lord', and it forms the primary task and duty of the parents.

In the Old Testament it is quite clear that the father was a kind of priest in his household and family; he represented God. He was responsible not only for the morals and the behaviour but for the instruction of his children. The Bible's emphasis everywhere is that this is the primary duty and task of the parents. And it remains so to this day. If we are Christians at all we must realize that this great emphasis is based upon those fundamental units ordained by God – marriage, family, and home. You cannot play fast and loose with them. It is vain to say, as most do about sending children to boarding-schools, 'Everyone is doing this, and it provides a wonderful system of education'. The all-important question is, Is it biblical, is it Christian, is it really ministering to the present and eternal interests of the soul of the child?

I venture the prophecy that the recovery of spirituality and of morals in Great Britain may well come along this line. Christian people will once more have to do their own thinking. We need to be pioneers once more, as God's people in times past have had to be, and the others will then follow. We should be considering to what extent the system of boarding children away from home is responsible for the breakdown of morals in this country. I am not thinking of particular sins only, but of the whole attitude of children towards their own home. A home should not be a place where children spend their holidays. But there are many children to whom home is nothing but a place where they spend their holidays; and their parents, instead of treating them as they should, tend to give them indulgent treatment because they are only home for a while. In that case the whole idea of discipline, and of bringing up the child 'in the nurture and admonition of the Lord', is lost to sight. But, it may be argued, there are many special circumstances. If special circumstances can be proved, I agree. But if there are no special circumstances, the principle I have stated should be the rule; and there are very few special circumstances. The primary task of the home and of the parents is quite clear.

What are parents to do? They are to supplement the teaching of the church, and they are to apply the teaching of the church. So little can be done in a sermon. It has to be applied, to be explained, to be extended, to be supplemented. That is where the parents play their part. And if this has been always right and important, how much more so today than ever before! I ask Christian parents: Have you ever given serious thought to this matter? You face a greater task, perhaps, than parents have ever done, and for the following reason. Consider what is now being taught the children in the schools. The theory and hypothesis of organic evolution is being taught them as a fact. They are not being presented with it as a mere theory which has not been proved, they are given the impression that it is an absolute fact, and that all people of scientific knowledge and learning believe it. And they are regarded as odd if they do not accept it. We have to meet that situation. Higher-criticism of the Bible is also being taught with its supposed 'assured results'. There are school teachers, to my own knowledge, who are using textbooks which were published thirty or forty years ago. Few of them are aware of the changes that have taken place, even among the Higher Critics. Children are being taught perverse things in the schools, and they hear them on the wireless, and see them on the television. The whole emphasis is anti-God, anti-Bible, anti-true Christianity, anti-miraculous, and anti-supernatural. Who is going to counter these trends? That is precisely the business of parents – 'Bring them up in the nurture and the admonition of the Lord'. It demands great effort by the parents at the present time because the forces against us are so great. Christian parents today have this unusually difficult task of protecting their children against these powerful adverse forces that are trying to indoctrinate them.

There, then, is the setting! To be practical, I wish, in the second place, to show how this is not to be done. There is a way of trying to deal with this situation which is quite disastrous, and does much more harm than good. How is this not to be done? It is never to be done in a mechanical abstract manner, almost 'by numbers', as if it were some sort of drill. I remember an experience of my own in this connection some ten years or so ago. I went to stay with some friends, while I was preaching in a certain place, and I found the wife, the mother of the family, in a state of acute distress. In conversation I discovered the cause of her distress. A certain lady had been there lecturing that very week, her theme being 'How to bring up all the children in your family as good Christians'. It was wonderful! She had five or six children, and she had so organized her home and her life that she finished all her domestic work by nine o'clock in the morning, and then gave herself to various Christian activities. All her children were fine Christians; and it was all so easy, so wonderful. The mother talking to me, who had two children, was in a state of real distress feeling that she was a complete and utter failure. What had I to say to her? This: I said, 'Wait a moment; how old are the children of this lady?' I happened to know the answer, and my friend knew also. Not one of them at that time was above the age of sixteen, or thereabouts. I went on: 'Wait and see. This lady tells you that they are all Christians, and that all you need is a scheme which you carry out regularly. Wait a while; the story may be different in a few years'. And, alas, it turned out to be very different. It is doubtful whether more than one of those children is a Christian. Several of them are openly anti-Christian and have turned their backs upon it all. You cannot bring up children to be Christians in that way. It is not a mechanical process, and in any case it was all so cold and clinical. I heard of the same lady giving her same lecture in another place. There, someone was present who had a little understanding and insight. Listening to the address, this other lady made what I thought was a very good comment. She turned to some friends on the way out and said, 'I thank God she was not my mother'! That is laughable, but at the same time there is something tragic about it. What the comment meant was that there was no love there, no warmth. Here was a woman who was proud of herself; she did it all 'by numbers', mechanically. What a wonderful mother she was! This other woman detected that there was no love there, there was no real understanding, there was nothing to warm the heart of a child. A child is not a machine, and so you cannot do this work mechanically.

Nor must the work ever be done in an entirely negative or repressive manner. If you give children the impression that to be religious is to be miserable, and that it consists of prohibitions and constant repression, you may well drive them into the arms of the devil, and into the world. Never be entirely negative and repressive. I meet tragedies constantly in this respect. People talk to me at the end of a service and they say, 'This is the first time I have been in a chapel for twenty years or so'. I ask, 'How is that?' Then they tell me that they had reacted against the harshness and the repressive character of the religion in which they were brought up. They had no conception of Christianity at all. What they saw was not Christianity, but a harsh man-made religion, a false Puritanism. There are still people, alas!, who only present a caricature of true Puritanism, and have never understood its real teaching. They have seen the negative but have never seen the positive. That does great harm.

Thirdly, in bringing up our children in 'the nurture and admonition of the Lord', we must never do so in such a way as to make little prigs and hypocrites of them. I have seen much of that also. To me it is very sad, and indeed revolting, to hear children using pious phrases which they do not understand. But their parents are proud of them and say, 'Listen to them, isn't it wonderful?' The children are too young to understand such things. I know that many children like to play at preaching. Such childish behaviour may be excusable, but when you get the parents thinking that it is wonderful, and putting up the children to do it before the admiring gaze of adults, then it is almost blasphemy. It is certainly very harmful to the child. It is to turn them into little prigs, to make little hypocrites of them.

My last negative at this point is that we must never force a child

[297]

to a decision. What trouble and havoc has been wrought by this! 'Isn't it marvellous?', say the parents, 'my little So-and-So, a mere youngster decided for Christ.' Pressure had been brought to bear in the meeting. But that should never be done; you are violating the personality of the child. In addition, of course, you are displaying a profound ignorance of the way of salvation. You can make a little child decide anything. You have the power and the ability to do so; but it is wrong, it is unchristian, it is not spiritual. In other words we must never be too direct in this matter, especially with a child, never be too emotional. If your child feels uncomfortable as you are talking to him about spiritual matters, or if you are talking to someone else's child and he feels uncomfortable, your method is obviously wrong. The child should never be made to feel uncomfortable. If he does it is because you are too direct, or you are too emotional, or you are bringing pressure to bear. That is not the way to do this work.

I have known some real tragedies in this respect also. I recollect the case of two young men in particular before they reached the age of fifteen or sixteen. Their parents were always pushing them forward. In the one case one of the parents used to write about her children and give the impression that they were outstanding Christians. Both these young men have repudiated the Christian faith utterly and entirely by today, and have no use for it. Christian parents must always remember that they are handling a life, a personality, a soul. My counsel is: Do not bring pressure to bear upon your children. Do not force them to a decision. I know the anxiety felt by a parent. It is very natural; but if we are spiritual, if we are 'filled with the Spirit', we shall never violate a personality, never bring any unfair pressure to bear upon a child. So our teaching must never be too direct, or too emotional. It must never be done in such a manner that the children are made to feel disloyal to us if they do not profess belief. That is unforgiveable.

What, then, is the true way? Let me give some suggestions. There used to be at one time in people's houses – and I still see them sometimes – a little card hanging on the wall with this sentence on it, 'Christ is the Head of this house'. I am not an advocate of putting up such cards or texts; but there was something good in the idea. In the Old Testament we read that instructions were given to the children of Israel to 'Write them (the words of the Lord) on the door-posts', the reason being that we are such forgetful creatures. The early

Protestants used to paint the Ten Commandments on the walls of their churches partly for the same reason. But whether you do, or do not, display a card, the important point is that the impression should always be given that Christ is the Head of the house or the home.

How is that impression given? Chiefly by your general conduct and example! The parents should be living in such a way that the children should always have a feeling that they themselves are under Christ, that Christ is their Head. The fact should be obvious in their conduct and behaviour. Above all, there should be an atmosphere of love. 'Be not drunk with wine, wherein is excess; but be filled with the Spirit.' That is our controlling text in this as in all these particular applications. The fruit of the Spirit is love, and if the home is filled with an atmosphere of the love produced by the Spirit, most of its problems are solved. That is what does the work, not the direct pressures and appeals, but an atmosphere of love.

What else? General conversation! At the table or wherever you are, general conversation is most important. We listen perhaps to the news on the radio, and conversation begins about the news. Great affairs are being mentioned – international affairs, politics, industrial troubles etc. A part of our task in bringing up our children in the nurture and admonition of the Lord is to see to it that even such general conversation is always conducted in Christian terms. We should always bring in the Christian point of view. The children will hear other people talking about the same things. They may be walking along the road, and they hear two men arguing about the very things that they had heard discussed at home. At once they will notice one big difference; the whole approach was different at home.

In other words the Christian point of view must be brought into the whole of life. Whether you are discussing international affairs or local affairs, personal matters or business matters – whatever it is, everything must be considered under this general heading of Christianity. This is a most vital point, for when this is done, the children unconsciously become aware of the fact that there is a governing principle in the lives of their parents; their thinking and everything else about them is different from all that they see and hear in the unbelieving world. The whole atmosphere is different. Thus the children, gradually and partly unconsciously, become aware that there is such a thing as a Christian point of view. That is a real achievement. Once they get hold of that fact the problem becomes much easier.

The next matter is the answering of questions. There the Christian parent gets a great opportunity. It is sometimes extremely difficult, I know; but we are given the opportunity of answering questions. I like the way in which the matter is introduced in the sixth chapter of Deuteronomy, in the twentieth verse: 'And when thy son asketh thee in time to come, saying, What mean the testimonies, and the statutes, and the judgments, which the Lord our God hath commanded you? Then thou shalt say unto thy son, We were Pharaoh's bondmen in Egypt: and the Lord brought us out of Egypt with a mighty hand', and so on. In other words, a day will come when the children will ask a question such as this: 'Why don't you do this or that? The father and mother of my little friend do this, why don't you?' There you have been given an opportunity of bringing up your child 'in the nurture and admonition of the Lord'. But if we are to take it, we must know the right answer, and be able to supply it. You cannot 'give a reason for the hope that is in you', you cannot bring up your children in the nurture and admonition of the Lord, unless you know your Bible and its teaching. 'Why don't you do this, why don't you do that? My friends' fathers spend their evenings in public houses; you don't. They spend their evenings in clubs, they spend their nights dancing; you don't. Why? What is the difference?' When questioned in that way you must not brush the child aside and say, 'Well, we are all different, you see, and this is how we prefer it'. No, you say rather to your child: 'We are all alike at heart to begin with; and we behave in this different way not because we are naturally better than others. That is not the explanation. It is not that I have one temperament and the other fathers have other temperaments. We are all "born in sin", we are all slaves by nature to various things. There is something wrong within us all, there is an evil principle in us all and none of us knows God truly. You see, the difference is this, that God has caused me to see how wrong certain things are. But I would still be like your friends' fathers, were it not that I believe and know that God sent His only Son, the Lord Jesus of whom you have heard, into the world to rescue us, to deliver us'. Thus you introduce the Gospel; you have to decide how much to give. It depends upon the age of the child. But answer his questions, let him know, let him know exactly, when he asks his question, why you live as you do. You must not foist it on him, you must not preach at him; but if he asks his question, then tell him, tell him very simply. Tell him more and more as he gets older; but always be ready to answer the questions. Know your facts, understand your Gospel, build yourself up in it, so that you can impart it and pass it on. Thus you will be able to bring up your children in 'the nurture and admonition of the Lord'.

Then you can guide their reading. Get them to read good biographies. Biographies will appeal to them. Guide their reading in various ways; turn their minds in the right direction, and familiarize them with the glories of the Christian faith in action.

What else? Be careful always, whenever you have a meal, to return thanks to God for it, and to ask His blessing upon it. This is rarely done today by any except those who are Christians. If your children become accustomed to hearing you thanking God, and returning thanks, and asking a blessing, it will do something for them. Go further. Have what is called a family altar, which means that once, at least, every day you should meet together as a family round the Word of God. The father as the head of the house should read a portion of Scripture and offer a simple prayer. It need not be long, but let him acknowledge God and let him thank God for the Lord Jesus Christ. Let the children hear the Word of God regularly. If they ask questions about it, answer them. Give them instruction as you are able to do so. Be wise, be judicious. Do not make of it something distasteful, hateful, or boring; make it such that they will look forward to it, something they will like and in which they find delight.

In other words – to sum it all up – what we have to do is to make Christianity attractive. We should give our children the impression that the most wonderful thing in the world is Christianity; and that there is nothing in life comparable to being a Christian. We should create within them the desire to be like us. They see us and they see the joy that we have in it, and the way we marvel and wonder at it all. They should be saying to themselves, I am longing to be as old as they are, so that I can enjoy it as they obviously do. Our method must never be mechanical, legal, repressive. Our testimony must never be forced, but in all we are and do and say, let them know that we ourselves are 'bond-slaves of Jesus Christ', that God in His grace has opened our eyes and awakened us to the most glorious thing in the world, and that our greatest desire for them is that they may enter into the same knowledge and have the same joy, and have the highest privilege possible in this world, that of serving the Lord and living to the praise of the glory of His grace. Whatever your work, whether business or profession or manual labour or preaching, do all things to the glory of God, and in that way you will bring up your children 'in the nurture and the admonition of the Lord'.

WORK

Ephesians 6:5–9

5 *Servants, be obedient to them that are* your *masters according to the flesh, with fear and trembling, in singleness of your heart, as unto Christ;*
6 *Not with eyeservice, as menpleasers; but as the servants of Christ, doing the will of God from the heart;*
7 *With good will doing service, as to the Lord, and not to men:*
8 *Knowing that whatsoever good thing any man doeth, the same shall he receive of the Lord, whether* he be *bond or free.*
9 *And, ye masters, do the same things unto them, forbearing threatening: knowing that your Master also is in heaven; neither is there respect of persons with him.*

22
The Things that are God's

Ephesians 6:5–9

Here we come to yet another application of the principle which the Apostle had laid down in the previous chapter, especially in verses 18 and 21. The controlling thought, as before, is, 'Be not drunk with wine, wherein is excess; but be filled with the Spirit'. Then the general principle of the outworking of that is found in verse 21, 'Submitting yourselves one to another in the fear of God'. It is essential that we should bear in mind that that is the background. Here we are looking at the third of the illustrations which the Apostle gives of how, being filled with the Spirit, we are to submit ourselves one to another.

These words are not addressed to the world as such. The world is incapable of doing what is taught here. A godly obedience is possible only to people who are 'filled with the Spirit'. Also, we are reminded again here of certain important truths. One is that our Christianity is to cover the whole of our life and affect our every relationship. Nothing that the Christian does is the same as that which is done by the non-Christian. The latter may do the same things, but he does them in a different way. Christianity is not confined to Sunday; it is something that manifests itself in the whole of life. There is nothing more practical in the world than the Christian faith and the Christian teaching. The way in which the Apostle takes the trouble to work out his central principle in these various departments of life is proof of that in and of itself. He is not content with saying, 'Now those of you who are filled with the Spirit should submit yourselves one to another' and leaving it at that. As a very wise teacher he knows that it is necessary to go into details, to take up these points one by one and apply them. So he takes these examples, and they are examples which are quite typical of daily life and especially where the stresses and the strains in life tend to manifest themselves most frequently. Clearly that was the rule which must have guided him in choosing these particular illustrations. The most delicate relationship of all is the marriage relationship, so, for that very reason, the tensions and the stresses and the strains are liable to be at their greatest there. Then next to that comes the family. Here again is a most delicate intimate relationship, and the devil is always busy in his efforts to disrupt the home and its sanctity.

The third relationship is that of masters and servants. This follows the other two as a sphere where tensions, stresses, and strains are particularly liable to be felt. The conditions prevailing in the industrial realm today are sufficient proof of that claim. But this particular relationship is one which has always caused much trouble throughout the history of the human race. The Old Testament and the secular history-books supply an abundance of illustrations. And it remains one of the acute problems confronting Britain and all the countries of the world at this present hour. I venture to go further; it always will be a great problem. While man is in sin, and while, as the result of that, he is always primarily and essentially selfish and self-centred, there will of necessity be tensions in this particular relationship. During this present century, indeed during the second half of the previous century also, we have multiplied the machinery for dealing with this particular problem in a quite exceptional manner. Organizations and Societies and Acts of Parliament have dealt with the whole problem of labour, the relationship of master and servant. Yet in spite of all it is still one of the major problems confronting employers and employed, politicians and many others. We should not be surprised at this, because man in sin is essentially self-centred and selfish. And as that is true of all, whatever their position in life, it is inevitable that there should be these problems and difficulties and stresses. Fortunately for us the Apostle takes the trouble to deal with the matter, and to do so in detail.

Certainly, this is a great and involved and very difficult subject. We must therefore approach it with particular care. I propose to give a series of points for consideration. Remember that not one of them says everything; it will be qualified by the rest. The main trouble in connection with this problem is that it is so frequently thought of in slogans which people hurl at one another. But slogans furnish no solutions. This matter has to be reasoned through and considered carefully in the full light of biblical teaching.

In the light of what the Apostle tells us here, I start by emphasizing that there are certain general characteristics of Christian teaching that bear upon this particular matter. The first is that it is quite unique. What we are considering is something that cannot be found anywhere else. There are other teachings that appear to be like it because they have borrowed from it. There are many types of philosophers who have borrowed from the Christian teaching. Though not Christians, they have seen the excellence of certain aspects of Christian teaching, and they have borrowed them and used them to suit their own purposes. So there are teachings which may simulate the Christian teaching but which always leave out the most vital thing of all. They thus establish the uniqueness of this teaching, and its essential difference from all else.

The second characteristic is that this teaching assumes that, because we are Christians, we have undergone a profound change at the very centre of our lives. I have already said that this teaching is not addressed to the world. It would be utterly pointless to take it and address it to gatherings of working people or of employers who are not Christians. To do that would mean that we do not believe in regeneration; it would mean that we do not believe that man by nature is entirely perverted as the result of sin; it would mean that we do not agree that man is essentially selfish and self-centred. But the whole of the biblical teaching is based upon that supposition. Therefore these epistles are only addressed to churches, to members of the Christian church. They are not comparable to newspaper articles in the daily Press. There were no newspapers in ancient days, but even if there had been, these epistles would never have appeared in them. These are epistles for churches, for church members, for Christians only, in other words for people who have been born again, who have a new nature, a new outlook, who are 'new creatures', people of whom it is true that 'old things are passed away; behold, all things are become new'.

The Apostle has reminded the Ephesians of these truths at length in the first three chapters. Then he summed it all up in chapter 4, beginning at verse 17, and especially in the phrase 'Ye have not so learned Christ'. Then again in chapter 5, verse 8: 'Ye were sometimes darkness, but now are ye light in the Lord'. The Ephesians were new creatures, and the Apostle assumes that in his teaching.

This principle has a particular significance today. There are people whose names and utterances are constantly appearing in the Press. They are regarded as experts on the Christian view of industry and similar matters, but their statements often indicate clearly that they have never grasped the principle I have enunciated. They think that Christianity is a teaching which can be offered to the world as it is; and they appeal to people to put it into practice. Thereby they are denying the first principles of Christianity, and wasting their breath. Their efforts never produce the desired results. 'Verily they have their reward' says our Lord of such people, and the reward is the publicity they receive; but they do not touch the situation; they fail to make any difference whatsoever to the course of events. But above all, as I say, their ideas are a complete denial of the whole basis of the Christian teaching, which assumes that a radical and tremendous change has taken place in the people to whom it addresses its appeals.

But then, thirdly, the teaching of the Apostle assumes something further, namely, that Christians have a knowledge of doctrine, and the ability to work out that doctrine. That knowledge and ability are pre-supposed in the New Testament teaching on Christian living. The New Testament does not come to us and say, 'As a Christian you are bound to have certain problems and difficulties. You will want to know how to behave as an employee, how to behave as an employer, what you are to do. Ah, the only thing to do is to "take it to the Lord", just pray about it, and then He will show you what to do; indeed He will do it for you'. But that is not New Testament teaching at all. In New Testament teaching we are first of all given the doctrine, the teaching; then we are told that we have to apply that to our personal circumstances. Obviously, if we do not know the doctrine we cannot apply it; if we lack an understanding of the teaching we cannot put it into operation. First of all we have the instruction; we must receive it and understand it; then we say, 'Now in the light of this, this is what I have to do'. That is the New Testament doctrine of sanctification; and what we have here is just one practical example and illustration of how we show in a practical way that we are being sanctified. Such is the sanctified life in this matter of 'servants and masters'. But without a knowledge and belief of the doctrine it cannot be done.

The last general observation I offer is a comment once more on the balance and the fairness of the teaching. It starts with the servants. The Apostle starts in each instance, you remember, with those who are called upon to subject themselves – the wife to the husband, the children to the parents, and now the servants to the masters according to the flesh. But how careful he is to put the two sides! There is never injustice, never unfairness. Husbands are told about their duties, fathers are told about their duties, and masters are reminded of theirs in this way – 'And you masters, do the same things unto them, forbearing threatening: knowing that your Master also is in heaven; neither is there respect of persons with Him'. I remind you of the balance because it is one of the great glories of this teaching; it is what makes it so utterly unique. There is no other teaching that does this as the Scripture does it. To me it is sufficient proof, in and of itself, that this is indeed the very Word of God. God looks down upon us all, and on all the divisions and distinctions of which we make so much; He puts them all at the right level, He shows us the right perspective, which is that everything is under Him.

Thus we find ourselves introduced to the great problem. 'Servants' – how do we interpret it? At this point our translations are somewhat unfortunate; they do not give us the true impression of the meaning of the word. It really means 'slaves'. Slaves! The Apostle was not dealing here with the case of hired servants. There were in the civilized world at that time hired servants; there were house servants who were hired and given their wages. But the Apostle is not dealing with them primarily; he is dealing with slaves. Slavery was universal in his day; and many of these early Christians were literally slaves. The word the Apostle used is proof enough of that in and of itself. He used the word that is always used for slaves, not for hired servants; but if any doubt remains it is settled by verse 8 – 'Knowing that whatsoever good thing any man doeth, the same shall he receive of the Lord, whether he be bond (bound)' – that is, a slave – 'or free' – that is, a free-man. So the contrast is between a slave and a free-man. In other words the Apostle is quite definitely and specifically dealing here with the question of slavery and how the slave is to conduct himself. Thus we cannot expound this paragraph without at once coming face to face with the problem of slavery, and in particular the biblical teaching with regard to slavery.

I need not say that we are looking at a highly difficult and controversial subject. There are people who say that their main reason for not being Christian is the attitude of the Bible and the New Testament in particular to slavery. They argue that that is enough to damn it, and therefore they can have nothing to do with it. It has indeed often been a cause of great perplexity to many Christian people. Imagine what the position must have been one hundred and sixty years ago when Wilberforce was waging his great campaign for the abolition of slavery in Britain's overseas possessions. Cast your minds back also to the 'sixties of the last century, when the Civil War in the United States was fought over this very subject. There you see at once what a subtle and difficult and involved problem this really is. And there is still a great deal of confusion with respect to it. But I would further remark that in looking at the question we are incidentally looking at a number of related problems also. We are looking at the whole problem of the relationship of the Christian to the State, at the whole problem of the relationship of the Christian to trade and business at the present time, and in particular to trade-unionism. We are looking, indeed, at the whole problem of the attitude of the Christian to social conditions, to politics, reform, and even possible revolution and rebellion. It is all implicit here.

The New Testament deals with great principles; it presses them upon our attention. It would be foolish for someone to say, 'Well, if that deals with slavery, what has it to do with me?' The answer is that slavery is only one of the possible relationships of man to man; and what the Apostle is concerned about is the behaviour, the conduct and the reaction, of Christian people who are in any position of subservience to others, Christians who are employed in any service. It goes further; we are all subservient to the State, to social enactments and social conditions. So this subject, if we are to look at it truly and thoroughly, will take us into all those various realms. Here the theme is slavery and the question arises, How should a Christian slave conduct himself? Has he to seek to free himself? Is he to try to abolish slavery? This at once leads to all the other questions, to all conceivable forms of employment, to all kinds of social and economic relationships. This is yet a further reason why we should thank God for the Scriptures. There are people who look at these things superficially and who say that to be a Christian does not help me to decide whether or not I should join a trade union, for there is nothing in the Bible about trade-unions simply because there were no trade-unions in ancient times. But the principle governing that question is here, in this very paragraph. Our business therefore is to understand the paragraph, to get hold of the principle, and then to apply it to the particular aspect of the problem with which we find ourselves confronted.

Undoubtedly the best way of approaching this whole complex matter is to gather together the relevant teaching of the Bible in its entirety. There are a number of passages that deal with it. Take, for instance, Matthew 22, verses 15–21, where we are told that certain of the Pharisees and Herodians came together to our Lord and put their catch question to Him, 'Shall we pay tribute to Caesar, or not?' Note our Lord's reply, 'Show me the tribute money'. He looked at it and said, 'Whose is this image and superscription?' They said, 'Caesar's'. Then He gave that decisive reply, 'Render therefore unto Caesar the things that are Caesar's, and' – a thing they had not asked Him about, but which He added – 'and unto God the things that are God's'. We are told that 'they marvelled, and left him, and went their way'. We can well understand their consternation. They had met with more than they had bargained for; they heard teaching that they had never anticipated.

Another very interesting example of this selfsame thing, and one which is often overlooked is found in Matthew, chapter 17, verses 24 to 27: 'When they were come to Capernaum, they that received tribute money came to Peter, and said, "Doth not your master pay tribute?" He saith, "Yes". And when he was come into the house, Jesus prevented (anticipated) him, saying, "What thinkest thou, Simon? of whom do the kings of the earth take custom or tribute? of their own children, or of strangers?" Peter saith unto him, "Of strangers". Jesus saith unto him, "Then are the children free. Notwithstanding, lest we should offend them, go thou to the sea, and cast an hook, and take up the fish that first cometh up; and when thou hast opened its mouth, thou shalt find a piece of money; that take, and give unto them for me and thee".'

Another crucial statement is that found in the Epistle to the Romans at the beginning of chapter 13: 'Let every soul be subject unto the higher powers. For there is no power but of God: the powers that be are ordained of God. Whosoever therefore resisteth the power, resisteth the ordinance of God; and they that resist shall receive to themselves damnation. For rulers are not a terror to good works, but to evil' and so on. Then we have the Epistle to Philemon which deals quite directly and specifically with this whole question of slavery. There is also a reference to the same matter, the same principle, in the First Epistle of Peter, chapter 2, beginning at verse 13: 'Submit yourselves to every ordinance of man for the Lord's sake; whether it be to the king, as supreme, or unto governors, as unto them that are sent by him for the punishment of evil-doers, and for the praise of them that do well'. Then he continues: 'As free, and not using your liberty for a cloak of maliciousness, but as the servants of God . . . Servants, be subject to your masters with all fear; not only to the good and gentle, but also to the froward'. And remember that these instructions about obeying 'the powers that be' were written when the Emperor was none other than that cruel despot Nero. Christians were told to be subject even to him and to all such powers.

There we have examples of direct teaching, but in addition, there is indirect teaching. For instance in the Book of Daniel we have an account of Daniel's conduct and behaviour, especially in chapters 3 and 6. There is also very interesting implied teaching, for instance, in the sixteenth chapter of the Book of the Acts of the Apostles, where the Apostle Paul and Silas were arrested, beaten and scourged, and thrown into the innermost prison. Later we are told that the authorities were going to set them free but the Apostle objected and said that as they were Roman citizens the magistrates who had wrongly subjected them to such treatment and imprisonment must themselves come in person and let them out. It is an interesting sidelight on this whole question. And there is a further example in Acts chapter 25 where the Apostle Paul appeals to Caesar. As a Roman citizen he had a right to do so, and he exercised his right.

As we look at these passages in the Scriptures I feel once more constrained to make some general comments. Firstly, have you ever been struck by the fact that there is comparatively very little teaching in the Scriptures on this subject, directly and specifically? It is mainly a matter of general teaching, and of the establishment of principles which are to govern this matter. But why is it that the Bible does not give more attention to such problems? Why does it not give us much more direct teaching respecting the problem immediately before us, that has been present age after age in the life of the human race? Why such paucity of teaching? The answer, surely, must be that the Bible's main interest throughout is in a man's relationship to God. All its stress, all its emphasis is given to *that* problem. As we see illustrated in our Lord's reply to the Pharisees and Herodians, it is that which makes the incident so significant. Those two sects were in many ways typical representatives of modern men. They asked, 'Master, is it lawful to pay tribute to Caesar or not?' Today it is, 'What has the church to say about apartheid? What has the church to say about economics? What has the church to say about war?' Though the actual subjects may change as regards their form, the principle behind the questions remains the same always. Never a word about man's relationship to God! The theme, in all its variations, is always man's relationship to man – man's rights, the treatment of man by his fellows, and so on. Our Lord's reply also is still the same. He introduces his 'AND' – the thing we have forgotten, that which gets us into a muddle about these particular problems – 'AND unto God the things that are God's'. That is a perfect example of the typical emphasis of the Bible. It is concerned about man's relationship to God. That is its great message, its first message.

Take another illustration. A scribe came to our Lord and asked, 'Which is the first and the greatest commandment?' He, again, like the Pharisees and Scribes, was one who spent much time in arguing about the details of the Law, and the question virtually was, Which is the greatest of these six hundred and thirteen? One said this, another said that; the arguments were endless. The man came to our Lord and asked, 'Which do you say is the greatest?' And our Lord replied, 'Thou shalt love the Lord thy God with all thy heart, and soul, and mind, and strength. That is the first and the chiefest commandment. And the second' – yes, but it is only second – 'is like unto it, Thou shalt love thy neighbour as thyself'. The Lord does not put the second first. Human relationships do not come first; they never come first in the Bible; it is always man's relationship to God first. Our Lord breaks through all the pettifogging legalistic attitude. He says that the trouble with the Pharisees and Scribes is, 'You tithe mint and rue and anise and cummin, and have forgotten the weightier matters of the law'. 'You compass sea and land to make one proselyte . . . but you have forgotten the love of God'. They were missing the principal thing, the great thing, the central thing, that which the Bible everywhere stresses. With these thoughts in mind, read again our passage in Ephesians 6: 'Servants, be obedient to them that are your masters according to the flesh, with fear and trembling, in singleness of your heart, as unto Christ: not with eye service, as men-pleasers, but as the servants of Christ, doing the will of God from the heart'. The Lord lifts the question up into the sphere of God and our relationship to Him. And he is careful to say the same to the masters, 'Knowing that your Master also is in heaven; neither is there respect of persons with Him'. Keep in mind, then, the invariable rule.

My second comment is one which is hated by many today who claim to be practical men of affairs. Life in this world is always regarded in the Bible as being of secondary importance; it is just a pilgrimage, a journey. What are we? 'We are strangers and pilgrims', says Peter. We find this emphasis in the whole of the Old Testament; it is summed up magnificently in the eleventh chapter of the Epistle to the Hebrews, that portrait gallery of the saints and heroes of the faith. It tells us that these men were 'looking for a city which hath foundations, whose builder and maker is God'. They regarded themselves but as 'strangers and pilgrims' on the earth. They were journeymen. That is why Moses, one of them, had his eye 'on the recompence of the reward'. He preferred therefore to endure hardship with Christ and His people rather than 'to enjoy the pleasures of sin for a season'. These men of the Bible rode very loosely to life in this world. They did not want to settle down in this world, they knew that they were meant for another. It is the other realm that matters, it is that other eternal realm that counts. This teaching is found everywhere in the New Testament. Our Lord's teaching abounds in it; and you find it in the epistles, as, for example, in the words: 'Set your affection on things above, not on things on the earth' (Colossians 3:2). It is the great theme of the Book of Revelation also.

It is very important for us to remember this, because it is the principle that controls the Bible's teaching about slavery and all these other matters. The guiding principle is man's relationship to God, and the view that this present life is something passing, temporary and evanescent. That does not mean, of course, that this life and this world are to be ignored; it does not mean that they are to be dismissed as having no importance at all. Still less does it mean that a Christian must decide to become a monk or a hermit or an anchorite, and segregate himself from the world. That, of course, was a complete misunderstanding of the teaching. But it does mean that we do not put this life first, we do not think about this world alone. This world is only considered and understood in the light of another world. We are pilgrims of eternity; we are 'a colony of heaven'; 'our citizenship is in heaven'; that is where we belong (Philippians 3:20-21). We are still living in this world, but our true home is in that world; our centre of interest is there, the seat of government for us is in heaven. I know of nothing that is more important at a time like this than that we should grasp that controlling principle – man in his relationship to God, man in his right relationship to this world. This world and man are secondary, not primary. God first, heaven first, 'the glory' first. This life is temporary, preparatory, impermanent. We are moving on. We do not neglect this world, we do not attempt to go out of the world; but we keep it in its right and subordinate position. It is in the light of such a principle, and that alone, that we can understand this teaching.

Our deduction from the foregoing is that this particular emphasis is always to be the primary characteristic of the church and her teaching. The business of the church is to expound the Scriptures; and these are the controlling principles which we find in the Scriptures. They must therefore be the controlling principles in the preaching and in the teaching of the church. The primary business of the church is not to deal with conditions in this world, but rather with the Christian's relationship to them, and with his conduct while he finds himself in them. As the Bible always puts its main and primary emphasis upon man in his relationship to God and his temporary relationship to this passing world, so must the church.

The church must not spend her time and energy in dealing with conditions as such in this world. That is not her primary task. And it is interesting to notice that she did not regard that as her task in the early centuries. There is no protest even against slavery in the New Testament. I repeat that the business of the church is not with conditions as such, but rather with the way in which the Christian is to work in existing conditions, and with the way in which he is to conduct and comport himself. This is something of which we must never lose sight. I suggest that the condition of the church today is very largely due to the fact that this great principle has been forgotten. I have no desire to be controversial – I am simply expounding Scripture – but I cannot find any justification in the Scripture for the notion of so-called spiritual lords in the House of Lords. I can see no justification in the Scripture for bishops and archbishops taking their seats in the House of Lords, and taking part in debates about politics and social affairs and conditions. Let me hasten to add this. There is as little justification for Free Church or Nonconformist ministers who spend their time preaching on politics and economics and social matters. Both groups are wrong, and they are equally wrong. The task of the church is to remind men constantly of their relationship to God, even as our Lord did. People come to us with their questions, and our business is to see that the emphasis is on God, and that their relationship to God is put in the first place, and that we also teach them their right attitude towards this present life and world. The tragedy of the world situation today is mainly that the majority do not see and realize that the world's malady is due to its paganism, its ungodliness, its irreligion. In Britain and in every other land men and women have forgotten God, their relationship to God, and their eternal destiny. While that is the position, the church is spending most of her time in dealing with the secondary matters, the passing matters, the matters that are only dealt with incidentally in the Scriptures, and that merely as illustrations of the great general principles. Is it not tragic that while church leaders, so-called, are always talking about these other matters which our Lord puts in a very subsidiary position, the great central need of man is passing by default?

There is one other general aspect of this question which I must mention before we can come to deal with the detailed teaching. There are those who as Christians have been tempted to contract altogether out of the world, as it were. There have been, and still are, those who say that it is wrong for a Christian to vote at a local election or a General Election. They regard it as sinful for a Christian to engage in politics at either local or national level.

Such an attitude is, again, a complete misunderstanding of the teaching; it is as bad as the other errors which I have mentioned, for it departs from Scripture's perfect balance. We are not to go out of the world, we do not cease to be citizens of this world; and we are to exercise certain functions as citizens while we are in this world. Yes, but we are to keep ourselves in the right place, in the right position. It is always a question of priorities, and of emphasis, of what comes first and of what comes second.

To sum up what we have seen: the subject is one which is surrounded by so many difficulties and perplexities that the only safe way to approach it is to look carefully at the Scriptures, to bring them all together, to compare Scripture with Scripture, and never to wrest a text out of its context. Every statement must be taken in its context, taken as a whole, then put together with all the others. Thus alone can we discover the great principles of biblical teaching. We must examine ourselves also in the light of the Word. If we cannot say that our first and chief concern is our relationship to God, then whatever we may believe about these various matters is more or less irrelevant. If we cannot say that we view our life in this world as temporary, passing, evanescent, again we are wrong. If in any shape or form in our thinking or in our talking we give the impression that this world and this life are everything to us, and that they must always be at the centre, I say we are no longer in a New Testament position. The problems are there, and we have to do something about them; we have to realize our relationship to them. But if we fail to do so in the way the Bible teaches; if we fail to remember that it is all fleeting and temporary, and that what really matters is that we belong to another realm also, we are not in the Christian position at all, and our deductions therefore almost certainly will be wrong.

These things having been said, we can now proceed to consider the teaching of the Scripture first and foremost with regard to slavery, but also, by implication, with regard to any one of these positions in which we are involved with other people – in employment, or under the State, or whatever it may be. And we must keep in our minds also the question as to whether rebellion is ever justified or justifiable. These problems have had to be met by our forefathers in past centuries; and there are many in the world who have to face these problems urgently at the present time. The fact that they may not be so acute in Great Britain is no reason why we should not think about them. We ought to know what we would do if such a position arose here. In any case we ought to be able to help others. You may have relations in other countries, who may write to you and say 'You are a Christian, tell me what am I to do?' It is our duty to know the biblical teaching so that we may apply it ourselves and help others to do so. May God give us grace to do that to the glory of His holy name!

23
The Christian's Priorities

Ephesians 6:5–9

Having taken note of the biblical principles involved in the obedience of a Christian to masters, employers, governments, and others, we next consider the practical application of the principles, remembering that the business of the church is not to deal with political or social or economic conditions as such. But some people object at this point and say, 'But what about the Old Testament prophets? Were not they always dealing with these practical problems and conditions?' The answer to that is quite simple. The nation of Israel was also the church. There was no division between the State and the church then; the State and the church were one. So that as the prophets address their remarks to the nation, they are addressing God's people, the believers. The business of the church always is to deal with conditions in the church, and as in those days the church and State were one, it was the church's business to deal with political and other matters. But the moment we come to the New Testament we find an entirely different position. Here the church is separated from the world, and gathered out of it. She has her relationship to the State, but is no longer one with the State. It is vital that we should observe this distinction. There is no contradiction between the Old and the New Testaments; the attention is always given to the church, to God's people, and to God's people in their relationship to Him as pilgrims of eternity.

The deduction we therefore draw is that the church's task primarily is to evangelize, and to bring people to a knowledge of God. Then, having done that, she is to teach them how to live their life under God as His people. The church is not here to reform the

[318]

world, for the world cannot be reformed. The business of the church is to evangelize, to preach the Gospel of salvation to men who are blinded by sin and under the domination and the power of the devil. The moment the church begins to enter into the details of politics and economics, she is doing something that militates against her primary task of evangelism.

As one obvious example, take the case of the church and communism. My contention is that it is not the business of the Christian church to be denouncing communism. She is actually spending a great deal of her time in doing this very thing at the present time. It is wrong for this reason, that the primary task of the church is to evangelize communists, to open their eyes, to bring them to conviction and to conversion. Whatever the position or political views of men, whether they are communists or capitalists or anything else, we are to regard them all as sinners, and equally sinners. They are all lost, they are all damned, they all need to be converted, they all need to be born again. So the church looks on the world and its peoples in an entirely different way from non-Christians. If the church therefore spends her time in denouncing communism she is more or less shutting the door of evangelism among communists as firmly as possible. The communist says, 'Your Christianity is just anti-communist and pro-capitalist; I am not going to listen to that message'. Therefore you cannot evangelize him. The church is not meant to deal with political and other positions directly, her task is to preach her Gospel to all and sundry whatever they are, and to bring them to a knowledge of Christ. She must refrain from entering into details lest her primary task of evangelism be impeded and hindered, and lest she herself shut the door against the very thing she claims she should be doing. That is what one deduces in general from the biblical teaching. We are always to do what the Apostle does here, what we saw our Lord Himself did, and what all the writers and teachers in the Bible do, whether in the Old Testament or the New.

But what are the more detailed principles that we deduce from all this?

The first principle is that Christianity obviously does not abolish our relationship to existing social, political and economic conditions. It is necessary to say that, because some of the early Christians erred at this point, and there are many who still do so. There are those who still think, as some of the early Christians did, that once a man became a Christian he no longer is bound to his wife if she is not a Christian. Hence Paul had to write the seventh chapter of the first Epistle to the Corinthians. It was happening on both sides. The man, for instance, would argue in this fashion: 'We were married when we were pagans in unbelief, but now I am a Christian and I see everything differently. My wife is not a Christian, so I am not bound to her any longer, for that would hinder my Christian life'. Similarly with the woman. The converted were tending to leave unconverted partners. But the Apostle writes to them and tells them not to do so. There were children who were tending to behave in the same way. They had been converted but their parents remained pagan, so they said, 'Of course our parents no longer have any control over us. They do not understand, they are pagans, and therefore we must no longer submit to them and their guidance'. But Paul teaches them otherwise. And so it was with this question of servants in their relationship to masters. Indeed, we find in the second Epistle to the Thessalonians, in the third chapter, that there were some Christians who even stopped working. They argued that they were now in a new realm and were to spend their time in looking for the return of the Lord. So they abandoned their daily tasks and were just looking to the heavens and waiting for the appearance of the Lord. The Apostle has to tell them quite plainly that 'if a man will not work, neither should he eat'. What they were doing was due to a complete misunderstanding of Christianity.

In the case of the relationship of servants and masters, the tendency was to argue wrongly from the fact that we all are equal in the eyes of the Lord, and to say, 'Does not the Apostle Paul teach that "there is neither Jew nor Greek, there is neither bond nor free, there is neither male nor female; ye are all one in Christ Jesus"? We are all equal now. There is no difference between men and women any longer, so let women be ministers of the Gospel and preach, and no longer should servants be subject to their masters. The fact that we are Christians has abolished the old relationships'. Again, a complete misunderstanding of Christianity! What the Apostle teaches is that there is no difference from the standpoint of the possibility of salvation. But that does not do away with the orders of society, it does not abolish the inherent difference between a man and a woman, or these various other relationships.

The history of the Christian church shows that people have

constantly fallen into this error. The sect known as the Anabaptists, that arose in the sixteenth century, did so, and said that Christians should have nothing to do with the State. They tried to cut themselves off, to segregate themselves from the world in every respect. There are still people who tend in that direction; some think it is wrong for a Christian to pay rates and taxes, and some for a Christian to take part in politics. They do not vote at the elections and so on. Now all that results from a failure to see this first principle – that the fact that we have become Christians does not dissolve or abolish our relationship to the State, and to social, political and economic conditions.

The Apostle even goes so far here as to say that our becoming Christians does not even automatically bring slavery to an end. He does not tell slaves that because they have become Christians the former conditions are abolished; indeed he says the exact opposite. The slaves are to go on as they were before, but with the new standpoint and attitude which he here teaches. His Epistle to Philemon teaches exactly the same thing. But perhaps the clearest statement of all is found in 1 Corinthians 7, verses 20-24: 'Let every man abide in the same calling wherein he was called. Art thou called being a servant (a slave)? Care not for it; but if thou mayest be made free, use it rather. For he that is called in the Lord, being a servant (a slave), is the Lord's freeman: likewise also he that is called, being free, is Christ's servant (slave). Ye are bought with a price; be not ye the servants (the slaves) of men. Brethren, let every man, wherein he is called, therein abide with God'. That is the classical statement on this whole matter. 'Art thou called being a slave? care not for it.' Do not allow that to be the big thing in your life; do not become anxious about it; do not let it absorb all your attention; do not allow it to occupy the centre of your thinking. 'Care not for it; but if thou mayest be made free, use it rather.' The fact that we have become Christians does not abolish our relationship to social, political and economic conditions.

The second principle at first sounds most astonishing. Christianity not only does not change our relationship to these conditions, it does not even condemn such things as slavery directly as being sinful. This has been a great stumblingblock to many people, and particularly during this last century. But our business is to expound Scripture. People argue that slavery is patently wrong and sinful, therefore Christianity must of necessity denounce it. They argue in

[321]

the same way about various other things at the present time, for example, fighting and war. They say, 'But it is obvious, everyone can see that it is wrong; even a man who is not a Christian can see it; any man who has a sense of fairness and righteousness, and a view of the dignity of man, must see at once that it is altogether wrong'. Yet the plain fact is that the Bible does not condemn slavery as such directly. If it intended to do so, Paul would surely do it here; but he does not. In writing to Philemon he does not do so, and he does not do so elsewhere. Our Lord did not do so.

This is something which the natural man simply cannot understand at all; and the rationalists and humanists of today – these critics of Christianity – think that they have an unanswerable point here. Of course the simple answer to them is that they have never even begun to see the two great controlling principles which we have already laid down. They cannot see that it is a man's relationship to God that matters fundamentally, and that once a man has seen that, everything else, including slavery, becomes different to to him. Though he be still a slave he does not view that as he did before; he is now 'Christ's freeman'. It is because these humanists are blind to the supernatural, blind to the spiritual, because they see nothing but this world, nothing but this life, that the whole of their thinking is vitiated. Christian thinking is unlike natural thinking at every point. That is why, to me, it is tragic to see men who call themselves Christians joining in with, and participating in the activities of these rationalist non-Christians at the present time. The whole approach, the entire mode of thinking is entirely different. We note then that Christianity does not even condemn slavery directly as being sinful; and that is doubtless why slavery persisted for many centuries.

Proceeding to our third principle we note that, while Christianity does not condone slavery it does not justify it either. Here, once more, there has been frequent misunderstanding. There have been Christians who have thought that Christianity is but a justification of the 'status quo'. I am amazed at the blindness of people who are falling into the Roman Catholic trap at the present time. Roman Catholicism is fighting Communism, and is inviting all Protestants, and all who use the name Christian to join with them in doing so. Those who accept the invitation do not see that Roman Catholicism is mainly concerned to defend her own particular form of totalitarianism. It is simply a case of one totalitarian system against another, a defending of the 'status quo'. Christianity never does that. It does not condemn slavery, but it does not condone or justify slavery. What is its attitude then? I have already explained: What Christianity is interested in is the way in which a Christian slave behaves himself towards his master, and how the master behaves towards his slave. It does not deal directly with the question of slavery per se.

The trouble today is that the leaders of the Christian church are spending much of their time in dealing with these things directly. They are always preaching about them, sending messages and protests to governments, taking part in processions. Direct action! The Bible never does that; what it is very concerned about is how the Christians on the two sides of the problem and the situation conduct themselves.

This is such vital teaching that I must put it in yet another way. Christianity is not concerned to condone such practices as slavery, it is not here as a defence of the status quo. We hear so much today about defending Western civilization against various forms of attack. That is all wrong! As a Christian I am not primarily interested in Western civilization, I am interested in the Kingdom of God; and I am as anxious that men behind the Iron Curtain should be saved as that men on this side of the Iron Curtain should be saved. We must not take up a position of antagonism towards those whom we want to win for Christ. If we spend the whole of our time talking against them we shall never win them. That is why I never preach a so-called Temperance sermon – I want to see drunkards converted. Our business is not to denounce drink; it is to get the poor drunkard to believe on the Lord Jesus Christ; because that alone can deliver him. But the church constantly mistakes this teaching and goes into these things in detail.

Another way of making the same point is to say that it is not the business of the Christian church to preach the divine right of kings. There was a time when the church did so. James the First was a very astute man. He said, 'No Bishop, no King'! So he and the episcopal church stood together, and the church became a defence and bulwark of the divine right of kings. By so doing she had abrogated her whole position, and she was being false to her teaching. The business of the Christian church is not to defend any particular system – political, social or economic. Christianity, I say, while it does not condemn slavery does not condone slavery. Its attitude is

[323]

the detached one which looks on and is concerned about principles.

That leads to the fourth principle. The Bible's concern, Christianity's concern, is as to how the Christian should react to these things, and how he is to live in such a world as this. That is the essence of the teaching, and we have it here. Paul, when he comes to 'servants and masters', does not begin to give his views as a Christian on the question of slavery. 'Servants', he says, 'be obedient to them that are your masters according to the flesh, with fear and trembling, in singleness of your heart, as unto Christ; not with eyeservice . . .' In other words his one interest is as to how they are to conduct themselves as Christians in that situation. Likewise with the masters. 'You masters, do the same unto them, forbearing threatening.' He does not tell them to give up their slaves; instead, he says, 'Do not threaten them, do not be unkind, do not be cruel to them, "knowing that your Master also is in heaven; neither is there respect of persons with Him". '

We have the same teaching in the first Epistle of Peter, chapter 2: 'Servants, be subject to your masters with all fear' – and notice – 'not only to the good and gentle, but also to the froward'. He does not tell slaves to rise up and rebel against the masters. The Bible never does so. But it is very interested to assert that a Christian man should never abuse his position – 'not using your liberty as a cloak for maliciousness'. That is the danger, that the Christian may use his Christian position as a cloak for the malice that is in his heart. That has often been done; things have been done in the name of Christianity that should never have been done at all. And that does untold harm to Christianity. It has happened on both sides. It is always because men and masters forget that their duty is to God, their Master who is in heaven, that the problems have arisen.

We could easily dilate on these problems. There are many people today who say that the so-called working classes are outside the church because the church of Victorian days was largely a church of the masters. Go to the mining districts of any part of Great Britain and you will be told that regularly. They will remind you that, last century, far too frequently the same man was the boss in the works as in the chapel, the head deacon was generally the manager of the works. That is why they say they have rebelled against Christianity and the church. That certainly happened to a great extent in Russia. The monarchy in Russia was under the close influence of the Russian Orthodox Church, with that evil monk Rasputin controlling the royal family. So the Russian people identified that horrible abuse with Christianity; and they threw out what they thought was Christianity. In reality they were doing nothing of the sort; they were rejecting a most horrible perversion of Christianity, that was not Christianity at all. But that has been done very often; it has been done on both sides; and that very largely because both sides have failed to implement and to understand the principle the Apostle is enunciating here. Our business is primarily to relate ourselves correctly to the positions in which we find ourselves.

In Romans chapter 13 we find exactly the same teaching. There the Apostle tells Christians 'to be subject to the powers that be, for the powers that be are ordained of God. Whosoever therefore resisteth the power, resisteth the ordinance of God; and they that resist shall receive to themselves damnation'. These words were written to people who were under the power of the Emperor Nero, of all men. But that is what the Christian has to do. His primary concern is to be a servant of God and of Christ. Whatever his position, whatever his circumstances, whether he is master or servant, whether he is king or subject, it does not matter. They are all to submit themselves together, and to see that in every way they are behaving as Christian people. They are not to be primarily concerned about the situations and the conditions as such; their concern as 'pilgrims of eternity', as 'strangers and pilgrims', is to be true to their Master, and to be preparing for their everlasting home.

But I proceed to a fifth and last principle. Someone may ask, 'Well then, what about improving conditions? Are you not in reality simply taking up, after all, a defence of that status quo? You say you are not doing that, but in effect you are doing so. You are saying that the Christian is not to be concerned about the conditions, but that he should concentrate on Christ-like behaviour in the conditions'. The answer to this question is quite plain. It is not the business of the church to be concerned about improving conditions; her business always is to be laying down the biblical principles I have been expounding. She should never attack the circumstances and the conditions directly. But, at the same time, that does not mean that the individual Christian as a citizen of a country should not be concerned about improving conditions. There, it seems to me, is the dividing line. The individual Christian is never to take the law into his own hands, he is never to act as an individual. But that does not mean that as a citizen of the country to which he belongs he is not entitled to take part in improving the circumstances and conditions in which he and others live.

It works in the following way. The Christian message is primarily concerned to produce Christians. It preaches its Gospel, it convicts men of sin, it calls them to Jesus' blood, it brings them to this Word by which they can be born again by the power of the Spirit, it changes men. Then, having changed them in that way, it goes on to teach them these great principles. That is the direct task and business of the church. But as the church does that, she is indirectly doing something else; she is obviously influencing the whole personality of such people – their mind, their thinking, their understanding. And the moment that begins to happen to men they begin to see things in a different way and they begin to apply their thinking to daily living.

An illustration of what I am saying is to be found, for instance, in the Evangelical Awakening of two hundred years ago. Prior to that time the majority of the common people of this country were ignorant, and illiterate, and living a life of sin and of squalor. The facts are to be found in the secular history-books. There were few schools; the people were in a state of ignorance, illiteracy, and gross and foul sin. Why did that situation become very different last century, and still more so this century? Was it because the Christian church conducted a great social and political campaign? That is not the explanation. There were always individual church leaders who were trying to do such things; but that never led to anything of value. The change was produced by the flaming, passionate evangelism of George Whitefield, the Wesleys, and others, and the situation became transformed. What was their message? What did Whitefield and the Wesleys preach to the masses, for instance to those miners living near Bristol? Did they talk about social conditions, about wages, about hours of work? Did they rouse them to agitate and protest against their miseries, and to rise up in rebellion? The answer is to be found in their Journals. Whitefield preached a message that brought men to see that they were sinners in the hands of an angry God who nevertheless had provided a way of forgiveness. He preached to them about their souls, not about their bodies, not about their circumstances and conditions. The first time John Wesley preached in the streets in the poorest district of Newcastle-on-Tyne, his text was from Isaiah 53, 'He was wounded for our transgressions, He was bruised for our iniquities; the chastisement of our peace was upon Him; and by His stripes we are healed'. The same happened everywhere. The evangelists were always dealing with men as men, and the result of their preaching was that people were changed and converted. They became Christians, they were born again. What was the result of that? They began to use their minds. They had not used them before; they had lived to drink, to gamble and to indulge in such cruel sports as cock-fighting. But now having been awakened spiritually, the whole man became awakened. They found that they had minds. The first thing they desired to do was to read the Bible, but many of them could not read, so they asked that they might be taught how to read; not in order that they might set up political societies and associations, but that they might read the Bible. And so they were taught to read. Thus they were awakened and enlightened, and they began to realize the truth about man, and man's personality and dignity. And having gone so far they went further; they began to look at the circumstances and conditions in which they were living. They began to ask whether such conditions were fair and just and right, and coming to the conclusion that they were not, they proceeded to take measures to change them.

That was right and good; and entirely in accord with the Scriptural teaching. That teaching does not denounce slavery, and it does not condone it. It does not expect men to rise up and change it; neither does it simply maintain the status quo. It deals with the man himself first, and then, under the influence of this teaching, and with this new understanding, the man himself begins to examine the position and to deal with it.

We can sum it up in the following way. The church does not command any of these changes; it has never done so. There is not a word in the Bible which tells men to abolish slavery; and yet we know that it was Christian men who eventually brought that to pass. And that is exactly in accordance with biblical teaching. There is no command to do it; the Bible does not deal with these things directly, and yet when men become Christians they begin to think, and they think on both sides of the question. I have given an example of how working men began to think. But on the other side look at William Wilberforce. He was a wealthy man, born in the lap of luxury. Why did he become concerned about the question of slavery? There is only one answer to the question. It was his conversion. William Wilberforce underwent a conversion as radical as that of the drunken miners outside Bristol. He was entirely changed, and from being a society fop he became a great reformer, and as his mind became more and more Christian, he began to look at the question of slavery and saw that slavery was wrong. Not because he found a specific command in the Bible but because of his general thinking and his general Christian outlook! The same was true of the Earl of Shaftesbury who was mainly responsible for the Factory Acts of the last century. He was another man, an aristocrat of the aristocrats, born in wealth and luxury, who underwent an evangelical conversion. But because his mind had been renewed in Christ he began to see everything differently and he became concerned about conditions in the factories and mines. The same was true of Dr. Barnardo, the founder of Homes for destitute children.

And so it has always happened! It is not the task of the church to deal directly with these problems. The tragedy today is that while the church is talking about these particular problems and dealing directly with politics and economics and social conditions, no Christians are being produced, and the conditions are worsening and the problems mounting. It is as the church produces Christians that she changes the conditions; but always indirectly.

I will give another illustration of this same point. I read in an article quite recently something I had known before but which somehow had escaped my memory. It concerned the great Charles Simeon, an Anglican clergyman in Cambridge from 1782 to 1836, who was one of the biggest influences in the Anglican Church until about 1860, and indeed beyond that. It was the following fact that the article called to mind. Charles Simeon was preaching in Cambridge throughout the entire period of the French Revolutionary and Napoleonic Wars, from about 1790 to 1815, and during the whole of that twenty-five years, despite all the crises and the alarms and fears, Charles Simeon did not preach once on the Wars. Not on a single occasion! He was criticized bitterly and severely for this. Why was he not dealing with such events? Why was he not taking up current affairs and dealing with them as a clergyman is supposed to do? There were many others who were doing so, but their names have long since been forgotten. Those topical preachers may have been popular in their age, but no one knows about them now – not even their names. They had no effect upon the conditions then; they made not the slightest difference to Napoleon or to the Wars or to anything else; but their names were in the newspapers and in the headlines! But it led to nothing, it was a waste of breath. The Anglican preacher who really influenced the life of the nation was Charles Simeon; and he did so in the biblical way, which is indirect. He did it by preaching the Gospel and changing men.

The church cannot change conditions; and she is not meant to change conditions. And the moment she tries to do so she is in various ways shutting the door of evangelistic opportunity. If I attack Communism, the communists are immediately on the defensive, and are not going to listen to my Gospel; they will not even give it a hearing. I must avoid that. I must not launch a direct attack on any of these things, whatever they may be. My concern as a preacher of the Gospel is with the souls of men, my business is to produce Christians; and the larger the number of Christians the greater will be the volume of Christian thinking. It is the business of individual Christians to enter Parliament, as Wilberforce did, or to speak in the House of Lords as did the Earl of Shaftesbury, or to seek election to a local Council, and in general to act as good citizens. You are still citizens – act accordingly. Do not let these activities absorb all your time; do not let them be the chief thing in your life. That has often been the mistake. I believe the state of our churches today is largely due to that fact. I am old enough to remember a time in this country when the main difference between the Anglican Church and the Nonconformist Chapel was the difference between Toryism and Liberalism. Toryism was defending the status quo and on the other side Nonconformity was introducing reforms. For Nonconformity it was the age of the preacher-politicians. As I have already said, the preacher-politician is as reprehensible as bishops and archbishops who have often been but court chaplains. Together they have often side-tracked the attention of the people from the message of the Word of God. They certainly failed to produce Christians; and it is because there are so few Christians in the world today that ungodliness prevails.

Thus far, then, we have considered the five biblical principles which control the relations of rulers and ruled, masters and servants, employers and employed. We must go on to discover how the Scripture gives us further guidance yet on how to implement these five principles. We need such guidance and, thank God, it is here for us. But if we miss the main emphasis, the central principles, any further consideration will be a sheer waste of time. The question I

[329]

would ask is, What is your primary concern? Is it the social and political conditions in which you find yourself, or is it your relationship to God and eternity? If you are obsessed by your present conditions; if you become agitated, passionate and bitter about them, and simply condemn people on one side or the other, you are already outside the New Testament position. The Christian's one burning concern is his relationship to God and to heaven and to eternity, and because that is so he looks upon all other matters as secondary. He looks at them coolly and quietly, realizing that his first business is to be related as a Christian to all that life involves. He is different from men who are not Christians. It is only when his spirit is thus right that he can begin to consider whether as a citizen living in the world he should be trying to change or improve or maintain this or that – whatever his point of view may happen to be. But the final and the vital concern is always this, 'My Master is in heaven'; whether I am servant or master, whether I am employee or employer, am I submitting myself to the Lord and living to His glory?

24
Saints in Society

Ephesians 6:5–9

I have been emphasizing that it is the work of the church of God to preach, not politics or social reconstruction, but the Gospel in its fulness. At the same time I have intimated that it is right and legitimate that evil conditions be changed and that the individual Christian should take part in that task. Someone may object at this point, however, and say, 'But what about the martyrs? what about the men in the past who have been put to death by the State – the early Christian martyrs for instance? Those martyrs refused to say that Caesar is Lord, and were thrown to the lions in the arena in Rome. What about the Protestant martyrs in the sixteenth century? What about the Puritan martyrs in England, and the Covenanters in Scotland in the seventeenth century?' My reply is, that those saints were not put to death because they were preaching politics, or because they were doing anything directly against the State. They died for the truth, they died for the faith. The early Christians did not attack the Roman Empire. They were not political agitators. All they desired was to preach the Gospel and to live the Christian life. Why, then, were they put to death? The answer is that the State came to them and tried to compel them to say 'Caesar is Lord'. They refused to do it. Why could they not say these words? Because they knew that 'Jesus is Lord', and that there is none other. They chose to die rather than yield. They were passive, not active resisters. They got into trouble, not because of their activity, but because of their refusal to commit sin even at the dictate of the State. The same was true of the Protestant martyrs in the sixteenth century, and the Covenanters and others in the seventeenth century. I admit that sometimes the line between the spiritual and the political was very fine; and, as all men are human, there was a tendency at times for the political element to intrude. But speaking generally, what I have just been saying is the simple historical truth.

This problem arose very acutely in the 1939–45 war, and it is arising in many countries today. God knows, it may arise in any of our countries in the not-distant future. That is one reason why it is so important to consider these matters. Take the position of Christians in pre-war Germany with Hitler and Nazism in control. What were they to do? It is very difficult to be scriptural in our view of all this. Some of us are naturally hero-worshippers. We admire a man of courage, a man who is prepared to fight and to stand for principles; and therefore our judgment is likely to be biased and we may arrive at an unscriptural position. We have all heard of certain pastors and preachers who took their stand in pre-war Germany and criticized their government and who were put into prison and concentration camps for doing so. We are filled with admiration for them as men of courage and men of conviction. But perhaps, after all, they are not the men whom we really should be admiring. There were many unknown pastors, whose names we have never heard of, in Germany and such countries, who were never put into prison or into concentration camps, but who went on preaching the Gospel faithfully Sunday by Sunday. The well-known personalities who were punished were generally condemned by the authorities because they were preaching politics, which, if our exposition is correct, they should not have done. That appeals to the natural man, of course, in terms of heroism. But we must raise the question as to whether that is scriptural. The Apostle Paul did not behave in that way; none of the apostles did so. Surely the men who conformed to the scriptural pattern were the pastors who went on preaching the Gospel of salvation Sunday by Sunday, adding to the number of Christian people, building up the saints, and helping them to withstand the tyranny and to adjust themselves to it. They were the men who were doing the really difficult and the truly Christian work. Let us thank God for, and remember in our prayers, many similar humble pastors who are doing the same thing today in many countries. We must be very careful at all times to exclude the purely political and natural, and to make sure that we are conducting ourselves in the light of the biblical teaching.

That brings us to another question or problem which has been much discussed and which perplexes many. They cannot understand the time-lag which has been so evident in history over this question of slavery, for instance. The problem is often put thus. People say that they cannot understand how it was that the church and Christian people seemed to raise no protest against slavery until about the eighteenth century. This is the familiar argument of the modern rationalist, the modern intellectual who is not a Christian. This is one of his stock reasons for not being a Christian. Is it not obvious at once, he argues, that slavery is wrong? Is it not altogether wrong in principle that one man should own another? It is so obvious, he says, that everyone sees it clearly, and agrees about it, today; and yet Christianity had been in existence for nearly eighteen centuries before anything at all was done about it.

How as Christians can we possibly explain this time-lag? It is a perfectly fair question. We shall meet it, and we have to face it. And it is very much in the forefront of thought at the present time, not now so much over the question of slavery, but over certain other questions where people use the same principle and approach. There is a great deal written these days, and in religious magazines especially, to the effect that the great need at the moment is that we should bring our theology up to date. Certain writers feel that many of the troubles in the past have been due to wrong theology. The church, they say, holding on to certain false views and teachings, has been a drag upon the development of the human race; and they say this is still true, in a sense. Our learning and knowledge in the realms of anthropology and sociology and science, and especially in respect of the development of the human frame, have brought new light, they say, but the church is still holding back.

To what are they referring? It is an unsavoury subject, but as it is being discussed freely, and Acts of Parliament are passed about these matters, I must mention it. I refer to what is being said, for instance, with regard to sexual perversions. The same is being said on the question of marriage and divorce, and also with regard to the question of ordaining women into the Christian ministry and allowing them to preach to mixed congregations. The argument runs thus. The church in the past has always been rigid on these matters; it has denounced homosexuality as being perversion and sin and evil and crime. It has said that women, by definition and by nature, should not be ordained in the Christian ministry and should not preach; and as regards marriage it has held to the indissolubility of

[333]

marriage. But by now, they say, we know that such attitudes have been wrong. With our new knowledge of man in terms of anatomy and physiology, psychology and anthropology, we know that what has always been regarded in the past as perversion and horrible and sinful, is normal and natural to some, and should not be regarded as crime. It should not even be regarded as sin; some go even as far as to say that it is beautiful. That old wrong view, they say, was based entirely on biblical teaching. So the conclusion is – and I read it recently in a religious publication – that the great need at the moment is to bring the theology of the church 'up to date', and into conformity with modern knowledge.

That, to me, is one of the most grievous departures from scriptural teaching that one can possibly imagine; and for this reason. It takes away entirely the claim of the Bible to be the final authority in all matters of faith and conduct. The Bible is no longer to be regarded as a revelation from God, of His truth, His will, and His mind. What is the new authority? Modern knowledge, modern advances in knowledge, and especially scientific knowledge. So everything in the past has been wrong; modern man alone is right. They are, of course, blind to the fact that the logic of their position is that in fifty years' time what they now assert dogmatically will be proved to be wrong. Logically, their claims amount to this, that eventually there is no such thing as right at all; we are on a sliding scale; today's right is tomorrow's wrong; absolute standards do not exist.

But, secondly, such arguing assumes that modern knowledge is always right. I answer that no scientific knowledge can prove that these horrible perversions are natural. To say so is mere dogmatic assertion. The same applies to the question of women preachers; and also to the question of marriage. The position still is that fundamental truth is only to be found in the Bible; and that our modern troubles and problems are due to the fact that the world will not accept its teaching. It is the modern views that are wrong. No change is needed; what is needed is a return to the Bible and its teaching. It is because men and women are departing from the Bible that we have the moral muddle in society today. That is why the streets of London are becoming increasingly dangerous at night, and why horrible things are disgracing and alarming the community.

But we are told that we must set the Bible aside or make it

conform to modern knowledge and the modern understanding. That is the ultimate depth of sin, and of rebellion against God and His holy Law. The great need is to return to the Bible. I am not denying that there have been times when Christian people have misinterpreted the Bible. Take, for example, the famous argument which some people imagine finally settles this matter. They say: 'You know, it was Christian people who opposed the modern view of the cosmos, and were so wrong about astronomy. They said that the earth was flat or even square, and they withstood the advances that were made some four hundred years ago'. The answer is quite simple. The Bible does not say that the earth is flat. Certain people, through not recognizing the nature of biblical imagery, and through following Greek philosophy, have in the past come to the conclusion that the Bible did speak in that way. But they have misinterpreted Scripture and read their own erroneous conceptions into it. But that does not mean that the Bible is wrong. The same holds good with respect to other matters. The biblical teaching is foundational, it is the truth of God. There is no contradiction between the truth of God and true science; there is much contradiction between the truth of God and the theories of men. But such theories are not true science; they belong to philosophy and the realm of speculation. That, then, is not the explanation of the time-lag.

What, then, is the explanation? Primarily, it is what we have been laying down from the beginning, namely, that the main interest of the Bible is man in his relationship to God and to eternity. But there is a second explanation, and that is, that the Kingdom of God is compared to 'leaven'. It is also compared to 'seed sown in the ground', and to a tree that grows. The point made, of course, by all those analogies is that the Kingdom of God spreads by a very slow process of permeation and growth and development. That is our Lord's teaching about the Kingdom everywhere in the New Testament. It does not suddenly change everything as it were by Acts of Parliament or some similar enactment. The Kingdom of God is not like that; it is like leaven, it takes time, it seems to be a very slow process. The same is true of God's method in nature; at times you would not think anything was happening; but development there is, though unseen. It is as our Lord said in a parable; a man puts seed into the ground, and goes to bed, and rises, and goes to bed again and again. Nothing seems to happen, but ere long you

[333]

see the result. The process has been gradual. That is true of the Kingdom of God. As you look back over the history of the last two thousand years you see this truth in operation.

Furthermore, the Christian faith has never said that its business is to reform and to change the world. It does not set out to do so, it is not meant to do so. All the changes and advances in civilization are indirect results of Christianity, not direct results. And indirect results always take much more time. In other words, the time-lag is due to one thing only, namely, the state of the world. Civilization has always been a very slow process. The history of the missionary enterprise proves it to be so. Preachers have gone to uncivilized countries and have preached the Gospel. There have been conversions; but it has taken a very long time to persuade such people that they have to change the whole of their life.

But in many ways the most important reason of all is that Christianity really solved the problem of slavery at the beginning. That is the message of the Epistle to Philemon. 'Philemon', says Paul in effect, 'I am sending back to you this run-away slave of yours, Onesimus. He happened to be in the same prison as I myself, and he has become a Christian. I am sending him back to you, not only as a slave, but now as a brother. You are a Christian, Philemon, and so is Onesimus. He is coming back to you to occupy the old position; but of course he is now a different man. Therefore though the actual situation, and the external relationship, has not changed, in reality everything has changed. Onesimus is now a beloved brother. Receive him as such'. Here we have the real solution of the problem of slavery; the two men, the master and the slave, have become Christians. But, you notice, that while it really 'solves' the problem in its essence, it leaves it in existence as a political and a social problem. That is the method of Christianity.

Why is that the method of Christianity? Here, it seems to me, is the real secret, the real answer to the problem. If Christianity had attempted anything else, anything drastic in a political and social sense, it would have been exterminated at the very beginning. Let us imagine that the Christian church, in addition to preaching the Gospel, had began to attack the whole institution of slavery. What would have happened? All Christians would undoubtedly have been put to death. The Roman Empire could have stamped upon Christianity. It would not only have denounced it, it would have exterminated it. Christians never interfered in political or social or economic matters, but history tells us that, even so, whenever any-thing went wrong in the Roman Empire the Christians were always blamed for it. The secular history books make this quite clear. Whenever anything went amiss in Rome, when Rome went on fire, or a war was lost, men said that it was due to the Christians who refused to worship the old gods. Christians were regarded as atheists because they did not believe in the various gods who were held to control the elements, and they were therefore blamed for earthquakes and pestilences. Thousands of them were put to death, not because they had done anything wrong, but because they were falsely charged with being rebels and assisting in insurrections. And it has often been the same since then in the history of the church. The early Methodists were maliciously and falsely charged with being Jacobites. So if Christianity had presented the first century with a great political and social programme, and had claimed that slavery was wrong, and had tried to reform the entire social system, it would undoubtedly have been exterminated immediately.

We see therefore the wisdom of God in this matter. In spite of the fact that the system of slavery remained, men and women were converted as the result of the preaching of the Gospel. Though many remained in slavery they 'rejoiced with joy unspeakable and full of glory' because they knew that they were citizens of heaven. That does not justify slavery but it does help us to understand why there was this time-lag. It was the world that took eighteen cen-turies to see the wrongness of slavery, not the Christian teaching. The Christian teaching realizes that it cannot transform society as a whole; it must go on trusting that gradually the teaching will act as a leaven, and that men will become more and more enlightened. The time-lag is not to be explained in terms of the failure of biblical teaching; it is to be explained in terms of the blindness of the world to Christian teaching. Christians have been given wisdom by God and the power to be patient, and to wait until the right time for action has arrived.

Such, then, are our controlling principles. But I must work this out a little in detail. It is difficult, it is involved; and some may wonder whether it is necessary to do so at all, as it is not a personal problem for them. But as I have already said, in this modern world, a Christian may well find himself in this kind of situation one day. In any case it is always our duty to think of others. What of Christians today in China, and in parts of Russia and other similar territories?

We must 'bear one another's burdens', we must be prepared to understand these things in order that we may help one another as well as help ourselves. The whole world of Christians may be facing them ere long, for we live in ominous days.

Here are some of the practical details which Christians should work out. I am referring, of course, to the individual Christian. He is to realize, primarily, that the State and government, and law and order in society are ordained by God. 'The powers that be are ordained of God' (Romans 13:1). It is God who has ordained magistrates and judges and all such authorities, primarily in order to restrain evil. Men did not invent the State, men did not invent kings and governors, magistrates and powers. God has ordained them in order to keep evil within bounds. They are not meant to do more that that; but they are certainly not to do less. If God had not ordained them the world would be in a state of complete anarchy. Conditions are bad enough as it is, but if there had been no law and order, no Acts of Parliament and police, the situation would have been infinitely worse. All this is God's contrivance to keep evil and sin within bounds, to prevent their festering and destroying life. The 'powers that be' are a basic requirement. Whatever the political conditions in which we may find ourselves as Christians, and however adverse to us they may be, we have to say, 'Well, after all, the State and all these powers have been put there by God'. I must not say 'Abolish the lot'. No, there must be order, there must be government, there must be system. That is God's contrivance.

Secondly, it must be realized that no system is perfect. The trouble in past times has often been that some have entertained the notion that their political system, and theirs alone, was perfect. Some have believed in an Oligarchy, others have believed in a Constitutional Monarchy, others believe in what they call Democracy, others believe in Republicanism, others in Communism, a classless state, and so on. And the trouble generally arises because these partisans claim that their ideas and their system is the only right one, and the only true one, the only perfect one; and they fight about these things.

The Christian looks out upon all this; he knows that none of these ideologies is perfect, not one of them. The Bible does not prescribe or advocate any one of them. All this is a matter for discussion, a matter of human opinion; and men must investigate these things as citizens of the State. How much nonsense has been talked about these matters on every side! Some have defended an Oligarchy or an absolute Monarchy, and talked about 'the divine right of kings'. The Bible shows us clearly that there is no such thing. We remember what God said to the children of Israel when they first desired to have a king. But then, at the other extreme, you get men rising up and saying, 'All men are equal'; there must be no divisions of function and no ruling and no ordering. That has often been the great slogan. But it simply is not true. All men are certainly equal in the sight of God; the Bible teaches that. But it does not say that all men are equal; for it is quite obvious that all men are not equal. No two men are identical. You cannot say that two men are equal when one is a very able person and the other is dull and stupid. You cannot say that all men have the same attributes and faculties and propensities. One man has a better mind than another; one man has an element of leadership which another lacks. They are born like that, and clearly they are not equal. The common and general wisdom of the human race has always realized that you have to accept certain divisions in order to organize society and to make life possible. Slogans are always dangerous.

All this is demonstrated at the present time in Russia where they believe in the theory of a classless society. But already there is a new class developing there – the Commissar, the leader, the man who is in the bureaucracy, the civil servant. A managerial class is rising. They may decide to abolish such differences, they may try to do away with all natural distinctions and divisions, but they will come back, they are bound to come back, because all men are not equal. A man of ability and intelligence is certain to forge ahead, and the others will very naturally look to him in a time of crisis. Great claims have likewise been made by the advocates of democracy. The French Revolutionists proclaimed 'liberty, equality, and fraternity', but it soon led to a tyranny and to atheism and many other evil consequences.

My point is that, as he looks out upon all these things, the individual Christian sees that no system is perfect. I must not 'lose my head' therefore, I must not give my whole life to the advocacy of any one system and claim that it is perfect and will solve all problems; because that is simply not true. The problems and troubles remain under every single and every conceivable system; and that will always be so. That is how the individual Christian must look at the problems of society.

[339]

The next step follows logically. Recognizing that there is no system which is perfect, the Christian desires to have the best that is possible, and to do everything he can to produce the best that is possible. He does not 'lose his head' about it, he does not become excited about it as, alas, so many of our forefathers have done. During the past one hundred years many of our Nonconformist fathers forgot the Gospel and really believed that the Liberal Party was going to introduce the kingdom of heaven on earth by social legislation. The Christian should never be guilty of such a colossal error. He believes that we must try to get the best possible, and he is prepared to work to that end; and that is in accord with biblical teaching.

The Christian then goes on to the last step. Tyranny and oppression and injustice, he argues, are patently false to the biblical teaching concerning the State and its functions. He therefore has a right to object to them. In so doing he is not setting himself up as a political agitator; he is saying that when the State is guilty of tyranny or oppression, or of perpetrating injustices, it is not conforming to what the Apostle Paul says in Romans chapter 13. He therefore joins with others in protesting against the fault, and trying to change it. The Apostle Paul himself behaved in that manner in connection with his unjust imprisonment at Philippi, as we have seen. He was not agitating against the law in doing so; he was simply saying that the law must be carried out, and carried out correctly. He was making a legitimate protest as a citizen. He did not preach about these things, but in actual practice, as a private individual, he insisted that the law under which he and others lived should be rightly administered. That is always right conduct for the individual Christian.

So a Christian has a perfect right as an individual to try to produce a change in order that he may obtain the best conditions possible for himself and others. I would even say that if it becomes necessary, and if there is a large body of opinion pointing in that direction, he is even justified in taking part in a rebellion or a revolution. He must not do so, as the people did at the time of the French Revolution; he must not worship 'Liberty, Equality and Fraternity'; he must not do away with God and say 'All men are equal'. Never! He must not act for any selfish or personal reason or motive. He must always seek the best for the State and for people. I am at this point thinking of the position of some of the Puritans in the seventeenth century. It was difficult for them to decide what to do. Should they join in the war against Charles I, or should they not? I am trying to justify the position of Cromwell and others in the rebellion. I am not justifying all that every individual did, but I am saying that, if a man takes the view that he and others are being subjected to tyranny and injustice which is opposed to the biblical teaching concerning the way in which kings and those who rule are to behave, he is in that case entitled to take part even in a rebellion and a revolution. But let him be careful as to how he does so.

That brings me to my last word. It is obviously, therefore, quite right for a Christian to take part in every movement or every arrangement which is designed to produce the best possible conditions for human beings while they are in this life and in this world. It is perfectly legitimate for a Christian to take part in politics, to enter into them, and not merely to vote, but to become a local councillor or a member of parliament. It is, on the same principle, equally right for a Christian to belong to a trade-union, for the State recognizes such unions. An Act of Parliament has made it legitimate for men to combine together to see that they get justice and fair play. They also have a legal right to strike, and withhold their services. The law also recognizes similar organizations formed by employers. To belong to one or the other is legitimate; it is right.

There are many Christians, however, who feel that it is sinful for them to belong to a trade-union; but that is entirely to misunderstand the biblical teaching. To belong to such a union is in no way a contravention of the apostolic teaching about servants and masters. This teaching says that I am always to conform in a legal way to the existing position, but that if I can legitimately change the conditions, I am entitled to do so. I am entitled to put an end to slavery if I can do so in the right and legitimate way. I must not do so in a precipitate or lawless manner. I must never bring the Christian cause into disrepute. But in the right and legitimate way, by exercising my vote, by speaking, by talking, by organizing, all of which is quite legitimate – I can do so. So the individual Christian can belong to these various societies and organizations and institutions and in doing so he is in no way violating his Christian principles. There are Christian people in the various political parties; and you can find them in the different social and industrial groups. All these divisions are quite consistent with a profession of the Christian faith.

[341]

It remains to emphasize a matter which is of extreme importance. The Christian, in his own particular situation, must be careful to conduct himself in a truly Christian manner. He must not become confused about these things. Because he may disagree with a system he must not take the law into his own hands and act against it. The Apostle exhorts us as believers to live always in a law-abiding manner whatever the circumstances and conditions. If a situation can be improved in a right and legitimate way, we are free to join with others to bring that about. But we are not to allow that to interfere with our present conduct. There were Christian people in the Roman Empire living under that horrible despot, the Emperor Nero. They were not told to rise up, and to rebel against him, and to bring him down. They were told to be obedient. But, taking a longer view, as individual Christians they were to be free to use any legitimate means and methods to abolish such tyrannies and to bring in the best conceivable form of government in this sinful and evil world.

We have now dealt with what is, undoubtedly, the most difficult aspect of this matter. We shall go on to look at it in a much simpler and more direct way. May God enlighten us, and teach us how to think in a Christian way, and to view everything in the light of these great principles that are enunciated in the Word of God! Who knows but that it may be your conduct as a servant, or as a master, that is going to be the means of arresting and apprehending someone and awakening him to the truth of this glorious Gospel, which changes a man and his entire outlook. Thus, by just doing your work, whatever it is, and whatever your sphere, and even perhaps by suffering wrong in a Christian manner, you may become an ambassador for Christ, an evangelist of the Kingdom of God.

25
Slaves of Christ

Ephesians 6:5–9

We have arrived at the general conclusion that it is the business of the Christian to conform to the circumstances and conditions in which he finds himself. He is not automatically to break loose or to try to break loose because he has become a Christian. We have also seen that he has a right to join with others to improve and to change the conditions of life. He does so within the limits of the law; and he is entitled to do so. But the over-riding principle is that the main task and object of the Christian should be to discover how to adjust himself, with this new understanding that he now has, to the circumstances in which he finds himself.

From all this we can draw certain conclusions. There is no sin involved when a Christian does things in connection with a system in which he is involved, though he might prefer personally not to do such things. For instance, here is a Christian who is involved in a situation such as that of the slaves at the time when the Apostle was writing. As Christians they would be required to do many things they would prefer not to do, things they might even regard as being definitely wrong; yet, it seems to me, the teaching is that they are to do those things. They are to render obedience because it is a part of the system in which they are involved. The slave was not told to try to free himself, to contract out of his situation. No, he had to conform, and he had to render obedience. This is a very important principle. Let me apply it to the conditions of today.

There are many Christian people involved in business or in industry who are called upon to work on Sunday. They are often very perplexed about this, and they ask 'Am I sinning by working on Sunday?' By way of answer I generally put the following

[343]

question to such a person: 'If you were at complete liberty, and had absolute freedom of choice in this matter, would you choose to work on Sundays? You tell me that you get double pay by working on Sunday. Very well, here is my question: If you were absolutely at liberty, would you forego that double pay in order to attend public worship in God's house?' And if the man tells me that he can say quite honestly that that is what he would choose, namely, to be in God's house, I then tell him that he is not sinning if he works on Sunday when that is a part of the system in which he is involved. If he refuses to work on Sunday he will lose his post, his job; and the Christian is not called upon to do that. He is involved in a system in which he may not believe, as these slaves were; but the injunction is that he is to give obedience within the system, though it may sometimes involve his doing things which he himself would not choose to do.

Let me give another illustration. A short while ago there was talk of the possibility of a strike on the part of the medical profession. Many Christian doctors were very much concerned about this, and they asked, 'Can we as Christians join in the strike?' My answer was, 'Of course; you are in no new or exceptional position'. The same question arises with any Christian involved in any occupation. When a strike is proposed, should the Christian take part in it? Again, the answer seems to me to be quite clear. Whatever his own opinion may be, he is involved in the system. Industry is so organized today that a workman does not have personal dealings with his masters; he is one of a group, and his masters probably belong to a group also. The personal element is disappearing, indeed has largely disappeared. The workman is part of a system; usually he has to belong to a trade-union in order to obtain a post. So the Christian really has no choice here; he has to conform to the system. And if the majority of the people with whom he is working come out on strike, he joins them whatever his personal views may be. Otherwise his life will become impossible, and ultimately he brings Christianity into disrepute because in the eyes of others he appears ridiculous. Every Christian must think the matter out and work it out, for himself. The general principle is that, clearly, the Christian has to be a part of the system in which he finds himself. He can do his best with others to change the system or to improve it; but he is not to act as a rebel, he is not to cut across the system as an individual simply because he is a Christian.

The second point – and I hasten to add it because it is a qualification of all I have been saying – is that there is one point at which the Christian must take an absolute stand. That is when he is asked to do something, or when he is involved in a situation, which affects his personal relationship to God and to the Lord Jesus Christ. There, he has to make an absolute stand whatever the consequences may be. If he is put into a situation where somehow he has to deny his Lord, he must refuse to do it. He has to be careful. He is governed by these two principles. He must not be guilty of a morbid scrupulosity, and yet he must always know where to draw this line. It is when it becomes a question of his personal relationship to the Lord and of the whole matter of salvation that he takes his stand. Those early Christians continued to serve as slaves; but they would not say 'Caesar is Lord'. They would die rather than say that.

There is a good illustration of this point in the first chapter of the Book of Daniel. Daniel felt that at a certain point he had to make a stand. He did so in a very reasonable way, and he gained his point. But every man must judge in each instance for himself. He must never do anything that involves a denial of his Lord, or in any way interferes with the question of his salvation.

That is the general aspect of the matter. That enables us now to go on to consider the more practical aspects of behaviour involving servants (slaves) and masters, as taught by the Apostle. The slaves are to continue as slaves, but how? How are they to conduct themselves? As Christians now, how do they reconcile their new point of view with the situation in which they still continue? The answer seems to divide itself very naturally into two sections. First, how are we to serve? Again the Apostle divides that up into two sections – I am taking his divisions, they are not mine. He goes to great trouble over this, and enters into detail. He first lays down a negative point. They are to be obedient to their masters; but 'not with eyeservice'. That is the negative at the beginning of verse 6.

How are we to understand 'not with eyeservice'? This is something with which we are all familiar. It means that servants are to obey their masters, but are not always to be keeping their eye on the master, not keeping their eye on the master more than on the particular task. In other words, they must not merely do the minimum, just sufficient to keep themselves out of trouble. There is a type of servant who, whatever he may be doing, always has his eye on the master, waiting to see whether he is coming or watching.

If no one is watching he either does nothing or else does the bare minimum; but when the master is present he works hard, and gives the impression that he is a very dutiful servant. That is 'eye-service'; and the Apostle says that the Christian must never behave in that way, doing the least possible that is compatible with his receiving his salary or any kind of reward. The Apostle is condemning the attitude that is merely concerned to keep out of trouble and to keep things going, the attitude that is not interested in the work at all, not concerned to do it, in fact concerned to do the very minimum possible, the attitude of the man who only works when he is watched. 'Eyeservice' says the Apostle, is utterly incompatible with a truly Christian attitude.

What then are we to do? We are to be the exact opposite of the eyeservice type. Notice the Apostle's method. He is never content with positives only. Many foolish people today do not like negatives. Yet the world is very largely as it is today because people do not observe negatives. It is as important that we should be told what not to do, as it is that we should be told what to do. How then are we to serve? 'Servants, be obedient to them that are your masters according to the flesh, with fear and trembling'. Notice that the Apostle uses the very same expression elsewhere, as, for instance, in 1 Corinthians 2:3, where he tells the Corinthians, 'I was with you in weakness and in fear, and in much trembling'. We have it again in 2 Corinthians 7:15, where, in reference to a visit of Titus to the Corinthians, he says, 'And his inward affection is more abundant toward you, whilst he remembereth the obedience of you all, how with fear and trembling ye received him'. Again, in the famous passage in Philippians 2:12: 'Wherefore, my beloved, as ye have always obeyed, not as in my presence only'. Here we meet with the same idea again. 'You have always obeyed', says Paul, 'not only when I was with you', that is to say, 'you are not rendering obedience with eyeservice or as menpleasers. I know', he says, 'that whether I am with you or not, you will still behave in this way. Wherefore, my beloved, as ye have always obeyed, not as in my presence only, but now much more in my absence, work out your own salvation with fear and trembling'.

The other passages quoted help us to interpret what is meant here. It does not mean that Paul is exhorting these slaves to live in a state of perpetual fear and trembling of their masters, to some kind of craven morbid fear – the fear of the poor slave who thinks of a master with a whip and its cruel lash. It does not mean that they should always be trembling in fear at what might happen to them. That is inconceivable, and impossible as an interpretation here and elsewhere.

To find what it does mean we must look at the Apostle himself as he went to preach in Corinth. He says that he went 'in weakness, and fear, and much trembling'. What was the cause of that fear, what made him tremble? Obviously it was not that he was afraid of the Corinthians. The Apostle was afraid of no one of that type. He was not afraid of the Epicureans and the Stoics in Athens, or of kings like Herod, or Roman Governors like Felix and Festus. He had no need to be afraid of any man. He was not only the intellectual peer of anyone who might be listening to him, he was intellectually superior. He did not fear anyone among the Jews in the matter of the knowledge of the Law, and he knew that the Gentiles were ignorant concerning God. It was not that kind of fear therefore.

The Apostle's fear was that he might somehow or other misrepresent his Lord and Master, and the Gospel which he had to preach. He always felt that it was a tremendous thing to be a preacher of this Gospel. He knew the danger of antagonizing people against it. Hence he feared and trembled. The Apostle regarded the preaching of the Gospel as a very serious matter. There are people who are ready to run into pulpits at any time. Not so the Apostle! Had it not been that he was constrained by the love of Christ, and that he could say 'Woe is unto me if I preach not the gospel'! he would never have preached. We 'work out our salvation' in the same way. Not that Christians are exhorted to be morbid; but that we must realize that what we do in this life and in this world is a tremendously important thing. 'We shall all appear before the judgment throne of Christ' – every one of us – 'and give an account of the deeds done in the body, whether good or bad.' That is what it means. It is the 'fear and trembling', then, of misrepresenting or of not doing something well. The Apostle says that slaves are to be obedient to 'their masters according to the flesh' in that kind of way. What a tremendous thing it is to be a Christian! It lifts everything – even this condition of slavery – and puts it into a higher context. Here, then, is the poor slave, doing a very menial manual task; he is told to do it in the same way and in the same spirit as the Apostle himself preached the Gospel.

The next term is, 'in singleness of your heart'. This is similar to

[347]

our Lord's saying in the Sermon on the Mount and elsewhere about the 'single eye'. It means the opposite of double vision; the opposite of doing two things, or seeing two things, at the same time. The 'single eye' denotes focusing, concentration. It means that we are to do what we have to do with undivided attention and effort. Here the Apostle is thinking about motives, and especially about having a single motive. Our motive should be to do the best work possible, in order that we may do it in the best way possible, and above all for the sake of pleasing the Master. Do we all, as Christians, always realize the application of this to ourselves? The Apostle is telling these slaves to do their work in that way; not as people who always have their eye on the master who may turn up at any moment, 'not with eyeservice'. Because they are Christians it should not matter whether the master is within sight or not, because they are to perform their appointed task with 'singleness of heart'. They are to concentrate on it, and to give it their undivided attention.

This means, among other things, that it is the business of the servant, the man who is employed – irrespective of who may employ him – to give himself utterly to his task and to his master while he is doing it. His time is not his own time, it is his master's time. The money he handles is not his, it is his master's. Everything connected with his work is his master's. In other words, I would say that a Christian is disobeying the Apostle's injunction if, during his master's time, and when he ought to be doing his master's work, he is directing his attention to any other interest.

I have no right to use my employer's time even to evangelize! There are many Christians who are guilty at this point. While they are paid to do their work they use part of the time – which is not theirs, but their master's – in talking about the Christian faith, about the soul, about salvation. They may spend hours doing this in the course of a week, and countless hours during a whole year. But that means complete disobedience to this injunction; it is dishonest, it is a form of theft. The Apostle says that we are to obey in 'singleness of heart', we are to concentrate, we are to give our undivided attention to duty. We have no right to appropriate to ourselves, however good our motive may be, that which belongs to our master. But a man says, 'Surely, if it is for the good of a man's soul it must be right'. But it is not! You were not employed to be an evangelist. That does not come into the terms of your agreement; it was not mentioned when you undertook the task. You have no

[348]

right to do it, you are not meant to do it, and you are doing harm to the Gospel ultimately if you behave in that way.

This applies to everything that belongs to an employer. I am shocked now and again when I receive an invitation to speak at a Christian Union in connection with a government department, or a great business house, to see that the invitation has been written on notepaper of the government or the business-house. This is serious, because it is a form of theft and robbery. A Christian has no right to transact the business of a Christian Union on the notepaper of the company or the office to which he belongs, unless he has been given specific authority to do so. He is appropriating to himself something that does not belong to him. It is no longer service with 'singleness of heart'. We must work this out in terms of time, possessions, and all other respects. The Christian has to be careful about these things.

The next term the Apostle uses is, 'Do it (the will of God) from the heart'. 'Not with eyeservice, as menpleasers; but as the servants of Christ, doing the will of God from the heart.' A better translation here would be 'from the soul'. Notice that the three terms used here are virtually those that our Lord used when He was asked which is the first and chief commandment. He said, 'Thou shalt love the Lord thy God with all thy heart, and all thy soul, and all thy mind'. We have already looked at the heart; now we are looking at the soul. Then under the term 'good will' you get the mind. In other words the emphasis is on the whole man. The Apostle is saying that the whole personality is to concentrate on the work. The expression 'from the soul' means, 'heartily', 'do it from the depth of your being'. 'Do not do it in a grudging manner.'

This, alas, calls attention to a common failure. People do their work in a grudging manner. They would prefer not to do it, and they wish they had not got to do it. There is no grace in the way they do it; they give the impression that it is all 'against the grain'. They do it in a surly manner; it has to be dragged out of them, as it were. The Apostle says that we are not to work in that way, but always 'from the heart', from the soul, from the depth of our being. We are to be 'all out', and to show that whole-heartedness. 'Whatsoever thy hand findeth to do, do it with thy might' (Ecclesiastes 9:10). Be one, be unified, let it come straight from the depth of your soul. In that way slaves are to obey their masters, says Paul. And that is how all of us in employment, whatever it is, are to conduct and to comport

[349]

ourselves; not in a grudging spirit, but in a free spirit and whole-heartedly.

The last phrase is 'with goodwill doing service'. Goodwill! This, as I have said, refers to the mind and to the understanding. In other words the Christian is to show that he has thought this thing right through; he is not in a muddle. Here again we have a theme that might very well occupy us for some time. People have often come to me with some such perplexity as the following: Here is someone who is teaching English literature. Suddenly he is converted, he becomes a Christian, and soon he is faced with a problem. 'Can I go on doing this work?' he asks. 'It is not specifically Christian. Here am I teaching Shakespeare to children who are not Christians, and Shakespeare has no specific Christian teaching. Is it right for me to continue in this way?' Thus Christians get into a muddle, and develop a divided mind. They are no longer doing their work with 'goodwill'. They are not quite sure. Something in them says it is wrong; something else says it is right. Thus they do not know what to do. The Apostle gives the answer to all such problems in the words, 'With goodwill'. Get matters clear in your mind, see the place of culture in the total Christian view of life; then you will be able to do your work with goodwill.

The problem merits further attention, for a time comes in the experience of many Christians when they feel that they must, as they put it, 'be whole-time Christian workers'. 'Because I am a Christian I must be doing nothing but Christian work.' That is quite contrary to the New Testament teaching. If you are called to do whole-time Christian service (so-called), well, go and do it. But if you are not called to it, stay where you are (1 Corinthians 7:20). You must not automatically say 'I must leave everything in order to live as a Christian'. I would not be a preacher and pastor if I had not been called to the work by God, if I could not say that I could do nothing else. If you can do anything else, keep on doing something else; and when you cannot, you can be sure that God has called you to a specific Christian task. What I am condemning is the notion that because you have become a Christian, and because the work you are doing is not directly Christian, that it is not compatible with your life as a Christian. It probably is! 'Servants, obey them that are your masters according to the flesh.' Get the matter clear in your mind and then you will be able to do your work with goodwill. Your understanding will be clear, your attitude towards it will be clear, you will not be hesitant, reluctant, you will not do it with a divided mind. 'Goodwill' – the whole of you will be in it, and you will do it in a good way.

That brings us to the second major section. Why does the Apostle exhort these slaves to conduct themselves in this way towards their masters? Why are *we* to work in this way? This question is important for this reason, that if we do not understand the teaching of this second section, we shall never be able to carry out the teaching of the first section. It is only as we understand this that we shall be enabled to do our work, 'not with eyeservice, but from the heart' and with 'goodwill' from the depth of the soul.

Once more the Apostle divides up his statement into a negative and a positive. It is not my division, it is his. Here is the negative: 'Not with eyeservice as menpleasers'. You must not do your work, he says, with that sort of 'eyeservice' that keeps its eye on the master, having as its main motive to keep in with the master, pleasing men. You must not do it as 'menpleasers'. He repeats the thought, because it is so important, in verse 7: 'With good will doing service, as to the Lord, and not to men'. The repetition of the negative is for the sake of emphasis. In other words, the first thing we have to realize is that our eye must not be on men at all. Is not that the whole trouble with the non-Christian and with the non-Christian life? He has his eye constantly on men – on self, on other men; he is constantly asking, How is this going to affect me?, to work out for me? And if, as a Christian, that is my motive, I shall have my eye on others always – What do they think of me? What do they think of my appearance? What do they think of me as a man? What do they think of my ability? What do they think of me as a preacher? What do they think of me in a hundred respects? These become the dominating considerations: What do the people next door think? What will the other people in the office or in the factory think? The whole life is thus controlled by men and their opinions. 'As unto men.' The whole of the life of the unbeliever, poor fellow, is entirely governed and bounded by man. He wants the praise of man, so he always has his eye on men, he is always watching other people. But that should not be true of the Christian – 'not as menpleasers'. It must not be our ambition to please men.

Turning to the positive we find that the Apostle has four phrases which are most interesting. The first is found in verse 5, 'as unto Christ.' 'Be obedient to your masters according to the flesh, with fear and trembling, in singleness of your heart, as unto Christ.' The next occurs in verse 6, 'Not with eyeservice, as menpleasers, but as the servants of Christ'. And the next, 'doing the will of God' – not of men – 'from the heart; with good will doing service, as to the Lord, and not to men'.

Remember that Paul has exhorted the wives in exactly the same way. 'Wives, submit yourselves unto your own husbands, as unto the Lord.' 'Husbands, love your wives, even as Christ loved . . .' 'Children, obey your parents in the Lord.' Everything is 'in the Lord'. So here, we find in connection with these slaves – 'as unto Christ', 'as the servants of Christ', 'doing the will of God', 'as to the Lord, and not unto men'. Here we have the key to the Apostle's entire position. No one can speak like this but a Christian. The man of the world is not interested in this, he does not understand it at all. But this is the very hallmark of the Christian. The moment a man becomes a Christian in any real sense of the term, he sees everything in a different way – his work, his wife, his children, his home, his most menial tasks. His entire outlook is changed. Nothing remains the same – 'Old things are passed away; behold, all things are become new'.

We can show how this works out by taking these terms and putting them in a different way. The main desire of the Christian is to do the will of God, 'doing the will of God from the heart'. To please God is the first and chief desire of the Christian. What is a Christian ? First of all, he is one who has come to the realization that he is a sinner. What is a sinner ? A sinner is not merely a man who does certain things he should not do; a sinner, primarily, is a man who does not live to the glory of God. 'This is the first and the great commandment, Thou shalt love the Lord thy God with all thy heart, and soul, and mind, and strength'. 'The chief end of man is to glorify God, and to enjoy Him for ever', as the Shorter Catechism tells us. What is sin ? Sin in its essence is refusal to do that. Sin means that a man is not living to do the will of God. When a man comes to the knowledge that he is a sinner he realizes that he has not been living for that great end and object. He has been living for himself and for his fellow-sinners, and he says, 'Woe is me! I have never lived for God, and to do the will of God. I have been pleasing everyone but God. I have never thought that to please God should be the first thing in my life'. But now he sees it. That is the first thing that is true of a Christian. He is a man who has come to see that his first consideration always in every realm and department of life should be to know, and to do the will of God; and he is determined to live in that way. His first consideration always must be, What is God's will for me? Is it that I continue as I am? Or am I to change to something else? Whatever he believes to be the will of God he proceeds to do.

But then look at the second striking phrase, 'Not with eyeservice as menpleasers, but as the servants of Christ'. 'Servants', should be translated as in verse 5 – 'slaves'. What the Apostle Paul says in effect is this, 'My dear Christian friend, you who are a slave in Caesar's household, or wherever you are; what I say to you is this. When you wake up tomorrow morning do not start by saying to yourself, "Well, comes another day. I have hard work to do, and shall be thrashed if I do not do it. I shall not be given enough food, I am just a slave; it is all wrong. These pagan masters do not understand, I am not going to put up with it, I am going to rebel". No', says Paul, 'you must not speak in that way. When you wake up tomorrow morning say to yourself, "I am, incidentally, the slave of this man; but, in reality, I am the slave of the Lord Jesus Christ and my service must all be done as to Him" '. This is what Paul always says about himself, especially in the introductions to his epistles: 'Paul, the servant of Jesus Christ'. By that, he means 'the bondslave of Jesus Christ'. In that frame of mind he did all his work, he was the bondslave of Christ. And he reminds these slaves that the same is true of them.

It is essential for us to realize that we have been 'bought with a price'; that we are no longer our own. As Christians we have no right to determine what we want to do, and what we think and say. By nature a Christian may be a politician or a social agitator; he may want to rouse the rabble, and to smash up systems. But he must no longer think or speak or behave in that way, says Paul. And if he is a master, he no longer thinks in that way either. He will no longer threaten his workmen, because he realizes that he himself is a slave also. As Christians we are all 'slaves of Jesus Christ'. He has died for us, His body was broken, His blood was shed for us. He has bought us out of the market, He has ransomed us, He has redeemed us; we belong to Him. I must not think my own thoughts any longer; I am to be controlled by Him in my thinking as well as in my practice. Never forget that you are 'slaves of Christ' says the Apostle.

The third principle which I deduce is that because the foregoing is true of him, the sole and the chief desire of the Christian is to please His Lord and Saviour, and to show forth His excellences and His praise. 'As unto Christ, with good will doing service as to the Lord, and not to men.' In other words, the chief motive of the Christian is to glorify God and Christ and to please God and Christ in everything.

Summing up the matter we can put it in this way. We show that we are governed by these three principles by the way in which we do our work. That is what the Apostle is saying. We show that our chief ambition in life is to do the will of God, to prove ourselves to be the slaves of Christ, bought with His precious blood. And that will be manifest by the way in which we perform our daily task.

All this is of exceptional importance at the present time. We are living in a country where only some ten per cent of the people ever attend a place of worship. So, however good the preachers may be, they cannot do much because the people do not go to listen to them. But the individual Christian is working with such people daily, he is ever among them; he therefore becomes the evangelist, as it were. How does he practise his evangelism? By the way he behaves as a servant in his work, whatever it may be! There lies his opportunity. It comes to this: bad work is the worst possible recommendation for Christianity; negligent work, scamped work, hurried work, half-hearted work is a thoroughly bad testimony. That is how the man of the world works! He does the minimum for the maximum reward. If he can get out of doing a piece of work he will do so. If the master is not there, he merely keeps up the appearance of working, so that if the master suddenly comes he is apparently doing his work. But the Christian is the exact opposite of that. Any kind of bad work in a Christian, any negligent work, is a very poor testimony; and it does harm to the Kingdom of God. This applies in every sphere. A bad workman, whatever his work may be, is 'letting down' the Son of God, and the Kingdom of Heaven.

I am always grieved and unhappy when a Christian student fails an examination. 'Ah but', he says, 'I have been spending my time in the work of the Christian Union; I have been doing a lot of evangelizing'. But a student does not go to college to evangelize; he goes there to get qualified, to get into a profession or some other calling; and if he uses the time and money of his parents and of the State that has helped him to get there, in doing that evangelistic work, to the neglect of his proper studies, he has really been letting down the Christian cause. Any failure in a Christian is a bad witness. The Christian is to do his work well always. This applies not only to manual work and to school and college examinations; it applies in the professions. A man who is casual in his professional work is doing a great disservice to the Kingdom of Christ. An unpleasant Christian, whether he is doctor or solicitor or business man or anything else – I mean unpleasant in his handling of others above him or below him – is bearing a very poor testimony, and is probably doing great harm. It matters little that he may preach a sermon or give a pious talk now and again. It is the ordinary conversation of the man, it is his regular behaviour that people notice; and they judge God and Christ by what they see in him.

But let me put it positively. The Christian should always be the best in every department. I am not suggesting that the Christian is always the most able man of his group. He may not be; there may be others, who are not Christians, who are much abler. Becoming a Christian does not make an unintelligent man intelligent. But what it does essentially is this – and this is the point the Apostle is making – it makes a man use whatever powers he has always to the maximum. That is the secret. The other man may have more powers; that is not the point. If the Christian uses the powers he has to the maximum he is probably doing better work than the other man. That is the exhortation. The Christian should be 'all out', always industrious, always honest, always truthful, always reliable, always helpful, always trustworthy. That is what should always stand out in the Christian. You cannot give him new ability, or new propensities; but a Christian, however unintelligent he may be, can be an honest man, an upright man, a reliable man, a man who keeps good time, a trustworthy man, a truthful man, a man whose word is his bond – always, a man upon whom you can rely. And all this, because he is a Christian. That is precisely what the Apostle teaches here. 'Slaves', he says, 'be at your best always, do your job as well as it can be done, put all you have into it, whatever it is; though you are slaves do your utmost, be all out.'

Why does the Christian feel that he should behave thus? The answer is obvious. In doing this the Christian honours God, and he pleases Him. This is God's will for him. Behaving thus he is approximating more and more to man as he was at the original creation, and God is pleased to see him like that. Again, it is, as I have said, a great missionary opportunity, and it is open to everyone.

We see this constantly illustrated in the Bible. Call to mind the story of Joseph. Joseph, though he was one of God's people, became the slave of pagans. Yet because he was a godly man he became a favourite wherever he worked, and he won promotion. Why? Not because he preached to others, but because, being a man of God, he did everything he was given to do with all his might. So when he was in the house of Potiphar he was promoted, when he was in jail he was promoted; wherever you put him this man always got into a position of favour because he was a godly man, and always served to his utmost whatever the task. The same was true of Daniel and of Nehemiah. There are examples of this throughout the Scriptures.

The same comes out clearly in the history of the early days of the Christian church in Rome. That is why ultimately the Emperor Constantine, in his astuteness, decided to become a Christian, and the Roman Empire became nominally Christian. Those astute politicians discovered that the most stabilizing factor in the Empire was the presence of Christian people. They were law-abiding, they were peaceful, they were quiet, they did their work, and so eventually they came into favour. That involved other problems, I know, but the principle holds good.

I am given to understand that the same thing happened in Russia during the war of 1939–45. I remember during the war reading in a newspaper that the laws and rules concerning Christianity in Russia were suddenly relaxed by Stalin, of all people. We were all amazed. The explanation, I am given to understand, was this, that even Stalin made the observation that the most reliable workpeople in the whole of his territory were Christians. He could rely upon them to do their job. He therefore decided not to be so harsh in his treatment of them. He had not become a Christian – far from it! – but he had made this observation. Christianity in practice was making an impression. It always does.

This is one of the best ways to evangelize. It largely explains how Christianity spread in the first centuries. They did not hold mammoth campaign meetings with great advertising on which they spent vast sums of money. Christianity spread by 'cellular infiltration' as Communism has since spread. A man speaks to his neighbour or to his workmate. That is one chief method by which evangelism must take place today. We all have the opportunity wherever we are, whatever we are. There are endless opportunities.

Lastly, I observe that there is nothing that so shows the importance, and the dignity, of all we do in life as this teaching. Everything we do as Christians is to be done as unto Christ, 'as unto the Lord', and as unto God. This was the startling discovery that Martin Luther made. He had been brought up in the false system of Roman Catholicism, with the idea that Christians were divided into two groups – the religious and the ordinary. If a man really wanted to be religious he left the world and became a monk; and so Luther became a monk. But he could not find peace or satisfaction. Suddenly he was awakened to the great doctrine of justification by faith alone; and that opened his eyes to the whole position. He now realized that when a servant-maid sweeps out a room she can be working for God. You do not need to become a monk and spend your time in a cell counting your beads and sweating and praying in order to work for God. Not at all! A servant girl sweeping a room can serve God equally well, if not much better! The whole of life was transformed for him by that discovery. We need not become monks or anchorites or hermits in order to be Christian. We need not all be preachers. Wherever we are, whatever our work, sweeping out a room or anything else, let us do it with all our might, from the heart, 'not as menpleasers, not with eyeservice', 'with good will doing service as unto the Lord, and not as unto men'. You never know when someone looking on may say, 'This man and this woman are different from others. I have never seen anyone work like this before. These people seem to be really interested, they are doing their best. What is this'? And so you may start a train of thought that will eventually lead them to the question, 'What must I do to be saved? What must I do to be like that?' It does not matter where you are. You may be like Paul and Silas in a prison with your feet fast in the stocks, but by just behaving as a Christian you convict others, and you cause them to ask questions, and you may bring them to Christ.

Such, then, is this great and most glorious teaching. Nothing the Christian does is insignificant. When you get up tomorrow morning, and go to your office, you are going there, remember, as the slave of Christ, as the servant of God. It is not only people like myself who preach in pulpits who are servants of God. If you are a Christian, you are a servant of God, you are the slave, the 'bond-slave of Christ', even as was this mighty Apostle. Show it in your work, show it in everything you do – in your home, in your pleasure, in your recreation, at your lunch, at your tea, everywhere, always, let this come out. So you will realize that, whatever your calling, whatever your lot or position in life, it is a glorious one. As George Herbert puts it in his well-known hymn:

> *A servant with this clause*
> *Makes drudgery divine;*
> *Who sweeps a room as for Thy laws*
> *Makes that and the action fine.*

Never feel a sense of drudgery again! Your job may be mechanical, repetitive, soul-less. If so, get hold of this idea – 'A servant with this clause makes drudgery divine'. Say to yourself 'I am going to be a drudge for Christ's sake. Perhaps someone looking at me and seeing me enjoying the drudgery, and doing it with a finesse, and with a glamour and a glory that the world can never produce, may suddenly be convinced and convicted of sin, and may become an enquirer after the way of salvation. Get rid of the notion that you have to be preaching or teaching explicitly in order to evangelize. You can evangelize where you are, just as you are. You do it primarily by your life, by the way in which you do your daily work. You prove that you are a Christian in that way, because only a Christian can possibly do it in that way. 'Servants, be obedient to them that are your masters according to the flesh, as unto Christ, as unto the Lord.'

26
Our Master in Heaven

Ephesians 6:5–9

As we complete our consideration of this great statement we must look at the way in which the Apostle reminds the masters also of their responsibilities, and of their part in this situation. 'And, ye masters' he says, 'do the same things to them, forbearing threatening: knowing that your Master also is in heaven; neither is there respect of persons with Him.' Once more we are impressed by the perfect balance of the Scripture, by this complete fairness. In that respect, of course, Scripture is unique. There is nothing in the world's literature which is in any way comparable to it. And in the Bible everywhere, from beginning to end, the balance is maintained perfectly. We have seen it already in the case of wives and husbands, and also in the case of parents and children. It can never be said that the Scripture is unfair; its balance, its fairness, its equity is one of its most striking and glorious features.

This is one of the ways in which the scriptural teaching solves the problems of society; it also helps to explain why nothing else can solve these problems. The world today bears eloquent testimony to my claim. What is the cause of all the troubles, the discords, the clashes? Clearly the knowledge and ability of men are incapable of dealing with them. There is only one agency that can solve this problem of 'relationships', and that is the Christian message, the Christian faith. It does so in its own amazing and unique manner. All is based upon the fundamental statement in the eighteenth verse of the fifth chapter, 'Be not drunk with wine, but be filled with the Spirit'. It is only as men are filled with the Spirit that they can really live in peace and concord, and practise this kind of life. For when

[359]

people are filled with the Spirit there is no bitterness. Bitterness is the curse of life, it is the main cause of trouble in all relationships. All men's efforts to solve the problems are hampered by bitterness. It is found on both sides of the disputes. You find it in the demagogue who often represents the servants. He desires to improve conditions, and rightly so, but he rarely attempts to do so without producing a great deal of bitterness. And there is equal bitterness on the other side. Men can never solve these problems because each man is out for himself, and sees his own side only. Bitterness arises because of selfishness: that is the very opposite of being filled with the Spirit. But when men are filled with the Spirit on both sides of a dispute there is hope of solving it because both are animated and governed by a common desire.

That is exactly what the Apostle is concerned to show at this point. He is saying in effect to the masters: 'Now all I have been saying to the slaves is equally applicable to you'. That is the secret of Christianity; it brings all to the same position. First of all, it brings us all under the same common denominator – we are all sinners, we are all under condemnation, we are all failures; there is no difference. 'There is neither Jew nor Gentile, barbarian, Scythian, bond nor free, male nor female' – 'all have sinned and come short of the glory of God.' Then we are pointed to the same Saviour, the same God, the same salvation. Thus there is a common principle that governs all, and this is able to solve the various problems.

Let us follow the Apostle as he works this out. He turns to the masters and says to them, 'You masters, do the same things'. The world can never speak like that because it always tends to polarize positions and differences. It addresses one appeal to the servants; and makes a different appeal to the masters. But the Apostle says, 'Do the same things'. It means that they have to behave in their relationship exactly as the servants do in theirs. They have to live 'with fear and trembling', though they are masters. The 'fear and trembling', remember, does not mean craven fear, but a fear of displeasing the heavenly Master, a fear of doing harm to the Gospel, and to the Kingdom of God. They have to live in 'fear and trembling' and they have also to behave with regard to their slaves 'in singleness of heart', exactly as the slaves have to do. They have to do it 'as unto Christ', and they have to do it 'as the servants of Christ, doing the will of God from the heart', and 'with good will doing service, as to the Lord, and not to men'. There is no difference in those respects between them and the slaves. All the principles that were laid down in the case of the slave are equally applicable in the case of the master.

Then the Apostle adds one negative, even as he had one negative in the case of the slaves. In the case of the slaves it was 'not with eyeservice'. We saw that that was the peculiar danger of a slave, to keep his eye always on his masters, to do the minimum and get the most out of it. But what is the peculiar temptation of the man on the other side – the master? 'Threatening'! So Paul adds, 'forbearing threatening'.

Here again we see the profound psychological insight of Christian teaching. There are many dangers confronting a man who is in the position of master, but his greatest danger is to become guilty of threatening. That the Christian master is not to deal with his servant unkindly, not to treat him cruelly, not to whip him or strike him or trample upon him, goes without saying. Even ordinary common human decency would dictate as much. But Christianity goes well beyond those limits. Not only are you not to do such things to them, says Paul, you are never even to threaten them; you are never to display a wrong spirit towards them, you are never deliberately to keep them down, never to keep on reminding them that they are slaves and you are master, because that is a form of threatening. It is possible to threaten people without saying a word, without doing anything at all to them. A harsh way of looking at them, or general brusque behaviour can amount to threatening. To keep them rigorously in their position of subordination, to let them know that that is where they belong, and that they are going to be kept there; to hint to them that they had better be careful – all this can be done though you may not raise a hand, or swear or curse or shout; you can do it by your spirit, by your whole demeanour. The Christian master, says the Apostle, must never behave in that way, he must never be unfair in spirit, leave alone in practice and in action.

The perfect commentary on all this is found, once more, in Paul's Epistle to Philemon, whom he tells to receive back his runaway slave Onesimus, not only as a slave but now as 'a brother beloved'. That is the relationship that is to exist between the servant and the master – 'forbearing threatening'. Never in any way whatsoever must the master take advantage of his position to crush the spirit of the one who is serving him.

The motive the Apostle supplies here is exactly the same as it was in the other case. Let me remind you of it. The servants (the slaves) were to serve 'with fear and trembling, in singleness of heart, with good will', and so on. And they were to do so in order that they might please the Lord, that they might win others to Him, that they might show forth His glory and His praise. In this way, so too must the master serve the Lord. It must be his greatest ambition in life, his most central motive. He, like his subordinate, is the slave of Jesus Christ, and he is living for His glory and His praise and His honour. That is the secret the Apostle reveals at this point; that is the first motive that he presents to the masters.

We come to the second motive; and this again applies on both sides. It is emphasized in verses 8 and 9 in particular, although the Apostle has already hinted at it in verse 5. The statement runs: 'Knowing that whatsoever good thing any man doeth, the same shall he receive of the Lord, whether he be bond or free. And, ye masters, do the same things unto them, forbearing threatening: knowing that your Master also is in heaven; neither is there respect of persons with Him'.

This is the second grand motive that should govern the whole of our Christian life and living; namely, our accountability to the Lord Jesus Christ. It is the realization of the fact that we are His slaves, and that we shall all have to render up an account to Him. This is a principle which many dislike at the present time; indeed a dislike of this whole idea of accountability and judgment has been characteristic of much religious thinking during the whole of this present century. It is disliked, and has become most unpopular. People say, 'Ah, but that is a very unworthy motive for living the Christian life'. You should live the Christian life, they say, because it is a noble and exalted life. You must not live it in terms of the fear of hell or of the hope of being in heaven. You must live the life for its own sake, because it is so good and so wonderful. You find that sentiment in some of the hymns. They condemn what they regard as a mercenary and a selfish motive.

There was an ancient story which was quoted frequently in sermons and books some fifty or sixty years ago. It told of a man somewhere in Arabia or some such place who was seen walking along one day with a bucket of fire in one hand and a bucket of water in the other. Someone went to him and asked him, 'What are you doing with that bucket of fire in one hand and that bucket of water in the other'? 'Well', said the man, 'I am carrying the one bucket to burn up heaven, and I am carrying the other to quench the fires of hell.' He was represented as being such a fine idealist, such a noble-hearted man, that he was not interested in avoiding hell or in gaining heaven; he believed in 'goodness, beauty, and truth' for their own sake.

That kind of teaching came in about the middle of the nineteenth century. Men called 'scholars' began to say that the Bible was not divinely inspired in a unique sense, and they began to substitute for it their own philosophy. They put up 'goodness, beauty, and truth' in the abstract as the great principles for which men were to live, and they said it was not desirable that you should think of yourself at all. But that is by no means the Christian position; it is philosophy, idealism, but not Christianity. I say so because of the teaching of the New Testament, indeed I say so because of the teaching of the whole Bible. The Bible from beginning to end holds before us the idea of heaven and hell. It is God who appointed the two mountains – Mount Gerizim and Mount Ebal – in order to teach a vital lesson to the Children of Israel when they entered their Promised Land. According to whether they obeyed Him or not they would have blessing or cursing.

Our Lord Himself taught this same truth, as seen in Luke chapter 12. The servants in His parable recorded in verses 42–48, are to be examined when the Master comes. Some are going to be beaten with a few stripes, some with many stripes. In other parables also He teaches the same truth, for example, the parable of the Foolish Virgins, the parable of the Talents in Matthew 25, and the parable of the Pounds in Luke 19. All were spoken in order to emphasize this idea of judgment and reward. In 1 Corinthians chapter 3 it is made quite plain and explicit – 'Every man's work shall be judged', says Paul. The Christian teacher as a builder must be careful how he builds on the foundation that has been laid, because 'every man's work shall be made manifest' (verses 11–15). Then, again in 2 Corinthians chapter 5 it is made very clear: 'We must all appear before the judgment seat of Christ' – we who are Christians – 'that every one may receive the things done in the body, whether good or bad' (verses 9–10). That is the New Testament teaching. We must therefore dismiss the false idealistic teaching. It is just here that it shows its cloven hoof. It represents itself as something better than the Scripture – a sheer impossibility!

But the highest, and most irrefutable argument in favour of this teaching is found in the Epistle to the Hebrews chapter 12, verse 3. There we read that even our blessed Lord Himself was sustained by the thought of that which awaited Him. We are exhorted to 'lay aside every weight and the sin that doth so easily beset us' as we run this race; 'looking unto Jesus, the author and the finisher of our faith; who for the joy that was set before Him endured the Cross, despising the shame'. 'For the joy that was set before Him!' That was what helped Him and sustained Him.

The Scripture does not mean, of course, that by doing these things you earn your salvation. No! salvation is entirely by grace, it is the free gift of God. The Scripture teaches that 'we are saved by grace, through faith, and that not of ourselves, it is the gift of God'. Man is justified by faith only, 'not by the deeds of the law'. We are all saved in exactly the same way, that is, by simple faith in the Lord Jesus Christ. It matters not whether we were good or bad before conversion in a moral sense, whether we had sinned much or little – we are all brought to the same level, and saved and justified through faith alone, by grace. But having made that abundantly clear, the Scripture goes on to say that there is to be an assessment of our Christian life and works, and that, though we are all equally saved, there is some kind of difference. The Apostle says very clearly that a man who has been building 'wood and hay and stubble' on the foundation, Christ Jesus, will find at the great day that all his work will be burnt up, and that 'he shall suffer loss; but he himself shall be saved; yet so as by fire' (1 Corinthians 3:11-15). In other words, though the man who built wood, hay and stubble remains justified by faith, he is going to suffer loss. How, we do not know. But we do know that there is to be a judgment for rewards, that we shall all appear before 'the judgment throne of Christ', and receive rewards according to the 'deeds done in the body, whether good or bad'. Such is the apostolic teaching, and it is precisely the teaching the Apostle gives to the slaves and masters in this peculiarly difficult relationship of employer and servant. It is teaching that should always be in our hearts, in all our thinking, and in all our living. It holds great encouragement for us.

As the Apostle continues his exhortation, he uses the word 'knowing', as he has done previously in verse 8. In talking to the servants he says 'knowing'; in talking to the masters he again says 'knowing'. It might very well be translated, 'knowing as you do

[364]

know'. In other words the Apostle takes this for granted. This is not some new and strange and wonderful doctrine which he is suddenly introducing. He says, 'You know'; that is to say, 'I take this for granted. This is something that I assume everyone who has any Christian instruction at all knows, and therefore, because he knows it, he should be governed by it'. He is only reminding them of something that they knew already.

What, then, did they know? Here we reach the climax of all the Apostle has been saying concerning this duty of submitting ourselves one to another. He began that theme in the twenty-first verse of chapter 5. A new statement begins at the tenth verse of chapter 6. But the ninth verse supplies the climax of the doctrine of submitting ourselves one to another because we are filled with the Spirit and not with the 'wine'. This is what we know – that all that happens to us in this life and in this world is only 'according to the flesh'. Paul starts with the statement in verse 5: 'Servants, be obedient to them that are your masters according to the flesh'. That really says all. It shows immediately the Christian way of facing the problem of slavery. Here is a poor fellow, a slave perhaps with chains hanging from his wrists, and possibly upon his feet also. His movements are restricted, and cruel task-masters are watching him, giving him too much to do, and ready to punish him. The Apostle says to him, 'Be obedient to your master according to the flesh'. That is only one relationship, says Paul; there is another and a superior relationship.

At this point comes in the grand principle. All that happens to us in this world belongs to the temporary order; these things only obtain while we are 'in the flesh', while we are 'in the body'. This is a passing transient life; this world is not the permanent world. We say we are 'moving on'.

> *Here in the body pent,*
> *Absent from Him I roam,*
> *Yet nightly pitch my moving tent*
> *A day's march nearer home.*

'According to the flesh'. So whatever your position is in this life and this world, let me remind you that it is only a temporary arrangement. It is not eternal. 'The things which are seen are temporal, but the things which are not seen are eternal.' Nothing is more important than to realize that distinction, whatever your position may be. This applies not only to servant and master, to

husband and wife, to children and parents, but to all other relationships and circumstances. You may be struggling with some terrible
problem that is almost crushing you at this moment; you may be in
some situation that is almost impossible for anyone to endure; or
your difficulty may be concerned with your health; it matters not
what it may be, remember that, whatever your position or problem,
it belongs to the temporary order only. It is passing, it is 'according
to the flesh'. It is not eternal. Thank God for that! The realization
of this truth has been the secret of the saints in all centuries, the
secret of the martyrs and the confessors, the men who would not
say 'Caesar is Lord', the men who smiled when they were thrown to
the lions in the arena, the men who thanked God that they had been
'accounted worthy to suffer shame for His name'.

Do not forget that the Lord said to His disciples, 'Be not afraid
of them that kill the body, and after that have no more that they can
do' (Luke 12:4). He was sending His disciples out 'to preach and to
teach and to cast out devils'. He warns them that they are not going
to be received everywhere with open arms, that there will be many
who will persecute them, and even some who will conspire
together to kill them. He tells them not to be frightened, not to go
back on their message and deny Him in order to save their lives. For
there is a limit to what men can do; they can kill the body but
beyond that there is nothing that they can do. And the Lord goes on
to say, 'Fear him which, after he hath killed, hath power to cast into
hell; yea, I say unto you, Fear him' – that is, God. So whatever your
position, always remind yourself that this life is only transient,
evanescent, passing. We are 'here today, and gone tomorrow' –
'according to the flesh'.

Paul's second phrase emphasizes the first, in a sense; it puts it
positively – 'in heaven'. He exhorts the masters to 'do the same
things, forbearing threatening', because they are only masters
'according to the flesh'. Then positively, 'Knowing that your
Master also is in heaven'. Here he introduces the eternal world, the
realm of the Spirit. *That* is the realm of reality; *this* is the world of
shadows and appearances. It is just here that men who do not
believe the Gospel are blind. They think and say that they are
realists, and talk contemptuously about 'pie-in-the-sky' and belief
in another world. Here we have reality, they say – money, houses,
motor-cars – solid tangible things. The truth is, of course, that it is
all dissolving even while they are using it and enjoying it. 'Change

and decay in all around I see'. This is true even of our physical bodies. We have none of the cells in our bodies which we had seven years ago; everything is changing and moving. No, this realm of the seen is an unreal, artificial realm; it is passing away, and is destined to dissolve and disappear. But then there is this other realm 'in heaven'–the unseen, the eternal, the realm of the absolutes, the realm of the endless and the perfect in every respect. 'In heaven!' The Christian is a man who lives with his eye on these things. Paul says to the Philippians 'Our citizenship is in heaven' (3:20). That is where we who are Christians belong. And in this Ephesian letter he tells these slaves that they belong to heaven. Their masters are but masters 'according to the flesh'; the present is but a passing phase; the permanent lies ahead. He likewise reminds the masters that that is the ultimate realm. It is on that realm that we are to fix our gaze. As the eleventh chapter of the Epistle to the Hebrews reminds us, the men of faith were always 'looking for a city which hath foundations, whose builder and maker is God'. There are no solid foundations in this passing world; they all are rocking at this present time, are they not? The atomic and hydrogen bombs are at last beginning to bring people to see that this world is not stable and eternal. This old world is quaking and is to disappear. The only solid and durable foundation is that which is to be found there – 'in heaven'.

That is what all Christians, and especially masters, are to keep in the forefront of their minds, says the Apostle; for it will lead them to remember that there is Someone there who is over all, and above all, the One who controls everything and 'changes not'. He is your Master, says Paul. He is also your Lord: 'Knowing that whatsoever good thing any man doeth, the same shall he receive of the Lord, whether he be bond or free'.

The only way to solve the problems of society is found here. At the mention of this blessed Person, Christian servants and masters get down on their knees together and look up into His face and submit themselves to Him. They do so because He is 'the Lord'. He is the Lord of lords, the King of kings. He is supreme both in this world and in the world to come. All authority has been given unto Him in heaven and in earth, and by Him 'all things consist'. The moment you look at Him, in heaven, then, as the Apostle says, the terms 'bond' and 'free' become comparatively unimportant and almost irrelevant. He says also, 'the same shall he receive of the

Lord, whether he be bond or free'. When you come into the realm of the absolute all other distinctions vanish, they cease to count; here 'masters according to the flesh' become servants and slaves exactly as the others. 'Bond' and 'free' are negative terms, and are only temporary.

Finally, to make quite certain that we understand it, the Apostle adds the phrase, 'Neither is there respect of persons with Him'. He does not look upon our earthly human divisions and distinctions as we do, He is not interested in them as we are. The world of today is as full of such distinctions and divisions as was the ancient world – Jews and Gentiles, chosen people and dogs, Greeks and barbarians. The whole world was and is divided up in various ways. But that is quite irrelevant in the sight of this Master, this Lord. His great interest is in a man's relationship to Himself; with Him the soul is paramount. It does not matter in His sight whether you are a Britisher or an American or a Russian, whether you belong to China or to Cuba, to a great city or obscure village. There is only one thing that matters – Have you seen that you are a sinner in the sight of God? Are you trusting utterly and entirely to the Lord Jesus Christ who has died for you and your sins? Do you know that you are a miserable sinner saved only by the grace of God, and given new life; and that the one thing that matters is that new life, not the old life?

I have been at pains to point out that while Christianity speaks in these terms, it does not immediately destroy and abolish all human contrivances and divisions and distinctions. But it does get us to look at them in the right way, and to put them into the right perspective, and so to handle them that they do not cause trouble and unhappiness and misery. Master and slave must realize together that there is 'no respect of persons' with the Lord. It will avail us nothing on that Great Day to say that we were this or that in the world, important or unimportant. It will not count at all. But the world does not know this; and we cannot expect it to do so. It cannot know it until it has this new mind that is in Christ. But for all who claim to be Christians to go on attaching significance or importance to these things is a denial of the Faith. If we think and live as do others, and fail to put Christian principles into practice, the people looking on will say, 'What difference does it make to be a Christian? They are behaving exactly as they did before. Where does Christianity come in?' And so we do disservice to the King-dom and to the Cause. But when the world sees the servant and the master speaking to one another as brothers, and worshipping together, and praying together, it says, 'What is this? I have never seen this happen before; this is unique'. And so they begin to enquire. And the master and the slave can tell them together, 'This is because we are new men in Christ Jesus. "Old things are passed away, behold, all things are become new". We are still economically and socially in the same relative positions as before, but we are "one in Christ", in the thing that matters; and we know that we are going to spend our eternity together'. 'Neither is there respect of persons with Him'. In Him, all our human distinctions and divisions are completely irrelevant.

Finally, it comes to this. The Christian is one who knows all that, and he knows that we shall all stand before this blessed Lord and Master and 'receive the things done in the body, whether good or bad'. The Apostle says that in the eighth verse: 'Knowing that whatsoever good thing any man doeth, the same shall he receive of the Lord'. He shall receive! There is the judgment issuing in rewards. That should be the over-ruling and over-riding consideration in all our thinking and behaviour in every respect. 'We must all appear before the judgment seat of Christ, that everyone may receive the things done in his body, according to that he hath done, whether good or bad' (2 Corinthians 5:10). Before we get there we receive a great deal in this life, do we not? We serve a very generous as well as a very just Master. He does reward, He does encourage. Is there anything in life, in the whole world, comparable to His smile upon us, His expression of His satisfaction in us?

But, especially, let us think of it all in terms of the ultimate judgment and standing before Him, and the question of reward or punishment. There is the element of punishment, or at any rate of deprivation, the few stripes, the many stripes, and the Apostle's expression, 'he shall suffer loss'. We do not understand it fully; we are not given sufficient detail concerning it; and we are obviously not meant to know exactly. But we do know as much as is written, and we should ever be conscious of it. The Apostle Paul himself, amid all his preaching and activity in the Kingdom of God, tells us that this truth was always present in his mind. It explains why he did everything 'with fear and trembling', it was because he knew 'the terror of the Lord' and that he would have to stand 'before the judgment seat of Christ' and give an account of the deeds done in the body.

I am often amazed at the way in which Christian people dare and venture to do certain things, and also at the way in which they fail to do certain other things. So many seem to imagine that, because they believe and are 'saved', that is the end; they entirely forget this matter of rewards. They go on doing the minimum in the Kingdom of God, and in the church of God, and seem to fail to understand their true relationship to Him. Never forget that everything you do, and everything you fail to do, is known to Him, and that you will have to face your own record again, and 'give an account of the deeds done in the body, whether good or bad'. The 'suffering of loss', to which the Apostle refers must be only temporary. I am speculating; I do not know; but there is a loss that can be suffered. I sometimes think that it is just a question of looking into His face and into His eyes. We remember how as children, when we had done something wrong, and were a bit fearful that we were going to be punished by our parents, the most terrible punishment we ever received was when they did nothing at all to us. They just looked at us, and there was an expression in their eyes which showed that they were disappointed in us. And we felt ashamed, and despised and hated ourselves. We felt that we had lost something very precious. They did not actually deprive us of anything, they did not punish us physically, but oh, the look! 'We shall see Him as He is'. We shall look into His eyes. We shall remember how we failed Him in our selfishness, in our smallness. God forbid that any of us should suffer loss!

But look at the other side. There is a reward. 'Well done, good and faithful servant, thou hast been faithful in a little'. So He gives him more. He has used his one pound well, he has traded with it. Give him more, add to it! What a reward! Is it conceivable that there can be anything more wonderful than just to hear those words from Him, 'Well done, thou good and faithful servant. I entrusted this gift to you, you honoured my trust, you increased my gift, you were a wonderful steward. I looked down from heaven, I took pride in you as you did it; I liked it, I rejoiced in it; and now I receive you, "Enter into the joy of your Lord" '. Promotion, unexpected! As we are reminded in the 'sheep and goats' passage in Matthew chapter 25, we may very well be unaware of what we have done. That makes no difference. He has kept the account; He knows all about it; and He will reward us richly.

The Apostle tells us in 2 Corinthians chapter 5, 'Knowing the terror of the Lord we persuade men'. There were two great motives urging the Apostle, driving him on, in all his travelling and preaching: 'The *love* of Christ constraineth me', and 'knowing the *terror* of the Lord'. Those two motives should always govern us as Christians, be we servants or masters. 'Knowing that whatsoever good thing any man doeth, the same shall he receive of the Lord, whether he be bond or free'. Though your earthly master may not reward you, though he may treat you most unjustly, and though others may laugh at you and deride you, and your fellow-servants may say you are a fool, do not worry; you will get your reward. Your heavenly Master is looking down upon you, and He never forgets. He will reward you richly and abundantly whatever your position. And the same is said to the masters. 'Masters, remember your Master also is in heaven, and there is no respect of persons with Him'. We Christians belong to eternity; we are citizens of the Kingdom of God, we belong to the realm of the spiritual. God forbid that any one of us should look at his or her work in terms of this world. This is only 'according to the flesh'. We are 'here today, gone tomorrow'. What matters is that 'We shall see Him face to face'. We must all appear before the judgment seat of Christ, to receive the things done in the body, whether good or bad. 'Therefore' – let us say it with the great Apostle – 'Therefore, knowing the terror of the Lord', we go on to implement the teaching with regard to slaves and masters, children and parents, husbands and wives – whatever the relationship. 'Knowing the terror of the Lord', let us live to Him, and to His glory; let us ever remember that that is the realm which really matters. This world though transient and passing nevertheless has its influence upon that other realm, and determines whether we shall suffer loss, or receive a great and wonderful reward. Let us therefore ever live in the light of eternity; let us live as knowing that we are always under the eye of, and in the presence of, 'our Master who is in heaven'.